HEALTHCARE TECHNOLOGIES SERIES 29

Blockchain and Machine Learning for e-Healthcare Systems

Other volumes in this series

Blockchain and Machine Learning for e-Healthcare Systems

Edited by
Balamurugan Balusamy, Naveen Chilamkurti,
Lucia Agnes Beena T and Poongodi T

The Institution of Engineering and Technology

Published by The Institution of Engineering and Technology, London, United Kingdom

The Institution of Engineering and Technology is registered as a Charity in England & Wales (no. 211014) and Scotland (no. SC038698).

The Institution of Engineering and Technology
Michael Faraday House
Six Hills Way, Stevenage
Herts, SG1 2AY, United Kingdom

www.theiet.org

British Library Cataloguing in Publication Data
A catalogue record for this product is available from the British Library

ISBN 978-1-83953-114-9 (hardback)
ISBN 978-1-83953-115-6 (PDF)

Typeset in India by MPS Limited
Printed in the UK by CPI Group (UK) Ltd, Croydon

Contents

Poongodi Thangamuthu, Indrakumari Ranganathan, Kiruthika Mani,
Suganthi Shanmugam and Suresh Palanimuthu

2 Privacy issues in blockchain   **25**

Prabha Selvaraj, Sumathi Doraikannan, Vijay Kumar Burugari and Kanmani Palaniappan

3 Reforming the traditional business network   **57**

Neethu Narayanan and K.P. Arjun

5 Machine learning   **109**

Deepa Chinnasamy and Saraswathi Devarajan

6 Machine learning in blockchain   **137**

Kolla Bhanu Prakash, Vadla Pradeep Kumar and
Venkata Raghavendra Naga Pawan

**16 Identification and classification of hepatitis C virus: an advance
   machine-learning-based approach**   393
*Janmenjoy Nayak, Pemmada Suresh Kumar,
Dukka Karun Kumar Reddy and Bighnaraj Naik*

**17 Data visualization using machine learning for efficient tracking
   of pandemic – COVID-19**   417
*Supriya Khaitan, Priyanka Shukla, Anamika Mitra,
T. Poongodi and Rashi Agarwal*

About the editors

Dr. Balamurugan Balusamy has served up to the position of Associate Professor in his stint of 14 years of experience with VIT University, Vellore, Tamil Nadu, India. He has completed his Bachelors, Masters and Ph.D. Degrees from top premier institutions. His passion is teaching and adapts different design thinking principles while delivering his lectures. He has done around 30 books on various technologies and visited more than 15 countries for his technical discourse. He has several top notch conferences in his resume and has published over 150 quality journal, conference and book chapters combined. He serves in the advisory committee for several startup and forums and does consultancy work for industry on Industrial IoT. He has given over 175 talks in various events and symposium. He is currently working as a professor in Galgotias University and teaches students, does research on blockchain and IoT.

Dr. Naveen Chilamkurti is currently Acting Head of Department, Computer Science and Computer Engineering, La Trobe University, Melbourne, VIC, Australia. He obtained his Ph.D. degree from La Trobe University. He is also the Inaugural Editor-in-Chief for *International Journal of Wireless Networks and Broadband Technologies* launched in July 2011. He has published about 165 journal and conference papers. His current research areas include intelligent transport systems (ITS), wireless multimedia, wireless sensor networks, and so on. He currently serves on the editorial boards of several international journals. He is a Senior Member of IEEE. He is also an Associate editor for *Wiley IJCS, SCN, Inderscience JETWI,* and *IJIPT.*

Dr. T. Lucia Agnes Beena is working as an Assistant Professor in the department of Information Technology, St. Joseph's College, Tiruchirappalli, Tamil Nadu, India. She has 18 years of teaching experience and 6 years of research experience. She has published number of research articles in *Scopus Indexed Journals.* She authored one book and published few chapters with reputed publishers. Her areas of interest are cloud computing, big data and psychology of computer programming.

Dr. T. Poongodi is working as an Associate Professor in the School of Computing Science and Engineering, Galgotias University, Delhi – NCR, India. She has completed Ph.D. in Information Technology (Information and Communication Engineering) from Anna University, Tamil Nadu, India. She is a pioneer researcher in the areas of big data, wireless ad-hoc network, internet of things, network security and blockchain technology. She has published more than 50 papers in various international journals, national/international conferences, and book chapters in CRC Press, IGI Global, Springer, Elsevier, Wiley, De Gruyter and edited books in CRC, IET, Wiley, Springer.

Preface

Blockchain and machine learning technologies can mitigate the issues such as slow access of medical data, system interoperability, patient agency, improved data quality and quantity for medical research. Blockchain technology facilitates to store information in such a way that doctors can see a patient's entire medical history, but researchers see only statistical data instead of any personal information. The ultra-secure and immutable ledgers, strong, consensus mechanisms, decentralization and self-sovereign identity of blockchain technologies have tremendous potential to rebalance and improve machine learning algorithms. In healthcare, blockchain is used to store correct information that is unaltered and permanent, and machine learning can make use of this data to notice patterns and give accurate predictions. This provides more support for the patients and also in research-related fields where there is a need for accurate data to predict credible results. This book explores the concepts and techniques of blockchain and machine learning. Also, the possibility of applying blockchain and machine learning for the enhancement of e-healthcare system is discussed. The specific highlight of this book will be on the application of blockchain technology in any area of supply chain, drug verification, reimbursement, control access and clinical trials of healthcare.

Chapter 1 provided a detailed study on the fundamentals of blockchain technology, types of blockchain technology and the relevance of blockchain in the healthcare industry along with several use cases. The research challenges and opportunities are also discussed in detail. In Chapter 2, the privacy issues on blockchain at the national and multinational corporate were discussed. It also deals with the blockchain approaches to data privacy in healthcare and security for health data. Chapter 3 studies both the present and most recent updates in the field of medical organizations by acknowledging blockchain as a model. In addition, they discuss the employments of blockchain, near to the difficulties opposed and future points of view. Chapter 4 gives an elevated level overview of Hyperledger, why it was made, how it is represented, and what it would like to accomplish. The core of this chapter presents five convincing uses for big business blockchain in various ventures. Basics of machine learning are dealt in Chapter 5. Blockchain and its ledger can record all data and variables that go through a decision made under machine learning.

Chapter 6 focuses on a few standard machine learning algorithms which are useful in supporting blockchain technology. Chapter 7 explores the abilities predictable at the integration of machine learning and blockchain, particularly in the field of healthcare, and examines the typical descriptions, advantages and trials of this coalition. The blockchain tools and applications help in ensuring the global integrity of the medical records. Each and every day the business industries especially medical and healthcare sectors are enhanced with the immense usage of adaptive technologies which are discussed in Chapter 8. Chapter 9 deals with the discussion of various emerging technologies for healthcare analytics and various software which help in analyzing the healthcare data and the challenges associated with the healthcare analytics. Chapter 10 brings out, in brief, healthcare sector statistics and major healthcare data breaches over the last 5 years. The healthcare domain encompasses not just the health data breaches but also takes into consideration all components associated with it like supply chain, medical professionals, health fake credentials and certifications, and fake medicine chain. These have been discussed with possible resolutions and association with blockchain technology.

The main focus of Chapter 11 is put up in a novel patient centric framework to make the effective patient engagement, data curation and regulated dissemination of accumulated information in a secure and interoperable environment. Chapter 12 covers the structure for accessing clinical records of patients in blockchain by exercising medications based on keen agreements. Be that as it may, blockchain is not a solution for malignant growth, yet it fills in as potential innovative instrument to battle against special diseases. In Chapter 13, initially the discussion is about the work happening in COVID-19 using ML algorithms and then the role of machine learning for analyzing and assessing various chronic diseases that were detailed. In Chapter 14, the healthcare sector's diagnosing system is discussed, and the intended machine learning algorithm is identified and applied to make the diagnosis system more accurate and error-free using supervised and unsupervised machine learning algorithms. Chapter 15 gives a brief description of the characteristics of data, and the significance of the data quality in healthcare. Data has to be extracted from various sources for better analysis. Hence, this chapter put forth an overview of challenges that must be resolved, and various types of extraction tools that can be used are discussed. In Chapter 16, experimental investigations on the study of various machine learning approaches for the diagnosis of associated risk factors, cofactors promoting its progression, complications in the prevention and control of hepatitis C virus in Egypt were depicted. Further, this chapter will focus on some of the basic machine learning strategies along with the challenges of handling the hepatitis C disease. Chapter 17 provides the details of different ways of processing and visualizing the huge amount data generated on COVID-19 pandemic. This includes the clusters on the basis of symptoms in different age groups, effects of COVID-19 on different countries.

B. Balamurugan, N. Chilamkurti,
T. Lucia Agnes Beena and T. Poongodi

Chapter 1

Blockchain technology and its relevance in healthcare

Poongodi Thangamuthu[1], Indrakumari Ranganathan[1], Kiruthika Mani[2], Suganthi Shanmugam[3] and Suresh Palanimuthu[4]

Blockchain technology is extensively used in the recent years to maintain data security for the digital asset transformation without any third-party intervention. Blockchain is a rapidly evolving and emerging technology that has gained more attention from industry, academia and government sectors because of its latent relevance and offering potential solutions. The characteristics of blockchain made it as a cutting-edge technology and can be leveraged to solve significant issues in many promising applications. A plethora of blockchain application leverages and revolutionizes several disciplines with the potential of large-scale exploration. There is a promising future for the blockchain in the healthcare domain because of scalability, traceability, fault tolerance and high security. The benefits, challenges and relevant use cases for incorporating blockchain in the healthcare domain are presented by performing studies with in-depth analysis. The chapter provided a detailed study on the fundamentals of blockchain technology, types of blockchain technology and the relevance of blockchain in the healthcare industry along with several use cases. The research challenges and opportunities are also discussed in detail.

1.1 Introduction

Blockchain technology can be defined as a distributed system in which transactional or historical data can be recorded, stored and maintained across a network. It is a non-changeable, public digital ledger similar to a database. Blockchain technology is a horizontal innovation that can be adopted by any industry. Blockchain

[1]School of Computing Science and Engineering, Galgotias University, Greater Noida, India
[2]Department of Computer Science and Engineering, Jansons Institute of Technology, Coimbatore, India
[3]PG and Research Department of Computer Science, Cauvery College for Women, Tiruchirappalli, India
[4]School of Mechanical Engineering, Galgotias University, Greater Noida, India

can be considered as a movement, more than a technology, where multiple industries are innovating and redefining the way they function. Industries, including supply chain industry, food industry, healthcare industry, are adopting blockchain technology to renovate their working structure. The blockchain technology is getting massive attention in healthcare [1–3]. Using blockchain technology in healthcare industry will save the data-breach-related costs, IT costs, personnel costs, etc. up to $100 billion per year by 2025. Also there will be a considerable reduction in frauds and forgery products. Furthermore, based on the survey conducted by World Economic Forum, blockchain will maintain 10% of GDP across the world.

Blockchain is a collection of computers connected together in a peer-to-peer (P2P) network. It is a disruptive rising technology that maintains a digital ledger which is decentralized, timestamped, transparent and immune to fraud. It is the combination of existing technologies such as cryptography, shared ledger and distributed network and functions on a P2P network. The traditional healthcare systems are vendor specific with incompatible health systems resulting in improper communication, fragmented data, insecure sharing of medical and financial data and medical workflows with missing parts. The blockchain technology provides a secure and efficient infrastructure in overcoming these difficulties. In blockchain, the digital data is grouped into blocks with each block storing transactions and linked with other blocks having similar information in the form of a chain. The healthcare systems make the use of private blockchains that are controlled by a central authority and only selected nodes participate in the network based on a consensus [4–7]. A transaction is represented by a user initiating a request to create a block and then the transaction being broadcasted for each node that is connected in the P2P network. Using consensus algorithms, all nodes validate each transaction along with the user details in the blockchain network. Once the transaction is validated, the block that is newly created can be added to the existing blockchain. The basic working procedure of blockchain is depicted in Figure 1.1.

1.1.1   Evolution of blockchain technology

In 1991, cryptographically secured blockchain was introduced; it prevents the tampering of data by attaching timestamps to the documents. The system was upgraded by incorporating a Merkle tree structure that enables one to collect and maintain more documents in a single block. In 2008, Satoshi Nakamoto revamped the concept to gain its relevance; he introduced bitcoin as a digital ledger during this period [8]. In 2009, an attempt was made to improve the digital trust in a decentralization perspective where no one would have a control to alter anything. Blockchain is a digital platform, where users are allowed to perform their transactions without any trusted arbitrator. It is a P2P distributed ledger used to record transactions in several computers simultaneously. Bitcoin and blockchain are the two different technologies that have cryptocurrency as the common underlying technology. Blockchain 1.0 was announced as a bitcoin emergence in 2008; the chains of blocks which contain several units of information and transaction are

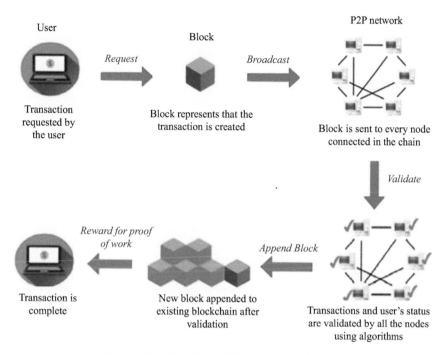

Figure 1.1   Working of blockchain technology

accessible, which leverages the capabilities of digital ledger in an electronic P2P system. In 2013, Blockchain 2.0 introduced a public blockchain named Ethereum blockchain that facilitates a user to record the assets as smart contracts. It acts as a platform for developing many decentralized applications. In 2015, Hyperledger was introduced as an open-source blockchain that promotes global industry collaboration by improving the reliability and performance of current systems [9]. Later, the blockchain networks involving private, public and federated (consortium) blockchains have started evolving in the recent years, which improves operational efficiency in blockchain technology applications. According to Gartner Trend Insight, in 2022, it is expected to have at least one business constructed on blockchain being valued over $10 billion. The research firm anticipates that the business value will grow more than $176 billion in the year 2025, and by 2030, it may exceed $3.1 trillion due to the exploitation of digital ledger technology.

1.1.2   Characteristics of blockchain technology

Blockchain technology has certain inherent features that can be utilized for diversified applications. The various characteristics include the following:

- *Decentralized*: The public blockchain is decentralized, and anyone connected in the blockchain has access to the database, by which the user can monitor, modify and update the data. The trusted third party or a central node is not involved in the validation of transactions and thereby reduces the cost and performance issues. The consistency and integrity is ensured by using consensus algorithms. However, consortium blockchain and private blockchain are partially and fully centralized, respectively [10].

- *Transparency*: The verification and tracking of data can be easily accomplished as the data is open to all the users on the network, i.e., public. The interactions among all participating nodes are verified by an authorized entity that automatically facilitates transparency.
- *Open source*: Because of its open nature, the users can also develop their own applications.
- *Persistence*: The transactions are distributed over all nodes that are validated and checked by other nodes using a consensus algorithm before it is being added to the block. Hence it is highly difficult to delete or alter any data. The public blockchain is immutable. However, if the majority of the nodes are interested in modifying the consortium and private blockchain, it can be altered [10].
- *Provenience*: Tracking of the origin of every transaction inside the blockchain ledger can be easily done. In blockchain, the authenticity of the data that is stored as a transaction is ensured by digital signatures.
- *Anonymity*: Users' real identity is not exposed as they participate with the generated address in the network.
- *Autonomy*: The nodes in the blockchain network are independent, and other nodes cannot intervene their functioning.
- *Distributed control*: The data stored in the blockchain is maintained in a distributed manner, which guarantees no single-point failure.

1.1.3 Overview of blockchain architecture

The blockchain architecture comprises five layers that act as an interface for providing blockchain-based services to support several industrial applications [11,12] that are described as follows:

- Data layer: In this layer, the data is encrypted using asymmetric cryptographic techniques and hash functions. The encrypted connected data blocks construct a blockchain once the blocks are validated. Different hash functions and cryptographic algorithms are used in various blockchain platforms. For example, SHA-256 and Elliptic Curve Digital Signature Algorithm (ECDSA) are used as a hash function and cryptographic algorithm in bitcoin.
- Network layer: The overlay P2P network comprises either physical or virtual connectivity among the nodes in the wired or wireless communication network. The nodes broadcast the transaction to other connected peer nodes. After receiving, the block of transactions will be verified locally. If the transaction becomes valid, then it is further propagated to the remaining nodes in the overlay network.

- Consensus layer: This layer is responsible in ensuring the trustfulness of a transaction block using consensus algorithm such as proof of work (PoW), proof of stake (PoS) and proof of elapsed time. The propagation mechanisms such as advertisement-based and relay networks are considered as the prerequisite for consensus protocols.
- Incentive layer: Its responsibility lies in accomplishing the tasks such as issuing digital currency, reward mechanisms for miners, managing transaction cost and, in particular, defining appropriate policy for digital currency creation and distribution of rewards to the participants involved in the mining process.
- Service layer: Providing services in terms of blockchains for several industrial sectors such as logistics, retail manufacturing, food industry, pharmaceutical industry, supply chains and utilities.

1.1.4   Merkle tree structure

A Merkle tree (binary hash tree) [13] is a complete binary tree associated with k-bits in each node. One-way function is followed for the values among the node and its children. Moreover, it facilitates the verification of a leaf node against the root value by providing the values of the pairs from the leaf node to the root node in the respective path. The Merkle tree structure is implemented in the blockchain to summarize the transactions efficiently. It produces $2 \times \log_2 N$ hashes for N number of transactions; hence it is considered as an efficient process to verify that a transaction exists in a block. To construct a Merkle tree, the process is initiated with the leaf nodes that hold the transaction hash. Although it is a complete binary tree, all internal nodes in the tree have two children that are at the same level. In the case of any odd number of transactions, the last transaction hash would be duplicated to make it even for further processing. For hashing, the leaves are grouped together to build a parent node. The same process will be continued till experiencing all the nodes, and thus, a root node known as Merkle root is generated.

To ensure that a transaction is available in a block, a particular path is provided in which the transaction is traversed through the tree. The complete path comprises the nodes of the same height in the binary tree. The hash enables rapid scan among thousands of transactions, and verification can be done only in a specific block; hence, it is not necessary to scan the complete block. If any particular node is interested in verifying a transaction, it requires the complete nodes assistance. The highlighted portion in Figure 1.2 shows the path to prove the set of transactions in a block. For example, to prove the transaction *C* on a block, *hash (D)*, *hash (AB)* and *hash (EFGH)* along with the block header will be sent to a simplified node. The Merkle tree root can be computed and compared with the root value existing in the block header. Furthermore, the simplified node computes *hash(C)* along with *hash (D)* and can compute the *hash (CD)*. By taking the value of *hash (AB)*, it obtains the *hash (ABCD)* and uses the *hash (EFGH)* to compute the root which is *hash (ABCDEFGH)*.

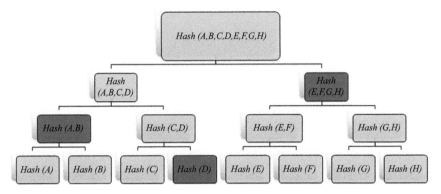

Figure 1.2   Merkle tree

1.2   Basic components of blockchain

1.2.1   *Cryptographic hash functions*

A mathematical algorithm is mainly used in cryptography that converts data such as text, image or file of any size into a bit string which is of fixed size and in compressed form. The output bit string can be known by the "hash," "hash value" or "message digest." This value is unique for that particular type of input data, and any changes in the data will be reflected by yielding a completely different hash value on applying the hash function. A random number generated by an authentication protocol called the cryptographic nonce (the number only used once) is added to an encrypted data to make it more difficult when rehashed. In blockchain, the hash functions are used for the derivation of address, creation of unique identifiers and authentication of block data and block headers.

1.2.2   *Asymmetric-key cryptography*

Asymmetric-key cryptography is an encryption process used in blockchain that guarantees security of data and is also known as the public-key cryptography. It uses two related keys called the public key and private key. All the users are made open to use the public key, but the private key is secure, which is only known to the owner. One can encrypt with a private key and decrypt with a public key. Also, encryption can be done using the public key and the encrypted message is decrypted only with the private key of the owner. It is often slow to compute. The integrity and authenticity of the transactions can be verified by this mechanism, and the transactions are made based on the trust among all users in the chain. In untrusted environments, digital signatures based on asymmetric key cryptography are used [12]. It uses ECDSA and provides double-layer protection with the help of private and public keys.

1.2.3 Transactions

Transaction is the interaction among parties by transferring data among different nodes. Transaction takes place when data is transmitted over the network that involves information such as the sender's identifier and public key, digital signature, transaction inputs and transaction outputs. The digital data to be transferred is called inputs. The transaction will have a reference to the origin or a source of the data to be transferred. It can be a reference to the previous past events or it can be the origin event in the case of new transactions. Transactions are not encrypted and so all technical details can be viewed by the users publicly. The receiver account that gets the digital assets is called outputs. It also contains details of receiver's identifier and how much data to be transferred.

1.2.4 Ledgers

Blockchain uses a distributed ledger that is a database containing a collection of transactions that is shared and synchronized across different locations and among multiple users. The transactions and contracts are accurately stored in a decentralized way using cryptographic techniques such as digital signatures. The validation and verification of transactions by a central authority can be eliminated. The records become immutable once they are stored; this makes them more resistant against cyberattacks. Also due to its distributed nature, the copies of records are distributed to several computers, and so changing a single record needs changing of all other copies of the record, which is impossible. It enhances the flow of information, thereby making audit trail easy to follow by the accountants.

1.2.5 Blocks

Blocks are records storing unalterable digital information related to transactions that together form a blockchain. Blocks are like ledger pages containing collection of zero or more transactions. Publishing node publishes a block, and the transactions are added to the block. A block usually consists of a block header and block data, and this may vary depending on the blockchain implementation.

A block header consists of the following:

- Block version indicates the group of block validation rules which is to be followed.
- Timestamp that contains current approval time as seconds in universal time, since January 1, 1970, for the particular block.
- Parent block hash is a 256-bit hash value pointing to the previous block.
- Merkle tree root hash is the hash value of all the transactions in the block.
- n Bits which is a 256-bit unsigned integer called the target threshold.
- Nonce which is a 4-byte field starting with 0 and increased for every hash calculation. It changes the hash output of the block contents.

Block data consists of the following:

- Transaction counter that maintains the total count of successfully completed transactions.
- Transaction data is the data stored in the field, which can be a business data, healthcare data or data related to bitcoins, etc. It depends upon the purpose of transactions performed.

As in the linked list, the blocks are chained together where each block contains the previous block's header hash value, thus forming the blockchain. Thus, if any data is changed in a block, it would change its hash value that is reflected in the subsequent blocks.

1.3 Consensus models

The absence of a central authority in blockchain necessitates the need of a consensus algorithm to maintain the consistency of the ledger transactions. The consensus algorithm plays a notable role in determining the efficiency and safety of the blockchain systems, and the type of algorithm chosen has a major influence on the performance of the system. Different approaches are used in the consensus algorithms which are as follows.

1.3.1 Proof of work

It is mainly used in bitcoins. The strategy is that a node is randomly selected from a group of competing nodes for publishing a block of transactions. Also, the node has to prove that it is legitimate by performing a lot of computational calculations and that it will not attack other nodes. The block header's hash value is computed by all the nodes in the network by modifying the nonce value frequently. The consensus is to select the node with a hash value equal to or less than certain target value. The one which attains the specified target hash value publishes the block, and all other nodes validate the hash value. Once validated, all other users add this block to their chain of blocks. This consumes a lot of effort from the user side.

1.3.2 Proof of stake

Stake means the amount of cryptocurrency that the participant in the blockchain network has invested into the system. It is based on the assumption that the more stake a user has invested into the system, the less likely to attack the system. Thus, a user with more stakes is given more chances to publish the block. However, it is unfair as users with the majority stake become dominant. But this can be overcome by altering the formula of strategy.

1.3.3 Practical byzantine fault tolerance

The byzantine faults are managed by using the algorithm that has the capability of handling up to one-third of malicious byzantine replicas [10]. In this algorithm, a primary node is selected, which is responsible for carrying the transactions based on certain criteria. The selection process has three phases: *pre-prepared, prepared* and *commit*. A node can pass through successive phases if two-thirds of votes are gained by it from all the nodes. There is no hashing procedure in practical byzantine fault tolerance [10].

1.3.4   Delegated proof of stake

Delegated PoS differs from PoS in such a way that the representatives or delegates are elected by their stakeholders for generating and validating blocks. The system is left with fewer nodes for validation and results in an easy confirmation of transactions. The delegates are rewarded and possess the status of publishing node, and so they do not act maliciously.

1.3.5   Round robin consensus model

In this approach, the nodes are given turns to publish their blocks. In case, a node is not available for its turn, other nodes are given chances to publish based on a time limit. It is used in permissioned blockchain systems, and if used in permissionless systems, a malicious user can continuously add the blocks leading to disruption in correct operation of the block.

1.3.6   Proof of authority (identity) model

It is used in permissioned systems. In this, the publishing user has the proof of identity verified and included in the blockchain. The user can build or lose the reputation depending on the behavior. The more reputation the user builds, the more likely the chance for publishing blocks.

1.3.7   Proof of elapsed time (PoET) consensus model

The publishing node requests wait time from the software of the system. After that the random wait time is allotted to stand idle for that particular time and starts publishing blocks. The randomly allotted wait time is given as a signed certificate in which the user can publish along with the block. The process is transparent, and this ensures that a malicious user cannot wait for a while to publish blocks.

1.4   Challenges and opportunities of blockchain technology

1.4.1   Security and privacy of the data

The data requiring security includes daily individual activities, medical records, corporate financial data and personally identifiable information [14]. Medical data holds sensitive information in which safety and privacy should be ensured. Blockchain uses decentralized system in which the data is shared among different services and nodes; hence, there is a potential chance of data leakage. Everyone on the chain has access to data unlike the centralized system in which authorization is provided by an intermediate trusted third party. Therefore, patients provide authorization to one or more reliable people to access the data that may pose a serious threat to the security of the data. So, proper data access control mechanisms should be implemented in the system. Blockchain relies heavily on cryptographic algorithms, smart contracts and software that may also have flaws and loopholes.

1.4.2   Storage

Blockchains have limited on-chain data storage with decentralization and hashing architecture [15]. In healthcare industry, voluminous amounts of medical data are generated, and so blockchain applications should be designed taking medical big data into consideration.

1.4.3   Standardization

For blockchain being used in different infrastructures and applications, a high level of standardization is required. The implementation of predefined standards for the size, format and nature of data is essential. As a relatively new technology in healthcare, potential benefits as well as related issues are unknown, and so it faces the problem of legal regulations acceptance from several countries [16].

1.4.4   Scalability

Blockchain technology should be capable of handling a large number of users and medical devices such as sensors, smart devices or Internet of Things (IoT) that are more prevalent in the health industry. In bitcoin, the rate of growth of the chain for every 10 min is 1 MB per block along with copies of data stored in the nodes [17]. If the number of users and the devices increases, the computational overhead also increases, which results in performance and synchronization issues.

1.4.5   Interoperability

The storage of medical data is done mainly in a centralized database server that leads to data fragmentation, reduced data quantity and quality for medical research, slow access and lack of system interoperability [16]. A single patient's medical record may be present at different locations in various systems. So, sharing and interoperability of data among various communicating providers and services is a major issue in blockchain. The transfer and sharing of data among various sources help health industry in providing improved services to the patients. Blockchain systems should be designed to be interoperable among different medical systems.

1.4.6   Key management

In blockchain technology, the data is distributed, and all users in the block have access to the data. Hence, in the cryptographic process, private and public keys are used to encrypt and decrypt the data. Currently, blockchain uses a single key for all blocks, and any leakage of this key may lead to the data in the whole block vulnerable [16].

1.4.7   Blockchain vulnerabilities

The inherent blockchain framework is vulnerable to various malicious attacks: a few to mention like 51% attack (in which a user dominates the other users with most of the computational resources), or double spending attack (in which a user spends the same cryptocurrency for more than one transactions).

1.4.8   Social challenges

Blockchain is a new and evolving technology, and so acceptance from people and shifting from the traditional technology being unaware of its pros and cons is a big challenge.

1.4.9   Accountability

The transparent, sharable and verifiable nature of data in blockchain plays an effective role in healthcare industry. It provides a multilayered data protection mechanism through decentralization, consensus and hashing algorithms. The documentation, billing and the procedures followed in the treatment of diseases are transparent and thus making all parties involved accountable.

1.4.10   Accuracy

The conventional health systems face the problem of data inconsistencies as the patient data may not be shared and updated by all parties involved in the system leading to inaccuracies and fragmented data. Rather in blockchain, the data can be shared and verified by all parties connected in the chain and updated immediately.

1.4.11   Agility

Medical data can be collected in real time through sensors, smart devices and wearable IoT used for providing personalized care and handling emergency situations in a timely manner [18–21]. The detection of pandemics and epidemics can be done easily and handled in an efficient way. Blockchain has the ability to transport, share and access these data from anywhere and from any device rapidly.

1.4.12   Fighting counterfeit drugs

Substandard drugs are more prevalent in low- and middle-income countries. Blockchain technology can be used for tracking drugs right from their production till the end users. Moreover, the supply chain distribution of drugs can be easily tracked and verified, thereby detecting medical frauds.

1.4.13   Cost efficient

The patient can make smart financial decisions with the help of accurate and documented information provided through blockchain. Furthermore, the operational cost of data analysis and distribution spent on third-party service providers is also eliminated.

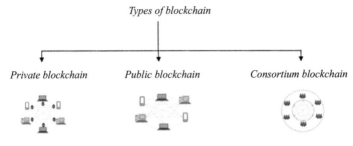

Figure 1.3   Types of blockchain

1.4.14   Improving research and development

Anonymity of the data in blockchain plays an effective role in conducting research. Currently, there are fake medical and genomic data which affects the research quality. Blockchain produces a transparent way in tracking these data from the real generators to the end users who analyze the data. Genomic information sharing mainly uses blockchain technology [15]. Blockchain technology coupled with artificial intelligence and machine learning can take research in healthcare to a higher altitude.

1.5   Types of blockchain

Blockchain holds a collection of information in interlinked blocks. Bitcoin, a concept of cryptocurrencies, initiated the notion of blockchain into the limelight, which protects the data from unauthorized tampering. The blockchain is an upcoming technology; hence it is hard for the users to recognize its working principle without stepping into its code and details. When compared to other technologies, blockchain is considered as the most secured network. Blockchain is an encrypted repository of digital information with a distributed and decentralized network of computers to facilitate the most secured transactions to avoid fraudulent activities [17]. Blockchain allows the user to track the asset individually. Blockchain is divided into two types:

1. Based on the nature of data accessibility
2. Based on the need of authorization

Based on the nature of data accessibility, the blockchain is categorized into three types and is shown in Figure 1.3:

(i)   Public blockchain
(ii)   Private blockchain
(iii) Consortium blockchain

1.5.1   Public blockchain

In public blockchain, every member in the network can access the block and can make transactions, and every participant can involve in the process of creating the consensus. In this case, there is neither an intermediatory register nor a trusted third party [22]. Public blockchains are transparent and open, so any participant can avail the blocks at any time. For instance, bitcoin, a cryptocurrency and P2P payment system introduced by Satoshi Nakamoto, is based on public blockchain. Bitcoin is the largest decentralized cryptographic currency with a capitalization close to 14 billion euros in 2016. It uses a decentralized mechanism to avoid the intervention of a third party. The decentralization mechanism is that each participant can draft the code, irrespective of the permission. Participants use their processing power to authenticate, save and protect transactions in the data blocks. This process is known as mining that allows the users to recompense for every new validated block, by creating bitcoins. Based on the law of supply and demand, the costs of the cryptocurrencies are fixed. The structure of public blockchain is shown in Figure 1.4.

Transactions among the participants are grouped into blocks, and every block is authenticated by the nodes present in the network, called the miners. In the bitcoin environment, it is called the proof of work that solves algorithmic problems. The validated blocks are timestamped and placed in the string of blocks, which is made visible to all participants in the network with an approximate time span. Public blockchains are trustless because of the mining process or PoW.

1.5.2   Private blockchain

Private blockchain is based on access control; hence, access is restricted to the users to take part in the network. Few entities are there in the network to control the access that makes the network reliable for third parties to transact. In this type of

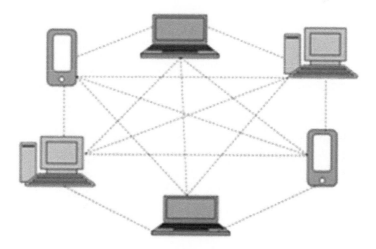

Figure 1.4   Public blockchain

blockchain, only the entities who are participating in the transactions would know about the details of the transaction. Linux Foundation and Hyperledger Fabric are examples of private blockchains. Private blockchains are applicable in database management and auditing in many fields. Mostly its uses are internal to a single company, where the privacy of the data should be preserved and not allowed to access publicly. Private blockchain serves better by abiding the privacy and security rules of the government and preserves data. The main advantages of private blockchain are data redundancies, easier data-handling, transaction cost and extra automated compliance functionalities. The structure of private blockchain is shown in Figure 1.5.

1.5.3   Consortium blockchain

Consortium blockchain is an amalgamation of public and private blockchains. Private blockchain is applicable for enterprise solutions to preserve business data. The consortium blockchain is considered as a semi-private blockchain with a restricted user group but available across various organizations. In other words, this type of blockchain can be utilized if organizations are ready to share the blockchain, but restrict data access to them, and retain it secure from public access. Thus, it possesses the features of both public and private blockchains. Consortium blockchain is a cross-discipline and cross-company solution provider with the support of many blockchain platforms. A blockchain consortium of concurring companies can leverage information to advance workflows, accountability and transparency. The structure of consortium blockchain is shown in Figure 1.6.

Figure 1.5   Private blockchain

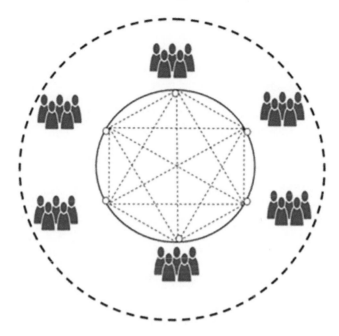

Figure 1.6   Consortium blockchain

The two categories of users practice consortium blockchain are as follows:

1. The participants who have their control over the blockchain can make a decision that who can access the blockchain network.
2. The participants who can access the blockchain network.

Here multiple authorities are present. For instance, consider that there are many companies that are collaboratively working and making decisions for the benefit of the entire group. Such groups are also termed consortiums or a federation blockchain. Consortium-blockchain-based applications are r3 and energy web foundation (EWF). The number of consortia for different sectors is given in Figure 1.7.

The comparison between public, private and consortium blockchains is given in Table 1.1.

Based on the need of authorization, the blockchain is divided into the following:

1. Permissionless blockchain
2. Permissioned blockchain

Permissionless and permissioned blockchain

(i) Permissioned blockchain requires former approval to use the system whereas permissionless blockchain allows everyone to participate in the network [23].

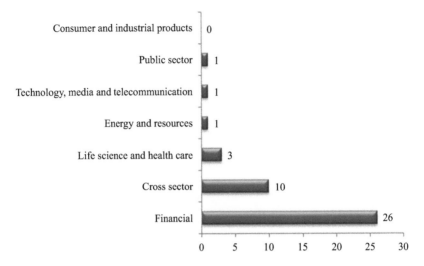

Figure 1.7   Number of consortia by sector (Source: Deloitte analysis)

Table 1.1   Public vs private vs consortium blockchain

Public blockchain	Private blockchain	Consortium or federated blockchain
Any participants in the network can run BTC/ETH full node in order to take part in the consensus	Not all participants can start mining to run a full node	Participants of the federation can start mining and run a full node
Any participants can do transactions on BTC/ETH full node	Not all participants can start transactions on the chain	Participants of the federation can make decisions on the chain
Any participants can audit the transaction	Not all participants can audit the blockchain in the network	Participants of the federation can audit the *blockchain* in the network
Example: Bitcoin, Litecoin	Example: Bankchain	Example: r3 and EWF

(ii)   Both these types are based on distributed ledger concept, which means various versions of similar data are stored at different places and connected through network.

(iii) Both these blockchains are immutable, and the blocks are connected by cryptographic hashes [24].

(iv)   Both these blockchains use consensus mechanism.

1.5.4   Permissioned blockchain

Permissioned blockchain is considered as an extra blockchain security system as it allows restricted identifiable participants to access the network. For this particular reason, these blockchains differ from private and public blockchains. Permissioned blockchains are useful for those who need security and role definition within the blockchain. Several methods are available to construct a blockchain, but some methods include special permissions to read, write and access data. The inherent configuration of this type of blockchain manages the transactions made by the participant by defining certain roles for them by maintaining the identity of each participant. Such blockchains are permissioned blockchains. Private blocks are different from permissioned blockchain. Private blockchain permits only the known nodes to contribute in the network. For instance, banks are using private blockchain that uses a selected number of participants to operate whereas in permissioned blockchains, anyone can join a network by verifying their role and identity.

Permissioned blockchains are preferred by business and industry-level people as they require role, security and identity. For example, a firm manufacturing a product can use a permissioned blockchain that also can participate in the supply chain management. The transactions may involve financing banks, logistics partners and some vendors in the process. Although the external parties are on the network, they do not have permission to see the cost the firm is fixing for its clients. These role-limited implementations are allowed by permissioned blockchain. The algorithm that constructs the permissioned blockchain allows certain participants to view selected record such as the name of the product, quantity but not the price. The access control layer maintains the profile and permission-related activities.

1.5.5   Permissionless blockchain

In permissionless blockchain, the popular applications such as Bitcoin, Ethereum, Dash, Litecoin and Monero come under this category. Permissionless blockchain permits any participants to do transactions and validation [25]. The copy of the ledgers can be accessed and stored globally. In this network, based on the purpose, the blockchains employ utility or monetary tokens. In permissionless network, the participants can permit one to access all information except certain information such as private keys that include transaction details and its processing. There is no centralized authority to monitor all activities such as editing the ledgers, changing the protocol and shutting down the network; due to this, it falls under decentralized network. It operates based on consensus protocol, so it needs 51% user consent to change the network type.

1.6   Relevance of blockchain for healthcare

The inherent features of blockchain technology such as decentralization, data immutability, data security and privacy, data availability, transparency make it appropriate for healthcare sector. Blockchain will shift the conventional institution-driven interoperability to patient-centered interoperability [26]. The various use cases of blockchain technology in healthcare industry are discussed in this section.

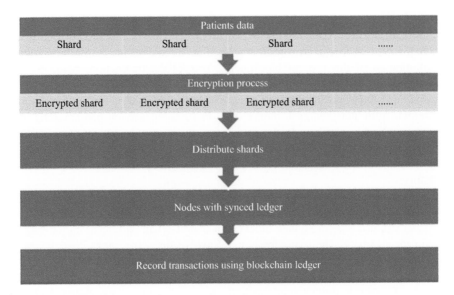

Figure 1.8   Medical record management using blockchain

1.6.1   Blockchain for medical record management

There is always a breach in securing patients records, and many patients' records are hacked over time. Using blockchain will eliminate the difficulty in maintaining doctor–patient confidentiality. There are many cases filed against healthcare practitioners for exposing the patients' health records. When blockchain is adopted into healthcare industry, the records of patients can be stored on blockchain, and the patients can decide upon who can access their data. The patients can also monitor for any data breaches in their record and if found, the unauthorized access can be easily stacked.

There are two issues in patient data management. The first issue is that each patient is unique. Although the diseases may be common between patients, there is no common treatment strategy among them. Therefore, there is a need to customize the treatment to each patient depending on their medical history. Healthcare is becoming more and more patient-centered. The second issue is the way how the information is shared among healthcare community. Today, sharing of patient's data from different places is done using social networks [27]. As known, medical data is very sensitive and a small change to the data may become a life threat. Sharing the information in a secure structure has become an essential factor in medical field.

Blockchain addresses the foresaid issues in addition to data ownership. Blockchain is used to provide a secure structure for data sharing, and the process is shown in Figure 1.8. Health workers of a particular organization collect data from the patients, including name, date of birth, blood group, family history, and the collected data is broken into small chunks. This process of breaking up data into small chunks is known as data sharding, and this is helpful for quick transfer. The shards are now encrypted and stored in a distributed manner. A unique ID is created for the patient, and a hash value is created for the collected information. Now the distributed data has a synced ledger that records the transactions. As blockchain is distributed, the patient can share the medical record with any other medical practitioners. The medical record of a patient may be needed by pharmaceutical companies, researchers, etc. The patients can decide who can access his/her information.

1.6.2 Blockchain for medicinal research

Medicine is a vast and dynamic field. Every day, many diseases keep on emerging, and thousands of health workers are fighting against the new diseases in innovative ways for the welfare of the patients. A number of researches and experiments are being done in healthcare industry. But there is no centralized system for handling these research-oriented data. Blockchain provides a distributed environment to store research data that can be shared with fellow researchers. Also, blockchain is secured, and the researchers all over the world, with patients' permission, can access the wide-ranging informative database. This will certainly increase the speed in the researches done in healthcare industry.

Clinical trials are performed to test the effectiveness and tolerance of a product on a particular group of patients. The tests are done for several years, and the outcomes are recorded properly. These results play an eminent role in releasing the tested drugs to the open market. Hence the recorded outcomes/results are very important and a minor change or error may lead to loss of billions of lives. Also, large groups of people are involved in clinical trials, leading ways to mistakes. Some mistakes are done intentionally, and this may include modifying or hiding data.

Blockchain can provide proof-of-existence for the clinical trial documents and allow anyone to verify the authenticity. When a person has to modify any data, then that transaction needs to be agreed by preponderance of the nodes that it is legitimate. Only then the modification can be carried out. When modifications need to be done, it has to be agreed by the majority of blockchain nodes. The data that is stored in a blockchain goes through a hash function and generates a unique hash key. Any alteration done to the data will produce a completely distinct hash value. Both public and private keys are used in blockchain. Hashing function in blockchain stands as a proof for data integrity, and the public key proves the ownership of the data. In order to check the authenticity of the data, the data with the user and data in the blockchain are given to the SHA256 calculator. There will be two hash values produced for two data. If the hash values of both the data are the same, then it can be proved that the data has not been modified. But if the hash values are different, then there is some change done to the data. This method is shown in Figure 1.9.

1.6.3 Blockchain for insurance claims

Blockchain technology is expected to improve the ways in which the insurance claim is done by the patients. Desired properties of blockchain, such as robustness

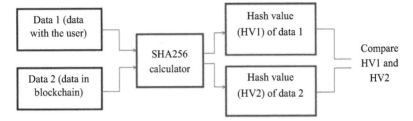

Figure 1.9   Clinical trials using blockchain

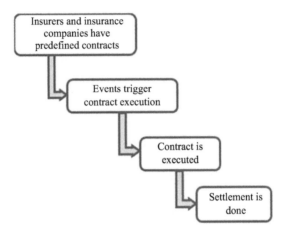

Figure 1.10   Insurance claims using blockchain

and distributed nature, make it useful for patients to claim insurance anywhere at the needful time. The settlement for claim can also be completely automated and secured using blockchain. Smart contracts can be used between the insurers and insurance companies where the contract can be executed involuntarily once the condition is met. When smart contracts are used, there is no need of middleman and no chaos occurs. Also, insurance fraud can be widely reduced using blockchain. According to a report published by BIS, the global healthcare market spend on blockchain is expected to hit $5.61 billion by 2025 [28].

According to the report provided by FBI, non-health insurance fraud in the United States is over $40 billion per year. This fraudulent activity can induce additional expense to the families by making them spend between $400 and $700 per year for their extra premiums [29]. As data in blockchain is immutable, any claims done before can be easily known by the insurers. The claim settlement can also be done in a jiffy using smart contracts. Terms are established between the insurers and the insurance company. The health insurance can be claimed by the insurer when he/she meets up the conditions specified in the agreement. Once the conditions are met, the contract is triggered and executed automatically. The claim settlement is carried out electronically using blockchain in a secured manner, without the involvement of a third party, and it is explained using Figure 1.10.

1.6.4   Blockchain for counterfeit drugs

Drug counterfeiting has become a major issue in the healthcare industries of developing countries. The World Health Organization states that the market of counterfeit medicines has reached billions of dollars every year [30]. The counterfeit drugs contain incorrect levels of ingredients and consuming them may even lead to death. Defective supply chain management in the pharmaceutical industry is the major reason for drug counterfeiting. The supply chain of drugs can be stated as in Figure 1.11.

In the current scenario, once the manufactures produce the drugs and give it to wholesalers, there is no information about their products. Also, the drugs become untraceable by the pharmaceutical regulatory authorities. Using blockchain technology in this supply chain may result in drug traceability and security. Reference [31] has proposed a system where the drugs can be traced starting from the manufacturers to consumers using permissioned blockchain. Data immutability and timestamping of data in blockchain helps one to track a drug in a reliable manner.

A private blockchain can be established between trustworthy companies to assure the authenticity. Hence, a company's access to this blockchain will act as a proof that the drugs they produce are authentic. Blockchain concept can be implemented by generating a hash value for a drug that is manufactured. This hash value contains all the relevant information about the drug. After production, the drug moves in the supply chain as stated earlier. Whenever the drug moves from one entity to another (e.g., from the manufacturer to the wholesaler), the information is stored on the blockchain, making it easy to track. This way, trusted companies in the blockchain can verify the drug supply any time. If any problems are detected in a batch of drugs produced, the manufacturers can withdraw their product easily as the drugs are traceable. Hence, using blockchain technologies, two issues are solved. First, it makes the drugs traceable down the supply chain. Second, it does not allow counterfeit drugs to enter the market.

A study published in the United States articulates that over 200,000 people expire every year because of the medical errors. These errors happen due to the changes that are made in the patient's record unknowingly. As blockchain data is immutable, data can only be added and cannot be erased/changed. Physicians suggest that this is the method how health information should be stored. Also, the patients' data can be accessed by the physicians anytime, and the medical record can tell the details of the patient from their very first hospital visit. Blockchain technology can be considered as a game-changer that enables patients to manage their healthcare needs. Blockchain has come as a rescuer to effectively dissipate the dilemma of errors by digitizing the health records of patients [32].

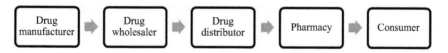

Figure 1.11   Supply chain of drugs

1.6.5   *Blockchain to prevent future pandemics*

The outbreak of the novel coronavirus, COVID-19, is the never seen before pandemic of the year 2020. The Center for Disease Control is taking various measures to solve the issues by partnering with the World Health Organization and IBM. It has initiated a project to employ blockchain technology for tracking, storing and distributing sensitive information to health centers at real time. This may result to an efficient and standardized management of pandemics all over the world.

1.6.6   *Blockchain to save cost*

Adoption of blockchain in the healthcare industry will certainly bring down the expense by tokenization. Tokenization can be termed a modern way of representing a digital asset. Using blockchain, the unnecessary third-party clients can be eliminated. Also counterfeit pharmaceutical drugs can be monitored. This way the industry would take an incredible drift, and the healthcare industry would transform to a completely transparent and accountable environment. This transformation will obviously save the expense spent by both healthcare firms and patients.

1.7   Conclusion

There is a tremendous and exponential growth of blockchain technology in various disciplines in the past recent decades. In such decentralized and distributed systems, obtaining consensus over a single data among all participating nodes is a challenging concern. The blockchain technology will strike many application domains by adopting appropriate consensus mechanisms that satisfy the intended properties to unlock the true potentiality. The main objective of this chapter is to draw attention of readers to understand the fundamentals of blockchain with its relevant components and the categories of it. Moreover, the literature study on the significant characteristics with the ongoing challenges is systematically analyzed. The blockchain technology plays a major role in the healthcare data management that addresses several issues related to counterfeit drug delivery, solutions to future pandemics, providing more security for data involved in clinical trials and single point of failure.

References

[1]   D. Yaga, P. Mell, N. Roby, and K. Scarfone. 'Blockchain technology overview'. *National Institute of Standards and Technology Internal Report 8202*, 66 pages. 2018. https://doi.org/10.6028/NIST.IR.8202.

[2]   E. Gökalp, M. O. Gökalp, S. Çoban, and P. E. Eren. 'Analysing opportunities and challenges of integrated blockchain technologies in healthcare'. *Information Systems: Research, Development, Applications, Education* Cham: Springer; pp. 174–183. 2018.

[3]   M. H. Kassab, J. DeFranco, T. Malas, P. Laplante, and V. V. G. Neto. 'Exploring research in blockchain for healthcare and a roadmap for the

future'. IEEE Transactions on Emerging Topics in Computing DOI: 10.1109/TETC.2019.2936881, 2019.

[4] J. A. Jaoude and R. G. Saade. 'Blockchain applications—Usage in different domains'. *IEEE Access*, vol. 7, pp. 45360–45381, 2019.

[5] D. Puthal, N. Malik, S. P. Mohanty, E. Kougianos, and G. Das. 'Everything you wanted to know about the blockchain: Its promise components processes and problems'. *IEEE Consumer Electronics Magazine*, vol. 7, pp. 6–14, 2018.

[6] T. Salman, M. Zolanvari, A. Erbad, R. Jain, and M. Samaka, 'Security services using blockchains: A state of the art survey'. *IEEE Communications Surveys and Tutorials*, vol. 21, no. 1, pp. 858–880, 2018.

[7] J. Xie, H. Tang, T. Huang, *et al.* 'A survey of blockchain technology applied to smart cities: Research issues and challenges'. *IEEE Communications Surveys and Tutorials*, vol. 21, no. 3, pp. 2794–2830, 3rd Quart. 2019.

[8] S. Nakamoto. *Bitcoin: A Peer-to-Peer Electronic Cash System*. 2008. [online] Available: https://bitcoin.org/bitcoin.pdf.

[9] V. Narayanan. *A Brief History in the Evolution of Blockchain Technology Platforms*. 2018. https://hackernoon.com/a-brief-history-inthe-evolution-of-blockchain-technology-platforms-1bb2b ad8960a.

[10] Z. Zheng, S. Xie, H.-N. Dai., X. Chen, and H. Wang. 'Blockchain challenges and opportunities: A survey'. *International Journal of Web and Grid Services*, vol. 14, no. 4, pp. 352, 2018.

[11] H.-N. Dai, Z. Zheng, and Y. Zhang. 'Blockchain for Internet of Things: A Survey'. *IEEE Internet of Things Journal*, vol. 6, no. 5, pp. 8076–8094, 2019.

[12] Z. Zheng, S. Xie, H. Dai, X. Chen, and H. Wang. 'An overview of blockchain technology: Architecture, consensus, and future trends'. *6th IEEE International Congress on Big Data*. Honolulu, HI, USA: IEEE; June 2017.

[13] R. C. Merkle. 'A digital signature based on a conventional encryption function'. *Proceedings of the Conference on the Theory and Application of Cryptographic Techniques. Advances in Cryptology—CRYPTO '87*, pp. 369–378. 1987.

[14] P. T. Duy, D. T. T. Hien, D. H. Hien, and V.-H. Pham. *A Survey on Opportunities and Challenges of Blockchain Technology Adoption for Revolutionary Innovation. Association for Computing Machinery*, pp. 200–207. 2018. Retrieved from https://doi.org/10.1145/3287921.3287978

[15] M. M. H. Onik., S. Aich, J. Yang., C.-S. Kim., and H.-C. Kim. 'Blockchain in healthcare challenges and solutions'. *Big Data Analytics for Intelligent Healthcare Management*. Elsevier, pp. 197–226. 2019. https://doi.org/10.1016/B978-0-12-818146-1.00008-8

[16] T. McGhin, K.-K. R. Choo, C. Z. Liu, and D. He. 'Blockchain in healthcare applications: Research challenges and opportunities'. *Journal of Network and Computer Applications*, vol. 135, pp. 62–75, 2019.

[17] R. Ana, M. Cristian, C. Jaime, S. Enrique, and D. Manuel. 'On blockchain and its integration with IoT challenges and opportunities'. *Future Generation Computer Systems*. Elsevier; vol. 88, pp. 173–190, 2018.

[18]   T. Poongodi, A. Rathee., R. Indrakumari, and P. Suresh. 'IoT sensing capabilities: Sensor deployment and node discovery, wearable sensors, wireless body area network (WBAN), data acquisition'. *Principles of Internet of Things (IoT) Ecosystem: Insight Paradigm*. Cham: Springer; vol. 174, pp. 127–151. 2020.

[19]   T. Poongodi, K. Rajalakshmi, R. Indrakumari, P. Suresh, and B. Balamurugan. 'Wearable devices and IoT'. *A Handbook of Internet of Things in Biomedical and Cyber Physical System. Intelligent Systems Reference Library*. Cham: Springer; vol. 165, pp. 245–273. 2020.

[20]   R. Indrakumari, T. Poongodi, P. Suresh, and B. Balamurugan. 'The growing role of Internet of Things in healthcare wearables'. *Emergence of Pharmaceutical Industry Growth with Industrial IoT Approach*. Academic Press; pp. 163–194. 2020.

[21]   R. Anu, T. Poongodi, Y. Monika, and B. Balamurugan. 'Internet of Things in healthcare wearable and implantable Body Sensor Network (WIBSNs)'. *Soft Computing in Wireless Sensor Networks*, pp. 193–224. 2018.

[22]   M. K. Shrivas and D. T. Yeboah. 'A critical review of cryptocurrency systems'. *Texila International Journal of Academic Research*, vol. 4, no. 2, pp. 116–131, 2017.

[23]   V. Buterin. 'On public and private blockchains'. *Ethereum Blog*. 2015. Retrieved from https://blog.ethereum.org/2020/06/07/on-public-and-private-blockchains/.

[24]   Z. Zheng, S. Xie, H. Dai, X. Chen, and H. Wang. 'Blockchain challenges and opportunities: A survey'. *International Journal of Web and Grid Services*, vol. 14, no. 4, pp. 352–375, 2017.

[25]   M. Crosby, P. Pattanayak, S. Verma, and V. Kalyanaraman. 'Blockchain technology: Beyond bitcoin'. *Applied Innovation Review*, vol. 2, pp. 6–19, 2016.

[26]   M. Swan. *Blockchain: Blueprint for a New Economy*. Beijing: O'Reilly. 2015.

[27]   T. Poongodi, R. Sujatha, D. Sumathi, P. Suresh, and B. Balamurugan. 'Blockchain in social networking'. *Cryptocurrencies and Blockchain Technology Applications*. Wiley Online library; pp. 55–76. 2020.

[28]   Gobal Bockchain in Heathcare Market, Focus on Industry Analysis and Opportunity Matrix – Analysis and Forecast, 2018-2025, 2018. Retrieved from https://bisresearch.com/industry-report/global-blockchain-in-healthcare-market-2025.html.

[29]   Blockchain in Insurance: Use Cases and Implementations. Retrieved from https://medium.com/swlh/blockchain-in-insurance-use-cases-and-imple-mentations-a42a00ebcd91

[30]   https://www.insurancejournal.com/news/national/2020/02/21/559057.htm

[31]   I. Haq and O. M. Esuka. 'Blockchain technology in pharmaceutical industry to prevent counterfeit drugs'. *International Journal of Computer Applications*, vol 975, pp. 8887, 2018.

[32]   M. Kang, E. Park, B. H. Cho, and K.-S. Lee. 'Recent patient health monitoring platforms incorporating internet of things-enabled smart devices'. *International Neurourology Journal*, vol. 22, no. Suppl 2, pp. S76–S82, 2018.

Chapter 2

Privacy issues in blockchain

Prabha Selvaraj[1], Sumathi Doraikannan[1], Vijay Kumar Burugari[2] and Kanmani Palaniappan[3]

Blockchain technology is a new innovation of secure computing without centralized authority in an open-networked system as explained by Nakamoto [1]. Blockchain stores the data in a distributed database that maintains a table of transaction record by arranging them into a hierarchical order of blocks. As far as security is concerned, blockchain is a decentralized peer-to-peer (P2P) network that is secured by an intelligent cryptography algorithm. Each node that is involved in the transaction is connected to the same blockchain data transaction itself since this has a distributed database. For example, in a digital currency, the blockchain is available to all such that entire transaction process can be monitored again to the first block. Bitcoin contains the false name in which the data nodes are not directly connected with the original data, but the repeated occurrences are associated with other. Blockchain is an innovation that is created by utilizing a mix of different strategies, for example, arithmetic, calculations, cryptography, and monetary models.

Blockchain is an open record of all cryptographic money transactions that are digitized and decentralized. All the transactions of digital forms of money are put away in sequential request to help clients in following the transactions without keeping up any focal record of the transactions. Application possibilities of blockchain are promising and have been conveying the outcome since its beginning. Blockchain innovation has advanced from starting digital currency to new-age shrewd agreements and has been actualized and applied in numerous fields. Albeit a ton of studies have been done on the security and protection issues of blockchain, a methodical assessment on the security of blockchain frameworks is as yet absent. Right now, we will attempt to exhibit a precise representation on the security dangers to blockchain and review the relating genuine assaults by analyzing well-known blockchain frameworks as explained in [2–4]. We will talk

[1]School of Computer Science and Engineering, VIT-AP University, Amaravati, India
[2]Department of Computer Science and Engineering, Koneru Lakshmaiah Education Foundation, K L University, Vijayawada, India
[3]Department of Computer Science and Engineering, K. S. Rangasamy College of Technology (Autonomous), Affiliated to Anna University, Chennai Namakkal, India

about the security and the protection of blockchain alongside their contact with respect to various patterns and applications right now. The section is expected to talk about key security assaults and the improvements that will help one grow better blockchain frameworks.

In recent years, blockchain, a distributed ledger technology (DLT), has attracted many fields, especially healthcare. The corporate scandals and crisis in financial section are all because of poor ineffective and inefficient corporate governance. Blockchain technology provides a solution to eliminate the problem by reducing the complexity involved in web of intermediaries for an exchange of money. In this chapter, we discuss about the national and multinational corporate support. It also deals with the blockchain approaches to data privacy in healthcare and security for health data.

2.1   National and Corporate Support

The identification of every trivial by sufficient pseudonymous location data is explained in a recent study in *The New York Times*. For few reasons, it is considered as a big concern for blockchain. Blockchain data is open for everyone—even for a malicious user who is trying to modify the information for the gain of finance to scrutinize data while app data which is cited in a *Times* article is not open. Once if credited to a user through any means, then it is exposed as linked to them for lifetime of pseudonymous transactions permanently. "This nature of blockchain accepts prospects for identification," said in an article on bitcoin examinations from the *Journal of Forensic Research*. With the help of Internet Protocol addresses, they monitor the communications between the nodes on the blockchain and the associated transactions.

To perform these analyses on public blockchain, applications have been developed. The cryptocurrency wallet software can also be legally analyzed [49] even though when it is not public, it requires no passphrases or keys that are required to use the wallet.

To play out these examinations on open blockchain, applications have been created. In spite of the fact that is not open, cryptocurrency wallet programming can likewise be legitimately examined even without the passphrases or keys that are required to utilize the wallet.

The most prominent utilization of these strategies was the capture of Ross Ulbricht for working the profound site "Silk Road," which was a commercial center for illicit medications, in addition to other things. The strategies permitted law implementation to recognize Ulbricht as the administrator of Silk Road. All the more fascinatingly, an internal revenue service (IRS) specialist was additionally ready to follow bitcoin dealings to establish that a United States (US) Drug Enforcement Administration operator engaged with that examination, Carl Force, was washing bitcoin identified with Silk Road.

A blockchain like bitcoin manages a slight security assurance. Aside from the open examination, people who depend on middle people, for example, a trade like

Coinbase, are liable to having their independences uncovered by the trade, for example, when the IRS requested Coinbase turnover-specific records, including digital money transactions. Even however protection is frequently the center when shortcomings of the blockchain are talked about; the innovation has some moderately hazardous security issues on blockchain security.

Nonetheless, a web search will create part of results pronouncing blockchain as reforming digital security; such articles are either regularly at elevated level that their cases cannot be sensibly centered or assessed around one of the parts of security and disregarding others. To assess security appropriately, we have to think about an innovation's capacity to safeguard the privacy, accessibility, and uprightness of the data. We previously tended to inadequacies of the blockchain, including to classification in the protection area above. Hence, accessibility and honesty are centered around this segment.

Circulated nature of blockchain is sufficient to safeguarding accessibility, a striking accomplishment for an untrusted decentralized system. There have been some disavowal of administration assaults concerning bitcoin, yet the significant ones have just happened against the trades, not against the system hubs themselves. These assaults are like the assaults on commonplace openly available sites and not demonstrative of an issue remarkable to blockchain; so here, we are not centered around them. Aside from denial of service (DOS) assaults, sure methods for the accessibility could be impacted [17]. There may likewise be different prospects; however, these all are by all accounts scholarly as they apply to bitcoin arrange; any of these has been completed for any huge interruption as there is no evidence.

The individuals who reason that the blockchain will upset the digital security regularly address respectability with the explanation that the blockchain guarantees the honesty with close to flawlessness and is permanent. On one hand, on the off chance that we have consideration just on the system itself, this is valid. For instance, in the event that you see an exchange bargain in the bitcoin organized in past square, specifically a more established square, you can be basically penny percent sure that exchange was substantial at that point. In spite of the fact that, for any down-to-earth outcome, uprightness should likewise be considered for the legitimacy of the exchange itself. This implies protecting against mixed up or fake exchanges just as making sure about from incidental misfortune.

Blockchain's unchallengeable record is regularly touted as showing its more terrific trustworthiness, then again it gives positively no barrier against mix-up or misrepresentation. Bitcoin execution resoundingly exhibits this significant uprightness issue. In July 2018, a cryptographic money exchange engineer assessed that 4,000,000 bitcoins were lost and another 2,000,000 were taken, while at the time under 18 million bitcoin existed. This implies that more than 33% of all the bitcoin were undermined. Remembering, bitcoin is prototypically blockchain execution and it is the most vigorous use case, which is a dumbfounding number, a higher hazard resistance than someone would acknowledge in planning a framework dealing with such basic trades.

This uprightness issue is not difficult to comprehend the individuals who has collaborated with the blockchain legitimately. The client accepts penny percent of the duty regarding securing what is in the digital money setting is a type of riches in its genuine decentralized structure. Yet, significantly less fortunate than holding monetary forms under a sleeping cushion, everything relies on computerized keys that when gotten to can be utilized to take the riches directly from under somebody with digital currency or can diminish it out of reach if the keys are lost. Due to the firm unchanging nature of the blockchain got together with the absence of brought together authority, there is irrefutably no plan of action. One more factor is that it makes the 33% figure far away and more terrible is the way that to date those that are connected straightforwardly with the bitcoin blockchain are obviously at the higher finish of the specialized and the PC capability. One can envision that the number would possibly get a lot more unfortunate, if the framework was utilized over the whole populace.

2.2   Asia trade and European trade

Blockchains accomplish the undertaking grade security and adaptability. We accept that blockchain will be at a few practical plans of action that reach out over the present increasingly tight contemplations of digital money, including trades and gracefully chain frameworks. At the point when digital forms of money rose, just about 10 years back, exercises were little scope. Their first pilots, for example, moving values or other money-related instruments in blockchain situations, will in general spotlight on finding ways that drive cost bankrupt procedures, by making exchanges progressively effective. Likewise, this could be incompletely a direct result of the extraordinary administering measures and high hazard associated with the financial services (FS) industry, as one error can prompt part of outcomes. While these might be profoundly esteemed utilizations, there may be more space to try different things with true applications, for example, shopper items and assembling, with money dug straightforwardly into the common exercises happening inside those business sectors. Interests in the blockchain innovations flooded. Governments in numerous Economic Commission for Africa (ECA) nations started trying different things with the blockchain to improve their comforts. Some national banks are contemplating the issues of the legitimate delicate as the advanced money, and monetary organizations are directing blockchain uses to join them in the current budgetary design. Blockchain advances, which place a high accentuation on making budgetary arbiters repetitive, are especially appealing in nations where trust in the money-related foundations is inadequate with regards to individuals' needs to maintain a strategic distance from the oversight, as monetary segments are immature. Nations where political flimsiness and defilement are higher, trust in the standard of law is lower, and administrative quality is lower will in general receive the bitcoin all the more quickly.

ASEAN are at different periods of their monetary turn of events, which designs open doors for nearby governments and organizations to find assorted use cases for blockchain. Ventures that are investigating the utilization of blockchain incorporate money-related administrations, flexibly chain and human services to improve the straightforwardness and proficiency. In the wake of giving a review of the block-chain utilized everywhere throughout the world, the report will profound jump into the blockchain scene in six ASEAN, perceiving the general patterns and key nearby upgrades. We trust that the report will give you a decent comprehension of the ramifications of blockchain and kick the trade-off on how this innovation can take care of issues and upgrade lives.

Specialized advancement, including blockchain, is a pertinent issue for Asian economies, which has a higher impact in the present open value markets. In the 20-year time frame, somewhere in the range of 1997–2017, the quantity of initial public share offering (IPOs) every year in the US and Europe has diminished while the quantity of the same in Asian markets has expanded. A significant piece of this achievement is skill IPOs, which have gotten all the more jutting in Asia. Of all out IPOs, the portion of innovation IPOs in Asia has expanded from 6% in 2012 to 10% in 2017, while comprehensively the portion of the same decreased from 23% in 2012 to 9% in 2017.

The disclosures of this report recommended that the national controllers and governments in Asia ought to be open, yet practice restriction while investigating new advances so as to keep up respectability and security of the open value markets. Blockchain innovation is still in its start and does not have the limit expected to meet prerequisites of the present market outlines and keep up current degree of the exchanges.

2.3   Multinational policies vs blockchain

Worldwide banks are chosen as a global innovation organization to utilize block-chain innovation to manufacture a universal exchanging framework called Digital Trade Chain. As indicated by an Accenture and McLagan report, blockchain may "decrease foundation costs for eight of the world's 10 biggest speculation banks by a normal of 30 percent, making an interpretation of to $8 billion to $12 billion in yearly cost investment funds for those banks." A significant car maker has coop-erated with MIT's Media Lab and others to recognize the employments of block-chain innovation in the vehicle business. A worldwide retailer collaborated with a global innovation organization and as of late reported the consequences of a test utilizing blockchain innovation in which it followed a nourishment item from ranch to retire like a flash, when contrasted with the days-long procedure without blockchain innovation. The Blockchain Insurance Industry Initiative B3i, which incorporates worldwide banks and budgetary administrations organizations, is investigating the use of blockchain innovation in the protection segment. In June, a significant backup plan and a significant global innovation organization declared a fruitful test case program of a blockchain-fueled "savvy protection strategy." Such shrewd protection arrangements would be intended to execute the agreement terms when determined conditions are met, accommodate information coherence, follow the starting point of a hazard, and diminish extortion, among different advantages. What is more, various new businesses are showcasing their blockchain-based stage to human services organizations.

2.3.1   Security of blockchain?

The changes to a blockchain are shown in real time and no focal client controls the record; blockchain is said to be significantly less helpless to hacking than a customary database. For example, if programmers needed to change data in a blockchain, they would initially need to hack into both the particular square and the entirety of the first and following squares in the blockchain over each record in the system simultaneously. Since agreement among the system members is required, the programmers' change would almost certainly be dismissed as it would strife with the other record sections on the system. Numerous onlookers accept this prompts an unmatched degree of security. Few security principles are as follows:

- penetration defense
- privilege reduction
- vulnerability management
- risks managements
- patches management

Be that as it may, blockchain innovation, similar to the Internet before it, will probably prompt unexpected dangers and exposures. The data safety is achieved by using encryption technique in bitcoin applications as explained by Tschorsch [5]. For instance, in 2013, Mt. Gox, a bitcoin trade taking care of 70% of all bitcoin exchanges at that point, endured a specialized glitch bringing about bitcoin's briefly shedding a fourth of its worth. That specialized glitch was a fork in the blockchain, which came about because of the utilization of contrasting variants of the bitcoin programming. In 2015, Interpol recognized an opening in blockchain utilized for cryptographic forms of money that programmers could adventure to move malware to PCs. What is more, blockchain is just as secure as its entrance focuses. On the off chance that the entrance frameworks utilized for blockchain are powerless against assault, the innovation's security might be undermined. In whole, blockchain is not without hazard and may not be programmer evidence. Given the worth and potential prominent of exchanges that may happen utilizing blockchain innovation, programmers will have motivators to design better approaches for utilizing the innovation for malevolent purposes in spite of its insurances.

Large banks, speculators, and other money-related organizations have put a large number of dollars in blockchain, trusting it could make exchanges quicker, simpler, and progressively secure. IBM has been joining forces with driving organizations in different businesses, including Danish vehicle organization Maersk, to make blockchain-based items that can streamline complex universal dealings across segments.

Blockchain innovation, which controls the advanced cash bitcoin, empowers information sharing over a system of individual PCs. It has increased overall notoriety because of its value in recording and monitoring resources or exchanges over all businesses.

Global protection inclusion is frequently lumbering a result of a labyrinth of worldwide guidelines, desk work, and installment terms. "There's a great deal of to and fro and it's everything through email chains circumventing the world, rather than a brought together framework," Carol Barton, President of AIG Multinational said in a meeting.

Different gatherings are engaged with a worldwide arrangement as "worldwide customers," "neighborhood customers," "worldwide brokers," "nearby brokers," "safety net provider home office," and "backup plan local office." The previously mentioned partners need to share information, including strategy, claims, and installment, and the vast majority of this correspondence occurs through messages, calls, and messages, rather than to confide in an incorporated framework.

At last, numerous observers are drawing matches between the development of blockchain innovation and the rise of the web in the late 1990s. Organizations that can make sense of how to beneficially saddle the monstrous intensity of blockchain could be the security exchange victors of things to come.

2.3.2   Shifting security to the end user

The mix of the unchanging nature and decentralized nature of the blockchain moves basically the entirety of the respectability obligation to the end client, at an elevated level on the grounds that there are no checks against misfortune, extortion, or mix-ups. There is an old PC principle "trash in trash out" that is by all accounts especially legitimate here. The trustworthiness of any of these present reality executions is experienced by its yield, which in the digital money usage is attached 1:1 to the respectability of its contributions of the exchange. On the off chance that the framework is built to such an extent that it gives no component of review as said in [6] and it helps deceitful exchanges, it has profound honesty blemishes.

2.3.3   Trade-offs

The study primarily centers around cryptographic money since it is the fundamental execution of the blockchain, and its investigation proves that the advantages of blockchain accompany few important protection and security issues. An apparently unavoidable event in the blockchain conversation centers around the center advantages without tending to whether the specialist protection, and security issues can be diminished to an appropriate hazard resistance. Another continuous event is an endeavor to address a portion of the protection and security issues by proposing "exchange offs" of parts of the innovation, without conceding that those exchange offs annihilate a portion of the "progressive" blockchain merits and begin making the innovation less discernible from heritage database innovation. At last, it is almost difficult to decide any portrayal of a utilization case that addresses these issues and afterward looks at all in cost of the execution to inheritance innovation that performs practically identical errand with impartially tantamount measurements.

Regarding the first problem of focusing on the center advantages and not giving equivalent thought of the difficulties, one of the chances is that there are some contradictory issues that cannot be tended to. In January 2016, Vitalik Buterin fellow benefactor of Ethereum composed a blog entry setting out some hypothetically conceivable ostensible ways to deal with blockchain security, which ranges from awfully wasteful to high possible for the private blockchains to one that being private of course however it uncovers the data to the outside world when there is a dispute [20]. One takeaway from Vitalik's post is that if this protection issue can be tended to reasonably, the arrangement will probably be far profoundly complex than even blockchain itself.

Over the protection Catch 22, some appears to recognize that there is a comparable security incongruence owed to the intrinsic dependence on clients for trustworthiness of the exchanges. A model is found in a white paper on free personality distributed in October 2018 by the Blockchain Bundesverband [21]. In portraying the focal capacities, the article expresses that they accept, all substances and people as identity owners have at least one with an unmistakable arrangement of private keys that control each. In the reference section, the article perceives the protection dangers, expressing if an aggressor can get the entrance to a character to the full authority over this character is missing and this may wind up with immense harm to personality subject. In consider with the gigantic harm that can happen, if—as the case with the bitcoin—there is a 2-fold digit misfortune rate and extortion of the keys is utilized to secure the characters, the framework will miss the mark concerning being practicable. In the meantime, the article depicts the hopeful highlights that should be executed, for example, usable key administration and high secure. There is no careful proposition on the best way to embrace this or do different necessities referenced in the article, for example, the subject must be allowed to recover power over their personality. Most relevant inquiry of how, and perchance more significantly whether, the objectives can be accomplished is not tended to.

Other basic topic of blockchain approval includes recognizing a potential exchange off because of the honesty or protection concern while not tending to the whole ramifications of the exchange off. A machine is conjuring the private permissioned blockchain as a reaction to security worries of open blockchain. Making a blockchain permissioned essentially presenting an administrative position and a layer of qualification the board. This acquaints the need with dependence that power includes concentrated protection and security vulnerabilities and opposes the trust less circulated nature of a blockchain that is referred to as the key novel feature as stated by Kalra [7]. Privately controlled square chain cannot ensure unchanging nature the way an open one like bitcoin can on the grounds that the substance or elements checking it could control the assent system. So also, it presents protection and security susceptibilities in light of the fact that the trade-off of a controlling substance can bargain the uprightness of whole framework. Sooner or later, with sufficient exchange offs, the inquiry becomes whether this as far as anyone knows progressive innovation is not quite the same as the current innovation whatsoever as explained by Malin [8].

With regards to cryptographic money blockchains like bitcoin, there is a slight inquiry that it was transformative in sense that no extra innovation arrangement exists where a privacy less decentralized system of self-intrigued entertainers can be boosted to cowork to empower exchanges. The need of examining the exchange offs in the former sections is that when the exchange offs are made for a particular use case, this advancement is disintegrated, and there are likely some other existing advances that can promptly play out the comparative usefulness. Private permissioned blockchain actualizing the exchanges within a solitary affiliation is practically undefined from the as-of-now executed circulated databases. In such case, the assessment of the slanting innovation should be a general relationship of advantages and expenses to the current innovation.

There is such a famous use situation where a huge vendor actualized the blockchain to follow nourishment gracefully. There are no inquiries that the specialized capacity for actualizing such a framework without blockchain existed well before as checked by delivery organizations' capacity to follow the bundles. Apparently, the execution of blockchain was a huge endeavor, which incorporates long stretches of testing. Still none of the articles about it shed any light on cost of this task and how the execution of blockchain was better than the options by any metrics as stated by Karafiloski [9]. Meanwhile, the merchant has made a few affirmations about how this arrangement can decrease the expense of a recall, as explained by Krawiec [10]; it does not contain any investigation of how elective arrangements could have furnished similar outcomes conceivably with less intricacy, shorter development time, and at a lower value point.

Expanded consideration from universal associations is the consequence of the development of blockchain innovation. Stock trades and universal organizations have started to examine with blockchain over different examinations and have distributed a few exhibition results to outline the benefits and conceivable administrative system for blockchain in the global money-related markets.

The International Fiscal Reserve and the Bank for International Settlements (BIS) have given a report on the distributed record innovation convincing national bosses to exercise reasonably and in budgetary administrations like installment clearing and settlement of store while surveying blockchain's training in worldwide markets.

Recalling the standards and potential acts of a blockchain vault, the BIS stresses the lacking idea of the innovation and the absence of true progressive potential given the current market foundation.

As of June 2018, ESMA had distributed three reports on DLT, one of which straightforwardly assessed the uses of DLT in money-related and open markets. In October 2018, the FSB discharged a report precision, the budgetary strength ramifications of digital currencies and initial coin offerings (ICOs). The report stressed that the G20 Finance Ministers and Central Bank Governors should remain to screen the dangers emerging from crypto-resources and ICOs. The Financial Action Task Force has a few territories of work in progress to empower the predictable and fitting protections for blockchain that will add to the control of the related tax evasion and the psychological oppressor financing risks while evading undesirable boundaries.

The OECD has discharged the focused on investigates blockchain identifying with its exercises in open administration, corporate administration, rivalry strategy, just as a preliminary giving a layout of the blockchain innovation in money. OECD's first worldwide strategy meeting on blockchain reasoned that the OECD will keep on including with professionals, specialists, and governments to empower coactivity in the global approach condition and recognize and share best practices for the administration to oversee and utilization of blockchain as said in [11].

With the advancement in electronic well-being-related information gathering, cloud health-care information stockpiling, and patient information security assurance guidelines, new open doors are opening for day-by-day well-being information executives, just as for comfort for patients to access and offer their own well-being information.

2.3.4   Key developments of blockchain for voting

- In April 2018, an Australian blockchain organization consolidated 96 million-part socio-strict affiliation Nahdlatul Ulama to execute a network voter stage in Sumatra for provincial and national government races.
- Apart from casting a ballot, the stage offers types of assistance, including the advanced financial offices, improving efficiency in farming.

2.3.5   Improving productivity in agriculture

- A blockchain-based information exchange stage gives the information on geo-labeling, field exercises, satellites, climate and land, and market data to ranchers. Ranchers get reward focuses for the data/information they give, which can be utilized to trade a markdown on agrarian necessities. There were 3,000 rancher members by July 2018.
- In November 2018, the organization communicated participation with a worldwide blockchain innovation arrangements originator together to convey blockchain-based purpose of dealing with gadgets to ranchers to encourage the information assortment and the money-related walled in area.

2.3.6   Guarantee straightforwardness, supportability in fishing

- Indonesia is a leading tuna producer which is ideal for using blockchain to improve the transparency in supply chains as explained by Gordon [31] and improve overfishing.
- A blockchain startup showed a 6-month pilot in 2016, where traditional fisherman sent messages to record a catch, creating a new skill on the blockchain. This allowed the tracking of audit information/data to prove that fishes were caught validly and sustainably.

2.3.7   Cryptocurrency regulations

- To bring increased regulatory clearness in cryptocurrencies, steps have been taken by Malaysia's economic regulators such as the issuance of Anti-Money Laundering and Counter Financing of Extremism Policy for Digital Currencies in February 2018. In order to operate cryptocurrency exchanges, this policy framework for crypto transaction providers is used in Malaysia. As of November 2018, more than 40 cryptocurrency firms had registered with BNM.

• As of November 2018, the Securities Commission Malaysia (SC) was developing an outline to regulate ICOs, set to be distributed in 2019.

2.3.8   Energy industry

Tenaga Nasional Berhad, the highest electricity utility in Malaysia, is discovering the use of blockchain in the energy industry. Information storage in healthcare has displayed assessment to customary health-care networks and shows other remarkable observations as a feature of an appropriated record usage. Blockchain innovation, by configuration, is planned to give a successful method for recording "transactions." While these transactions are frequently connected with money-related exercises, they can be applied to health conveyance governments or related to conventional health data trade, for example, the sharing of data identified with a clinical experience, lab results, benefits the executives, or character.

Blockchains are upgraded to catch a discrete informational index that records the basic components of the kind of transaction. This methodology is generally known as the "minimal necessary principle" of blockchain arrangement. This guideline is applied dependent on the chose blockchain convention and as a major aspect of the plan of the blockchain arrange, catching just those information components required for each distinguished work process.

While blockchain structures can in fact reinforce any information fundamental for the transaction, exceptionally huge information records (or the amassing of huge documents for a given transaction) can present inertness and affect disseminated record execution. Thus, blockchain transactions in a health-care situation present extraordinary difficulties for the base important standard.

2.4   Blockchain approaches to data privacy in healthcare

Health researchers require the information like datasets to understanding the disease, and to know about the biomedical discovery, to develop the drugs and medicines and to plan basis on the patient situation, genetics, and environment. Blockchain would expand by updating the data of populations of people who are getting the treatment by medical agencies. The data that is shared among the blockchain environment makes easier to reach the patients and it shows the more positive results of public.

Many benefits are there when comparing blockchain with the existing traditional health-care database management systems as explained by Kuo [13]. They are as follows:

1. Decentralization of management in blockchains is suitable for the applications such as hospitals, patients who want to cooperate with each other without the involvement of a central management.

2. Audit trails that are immutable are provided by blockchains, which means they are appropriate for unchangeable databases such as insurance claim records for recording critical information.
3. Enabling data provenance by blockchain which suits for use in managing digital assets—for example, patient details in clinical trials. The ownership can only be changed by the owner using cryptographic protocols. In addition, the sources of the data and records can be confirmed, increasing the reusability of verified data as explained by Craig [14]. Availability and robustness of the data is given by blockchains which is suitable for the preservation and continuous availability of records. For example, the electronic health records (EHRs) of the patient [54] will be stored permanently in the hospital database [16]. The privacy and security is provided by blockchain for the data by encrypting the data and using the private keys of patient they can decrypt. It protects the data from the malicious party, even if the network is hacked; also there is no possibility of reading the data.

Bitcoin depends on open-source cryptographic conventions and has demonstrated to be an exceptionally protected stage for cryptocurrency trade. While the personalities behind some bitcoin exchanges stay unclear, the stage gives straightforwardness as anybody can get to the blockchain and visualize exchanges for any bitcoin address. It is definitely not a stretch to express that blockchain can exist any place where human administrations are required. Its application to social protection has not shown up at its greatest limit, yet the results may be noteworthy as it grows up, as demonstrated by industry insiders as said in [15]. It is anything but a stretch to state that blockchains can exist wherever human services are needed. Its application to social insurance has not arrived at its maximum capacity, yet the outcomes might be significant as it grows up, as indicated by industry insiders.

At the point when a specialist needs to endorse a treatment, the specialist basically permits the shrewd agreement to see the required patient records and the payer's brilliant agreement naturally analyzes those records to the insurer's health plan data, makes an assurance, and promptly transfers the outcome back to the specialist. This gives exact, real-time conclusions that spare assets and forestall delays in care. A blockchain-based way to deal with the business, in any case, would allow people to transfer this information in a safe way, with the alternative to secretly share it for the motivations behind medication improvement, clinical research, or general health examines. It further empowers them to adapt such information. Blockchain innovation's far reach is the eventual fate of clinical development. Boosting clients not just attracts a more extensive information pool to make ground-breaking informational indexes, yet guarantees that analysts are continually on the cutting edge. Man-made intelligence, machine learning (ML), and blockchain in human services are quick advancing. The intersection purpose of these headways is new, and a lot faster advancing. Constant information would likewise allow specialists and general well-being advantages for rapidly distinguish, segregate, and drive change for biological conditions that influence general well-being. Blockchain ways deal with information protection in healthcare. Due to the progress in electronic healthcare, data that has been collected in various ways is used to resolve various issues. Certain issues such as security, privacy, and accessing data become a critical task.

2.4.1 Blockchain for electronic medical record (EMR) data management

The possibility of developments in blockchain is found to be enhanced in a couple of trial models. A year back in the US, Booz Allen Hamilton Consulting made and executed a blockchain-based initial phase in the department of Food and Drug Administration's Office of Translational Sciences, which demonstrates the advancement for social protection data on the board. The pilot adventure is at present being promptly executed at four noteworthy facilities.

Deployment of Ethereum to administer data is made by methods for virtual private frameworks. The errand depends on the IPFS to utilize encryption and decrease data replication by methods for off-chain cloud leaves behind cryptographic counts to make customer sharing as said by Cyran [16].

2.4.1.1 Blockchain and health-care data protection

In Europe, the association between blockchains and the General Data Protection Regulation (GDPR) is to some extent questionable. It is observed that blockchain does not solve issues that are pertained with GDPR (concerning data transportability, e.g., or consent the board, data perceptibility and lawful access auditability), but issues can be perceived (with respect to choice to be neglected, yet furthermore when the specific use through sharp understandings may incapacitate the veritable authority over data, through modified execution). One choice to deal with this issue is "dynamic consent the board," which is totally as per the GDPR course of action concerning consent as demonstrated by Kaye [17]. Also, it is seen that "private blockchains," e.g., Enterprise Blockchain can do it without a bit of stretch fit with GDPR orders since the trades of the propelled records of the set aside information can be balanced and destroyed by private components or authorities which can have and regulate this stage, using a particular class of accord count. This kind of private blockchain is constrained through a singular association or affiliation, anyway they endow access to customers, regularly affiliations, that accomplish certain pre-developed accreditations or rules as explained by Lima [18]. Such systems would be relatively directed to the extent that how an association achieves its private web applications. Their use cases could combine with various activities like storage of records by government officials at workplaces, record owners, and furthermost administration providers as said in [19]. Later on, these private blockchain results in the most basic impact on human administrations course of action and the board. The ability of blockchains is moreover tended to succeed by the European Commission Research and Innovation Program IMI (Innovative Medicine Initiative) Pilot adventure named "Blockchain Enabled Healthcare" led by Novartis, which expects to utilize existing rules, for instance, Ethereum, and to make equal measures at whatever point required. The consideration is on enabling organizations that direct favorable position patients as explained in [20].

2.4.2   Blockchain for personal health record (PHR) data management

Data associated with various health metrics that could be obtained with the help of wearable sensors or clinical IoT devices as close and particular well-being records (PHR) [57]. Constant man-made mental aptitude (artificial intelligence (AI))-controlled restorative administrations examinations would be produced, which are related to customers, including patients, specialists, pharmaceutical experts, and payers as said by Dimitrov [21] and Salah [22]. This entire PHR organization course is transforming into a noteworthy wellspring of data for blockchain expert associations.

Appropriated or decentralized applications (Dapps) made on the blockchain engage specialists and patients to conveniently play a part in telemedicine without going between costs adjacent to the insignificant costs of the Ethereum compose, thus improving patient reinforcing.

2.4.3   Blockchain for point-of-care genomics

As shown by Timi Inc., which is a blockchain stage association, accessing a patient's data costs around USD 7,000 consistently as said in [23]. An enormous bit of the mHealth associations making blockchain organizations center around the ability of patients to have and sell their well-being data with a consideration on close and personal EHRs and cumulative data from sensors deployed in the body as said in [24]. Likewise, various client associations have been offering DNA sequencing for a long time. The association "23andMe," which was set up in 2006, is the most beneficial which providers direct-to-purchaser inherited testing organizations as said in [25]. Nevertheless, security is a noteworthy concern in the restorative administrations industry. A year prior, "23andMe" proclaimed that trading of a USD 300 million stakes with reference to the pharmaceutical goliath GlaxoSmithKline, provides access to the customers' data, but later it ignores since it contains exome data. These types of issues could be resolved by recommendations of blockchain in new organizations in human administrations in such a way that they give assurance to offer a response for buyers expecting to conduct a DNA test in spite of preserving the data ownership. They suggest that the decision of data adjustment could be performed through blockchain-reinforced providers. For example, a start-up called Nebula Genomics provides the complete genome sequence to no end, as a way to deal with stock up for its genuine ploy: a blockchain-based innate business community as said in [26]. At the point when customers have their genome sequence, they can demand the cost in terms of tokens from the corresponding person who is in need.

As the first phase, those tokens can be regained for surplus tests and things that will furthermore unravel DNA. Genomes.io is another genomics blockchain association that grants security to the genome right from the sequence stage to the access stage. The idea is to hinder inherent information getting into an unauthorized person, while permitting buyers the opportunity to sell their inherited data a small piece at once if they wish to do so as said in [27].

2.4.4   Blockchain for EHR data management

Blockchain technology is a feasible option for personal EHR management. Smart contracts are used for sharing the data of a patient in terms of tokens. For example, Health Wizz is piloting a blockchain- and Fast Healthcare Interoperability Resources (FHIR)-enabled EHR aggregator mobile app to make use of blockchain for the tokenization of data. This facilitates patients to provide security and privacy to the data, establish, and collect their personal medical records as said in [28,55]. The objective is to provide a good communication among the caregivers and health-care organizations to enable them in providing special and standard care to the patients based on the collected health data. It is observed that from an EHR blockchain company medical chain [50] works on empowering various agents such as laboratories, doctors, and pharmacists to demand access for the data pertained to the patient's health for better treatment as said in [29]. Also, this enables agents to communicate among themselves for an effective decision process. All these interactions are stored in the distributed ledger maintained by the company.

Certain limitations associated with public blockchain are as follows:

- Deficiency in data privacy
- Nonexistence of robustness

As a result of this, public blockchain is not appropriate for managing health since the data has to be stored and accessed in a secured manner. Private blockchains have issues associated with privacy, scalability, and security, but there are other challenges like non-usage of open standards, which do not remain neutral in handling cases.

Blockchain technology provides many advantages for healthcare. Features such as open-source software, commodity hardware, and open application programming interface (API) of IT blockchain enable rapid and easy interoperability between systems. The special characteristic is managing huge volume of data and blockchain users. Due to the availability of fault tolerance, data security, disaster recovery, and cryptographic techniques, it is most widely deployed in health-care department. Applications developed by experts for health blockchain provide benefits to the users in such a way that the needs and necessities are satisfied.

Blockchain runs on extensively used and reliable commodity hardware. Computations at flexible cost are developed by numerous vendors to compete in the market. Excess blockchain hardware capacity could be shared with health researchers, which aids in rapid exploration of new drugs and treatments.

By blockchain data structures, we decrease the risks of public by sharing the data immediately and increase the benefits [56] to give the treatment to patients as soon as possible. Furthermore, by combining the health data from mobile applications, it is made easy to classify into subgroups and to individuals, which makes one to get the individual personal care of patient and treatment plans.

Blockchain makes certain continuous available real-time data that makes the best coordination between patient and medical communities in emergency situations. It makes it easier to get the preventive measures of any virus before it spreads in the environment.

The availability of mobile applications and wearable sensors data from the blockchain makes it easier to deal with the severe and emergency cases easily without any risk. It is the best way to find and reach the care teams of patients. A health-care blockchain is the new milestone in technology that promotes the latest medical research and develops personalized treatment ways. It is the best option to give treatment to a patient and to communicate between a patient and health agency based on research other than intuition. Trust aspect, productivity, and compliance are main benefits of it. Blockchain technology is key to the de-centralized systems. It truly distributes the power to all the nodes in the system with the help of a predefined and agreed protocol. A web based health ledger works on network Baas in explained in [60].

2.4.5   *Fast health-care interoperability resources*

A standard that emerges and gives the data formats and its elements is FHIR and to exchange EHRs it gives public accessible APIs. It is developed and maintained by the Health Level Seven International health-care standards organization as said in [27–30,44]. The major problem with health-care industry is the lack of interoperability of health records among the hospitals. The reason for this is health-care data is sensitive and thus hospitals avoid sharing this and use a highly secure and centralized server to store it.

2.4.6   *Health-care blockchain*

Blockchain could solve this problem by using a DLT to create a safe and secure cloud environment [48] to facilitate the exchange of health records among various hospitals.

A transaction has the following characteristics:

Any transaction on blockchain is at the core creating a new block on the network hashed using a definitive agreed hashing technique.

- Hash of previous block
- Data being added

A transaction consists of the previous data hashed and added as a block by the various miners on the network.

2.4.7   *On-chain*

2.4.7.1   **High-level data**

The perfect blockchain transaction ordinarily appears as more elevated level information, metadata, transactional data, review records, pointers, and hash codes.

2.4.8   Off-chain

2.4.8.1   Large data files

The engineering of the dispersed record should keep huge volumes of clinical data off the blockchain and in secure access-controlled undertaking frameworks where they exist today and reference these information records as required from the blockchain with pointers and hash codes that can be utilized to check their integrity. Usage of existing information stores permits associations to use their current information stockpiling speculation while exploiting the benefits of blockchain for decentralized information trade.

2.4.8.2   Large data files

The secured access-controlled enterprise system is used to store personally identifiable information and protected health information. These records are useful and have benefits since it is obtained from blockchain.

2.4.9   Network is the concern not a database

Blockchain is a sort of Business-to-Business (B2B) middleware. It is anything but a trade for a database inside a given association. It rushes to concoct a blockchain use case. It takes more time to concoct a business organized around the utilization case. There is as on close term openings with blockchain based on existing B2B networks, for instance clearinghouses, or tranquilize supply chains, and so on. Longer term, new, and progressive use cases for blockchain will rise, with new kinds of members and networks; however, these will take more time to set up. Existing B2B networks may have a delegate. As opposed to disintermediate the middle person, what is bound to happen is for blockchain to change the job of the mediator from a potential bottleneck of transactions and single purpose of inability to a greater amount of an enablement, facilitator, and bolster job.

2.4.10   Clear definition of use cases

A fundamental element for progress with blockchain is away from utilization cases, members in the B2B system, and worth props to all partners. Conversely, a methodology of how about we put all the information on blockchain and make sense of later how to utilize it is probably going to fall flat for some reasons, including the absence of business purchase in protection and security concerns, administrative/information assurance law/consistence prerequisites, and potential execution and versatility challenges for enormous informational indexes. A great deal of the worth props declared for blockchain will in general be optimistic. Organizations need to have genuine business esteem props and return on investment (ROI) so as to increase and provoke their cooperation in sourcing and expending transactions to/from a blockchain. These impetuses, inspirations, and ROI are as of now settled and all around evaluated in existing B2B networks, which is again why existing B2B networks are better close term open doors for blockchain. In any case, business groups should be locked on right time in blockchain activities.

2.4.11   Throughput and scalability

Blockchains typically throughput depend on how they are implemented and the algorithm used for performing hundreds, or thousands of transactions per second range. Throughput should be within the range for blockchain. In some cases, millions of transactions/second blockchain may not be the best choice. Other techniques like expressing urgent and high priority transactions through the queue, queuing transactions, and batching transactions into blocks can improve throughput.

2.4.12   Adequate data

Information put on the blockchain "B2B middleware" between associations in a B2B arrange goes outside of the edge of your health-care association and is presented to new dangers to its classification, respectability, and accessibility. Information on blockchains may likewise experience new administrative or information assurance law consistence necessities relying upon the sort of information put on the blockchain and areas of the blockchain arrange hubs, or endpoints where the decentralized records and information live. Huge information types, for example, huge pictures, genomes, and so forth could have significant effect on the presentation of your blockchain and subsequently are commonly best left off-chain, referenced by pointers and hash codes (of the off-bind information to secure respectability), set on the blockchain. These worries can impact and affect the use cases and information on the blockchain and in this manner cannot be managed as a "bandage" after the blockchain is actualized. Protection, security, and consistence groups should be locked on right time in blockchain activities.

2.4.13   Blockchain privacy poisoning

The expression "blockchain privacy poisoning" alludes to the inclusion of individual information into an open blockchain, along these lines making that blockchain remains unaffected under the European GDPR. As per the GDPR, all people reserve "the option to be overlooked," so you can quickly observe why blockchain innovation speaks to such an issue: by their very nature, blockchains are intended to be totally unchangeable and permanent. Singular information cannot be erased without haggling the chain.

So far, blockchain insurance poisoning had not been a huge problem in light of the fact that most data being taken care of on a blockchain was strange trade data. For example, bitcoin uses an open blockchain access database to store information essentially trades. Be that as it may, no near and dear data of any kind is taken care of on the blockchain. This has a couple of great conditions—it infers that the specific character of any individual holding bitcoin is absolutely mysterious, and it furthermore suggests that nobody can ever evacuate your bitcoin by changing the bitcoin blockchain. Beginning at now, nobody has ever made sense of how to alter a blockchain by changing or deleting increasingly prepared "blocks" in the chain. Speculatively, that is what that keeps our bitcoin secure.

Nonetheless, simultaneously, industries are beginning to store increasingly more data on their open blockchains, and that is what is prompting the worry that individual information may wind upon the blockchain sooner or later. This individual information may exist in corporate data about incessantly sick patients, charge card numbers, or addresses of people. Particularly for monetary administrations associations, there is a scarcely discernible difference between putting away anonymized exchange information and putting away close to home money related data on the blockchain.

2.4.14   Consent management and the blockchain

As indicated by Gartner, one factor included blockchain privacy poisoning is that associations are utilizing blockchain now for confirmation of-assent usage. By 2023, more than 25% of GDPR-driven evidence of assent usage will include blockchain innovation. That is a lofty increment from the figure of under 2% today.

Subsequently, the use of blockchain innovation to the as-sent executives is, from numerous points of view, a 2-fold edged sword. On one hand, it could give following and inspecting required to agree to information security and privacy enactment. Then again, it makes it difficult to change any information that has been entered onto the blockchain.

At this moment, regarding blockchain and assent, the board is still in the beginning period of experimentation; however unmistakably worries over blockchain privacy poisoning could drastically change current stand considering the most ideal approach to actualize blockchain ventures without risking getting rebellious with privacy laws and general information insurance guidelines.

2.5   Blockchain privacy poisoning in the context of other privacy issues

For any association considering executing blockchain frameworks, there certainly should be coordination between the tech improvement group and the privacy group. That is on the grounds that there are a lot of other privacy chances that are connected to the way that associations basically store, record, procedure and change their information [58,59]. In its report of highlighting blockchain privacy poisoning, for instance, Gartner additionally dove into different kinds of related privacy dangers. By 2020, the biggest territory of privacy hazard will include the reinforcement and documenting of individual information. As per Gartner, this privacy hazard will affect 70% of all things considered and could prompt a sharp increment in online expenses for those associations.

A huge money-related administrations association, for instance, may choose to begin putting away exchange information on the blockchain. Without anyone else, exchange information put away on the blockchain would not speak to a privacy chance under the GDPR. In the case of an information rupture by an outside programmer, the way that this information is put away on the blockchain would really give an important reinforcement of the information. Nonetheless, this could risk connecting individual data to the exchanges, which would be the situation with financial balances or names of record holders. All things considered, the open blockchain would be harmed.

Working blockchain frameworks without overseeing privacy hazards, at that point, is never again conceivable in the post-GDPR period. Blockchains harmed with individual information will be a significant subject among no wand 2022, so associations are best off to begin thinking about the suggestions now. Open blockchains will endure if this issue cannot be worked out without trading off chain trust worthiness.

2.5.1   Who should be accountable for blockchain privacy poisoning?

The subject of blockchain privacy poisoning is new to the point that even privacy specialists are not actually sure where it is going. All things considered, the thought of a blockchain harmed with individual data alludes explicitly to "open" blockchains. Nonetheless, there are additionally "private" blockchains, and it is questionable if the GDPR would apply here. For instance, if an organization chooses to put its whole inventory network on the blockchain, it is likely (for serious reasons) that it would make a private blockchain in which you would require authorization to add squares to the chain. These private blockchains would almost certainly incorporate hierarchical information, business information, and business information—yet not close to home information. Also, regardless of whether somebody carelessly embedded individual information that renders the blockchain "harmed"—would it truly matter since none of that information would be open to the general population? Until this point, there have been no reported instances of blockchain privacy poisoning, so any new case that emerges will start a trend. While there is presently a lot of vulnerability over what happens when an executed blockchain will endure privacy poisoning, one thing is sure: new privacy guidelines are significantly affecting the procedure and approach for putting away and handling individual information.

2.5.2   Problems of blockchain security/privacy

Exchanges are comprehensively distributed and are not encoded in many applications. In the event that this information is close to home information, for instance "clinical or budgetary information," this prompts administrative and lawful issues, particularly in Germany. One arrangement is to store just encoded in formation in the blockchain, which prompts another issue: If the way to decode explicit data is lost, the information may not be recouped precisely. Moreover, if a key is taken and distributed, all the information is everlastingly decoded in the blockchain since the information cannot be adjusted. Be that as it may, blockchain can likewise assist with improving guarded cyber security methodologies, particularly regarding personality and access.

2.5.2.1 MITM attacks

One attack plot for man-in-the-middle (MITM) assaults is to get the certificate authority (CA) to give the client fashioned open keys (open key substitution MITM assault). This can prompt the decoding of delicate data. In a blockchain approach where their open keys are put by clients in distributed obstructs, the data is circulated over the taking part hubs with connections to past and following squares. This makes the open key unchanging and it gets more earnestly for assailants to distribute counterfeit keys. Besides, the single purpose of disappointment, the CA, is additionally circulated, which means it is more earnestly to cut this administration down.

2.5.2.2 Data tampering

Since each transaction is marked and dispersed over all blockchain hubs, it is basically difficult to control information without the system thinking about it. In medicinal services, the blockchain could be utilized to make permanent review trails, keep up the uprightness of wellbeing preliminaries, and guarantee the respectability of patient information shared across various clinical conditions.

2.5.2.3 DDoS attacks

On the off chance that DNS frameworks depended on blockchain innovation, assaults like the one from the Mirai botnet would be more diligently to effectively finish. Such a framework would give straight forwardness and security. The DNS framework could not be focused on the off chance that it was a dispersed framework, since the information is appropriated and the information sections cannot be altered, due to the nature of the blockchain. The undertaking of Turtle is likewise understanding a blockchain-based DNS administration.

2.5.2.4 Privacy

The blockchain innovation is an incredible model for the randomness of security (at any rate as far as permanence) and protection. While it is conceivable to structure a changeless, alter safe transaction, this transaction can be seen all through the entirety of the hubs on the system. The most encouraging exploration on security (or private transactions) for blockchain innovation is at present zk-SNARKs, which are executed by zCash and Ethereum (zCash on Ethereum). The blend of the two advances makes it conceivable to execute unknown installments, daze closeouts, and casting a ballot framework. Since the systems behind zk-SNARKs are not paltry, they cannot be portrayed right now. The need for improved new techniques for developing and evaluating with digital interventions is discussed in [46].

2.5.3 Challenges

Despite the fact that security improving innovations are conveyed, they produce metadata. Measurable investigation will uncover "a few" data, regardless of whether the information itself is encoded, making, e.g., design acknowledgment conceivable. Moreover, adaptability is a developing test, since the accord procedure is as of now excessively costly. In the event that money or some other worth is exchanged on a blockchain-based application, a lot higher transaction speed is required. Ethereum is at present equipped for 2.8 transactions every second, while bitcoin is prepared to do around 3.2 transactions every second. It takes such a long time in view of the perplexing agreement process for every transaction (presently proof of work or stake) as explained in [47]. Another assault to remember is the 51%-assaulter "greater part hash rate attack." On the off chance that an association or individual has 51% of the hash power, the assailant can invert transactions he sent, keep transactions from picking up affirmations, and keep different excavators from mining [45].

2.6   Blockchain security for health data: promises, risks, and future development: blockchain security issues

A security profits are gained due to the decentralization characteristic of its hubs. Due to the open access of transaction records, changes would not be made. The specific feature is that any changes made in the record need the authorization. Due to the structure of blockchain advancement, all open blockchains are prone to 51% attacks.

When the programmer provides an additional 50% of a blockchain's power, then it is considered as a 51% attack. Due to the additional contribution, they anticipate that the whole control of the blockchain must be with them, allows hackers to perform the 2-fold spend coins, maintains various miners and prediction of transactions. The threat level is more protuberant for littler blockchains with less excavators as the extent of figuring power expected to regulate 51% is less.

Moreover, some blockchain models are really defenseless against less—like on account of IOTA's Tangle, which is powerless to 34% assaults. On account of the decentralization of the information, anybody who has the power of hashing force of 34% could make use of blockchain. Apart from the blockchain, several other issues related to the security need solutions. Among these, one such issue that needs more focus is the trade security, and it has a great past about digital money hacks. Moderation of powerless trade is done up to some extent by employing cold storing for your coins. (See our rundown of best chilly wallets for digital money!)

A blockchain is a decentralized online record (database), first portrayed as a form of doing transactions in digital money, bitcoin as said by Nakamoto [1]. Its functions by supplanting confide outsider signatories of a transaction (in a money-related setting, ordinarily a "middle man" installment supplier, e.g., Visa) with computational (cryptographic) evidence to approve transactions. This approval is completed by a system of clients ("full hubs") who on the whole cling to recently concurred rules, which are executed by the product. This strategy spares both the expense of intercession, as a blockchain includes no arbiter, and the expense related with switching transactions when debates emerge, as blockchain transactions are basically irreversible. The transaction records are assembled into hinders, every one of which is bolted to the following with a cryptographic hash. When recorded, information in some random square cannot be adjusted without modifying every resulting obstruct (as each square's hash relies upon the last), nor without the understanding of a greater part of the individuals from the system. Just as in money-related administrations, dispersed record innovation has likewise been applied in the assembling business to follow merchandise inside a stored network as said in [10,21], in governments for casting a ballot and open records as said in [31,32], and in retail for unmediated products exchanging as stated by Lamport [33] and to permit progressively advanced dedication bundles as explained in [33,34].

The framework is additionally adaptable enough to permit the option of subjective rationale to process, approve, and get to the information. This is actualized through segments of business rationale known as savvy contracts, which dwell on the blockchain and are synchronized over all hubs. A keen agreement is a string of PC code that executes at whatever point certain conditions are met, guaranteeing security and approved access as said in [35]. The capacity to make shrewd agreements makes blockchain appropriate for human services, where severe guidelines oversee how delicate information can be utilized as said in [36,37]. Data trade utilizing brilliant agreements is straightforward and strife free and kills the requirement for a broker, as the blockchain executes the information sharing dependent on the pre-agreed states of the agreement as said in [38,39,51].

Possession and protection of information are significant issues that blockchain could comprehend. It is at present discussed whether the human services supplier or the patient claims social insurance information identifying with a patient (in spite of the fact that patients have a distinct option to get to the information as said in [40]). Notwithstanding proprietorship issues, with the presentation of the GDPR in the European Union, it is significant for patients to know how their own data is being taken care of. Knowledge contracts actualized by a blockchain would improve the assent procedure for information access by specialists as demonstrated in [15,36]. The present assent process is not institutionalized or customized, which makes it hard for a patient to communicate plainly by means of an entrance control strategy, which may, for instance, include permitting chosen access to specific experts. CareChain is modeled to provide support for integrating telehealth data [53].

Another worry with clinical records is the expense as of now connected with moving records between areas. Continued imaging contemplates did on account of inaccessibility of earlier outcomes can be hazardous as far as deferred treatment just as economically expensive. Sending information by means of email is viewed as a security chance, and there is clear wastefulness inborn in interpreting a computerized resource onto optical media that is generally perused just a single time at the getting site. A framework incorporating tolerant assent just as access to approved people would save money on these expenses.

Clinical data is never again restricted to composed reports, imaging studies, and blood tests. Genomic information that are gathered by wearable gadgets, for example, wrist trinkets and watches implanted with sensors, are progressively aggregated. Whenever abused successfully, the accessibility of these new types of information may prompt improved treatment alternatives and results, which may likewise be analyzed by medical coverage organizations offering limits for "sound" conduct. Further advantages emerge in the domain of man-made consciousness. At the point when given the proper information, this can derive patterns from the information that are then used to create populace level knowledge thus accomplish populace well-being in general. These new information groups, be that as it may, will require cautious incorporation to permit proper examination while keeping up persistent protection and protection from programmers.

In spite of the fact that digitization of records has been set up in the general professional division for more than 30 years (yet inadequate with regards to basic information sharing and trading abilities), auxiliary consideration has not yet effectively accomplished this accepted standard. Conveyed record innovation, started and exemplified by the bitcoin blockchain, is growingly affecting IT situations in which compliance to authoritative guidelines and upkeep of open trust [52] are progressively central, and it might be utilized in acknowledging NHS Digital's objective as explained by Wachter [41]. The point of this survey was to abridge the proof identifying with the execution of blockchain to oversee health records that are maintained in electronic form and to check with the efficiency of storage so that if it would be enhanced effectively.

Though blockchain has some interesting security capabilities with regard to its integrity and availability side, a secured framework is required. Several preventive measures are required to secure the blockchain. David Houlding, the director of health-care privacy and security at Intel Health and Life Sciences, told that blockchain, one of the distributed technologies nowadays, is not only supporting cryptocurrencies but also has the potential for securing health data exchanges. He also adds that this has many limitations that the organizations have to keep in mind. In a discussion with Information Security Media Group, he also says that today most of the health data is found to be in silos and enterprise systems. There is a huge unexploited probability in sharing the data in such a way that the quality of handling the data could be enriched and security could be enhanced. He also says, "Blockchain will not replace any database in healthcare but blockchain acts as business-to-business middleware." He claims that any network of health-care organizations that involves the organizations which exchange the health information, organizations that facilitate the payments exchange, medicine supply, submission of credentials by physicians in the network, and medical devices that are utilized for tracking for sharing the required data adds additional value to the blockchain.

Blockchain technology also deals with the interoperability challenges within the health IT ecosystem. Health IT systems would use Open APIs that match with industry compliances to combine and share the data. Consequently, the necessity for the complex point-to-point data amalgamations among the various systems would be eradicated, which makes the work easier.

Blockchain is useful for multiple accesses by health-care communities, patients, and researchers by one shared data which gives the source within time, accurate and gives the detailed information of patient health data. Data structures include the data from various sources that include information from various sources such as images, documents, sensors that are deployed in the body, and mobile applications. Extensive and easily understandable data are able to get that to deal with unforeseen data in future.

Data is growing from cheap mobile devices and sensors. Distributed architectures which are taken on the basis of hardware give the cost efficient and scalable. By increasing the data to the blockchain, it is easy to handle the increased load. The vital importance in blockchain-distributed architecture is recovery, which is unaffected. Data is distributed to more number of servers that are located geographically. Single point of failure in terms of server is not possible, since failure in single point leads to disaster on the whole system of all locations at a time.

Efficient algorithms and protocols are selected in blockchains for data encryption and cryptographic techniques. These technologies are highly scalable, analyzed, secured, and used in many government agencies and industries all over the world.

Blockchain technology has many advantages that are useful to the people belonging to different sectors like medical researchers, health-care providers, and people. Data could be accessed on the basis of the access permissions from the single point of storage.

2.6.1   Challenges and limitations

2.6.1.1   Data ownership and privacy

Accomplishing interoperability of patient's information and utilization lies within the responsibility of the person, which are the essential features of blockchain. Albeit moving information proprietorship from the legislature and organizations to patients requires broad reengineering of inheritance frameworks to present a blockchain, it would increase patients to develop dynamic specialists in their own consideration by providing information to acquire the most ideal treatment. The blockchain would likewise provide people the sole capacity to approve information access to different suppliers at their watchfulness, disposing of deferrals related with the present administration, and guaranteeing tolerant protection. These advantages presented by blockchain remain to engage patients with power over their information, another desire in when mutualistic and consumerist understanding specialist connections are turning into the standard. Patients could likewise specifically impart information to analysts utilizing blockchain, either for the more prominent logical reasons or for empowering concentration on their kind condition. The framework would ensure their assent, a factor key to setting up self-rule and patient-focused consideration. An ongoing case of patient independence over well-being information is 23, and 80% of whose clients decided to make their genomic information accessible to scientists. This exhibits that patients will be glad to share information for research should they remain to profit. Empowering direct patient association in controlling the utilization of their records right in a secure way empowered by blockchain will upgrade the take-up of such stages and conceivably lead to improved well-being results. Sharing information might be refined to confide is a framework, however as an incentive, can be given if there are "healthy and improving" patients, for example, with cheap insurance premiums. This and other comparable thoughts should be guided to decide how adequately they will beat this challenge.

2.6.1.2   Legal

Under GDPR articles, the Organization of Economic Cooperation and Development security rule, the Health Insurance Portability and Accountability Act (HIPAA) privacy rule, and others, individuals might demand information that needs an eradication. This is feasible when the records are not put away on the blockchain. Besides, a record that holds the past information might be put into the chain irrespective of its deletion. The legitimate inquiry emerging from this identifies with the availability of data about personal and other information related to home.

In any case, the way that information in the framework would regardless be constrained by the patient is a positive indication of progress. An impending limitation is that the utilization of a private or consortium-drove blockchain, since information security concerns, should be directed to make the administrations consistent and seller nonpartisan. This might be accomplished by having an administering authority uphold open measures. In spite of the fact that these sorts of administrative limitations are important to guarantee such proper utilization of data, it has slow advancement in the field. HIPAA, for instance, necessitates that an institutional survey board endorses the utilization of information as stated in [42]. Such postponement that would be considerable is anyway improbable, thus consistence with these guidelines is fundamental to the achievement of blockchain.

2.6.1.3   Security

Sensitive Certain Subtle Information must be remained careful from busybodies and gatecrashers. Breaks negatively affect the open view of the medicinal services field and take steps to ruin future research through increasingly stringent administrative limitations. The WannaCry assault of May 2017 tainted a large number of PCs around the world, including those of the NHS as demonstrated by Greenhalgh [43]. One prior assault in Los Angeles focused on EHRs specifically, requesting a huge number of dollars in recover. A blockchain is secure than inheritance techniques, which would give patients with accreditations. It accomplishes this feature by the utilization of open-key cryptography (rather than symmetric-key cryptography, the strategy regularly utilized for encryption). This includes creating an open and private key for every client utilizing a single direction encryption work, known as a hash. It is extremely unlikely for anybody yet the beneficiary to see data sent over the blockchain, as it is made sure about by their private key. The main security fault that may emerge with a blockchain is randomly generated and happens if an open blockchain is utilized: programmers could conspire in a "51% attack," bringing about the reworking of the chain structure. Accordingly, to understand the benefits of a distributed framework, patients must possess trust that in any event half of mining hubs would not have any desire to disregard the unchanging nature of the blockchain. The open blockchain additionally prompts the chance of patient recognizable proof, which should be evaded by pseudonymizing information to secure patients' characters. On the off chance that a private or consortium blockchain was to be utilized, in any case, mining hubs would be restricted to emergency clinics and other confided in wellbeing suppliers, disposing of these security defects. The capacity and sharing of clinical information (creating interoperability) are fundamental for improved security results, regarding protection of delicate data while doing this remaining part a major test in human services. The script shows that with the suitable administrative rules and use of principles, blockchain can go about as a vehicle to oversee assented access to EHRs. This will build interoperability without trading off security, while additionally ensuring tolerant protection. These issues would most adequately be handled by the utilization of a private or consortium-driven blockchain; in any case, this should be controlled to guarantee proper utilization of information. The improved interoperability and diminished long-haul authoritative expenses would prompt improved well-being results.

2.6.1.4 Future of blockchain

As of today, blockchain tech is at a very nascent stage. The software industry has been moving toward an open-source community due to factors like affordability and security. In a world moving toward open source, implementation of blockchain could be the next big thing as this technology provides a secure way to decentralize an application. To further understand the future of this technology, let us have a look at how it all began. Popular P2P applications like torrent, Napster have existed for a long time, but the true revolution in this space was brought by the introduction of a decentralized P2P currency bitcoin; it enabled the transaction of goods primarily online without any governing central authority like bank. The rise of bitcoin made many more people to look further into this area. Then came Ethereum that took this technology to the next level. It was not just a currency but it also had a feature called smart-contract where a developer could run a piece of code on the computation power of the Ethereum network in exchange for some other which was bought using dollars. Ethereum revolutionized blockchain. Smart-contracts enabled many developers to make secure Dapps running over a network hosted by several nodes on Ethereum. This smart-contracts way of developing application was not suitable for large enterprise level blockchain solutions. Enterprises started working on a more fitting solution to this problem and as a result of this, several blockchain frameworks have sprung up each suitable for a set of problems and environment like Iroha for mobile applications, Besu for Java based tools, etc. The open-source community, Linux Foundation took all these frameworks under its umbrella, thus creating the HyperLedger Foundation.

One such tool developed by Hyperledger Fabric was an enterprise grade DLT which also provided extensive privacy support. Fabric fueled the growth of several Dapps as now it was easier to define a network and thus host it using a BaaS platform like AWS or AZURE. This was truly an enterprise solution.

However, the main future of blockchain lies in financial and medical industry. The financial industry is primarily run by the big banks that act as a central authority governing all the transactions, however blockchain-based currencies like bitcoin and Ethereum challenge this conventional way of transactions. They give the trader a true digital currency entirely hosted on a de-centralized network without an authority. Medical field deals with very sensitive data; therefore, hospitals store it in a very secure fashion and do not share it with any third party, thus creating a barrier where hospitals cannot share information with each other and also with medical researchers. Implementing a secure blockchain network among a set of participants like researchers and doctors could solve this problem. Aggregate blockchains nested blockchains can be used to extend the reach of sharing and collaborating outside local networks. Blockchain technology with the rapid growth of computational power along with ML algorithms can give a mechanism that can serve as an alternative to AI.

2.7 Conclusion

Blockchain steps into another type of innovation wherein the present data is inadequate and no utilization context or measurable correlations with customary frameworks exist. There are costs related with another framework transformation, and in education experts and patients on how best to exploit it for improved well-being. Funds in to new frameworks would, in any case, be exceeded through returns. In the essential phases of usage, the useful convenience of the proposed framework will probably rely upon the end-client experience—the complexities-based blockchain should be held up behind an adequately easy to understand interface, for example, an on the web or portable application to be embraced effectively. Transient preliminaries illustrate the best approaches to actualize such an easy to use understanding, which might be extended from that point. Blockchain technology has some difficulty in implementing it, practically due to security and privacy threat and there is necessity to address this. In future, many applications are expected to continue, but the scope will be limited.

References

[1] Nakamoto S. Bitcoin: A Peer-to-Peer Electronic Cash System; (2008) p. 1–9. Available online at: https://bitcoin.org/bitcoin.pdf (accessed May 2019).

[2] Ekblaw AL, Azaria A, and Halamka JD, *et al.* A Case Study for Blockchain in Healthcare: 'MedRec' Prototype for Electronic Health Records and Medical Research Data. Proc IEEE Open Big Data Conf., Boston, MA. (2016); 13: 13

[3] Peterson K, Deeduvanu R, Kanjamala P, and Boles K. A Blockchain-Based Approach to Health Information Exchange Networks, Mayo Clinic. HealthIT.Gov;   2020.   https://www.healthit.gov/sites/default/files/12-55-blockchain-based-approachfinal.pdf.

[4] Zhang J, Xue N, and Huang X. 'A secure system for pervasive social network-based healthcare'. IEEE Access. (2016);4: 9239–9250.

[5]   Tschorsch F and Scheuermann B. 'Bitcoin and beyond: a technical survey on decentralized digital currencies'. IEEE Communications Surveys & Tutorials. (2016);18:2084–2123.

[6]   Cochrane Review, eHealth Stakeholder Group. Patient access to electronic health records. Cochrane Database of Systematic Reviews. (2013);6:1–17. doi: 10.1002/14651858.CD012707.

[7]   Kalra D, Stroetmann V, Sundgren M, *et al.* 'The European Institute for Innovation through Health Data'. Learning Health Systems. (2017);1: e10008. doi: 10.1002/lrh2.10008.

[8]   Malin B, Goodman K, and Section Editors for the IMIA Yearbook Special Section. 'Between access and privacy: challenges in sharing health data'. Yearbook of Medical Informatics. (2018);27:55–59. doi: 10.1055/s-0038-1641216.

[9]   Karafiloski E and Anastas M. 'Blockchain solutions for big data challenges: a literature review'. In: IEEE EUROCON 2017 – 17th International Conference on Smart Technologies. Ohrid: IEEE (2017).

[10] Krawiec RJ, Housman D, White M, *et al.* Blockchain: Opportunities for Health Care; 2016. Available online at: https://www2.deloitte.com/content/dam/Deloitte/us/Documents/public-sector/usblockchain-opportunities-for-health-care.pdf (accessed May 2019).

[11] OECD. 'The potential for blockchain technology in public equity markets in Asia', in OECD Equity Market Review of Asia 2018; 2018. Available online at: www.oecd.org/corporate/OECD-Equity-Market-Review-Asia-2018.pdf

[12] Phillips S. National Information Board. Personalised Health and Care 2020; 2014. Available online at: https://assets.publishing.service.gov.uk/government/uploads/system/uploads/attachment_data/ file/ 384650/NIB_Report.pdf.

[13] Kuo TT, Kim HE, and Ohno-Machado L. 'Blockchain distributed ledger technologies for biomedical and health care applications'. Journal of the American Medical Informatics Association. (2017);24:1211–1220.

[14] Craig J and Shore J. RX137: Evidence Generation Guide for Apps and Wearables Developers: Study Designs Including Applied Examples; 2016. Available online at: https://www.yhec.co.uk/yhec-content/uploads/2017/03/YHEC-Study-Designs-28.03.17.pdf.

[15] Williams-Grut O. Estonia is Using the Technology Behind Bitcoin to Secure 1 Million Health Records. Business Insider. Guardtime Secures Estonian Health Records;2016; Available online at: https://www.businessinsider.in/Estonia-is-using-the-technology-behind-bitcoin-to-secure-1-million-health-records/articleshow/51246942.cms

[16] Cyran MA. 'Blockchain as a foundation for sharing healthcare data'. Blockchain in Healthcare Today. (2018):1–13. [Google Scholar].

[17] Kaye J, Whitley EA, Lund D, Morrison M, Teare H, and Melham K. 'Dynamic consent: a patient interface for twenty-first century research networks'. European Journal of Human Genetics. (2015);23(2):141–146. [PMC free article] [PubMed] [Google Scholar].

[18]   Lima C. Blockchain-GDPR Privacy by Design: How Decentralized Blockchain Internet Will Comply with GDPR Data Privacy; 2018. [cited at 2019 Jan 15]. Available online at: https://blockchain.ieee.org/images/files/pdf/blockchaingdpr-privacy-by-design.pdf. [Google Scholar].

[19]   Commission Nationale de l'Informatique et des Libertes. Blockchain and the GDPR: Solutions for a Responsible Use of the Blockchain in the Context of Personal Data [Internet] Paris, France: Commission Nationale de l'Informatique et des Libertes; 2018. [cited at 2019 Jan 15]. Available online at: https://www.cnil.fr/en/blockchain-and-gdpr-solutions-responsible-use-blockchain-context-personal-data.

[20]   Innovative Medicines Initiative. Topic: Blockchain Enabled Healthcare [Internet] Brussels, Belgium: Innovative Medicines Initiative; 2018. [cited at 2019 Jan 15]. Available online at: https://www.imi.europa.eu/sites/default/files/uploads/documents/apply-for-funding/futuretopics/Blockchain_vJune 2018.pdf. [Google Scholar].

[21]   Dimitrov DV. 'Medical Internet of Things and big data in healthcare'. Journal of Healthcare Informatics Research. (2016);22(3):156–163.

[22]   Salah K, Rehman MH, Nizamuddin N, and Al-Fuqaha A. 'Blockchain for AI: review and open research challenges'. IEEE Access. (2019);7:10127–10149. [Google Scholar].

[23]   Timicoin. Timi Group Incorporation; 2018. [cited at 2019 Jan 15]. Available online at: https://www.timicoin.io. [Google Scholar].

[24]   Zajc T. F020 Blockchain, Value of Data, and the Role of Legislation With Adoption (Ray Dogum, Health Unchained); 2018. [cited at 2019 Jan 15]. Available online at: https://medium.com/faces-of-digital-health/f020-block-chain-value-of-data-and-the-role-of-legislation-withadoption-ray-dogum-health-80919d909e97. [Google Scholar].

[25]   Bates M. 'Direct-to-consumer genetic testing: is the public ready for simple, at-home DNA tests to detect disease risk?'. IEEE Pulse. (2018);9(6):11–14. [PubMed] [Google Scholar].

[26]   Nebula Genomics. Nebular Genomics [Internet] San Francisco, CA; 2018. [cited at 2019 Jan 15]. Available online at: http://www.nebula.org. [Google Scholar].

[27]   Genomes.io. Genomes.io [Internet]; 2018. [cited at 2019 Jan 15]. Available online at: https://www.genomes.io. [Google Scholar].

[28]   HL7. Fast Healthcare Interoperability Resources (FHIR); 2016. Available online at: https://www.hl7.org/fhir/ (accessed: 2016-08-01).

[29]   Leftwich R. The Path to Deriving Clinical Value from FHIR. InterSystems; 2016. Available online at: http://www.intersystems.com/library/library-item/pathderiving- clinica., -value-fhir/ (accessed: 2016-08-06).

[30]   iNTERFACEWARE Inc. What is 'FHIR' and why you should care?; 2016. Available online at: http://www.interfaceware.com/blog/what-is-fhir-andwhy-should-you-care/ (accessed: 2016-08-06).

[31]   Gordon WJ and Catalini C. 'Blockchain technology for healthcare: facilitating the transition to patient-driven interoperability'. Computational and

Structural Biotechnology Journal. (2018);16:224–230. doi: 10.1016/j. csbj.2018.06.003.

[32]   Iansiti M and Lakhani KR. The truth about blockchain. *Harvard Business Review*. Boston, MA: Harvard University, 2017.

[33]   Lamport L, Robert S, and Marshall P. 'The Byzantine general's problem'. ACM Transactions on Programming Languages and Systems. (1982);4.3:382–401.

[34]   Buterin V. A Next-Generation Smart Contract and Decentralized Application Platform; 2014. Available online at: https://github.com/ethereum/wiki/wiki/White-Paper (accessed May 2019).

[35]   Matakis L. Following a Tuna from Fiji to Brooklyn – on the Blockchain. Wired; 2018. Available online at: https://www.wired.com/story/following-a-tunafrom-fiji-to-brooklynon-the-blockchain/ (accessed May 2019).

[36]   Grellet V, Godfrey R, Rhodes Y, *et al.* Leveraging the Ethereum Blockchain for Social Good. Blockchain for social coalition; 2018. Available online at: https://www.blockchainforsocialimpact.com/ (accessed October 2018).

[37]   Cachin C. 'Architecture of the Hyperledger blockchain fabric'. In: Workshop on Distributed Cryptocurrencies and Consensus Ledgers. Vol. 310. Rennes (2016).

[38]   Fall KR and Stevens WR. TCP/IP illustrated. Vol. 1. The Protocols. Addison-Wesley Professional Computing Series; 2011.

[39]   Godlee F. 'What can we salvage from care. data?'. BMJ. (2016);354:i3907. doi: 10.1136/bmj.i3907.

[40]   Lipman A, Ekblaw A, Cameron A, Johnson B, Retzepi K, and Nchinda N. MedRec: Medical Data Management on the Blockchain. A beginner's guide to Ethereum Ethereum white paper Harvard Business Review on Blockchain MIT Digital Currency Initiative. 2016; Available online at: https://medrec. media.mit.edu.

[41]   Wachter R. Making IT Work: Harnessing the Power of Health Information Technology to Improve Care in England. Report to the National Advisory Group on Health Information Technology in England. London: The Stationery O ce;2016.

[42]   Centers for Disease Control and Prevention. 'HIPAA privacy rule and public health. Guidance from CDC and the US Department of Health and Human Services'. Morbidity and Mortality Weekly Report. (2003);52(Suppl. 1):1–17.

[43]   Greenhalgh T and Keen J. '"Personalising" NHS information technology in England'. BMJ. (2014);349:g7341. doi: 10.1136/bmj.g7341.

[44]   Benson T. Principles of Health Interoperability HL7 and SNOMED. Springer-Verlag London: Springer Science & Business Media; 2012.

[45]   Taylor K. Connected Health: How Digital Technology Is Transforming Health and Social Care. London: Deloitte Centre for Health Solutions; 2015.

[46]   Michie S, Yardley L, West R, Patrick K, and Greaves F. 'Developing and evaluating digital interventions to promote behavior change in health and health care: recommendations resulting from an international workshop'.

Journal of Medical Internet Research. (2017);19:e232. doi: 10.2196/jmir.7126.

[47] Brailer DJ. 'Interoperability: the key to the future health care system: interoperability will bind together a wide network of real-time, life-critical data that not only transform but become health care'. Health Affairs. (2005);24(Suppl. 1):W5–W19. doi: 10.1377/hlthaff.2012.1199.

[48] Van Staa TP, Goldacre B, Buchan I, and Smeeth L. 'Big health data: the need to earn public trust'. British Medical Journal. (2016);354:i3636. doi: 10.1136/bmj.i3636.

[49] Riordan F, Papoutsi C, Reed JE, Marston C, Bell D, and Majeed A. 'Patient and public attitudes towards informed consent models and levels of awareness of Electronic Health Records in the UK'. International Journal of Medical Informatics. (2015);84:237–247. doi: 10.1016/j.ijmedinf.2015.01.008.

[50] Albeyatti A. MedicalChain. 2018; White Paper. Available online at: https://medicalchain.com/en/whitepaper.

[51] Caldicott F. Review of Data Security, Consent and Opt-Outs; 2016. Available online at: https://www.gov.uk/government/publications/review-ofdata-security-consent-and-opt-outs (accessed November 2018).

[52] Drury RL. 'Unraveling health as a complex adaptive system: data mining, cloud computing, machine learning and biosensors as synergistic technologies'. International Journal of Data Mining and Bioinformatics. (2017);2017: J105. doi: 10.29011/2577-0616.000105.

[53] Sellström J and Farestam S. CareChain. 2018; Available online at: https://www.carechain.io/files/CareChain_The_Infrastructure_Consortium.pdf (accessed October 2018).

[54] Vestbo J, Leather D, Bakerly ND, *et al.* 'Effectiveness of fluticasone furoate–vilanterol for COPD in clinical practice'. The New England Journal of Medicine. (2016);375:1253–1260. doi: 10.1056/NEJMoa1608033.

[55] Ipsos M. Report prepared for the welcome trust. The One-Way Mirror: Public Attitudes to Commercial Access to Health Data. London, Wellcome Trust; 2016.

[56] Tully M, Hassan L, Oswald M, and Ainsworth M. Commercial Use of Health Data – A Public "Trial" by Citizens' Jury. International Journal for Population Data Science. (2018);3(4). doi: 10.23889/ijpds.v3i4.598.

[57] Kahn JS, Veenu A, and Adam B. 'What it takes: characteristics of the ideal personal health record'. Health Affairs. (2009);28:369–376. doi: 10.1377/hlthaff.28.2.369.

[58] Wyatt J, Sathanandam S, Rastall P, Hoogewerf J, and Wooldridge D. Personal Health Record (PHR) Landscape Review Final Report. London, Royal College of Physicians; 2016.

[59] Iacobucci G. 'Computer error may have led to incorrect prescribing of statins'. British Medical Journal. (2016);353:i2742. doi: 10.1136/bmj.i2742.

[60] Kapu N, Selvaraj P, Burugari VK, and Namburi A. 'Secured electronic health ledger using block chain as a service'. Journal of critical review. (2020);7(6):2176–2185.

Chapter 3

Reforming the traditional business network

Neethu Narayanan[1] and K.P. Arjun[2]

Blockchain development has expanded amazing thought, with an elevating eagerness for a lot of different applications, running from data the administrators, cash-related organizations, advanced cybersecurity, Internet of Things (IoT), and sustenance science to social protection industry and psyche inspect. The board has identified a stunning interest in using blockchain work opportunities for the transfer of sealed and secure social protection data. Already, there is a blockchain that is improving the standard social insurance practices to a legitimately solid recommendation, like successful end and treatment through guaranteed and secure information sharing. Later on, blockchain could be improved, which may conceivably help in changed, authentic, and secure remedial administrations by consolidating the whole consistent clinical information of a patient's prosperity and introducing it in a top-tier secure medical organizations course of the plan. In this work, we study both the present and most recent updates in the field of medical organizations by acknowledging blockchain as a model. We, in addition, talk about the employments of blockchain, near to the difficulties opposed and future points of view. The biggest problem connected with blockchain is a lack of technical knowledge. Trust is built in the network and blockchain invention, and less in the individual participants or the sharing of accomplices. High structure and operational consistency thus maintain the namelessness and pseudonymity of the participants. It reduces the lopsided characteristics of power, and the man handles and the arbitrary decisions.

3.1 Introduction

Social protection is a real clinical data space where a huge proportion of data is produced, accessed, and dispersed continuously. Taking care of and spreading this tremendous proportion of data is basic, similarly as in a general sense testing, in light of the tricky thought of data and obliging factors, for instance, security and assurance. Ensuring safe, secure, and efficient data exchange in the area of medical

[1]Department of Vocational Studies Software Development, St. Mary's College, Thrissur, India
[2]School of Computing Science and Engineering, Galgotias University, Greater Noida, India

management and clinical environments is of the utmost importance for the prosecution, as is the case in the current professional dynamic [1]. Information management activity is of the utmost significance to assist health professionals in transferring the therapeutic details of their patients to the appropriate master for an effective turn of events. Recommendations by observers and General Managers will be prepared to transfer the health details of their customers in an endlessly flexible and supportive way and guarantee that all external activities are completed and front-line knowledge on the circumstances of patient well-being.

In these two digital clinical courses of preparation [2], medical knowledge is transferred either by developmental collection and routing methods or automated comprehensive patient surveillance (e.g., tele-watching and telemetry). In these electronic healthcare environments, patients are electronically disassembled and handled by health experts by exchanging confidential details procedures. For all these clinical methodologies, health, effectiveness, and security of clinical details are some of the fundamental difficulties that can occur, considering the case-delicate existence of patient information. In this sense, the opportunity to share knowledge in a safe, secure, and flexible manner is, in turn, enormous to enable robust and vital therapeutic transfers of remote patients. As there is often a safe, useful sharing of knowledge in clinical communications, it helps one to pull together ideas or affirmations from clinical masters that consider increased consistent accuracy and successful diagnosis. In addition, there are various interoperability challenges that are constantly facing the right area at the moment. For example, the guaranteed, secure, and gainful trade of clinical information between human organizations affiliations or research establishments can present over the top difficulties in important activity. Such exchange of clinical information requires huge, solid, and sound encouraged effort between the substances included. Among the potential essentials that are looked into right now, the chance of clinical information, affectability, information-sharing understandings, systems, complex patient sorting out calculations, moral strategies, and controlling standards are the challenges. These are a fragment of the basic worries that should be settled upon normally, before completing any clinical information exchange fundamentally.

Over the years, masters have endeavored to conduct pit, automatic reasoning, artificial intelligence (AI) [3,4], and machine vision activities to energize pros and health professionals in the confirmation and care of different continuous infections. Astonishing technology for the usage of blockchains for the transport of safe and protected social security info, biomedical and e-prosperity data exchange, mind entertainment, and learning has begun late. A network leads the founder of P2P. This is fundamentally a diffused integrated multi-field composition system, made up of encryption, numbers, and conceptual descriptions that have been designed for the illumination of regular simulated database synchronization criteria utilizing computational computing. The blockchain development essentially includes six main sections shown in Table 3.1.

An individual who is a piece of this system needs to check each new exchange made. As every exchange in a square of a blockchain is checked by the entirety of

Table 3.1   Characteristics of blockchain technology

Key elements	Functionality description
Decentralized	An open-access software system for those connected with the network. Knowledge can be downloaded, verified, processed, and modified on various systems
Transparent	The documented and processed knowledge on blockchain is open to future customers and can be modified without any issues. The clear principle of blockchains will definitely protect knowledge from being changed or stolen
Immutable	Records, once created, are retained indefinitely and cannot be updated easily without the intervention of more than 51% of the node at the same time
Autonomy	The blockchain platform is autonomous and decentralized, meaning that any node in the blockchain network can safely access, transfer, store, and upgrade information, rendering it efficient and free from any outside interference
Open source	The invention of the blockchain is described in a manner that allows anyone involved with the network exposure to the open source. This inimitable versatility entitles everyone, not only to publicly review the documents, but also to build numerous impending applications
Anonymity	As knowledge travels between node and node, the identity of the person stays secret, rendering it increasingly safe and accurate

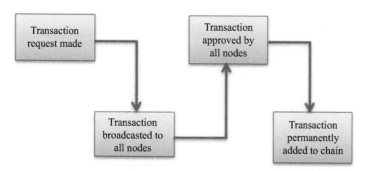

Figure 3.1   Simplified processes for the blockchain procedure

the hubs in the system, it turns out to be an ever-increasing extent permanent. Figure 3.1 shows the work stream of blockchain process.

In the future, blockchain might be an advancement that will hopefully assist for personalized, reliable, yet even safe health care, through consolidating all the constant therapeutic knowledge on the well-being of the patient and through implementing it as a state-of-the-art protected human resources system.

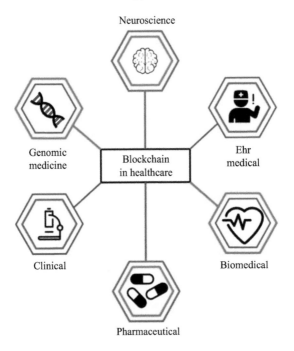

Figure 3.2   Applications of blockchain in healthcare

3.2   Applications of blockchain

Originally, blockchain technology (BCT) was designed for its most common application in financial relations and digital sources of finance, but today its usage is increasing in a variety of different areas, including the biomedical sector. The potential of blockchain innovation can be seen in Figure 3.2. Its system of balancing out and making sure about the informational collection with which clients can communicate through various kinds of exchanges is shown in Figure 3.2.

3.2.1   Blockchains in electronic health records (EHR)

Electronics Patient Journal (*EPJ*) is the Norwegian Electronic Patient Record position that records well-being data of clients and has been principally utilized by well-being suppliers in Norway. An EPJ framework stores EPJ documents in databases and offers an interface for enlisting, looking, and showing data from the EPJ records, and so forth. Such databases are (somewhat) open to clients and different suppliers with various determined consents. At present, this EPJ framework, similar to the Electronic Health Record (EHR) frameworks in numerous different nations, is divided across well-being suppliers and the whole framework still does not seem to be coordinated [5]. The well-being records of a client are kept up in various well-being suppliers' databases; in this way, the suppliers cannot have an extensive review of the considerable number of records of a solitary client.

The e-healthcare system is acknowledged as one of the domains where blockchain has enormous promise due to its inherent qualities, in particular for the maintenance of online well-being data. Noteworthy research endeavors have been made toward this path over the most recent couple of years. Azaria *et al.* [6] proposed a decentralized record of the executives framework, named MedRec, which was based on the Ethereum stage and used Ethereum's keen agreements to make a shrewd portrayal of existing clinical records put away inside individual hubs on the network. Patients have command over their clinical records across suppliers and medicines destinations in this framework. While clinical partners, for example, specialists and general well-being specialists, are boosted to take part in the mining of the blockchain, the blockchain record keeps an auditable history of clinical communications of patients, suppliers, and controllers. This arrangement achieves inquiries to which levels that patients should claim their clinical data and to which degrees that the information can be shared. The related guidelines have been talked about under different conditions and, much of the time, are chosen by well-being specialists. Thus, the accessible variety of the framework ought to likewise be taken into the thought that patients have not full authority over their clinical records and information are shared at various levels among every clinical partner.

Around the same time, Yue *et al.* [7] proposed a blockchain-based cell phone application design, named Healthcare Data Gateway, to improve the security part of sharing private patient data. The proposed engineering comprises three layers: crude information are encoded and put away in the private blockchain cloud at the capacity layer; database for the executives, including information get to the board is set at the administration layer; and utilization layer is the place medicinal services information are used, e.g., for the clinical records framework, and information investigation. In this design, a private blockchain is actualized. Dissimilar to an open blockchain that anybody can join the system, the private blockchain is a permissioned blockchain with limitations on who is permitted to take an interest and to which activities/activities.

Another way to deal with improving protection issues when sharing human services information between various partners was proposed by Peterson *et al.* [8]; the difficulties of picking basic interoperable information linguistic uses and security conventions, and ways to deal with settling these difficulties were discussed. Another agreement system, named evidence interoperability, alongside a calculation depicting the procedure, is proposed. Information must adjust to both basic and semantic requirements to be checked to arrive at the agreement. In this investigation, the EHR framework uses Fast Healthcare Interoperability Resources (FHIR) standard information design, and the proposed accord component correspondingly utilizes the profile of the FHIR as the interoperability imperatives. For various arrangements that other EHR frameworks are using, a lot of auxiliary and semantic imperatives should be assigned in advance to actualize this accord component.

In this way, Ma *et al.* [9] acquainted blockchain with the biomedical/social insurance domains. The article describes point by point the advantages of applying blockchain in biomedicine/medicinal services by contrasting it and conventional conveyed databases. It likewise talked about the potential difficulties and proposed answers for receiving blockchain advances in these areas. This work gives a general acquaintance about blockchain advancements with the biomedical and medicinal services informatics analysts. Liang *et al.* [10] proposed a user-centric well-being information-sharing arrangement by using a decentralized and permissioned blockchain. In this work, a portable application was sent to gather well-being information from individual wearable gadgets. The gathered information were synchronized to the cloud and afterward imparted to medicinal services suppliers and medical coverage organizations. The blockchain arrange is sent for information respectability insurance, notwithstanding which, it additionally stores to get to control strategies and all entrance exercises of the individual well-being information. Be that as it may, the versatile application gathers individual well-being information from either the sensors of the wearable gadgets or manual contribution by clients. In this manner, the methodology has its confinement of usage in EHR frameworks where information are essentially gotten to by well-being experts and recorded in normalized groups.

Recently, Kokoris-Kogias *et al.* [11] introduced a versatile disseminated record, the OmniLedger, where they utilized a method known as sharding, to make subsets of hubs for equal state and exchange handling. By executing this methodology, the preparing limit increments as the system scales out and conquers the limit issue of the conventional record, where the handling limit diminishes as bigger agreement bunches likely create more overheads. The need of sheer augmentation in digitizing clinical well-being records was brought about by clinical experts, medical clinics, and social insurance gadgets, as digitization of this information empowers simple access and sharing and is likewise a premise of better and speedy dynamic. The most well-known uses of blockchain advancements in social insurance are as of now in the territory of electronic clinical records shown in Figure 3.3.

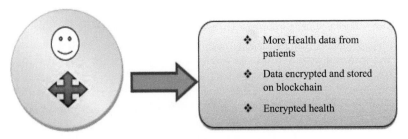

Figure 3.3   Featuring connections between EHR, smart healthcare applications,
blockchain technology, and preventive care

3.2.2 Blockchains in clinical research

A variety of problems, including privacy security, respectability of privacy, exchange of information, record keeping, continuous enrolment, can occur in the field of clinical trials. Blockchain, as the new generation of the internet, will provide realistic answers to such problems. Human resources experts are chipping away with the aid of digital technologies to address these problems. The human resources sector would likely be shocked by the usage of cryptocurrency, combined with AI and automation. In the analysis suggested by Clauson *et al.* [12], approved Ethereum, a protocol that offers genius agreement utility in blockchain is used corresponding to center-dependent knowledge executive frameworks. The primary aim of the inquiry was to resolve the problem of patient enrolment. The results of the study found that Ethereum contributed to snappier trades, as shown in bitcoin, and henceforth the finality suggested the usage of Ethereum's clear agreements for the convenience of the board's knowledge in clinical preliminary studies. Tolerant enrolment using blockchains is also one of the emerging applications of this technique in clinical science. A further study was performed by Benchouf [13]. A mechanism was placed in motion to take the informed consent of patients to comply and delete it so that it is safe, free of charge, and unfalsifiable. They used blockchain software to allow their work cycle run. Extensive application of blockchains in the healthcare sector covers the medical pharmacy store network of executives. Supplying managers is a crucial topic to be protected in all fields; however, due to its multifaceted existence, it has a more influential position in social insurance. This is because every exchange in the healthcare distribution network has an effect on the well-being of the customer. Supply chains are defenseless, despite openings for fake attacks, because they contain through moving pieces and people. Blockchains offer a safe and stable stage to destroy this problem and, at times, to avoid misappropriation, by providing better clarification of details and enhanced identification of the object. Because a record in blockchain must be accepted and refreshed by a clear agreement, managing the blockchain is not easy.

3.2.3 Blockchains in medical fraud detection

The widespread application of blockchains in the healthcare sector involves the executives' restorative product distribution network. Supplying the board is a crucial problem to secure in both fields, but it has a more important role to play in social security because of the growing importance [14]. That is because every transaction in the social security network has an effect on the well-being of the recipient. Supply chains are weak, what is more, they are composed of holes in deceitful attacks, like multiple moving pieces and persons. Blockchains offer a sheltered and safe stage for the removal of this problem and, now and then, depreciation even by providing higher knowledge accessibility and increased detectability of objects. Because a record in blockchain needs to be accepted and renewed by a genius arrangement, managing the blockchain is not straightforward.

3.2.4   Blockchains in neuroscience

Blockchains is the indicator of news and investigation dedicated to blockchain applications, and the field of neuroscience discipline is definitely included. Present-day neural advancements aim to create another mindset that prevents a technological link to the welcoming base, which enables one to monitor gadgets which knowledge by mental commands. These neural gadgets will decode the indications of mind behavior and translate them in orders to monitor the outer gadgets, as well as to identify the present mental state of a person, in the light of the knowledge of their mind activity.

The exceptional errand of perusing even, deciphering mind messages is illuminated by neural interface gadgets fitted with a few contact buttons, computing processors, and remote correspondence [15]. They translate the electrical activity of the cerebrum, which is then deciphered and sent to the leveled equipment. The whole lot happens in one device that the person carries on his head. Complex calculations and massive knowledge can use blockchain theory to store certain mind flags on the neural interface. One of the companies that states that they will be using BCTs is Neurogress. Enlisted in Geneva and set up in 2017, the company focuses on developing neural-control systems, allowing consumers to monitor digital weapons, rambles, shrewd apps, and AR/VR (augmented reality/virtual reality) tools through their own muses.

The Neurogress control system is focused around the usage of AI to boost the consistency of the memory and allows 90% of the memory knowledge to be stored in order to plan the AI being utilized by the device. As such, huge information of client neural action is required, with the organization's whitepaper relating to the Human Brain Project's demand for exabytes (1 exabyte=1 billion gigabytes) of memory, such as the scale of the storage maximum. It is obvious in this way that Neurogress aims to use blockchain, which it agrees to fix adequately the problem of encryption and safety of knowledge power. By storing client details on a shared ledger, these details become impervious to intrusion attempts and eventually confidential along these lines. Simultaneously, the usage of blockchain software makes the Neurogress platform accessible and transparent for future Neurogress administration clients. Because any unusual activity will be effectively discernible, the system would guarantee protection, what is more, the classification of individual knowledge.

It is also clear that blockchains [16] are a form of computer invention with a few important future uses, ideal for mind amplification, brain regeneration, and brain learning. Digitizing the whole human mind clearly requires some medium where to store it, what is more, it is here that blockchain innovation raises its head by and by. One proposition is the removal of mind files, which would result in the creation of information squares in close proximity to home reasoning chains, which can be shared in a distributed system document framework that allows verifiable forming. This kind of blockchain philosophy is presented as the material of the trains of the digital system for yield, with a few highlights of the loan incentive for man-made awareness, individual change, and their future reconciliation.

Blockchain enables the integrated PC network to shake hands at timestamped intervals to accept the origins and the validity of the ledger.

If, however, we were to build a mind from the earliest level, this kind of confidence aspect might allow the neurons' nets to store and evaluate data with precision and confidence of what is emotional versus the target of a given encounter. Multifaceted authentication correlated with a person insight chain, such as blockchain usage, will activate the open door to the sheltered framework of an assessed self-information center for individuals. Such a knowledge house diminishes the siloes of human intelligence, while at the same time enabling any human being to remain accountable for protection or sharing his or her expertise, theoretically gaining money-related benefit through the need of an expert or a joint authority. Perhaps not so far out, through an expanded variant of this technique, where at least two people witness the same minute, albeit from an emotional point of view, we might reassemble their experiences and be more impartial regarding the activities of the minute.

Preferably, it will facilitate the creation of simulated reproductions for past recollections, and the prospect of thinking emotions from someone else's point of view. When we still have a better functional perception of human mappings of emotions, concrete experiences as a reference to a specific experience will transfer knowledge from faculties to a potential blockchain (i.e., sight and smell). What is more, the fact of the matter is that the developments are being made to render that a reality. Not long from now, we will begin capturing our sensory experiences by the use of wearable tech, the present state of mind and nerve implants, biofeedback imaging, and all other sensors that authorize a multifaceted, special finger printing specific to a human record of brief interaction. Using such developments as an early step, work should be carried out to enhance processes, understanding, analysis, and healing conventions.

3.2.5   Blockchains in pharmaceutical industry and research

Pharmaceuticals are one of the main manufacturers and are the key component of the cutting edge of social security transport. The pharmaceutical component [17] not only deals with the arrival of fresh and future medicines to the market, it also seeks to maintain the quality and reliability of the clinical products delivered to the end-customer. What is more, the pharmaceutical division moreover helps in evaluation likewise, treatment of safe drugs, which helps finally in snappier patient recovery. In the regular cases, quiet associations face the challenges of following their things propitious, which now and again prompts present outrageous perils by allowing falsifiers to deal the creation, or assault fake drugs into the structure. Along these lines, the creation and spread of fake medication drugs has obtained one of the major and overall prosperity risks, particularly in making countries. During the creation, similar to imaginative work (R&D), of these meds, blockchain could be a best fit advancement, which can be used for evaluating, checking, and ensuring the creation methods of potential meds. Starting late, Hyperledger, an investigation foundation, impelled a fake medication drug prescription endeavor using blockchain development as a first instrument, for surveying and fighting the making of fake medication drugs. Right when it comes to fruitful transport of reliable and genuine meds to patients, there is a urgent need to screen, evaluate, and ensure the general technique of making and giving pharmaceutical drugs through the use of cutting edge progresses far and wide, and particularly in making countries. At this moment, a propelled drug control structure could be a solid course of action toward the shirking of fake medication drug prescriptions. Using a blockchain-based Digital Document Customizing System, gigantic pharmaceutical endeavors (Sanofi, Pfizer, and Amgen) moved a joint pilot adventure for assessment and the appraisal of new meds. Using blockchain as a technique, it is possible not to simply track the creation and territory of the medications at some irregular time, yet notwithstanding improving the traceability of misshaped meds, security of the drug gracefully system, and guaranteeing the idea of prescriptions given to purchasers or end-customers.

3.3   Business benefits of blockchain

The blockchain is a cryptographic innovation that decentralizes the handling of exchanges. It tends to be utilized to move data all the more rapidly, improve security, and convey another type of business process robotization through smart contracts [19]. These agreements use bits of code that receive the blockchain as a database and lines of code for process administration and execution. They make another worldview in business forms, improving execution and security. The difficulty is that numerous individuals in business experience issues in understanding the blockchain. This is the reason we will attempt to show, in the most down to business way that is available, what are the genuine advantages that lie behind this new idea.

Demystifying the regular publicity around blockchain, we can essentially avow that it is only a database, a safe, decentralized, and straightforward compartment of information that presents a keen idea—connect every datum with the past information utilizing cryptography. In this way, every exchange is connected to the past exchange by means of the hash calculations that lessen the measure of information contained in the exchange to a solitary and fixed-length string. This string is then added to the following exchange and recalculated making the chain.

Nonetheless, as opposed to investigating how blockchain functions, how about we dive into how it tends to be embraced in the endeavor plan of action to tackle the numerous advantages this intriguing innovation brings to the table. Since an undertaking is a mind-boggling setup, it includes procedures to interface individuals and their utilization of data for different everyday purposes. At the point when we talk about procedures, we are alluding to formal method used to satisfy a particular activity or exchange [20]. Now and then the procedures may just need coordination with individuals inside the association, and at different occasions these procedures may require joint effort with different associations to accomplish business objectives. These business processes, as regularly named in an authoritative air, could be requests, solicitations, or installments—all exchanges that include individuals and information. Here the blockchain becomes an integral factor, helping associations secure every one of these exchanges.

3.4   Reliance on blockchain usage

Few out of every odd organization will acknowledge bitcoin as a potential speculation. In any case, organizations cannot preclude the potential from securing the innovation behind the digital currency [20]. Blockchain's carefully designed nature is not just gainful for recording bitcoin exchanges but can also likewise be utilized to smooth out business activities. Walmart and Amazon are among the internationally perceived organizations that are currently considering blockchain to improve their methods.

Blockchain-related new businesses are getting millions in subsidizing from financial speculators, which is driving organizations to discover better approaches to utilize the innovation. Blockchain can update business activities to improve things, and underneath are a portion of the ventures that will profit extraordinarily from the innovation's capacity to smooth out the work process.

3.4.1   Protection claims

One of the significant segments that could profit by blockchain is the protection business. Through utilizing blockchain, insurance agencies will have the option to rebuild their technique for claims and guarantee the exact and speedy return of installments. Blockchain can likewise be utilized to make keen agreements, which will bring about faster and increasingly secure settlements.

3.4.2   Gold supply chain

The gold business would likewise profit significantly from blockchain. By carefully encoding each phase of the gold store network, venders of the valuable yellow metal will have the option to ensure the great conveyance status of each bit of gold, just as note where it was sourced. CNBC states that at any rate one tech organization called Emergent Technology Holdings is creating blockchain for this reason. Rising states that once they have finished their task, gold excavators and merchants will have the option to utilize a portable application that outputs keen chips in carefully designed seals, records moves of authority, and observes some other information identified with the deal and moving of gold.

Gold is one of the most costly items being exchanged every day. The FXCM's gold value diagram shows that the valuable metal is at present fluctuating at around $1,310 per ounce. Through blockchain, gold's deals, and delivery will be increasingly secure. The information contained inside the blockchain can never be changed, which implies that the gold being sold will consistently have the right data, for example, weight, size, and root.

3.4.3   Coordination's activities

Organizations in the coordination's business are among the early adopters of blockchain. Aside from utilizing shrewd agreements to take care of business, the industry is utilizing blockchain to be increasingly straightforward with their clients. Coordination's behemoth uninterruptible power supply (UPS) claims that later on, blockchain guidelines and intercompany joint effort will help coordination's benefits and empower clients to take part in exchanging and money. Linda Weakland, a UPS executive of big business engineering and advancement, stated that the innovation can possibly expand straightforwardness and productivity among shippers, transporters, merchants, customers, sellers, and other store network partners. Fedex, then again, anticipates utilizing blockchain to determine client grievances quicker. The data that the organization will implant on a blockchain record will be utilized to help cure client issues.

The earlier models show what the innovation could do to smooth out activities. World Wide Organizations are presently utilizing blockchain to make work forms considerably more proficient, and it will just involve time before it is utilized broadly over a wide range of business.

3.5   Market resistance to blockchain

Price resistance relates to a process in which sales at a given price point stops a price from reaching that amount. Investors often analyze when resistance appears to be taking place to determine if it is worth purchasing a stock at a cheaper price or selling it at the point of resistance.

3.5.1   Resistance

If a benefit is seen as exaggerated at a specific value level, dealers will make certain to exploit. Here, those enormous purchasers will hope to leave their position and take benefit. It is likewise that potential merchants will enter short positions at this level, given the apparent overvaluation, expanding the market's sell pressure [21]. Much the same as when there was high purchase pressure, this centralization of sell weight will compel the value level to go about as a hindrance, with the exception of this time it will go about as a roof, as opposed to a story, known as obstruction.

3.5.2   Level support and resistance

The most significant and simplest to recognize backing and opposition levels take the state of flat lines, thus a pattern being dismissed over and again at a fundamentally the same as value point. Even help or obstruction lines can be made by just drawing an obvious conclusion regarding pattern pinnacles or valleys as found in the diagram beneath.

In the upper edge of Figure 3.4, dealers of XMR/BTC constantly push down cost from the 0.00451/BTC zone, setting up it as solid opposition. Basically,

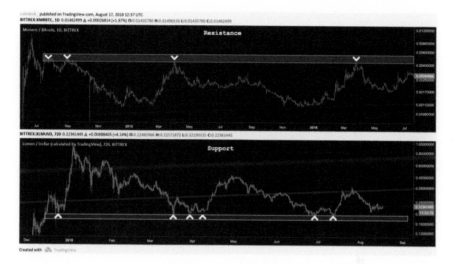

Figure 3.4   Resistance

brokers kept on exploiting this zone of concentrated sell pressure. In bringing down the casing, purchasers constantly held up the cost of XLM/USD at $0.17, bracing it as solid help. The dealers over and over exploited the level given in the diagram of Figure 3.4 which has revealed to them that consistent cost is bound to bob rather fail to work out.

3.5.3   Polarity

As referenced before, these hindrances do in the end break once either the purchasing or selling endeavors have been totally consumed by the market. At the point when this happens, a significant move in opinion can occur—an idea known as extremity. At the point when the selling behind a setup opposition level is completely ingested, it is not, at this point, apparent as an ideal point to take benefit, rather it is seen as a decent passage point for purchasers because of the vanishing of sell pressure, thus transforming the obstruction level into help. On the other hand, when the purchasing pressure behind a help level is completely retained, it will go to an opposition level given merchants are not, at this point, keen on purchasing at this cost.

Note that when the value gets through significant help, it is viewed as bearish turn of events, that is, a benefit normally drops further until venders arrive at a state of fatigue. The ensuing bounce-back because of benefit taking or deal chasing winds up making another help level. Alternately, outperforming obstruction is bullish in nature and value will in general follow the breakout until its next opposition level is distinguished.

Figure 3.5 outline delineates the impact extremity had on the cost of XMR/USD once its opposition level of 0.00451/BTC was broken. You can see that what was once settled as solid opposition, given it dismissed value activity on a few

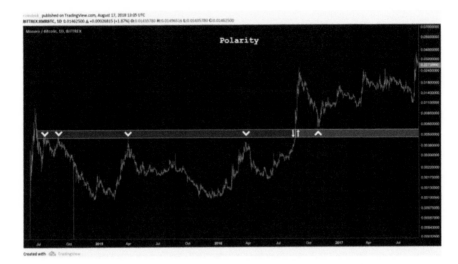

Figure 3.5   Polarity

events, became more vulnerable the more it was tried until it could no longer hold down costs. The value rose determinedly once the opposition was penetrated because of the enormous move in showcase assumption that was occurring. Considerably after costs activity chilled, it tumbled to the earlier obstruction left; however, this time it held as help—the substance of extremity. Value patterns are relied upon to cool off when coming in contact backing or opposition lines because of the grouping of purchasing or selling pressure that is standing by. While the levels can go about as a boundary to value activity for a long period, they do not keep going forever as the market will inevitably ingest their endeavors. When this happens, extremity produces results and changes over the help to opposition and the other way around.

Long story short, backing and obstruction levels help distinguish zones of solid market interest. Along these lines, distinguishing significant backings and protections is seen by numerous individuals to be the most significant part of exchanging.

3.6   Role of blockchain in healthcare

Blockchain innovation can take care of pretty much every issue out there. It is right now being utilized by banks, fund, and even human services [22,23]. Medicinal services are a major industry with a ton of issues that despite everything should be fathomed. Blockchain, on different hands, has pushed the limit enough to take care of its issues. In the present chapter, we will talk about some great use instances of blockchain innovation in the social insurance industry. To comprehend its utilization case, we first need to know how it is esteemed at this moment. Right now, the use every year in the USA alone is $3.55 trillion. By 2025, it will develop to $5.5.

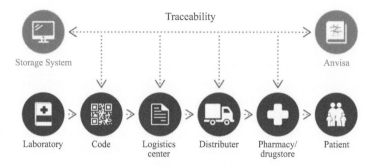

Figure 3.6 Drug traceability image source

Be that as it may, these numbers comprise waste riches as indicated by Institute of Medicine, very nearly 20%–30% of the consumption is a waste. Numerous new businesses have just begun chipping away at the utilization cases. This is the reason we will utilize a few models while talking about the utilization cases beneath.

3.6.1 Drug supply chain

The store network is constantly a major test for any industry. The equivalent is valid for human services. With blockchain, the entire medication store network issue can be improved. One such startup, FarmaTrust is moving in the direction of an answer for medicate store network. The point of the task is to dispose of the maltreatment of medications and consequently spare lives. It will likewise control the fake medications that are appropriated in the market. Not just that it will ensure you to dispense with squandered medications. Last, yet not the least, they will likewise give straightforwardness to the medication inventory network. To accomplish the entirety of this, a remarkable ID will be joined an organization's advanced store network. Figure 3.6 shows the different stages of drug traceability image source.

3.6.2 Clinical data exchange and interoperability

Another basic utilization of the blockchain identifies with clinical information trade. Medicalchain is a start-up that is moving in the direction of giving a decentralized stage [24]. The stage will take care of the well-being information trade issue. It will make a system of information where anybody, including research facilities, medical clinics, specialists, attendants, can get to records. Of course, authorization access will be required to do as such. It will likewise address protection issues.

3.6.3 Billing and claims management

Solve.Care is one of the kind thoughts that plans to fathom authoritative issues for social insurance. This implies it will fathom preparing issues just as charging and claims the board. It is made conceivable simply because of the straightforwardness and uprightness that blockchain gives. It will likewise process installments and guarantee that additional charging by elements can be annihilated.

3.6.4   Cybersecurity and healthcare IoT

Human services are likewise an objective for cybercriminals, particularly when they can bolt up the entire database in return for cash. Information burglary is additionally a serious issue where cybercriminals take the information and sell it in the market. In any case, one such start-up, Patientory, is en route to assemble a blockchain-controlled health information exchange that is HIPPA-agreeable. This implies it will be utilized to improve cybersecurity conventions and electronic medical record (EMR) interoperability to make sure about significant information.

3.6.5   Population health research and pharma clinical trials

The last use case that we will examine is the populace well-being exploration and pharma clinical characteristics. The principle target of this is to improve the clinical preliminaries. The blockchain activity will assist clinical personals with collaborating worldwide and do populace well-being research. It will say to coordinate new information and furthermore save old information. This will likewise help the utilization of better and quicker endorsements and administrative consistence. At the present time, no dynamic start-up is taking a shot at this utilization case. Figure 3.7 shows the population health management system.

Figure 3.7   Population health management analytic

3.7   Blockchain in hospital management services

Standing by interminably in clinics is the same old thing for us [25]. Be that as it may, why stand by unendingly to get to persistent clinical records or reports or to top off similar structures over and over at medical clinics? This can be cured by starting a tremendous social insurance change by executing blockchain in emergency clinic the board. The blockchain is changing healthcare, 16% of medical clinics have just executed blockchain by 2017 and 56% of the emergency clinics will actualize blockchain by 2020. So what is blockchain and how might it change human services? These are to be investigated.

Blockchains are dispersed frameworks that store data as between connected value-based records encoded on an advanced record. Each square is connected to the past one with a cryptographic hash and a timestamp and contains data. With no focal power, blockchains actualize elevated-level security by permitting clients to refresh just the information to which they approach and imitating the changes in every resulting square. With precise date and time stepping, all the exchanges are recorded and can be checked anytime. This interoperability and high security demonstrate that there is massive potential for blockchain in human services.

3.7.1   Blockchain in healthcare

Medicinal services for the executives' administrations are proclaiming the approach of blockchain as a definitive answer for some emergency clinic the executives' hiccups. Decreasing time, expenses and dangers is only one of the numerous advantages of blockchain for the executives. Blockchain for the executives counseling firms have recorded the accompanying regions as the space of blockchain in medicinal services.

3.7.2   New business opportunities

Generally, 60% of the social insurance suppliers feel that blockchain can open up new markets and openings by supplanting the go-betweens who were once required for information assurance. Little medicinal services administrators can total with greater well-being environments to meet contenders head-on. With disappearing middle people and data limits, difficult to reach markets would now be able to be tapped regardless of topographical separation.

3.7.3   Electronic medical records

Sharing of clinical data as EMRs is relied upon to spare $93 billion for US emergency clinics in 5 years alone. About 72% of the medicinal services suppliers vouch for the immense effect of square chain empowered electronic clinical records. With blockchain, a patient or his doctor can get to his clinical records whenever and anywhere with all-out security. This interoperability spares time and cost as well as guarantees speedy remedial help which is a definitive objective of human services.

3.7.4   Guideline compliance

Clinical administrations and exchanges need to hold fast to guidelines and obligatorily. The blockchain is confided in instrument to accomplish administrative consistence in social insurance frameworks. Because of their high security, information can be checked through a review trail progressively. They likewise identify resistant occasions and caution quickly in this way guaranteeing all-out guideline requirement.

3.7.5   Decreased billing and speedy claim settlement

Charging and claims are the gigantic worries of patients in social insurance. Blockchain in social insurance can drastically ease these concerns by empowering straightforward and complete access to treatment data by the patient. Square chain can likewise anticipate unexpected costs for the patient before they select the clinic or experience treatment. By this, patients would now be able to pick up knowledge on shrouded charges and set aside cash. For social insurance foundations, blockchain assists with uncovering uncollected installments and aides in their rapid recuperation.

3.7.6   Decrease in information risks

No all the more altering of information in medicinal services. Blockchain guarantees that all clinical data is safely put away forestalling hacking. Every single clinical occasion is date stepped forestalling any misbehavior.

3.7.7   Coordination of data

A large portion of the patient's parameters such as pulse, glucose level, circulatory strain are accessible outside the clinic setting and must be observed at home. This information gathered utilizing wearables can be handily incorporated utilizing blockchains that assist doctors with giving the correct treatment. Social insurance counseling firms see blockchain as an aid for human services as it implements security and straightforwardness of clinical data and strengthens trust in medication.

3.8   Blockchain—the new age business disruptor

Blockchain innovation holds unending potential to significantly upset an expansive range of ventures past the capacity and move of significant worth. Cryptographic forms of money might be the most clear utilization of the blockchain; however, the straightforward and changeless nature of the dispersed record innovation presents a huge number of down-to-earth use cases. The key advantage of blockchain innovation is the potential it holds to decentralize for all intents and purposes any framework [26]. By permitting people to execute in a trustless way without the obstruction of concentrated outsiders, blockchain innovation is catalyzing the development of another mechanical environment that technologists and crypto-defenders have named "Web 3.0."

The Web 2.0 change in outlook saw the web move from a profoundly specialized specialty system to an interoperable, exceptionally usable, and open community-oriented medium, starting the formation of web-based life, facilitated administrations, and web applications. The Web 3.0 development, fueled by blockchain-controlled decentralization, is set to destroy the vertical associations that rose up out of the Web 2.0 move, advancing interoperability and cooperation over all businesses [27]. The Web 3.0 environment right now comprises thousands of various cryptographic forms of money and utility tokens, circulated applications, exchanging stages, industry coalitions, and blockchain-based stages. While blockchain innovation may at present be in a beginning time of advancement, the all-out market top for the blockchain business as of now surpasses several billions of dollars.

3.8.1 3D printing

Blockchain innovation may not be pervasive yet, it is as of now disturbing various exceptionally brought together ventures, showing down to earth use cases that change the manner in which business completes. In this piece, we will separate how blockchain is decentralizing and enhancing about each vertical. Note that we perceive, blockchain is not a panacea for each issue, rather, enumerating the different ways it impacts business use cases will help illustrate where the innovation is going and where it will be best. Blockchain innovation is rising as the perfect engineering for decentralized frameworks, for example, the quickly creating system of IoT gadgets that are getting ordinary in homes far and wide. The inescapable decentralization of assembling, encouraged by the coming of the 3D printing age, could see blockchain innovation catalyzing another worldview of on-request assembling and creation.

3D printing is a mechanically concentrated procedure. It includes the transmission of information important for make, which, thusly, requires the dispersion and following of information. Blockchain systems, perfect for the trustless trade of information for capital, are set to turn into the foundation of dispersed shared 3D displaying and printing commercial centers. Deloitte looks into features of the requirement for an "advanced string" inside the 3D printing industry that capacitates as a solitary, consistent strand of information that connects any underlying 3D printing structure idea to the completed part. All together for the 3D printing industry to scale, complex information-driven occasions must happen, be followed, and be signed on a changeless record.

The disseminated idea of blockchain systems incorporates conveniently with the decentralized inventory network that is relied upon to emerge from the developing 3D printing industry. The close to continuous settlement and trade usefulness of the blockchain takes into account immediate structure changes. The Genesis of Things venture intends to meld blockchain and 3D printing innovation, making a decentralized worldwide manufacturing plant that permits clients to discover and contract topographically pertinent 3D printers that meet their creation needs. Beginning of things likewise centers around setting up brilliant agreements that administer coordinations, rights, installments, access, and use, just as labeling made items with a permanent and recognizable item memory recorded on the blockchain. Other remarkable blockchain-based 3D printing new companies incorporate Italy-based stage Politronica Srl, which plans to make a tokenized worldwide dispersed 3D printing industrial facility.

3.8.2   Accounting

One could contend that bookkeeping brought forth the idea of a blockchain. Therefore, bookkeeping is one of the most clear instances of an industry that blockchain can possibly totally upset. On the off chance that you know anything about bookkeeping you realize that the entire business is based on a progression of strategies and ways of thinking encompassing how to record money-related data sources and yields inside a framework. Regardless of whether you are not in the field, you do a smidgen of bookkeeping each time you survey your financial balance. What you are taking at a gander is a record of credits and charges to your record, a record of what cash you have gotten, and what cash you have sent somewhere else. Blockchain is a distributed ledger technology (DLT) and thusly in straightforward terms is only a decentralized or dispersed adaptation of the records we are all acquainted within both individual and open bookkeeping.

DLTs will overturn the present bookkeeping industry since they basically guarantee to mechanize the fundamental capacities that bookkeepers serve. Guaranteed Public Accountants are experts that we trust to record our monetary information and report those records to offices like the IRS as a precise portrayal of where cash streamed. Blockchain mechanizes this capacity by recording each exchange on an open appropriated record that is permanent since any adulteration would be rectified by the remainder of the system. Set forth plainly, while blockchain will not put bookkeepers bankrupt, it will lessen the quantity of hours required from them and it will change a portion of their center capacities.

A report from Deloitte contended that blockchain records are likely assistance with straightforwardness and normalization in the bookkeeping field. The future bookkeeping firm will be a lot littler and will concentrate on recruiting bookkeepers who comprehend coding conventions and can construct stages that mechanize the gathering and detailing of incomes. People will serve fundamentally as software engineers and an order layer over the framework, which does all the preparing people used to do.

3.8.3   Agriculture

Many people stop at nourishment supply chains while considering applications for blockchain innovation in the agribusiness business, which is childish, best case scenario. World horticulture has experienced various changes in the course of the only remaining century, beginning with Fritz Haber's revelations in 1918. All the more as of late, worldwide transportation courses and developing financial and political soundness worldwide have opened new regions to farming exchange. That being stated, barely any frameworks have effectively been built up that serve everybody in the store network. Little cultivators get a wage for what they sell in creating countries, and even the United States, a horticultural monster, needs to sponsor corn ranchers to keep them delivering. Blockchain may offer answers for cultivators that go past basic endowments. An incredible number of ranchers in creating countries might not approach the equivalent money-related devices that in first world economies are available to them. All things considered, it tends to be hard for them to take an interest in the inexorably worldwide agribusiness advertise.

A convincing alternative for blockchain advancement in horticulture could be immediate and reasonable exchange stages that reward ranchers with micropayments when their items are sold or increased in value by buyers around the globe. A great deal of the cases around crypto serving the unbanked sectors appear to be somewhat hopeful for the close to term, yet in horticulture, nourishment provenance on the blockchain is in progress. It is anything but a far vehicle to add to those frameworks with expectations of all the more straightforwardly remunerating cultivators for their endeavors.

3.8.4   Art

The craftsmanship business has not changed a lot through the span of history. All specialists now and again battle to associate their craft with intrigued purchasers, and most craftsmanship is bought by well off authorities, displays, or exhibition halls. One investigation found that 90% of all work of art is sold through concentrated sale houses and exhibitions. Truth be told, discussions around the matter of workmanship every now and again raise doubt about whether the manner in which the business capacities is in opposition to the beliefs of the specialists filling it. Blockchain offers various convincing arrangements that may overturn not just the manners in which we purchase and sell craftsmanship yet additionally how we make it.

One of the wells on the way to cause a ripple effect in the close to term is blockchain's reasonableness for decentralized commercial centers. Costs in the workmanship world are now and again determined by bringing entertainers together and go between who control exhibitions or other dissemination channels. Since individuals are restricted to getting to pieces through these customary channels, they have little state on the cost of a work. The equivalent one goes for specialists, who every now and again offer their work to an exhibition with negligible authority over the resale cost.

Decentralized craftsmanship commercial centers could totally supplant this framework. By giving computerized showrooms, blockchain-based displays could give more straightforward installment choices to specialists and purchasers and possibly join things like network subsidizing or request-driven valuing models.

In case you are an aficionado of the workmanship world, you may have found out about Banksy's latest trick, a masterpiece that devastated itself not long after purchase. Think pieces like this could turn out to be increasingly typical, as blockchain empowers progressively unknown cooperation and the opportunities for self-subsidized independent centerpieces. Specialists could likewise make cryptographic money-driven ventures that plan to act naturally continuing by performing errands like digging or requesting crypto gifts. The chances to overcome any barrier between the physical and advanced craftsmanship domains are expanding and the outcome will not simply be crypto collectibles like Crypto Kitties. We will see an ever-increasing number of craftsmen playing with that meager line among fiction and reality, utilizing blockchain innovation to do it.

3.8.5 Credit management

The credit business is exceptionally incorporated, depending on the intensely controlled activities of solid credit of the board organizations, for example, Equifax, Experian, and TransUnion and the FICO scores they give. Over 90% of US-based loaning establishments use FICO scores when deciding credit qualification. The delicate idea of credit data has prompted the separation, compartmentalization, and guideline of the credit business. Moneylenders, concentrated on the minimization of hazard when surveying advance qualification, depend on the FICO assessment conveyed by these outsider organizations as a changeless wellspring of secure information.

Credit office information of the board, be that as it may, experiences a similar significant imperfection as any unified association—incorporated security for the executives. Equifax endured a significant information break in 2017 that was depicted by US Representative Richard Blumenthal as "a notable information catastrophe," influencing more than 143 million individuals. The Equifax break was gone before by the 2015 Experian information penetrate, which uncovered the private credit information of 123 million US families.

Blockchain innovation can significantly decrease the risk of security that penetrates and assaults the target-siloed credit yet additionally presents the chance to limit the expenses related with information confirmation during the advance qualification evaluation process. Advancing interoperability by putting away normalized credit information on-chain will limit the charges paid by banks to get to credit information, at last bringing down the expense of retail money for the end client. Lumenous is one of the first blockchain-based stages to bring credit information onto an appropriated record organized, utilizing a cooperative labeling and investigation framework that permits clients to make and specifically share acknowledge information for leasers, accomplices, and clients.

The Polish Credit Office, which works as the biggest credit agency in Central and Eastern Europe, coordinated blockchain innovation into information stockpiling conventions in May 2018, making a blockchain-based money-related database that meets the tough prerequisites of EU General Data Protection Regulation.

3.8.6 Compliance

Consistence is one of those venture necessities that a couple of organizations are eager to spending plan for; however that could decimate your business whenever disregarded. Furthermore, most business visionaries, financial specialists, and officials realize that consistence divisions are left with costly inheritance programming, either by contract or by abstaining from experiencing the agony of moving to a more up-to-date, increasingly nimble framework.

That being stated, the advantage of a solid consistence culture is self-evident. The Association of Certified Fraud Examiners found that organizations which proactively screen their consistence programs experience a 54% decrease in consistence-driven misfortunes. Notwithstanding that, most organizations despite everything hold back on consistence spending plans. One examination by Deloitte found that 59% of respondents had all out consistence spending plans, covering individuals, procedure, and innovation, of $5 million or less.

Blockchain will reform the consistence innovation part in various manners. The main way it will make a sprinkle is by bringing an interoperability layer to consistence programming and information that has been formerly ailing in the business. Deloitte likewise found that 30% of consistence experts have no strategies for evaluating or following the achievement of their consistence programs. Consistence information generally sits in storehouses whether they be advanced or paper and is hard to cross-reference. Blockchain could help by making shared information conventions, and secure, changeless informational indexes that can be effectively perused by any significant program or evaluator.

Consistence stages based on the blockchain will likewise increase present expectations for trust in the business. Claims for consistence infringement are an incessant event and can cost organizations millions in the two punishments and harms. Savvy contract arrangements can guarantee that different procedures or arrangements cannot be finished until all terms or guidelines have been tended to. This implies associations can forestall infringement before they happen and rapidly distinguish the wellspring of any issues in their procedure. Furthermore, via computerizing consistence procedures, and making them progressively straightforward, organizations can all the more promptly show that their strategic approaches are above board, with no inquiries concerning the honesty of their information. Regardless of whether it is ecological, ADA, work consistence, or something else, blockchain arrangements could assist organizations with keeping up a stricter adherence to guideline without using up every last cent.

3.8.7 The Internet of Things (IoT)—connected devices

The IoT is decentralized essentially. The IoT biological system is approximately characterized as the progressing multiplication of constantly online web empowered information gathering gadgets that are getting progressively common in everyday life. IoT gadgets are basically keen machines—anything from cell

Figure 3.8   Internet of Things (IoT)-connected devices

phones, wellness trackers, and family unit apparatuses to mechanical hardware or fly motors. Figure 3.8 shows how IoT technology connected to all over the world.

Universal examination firm Gartner predicts the presence of more than 26 billion interconnected IoT gadgets by 2020. As a greatly conveyed framework, this system of IoT gadgets is undeniably overseen by a decentralized system—blockchain innovation. The crucial plan of the blockchain is designed for applications that include a lot of exchanges and associations, for example, those present in the IoT biological system.

The immense measure of information that moves between IoT gadgets requires the production of a safe texture resistant to the unplanned or purposeful arrival of touchy client data. IBM is as of now progressing in the direction of a huge scope execution of blockchain innovation concentrated on IoT—the Watson IoT stage permits associations to make secure private blockchain records that encourage the safe exchange of IoT information without unified control or the board.

One of the most intriguing utilizations of blockchain innovation in the IoT business is the IOTA stage. Particle utilizes a kind strategy for getting accord between arrange members—called the "Tangle"—that makes all clients hubs inside the system, at the same time preparing and making exchanges. The IOTA venture imagines a future mechanized machine economy wherein shrewd IoT gadgets execute between each other without human intercession. For instance, IOTA-empowered IoT electric driverless vehicles may utilize the IOTA system to get to decentralized ridesharing total DApps, pay robotized charging stations for vitality, or even request new parts without contribution from a human.

3.9 Conclusion

Blockchain innovation is as of now being utilized by numerous undertakings what is more, activities, planning to set up a demonstrated and confided in condition to construct a straightforward and increasingly maintainable nourishment creation and circulation, coordinating key partners into the stock chain. Notwithstanding, till now various issues and moves are there that should be settled, past those at particular level. To diminish limits of usage, governments must show others how it is done and empower the digitalization of the open association. They should moreover place more in innovative work, similarly as in guidance and planning, in order to make and show confirmation for the potential points of interest of this development. The conceivable progress of governments toward the utilization of the blockchain, taking note of the way that administrations and their pertinent offices ought to watch and comprehend the specific torment focuses, tending to them in like manner. From an arrangement point of view, different moves can be made, for example, empowering the development of blockchain-disapproved environments in agri-natural ways of life, supporting the innovation as a component of the general objectives of improving the seriousness and guaranteeing the supportability of the agri-nourishment inventory network, just as structuring a reasonable administrative system for blockchain usage. The monetary supportability of the current activities, as they have been introduced in this despite everything should be evaluated and the results of these financial examinations are relied upon to impact of the prevalence of the blockchain innovation sooner rather than later, applied in the nourishment production network area. Summing up, blockchain is a promising development toward a direct creation system of nourishment, regardless, various limits difficulties in spite of everything exist, which prevent its increasingly broad notoriety among ranchers what is more, nourishment flexibly structures. The not-all-that-far-off future will show up if and how these troubles could be tended to by managerial and private undertakings, in order to set up blockchain advancement as a secured, reliable, and clear way to deal with ensure sanitation and respectability. It is very excitement to see how blockchain will be obtained together with other rising developments like enormous data, mechanical innovation, IoT, radio frequency identification (RFID), near field communication (NFC), hyperspectral imaging toward higher automation of the sustenance gracefully shapes, improved with full straightforwardness and obviousness.

References

[1] Abelseth, B. (2018). Blockchain tracking and cannabis regulation: Developing a permissioned blockchain network to track Canada's cannabis supply chain. Dalhousie Journal of Interdisciplinary Management, 14.

[2] Peter, A. (2017). In China, You Can Track Your Chicken On–You Guessed It– The Blockchain. Fast Company.

[3]   Louisa, B.-T. (2018). Maersk Leads Blockchain of Food Startup Ripe.io
       $2.4m Seed Round. AgFunder Network Partners.

[4]   Kamilaris, A., Fonts, A., and Prenafeta-Boldú, F. X. (2019). The rise of
       blockchain technology in agriculture and food supply chains. Trends in Food
       Science & Technology, 91, 640–652.

[5]   Zwitter, A. and Boisse-Despiaux, M. (2018). Blockchain for humanitarian
       action and development aid. Journal of International Humanitarian Action,
       3, 16.

[6]   Azaria, A., Ekblaw, A., Vieira, T., and Lippman, A. (2016). MedRec: Using
       blockchain for medical data access and permission management. In: 2016
       2nd International Conference on Open and Big Data (OBD).

[7]   Yue, X., Wang, H., Jin, D., Li, M., and Jiang, W. (2016). Healthcare data
       gateways: Found healthcare intelligence on blockchain with novel privacy
       risk control. Journal of Medical Systems, 40(10), 218.

[8]   Peterson, K. J., Deeduvanu, R., Kanjamala, P., and Mayo, K. (2016). A
       Blockchain-Based Approach to Health Information Exchange Networks.
       Semantic Scholar.

[9]   Ma, Y., Sun, Y., Lei, Y., Qin, N., and Lu, J. (2020). A survey of blockchain
       technology on security, privacy, and trust in crowdsourcing services. World
       Wide Web, 23, 393–419.

[10]   Liang, X., Zhao, J., Shetty, S., Liu, J., and Li, D. (2017). Integrating
       Blockchain for data sharing and collaboration in mobile healthcare appli-
       cations. In Proceedings of the 2017 IEEE 28th Annual International
       Symposium on Personal, Indoor, and Mobile Radio Communications
       (PIMRC), Montreal, QC, Canada, 8–13 October 2017, pp. 1–5.

[11]   Kokoris-Kogias, E., Jovanovic, P., Gasser, L., Gailly, N., Syta, E., and Ford,
       B. (2018). OmniLedger: A secure, scale-out, decentralized ledger via
       sharding. In 2018 IEEE Symposium on Security and Privacy (S&P),
       pp. 19–34.

[12]   Clauson, K., Breeden, E., Davidson, C., and Mackey, T. (2018). Leveraging
       Blockchain Technology to Enhance Supply Chain Management in
       Healthcare. Blockchain in Healthcare Today, 1.

[13]   Benchoufi, M. and Ravaud, P. (2017). Blockchain technology for improving
       clinical research quality. Trials, 18, 335.

[14]   Hasselgren, A., Kralevska, K., Gligoroski, D., Pedersen, S. A., and Faxvaag,
       A. (2020). Blockchain in healthcare and health sciences—A scoping review.
       International Journal of Medical Informatics, 134, 104040.

[15]   Siyal, A., Junejo, A., Zawish, M., Ahmed, K., Khalil, A., and Soursou, G.
       (2019). Applications of blockchain technology in medicine and healthcare:
       Challenges and future perspectives. Cryptography, 3(1), 3.

[16]   Swan, M. (2015). Blockchain thinking: The brain as a decentralized auton-
       omous corporation [commentary]. IEEE Technology and Society Magazine,
       34(4), 41–52.

[17]   Jamil, F., Hang, L., Kim, K., and Kim, D. (2019). A novel medical block-chain model for drug supply chain integrity management in a smart hospital. Electronics, 8(5), 505.

[18]   Pandey, P. and Litoriya, R. (2020). Securing E-health networks from counterfeit medicine penetration using blockchain. Wireless Personal Communications.

[19]   Benisi, N. Z., Aminian, M., and Javadi, B. (2020). Blockchain-based decentralized storage networks: A survey. Journal of Network and Computer Applications, 162, 102656.

[20]   Casino, F., Dasaklis, T. K., and Patsakis, C. (2018). A systematic literature review of blockchain-based applications: Current status, classification and open issues. Telematics and Informatics, 36, 55–81.

[21]   Bano, S. (2017). Consensus in the age of blockchains. Cryptography and Security.

[22]   Becker, J., Breuker, D., Heide, T., Holler, J., Rauer, H. P., and Böhme, R. (2013). Can we afford integrity by proof-of-work? scenarios inspired by the bitcoin currency. Economics of Information Security and Privacy. Berlin, Heidelberg: Springer. 135–156.

[23]   Dhillon, V. (2020). Blockchain Based Peer-Review Interfaces for Digital Medicine. Frontiers in Blockchain, 3.

[24]   Clark, J., Meiklejohn, S., Ryan, P. Y. A., Wallach, D., Brenner, M., and Rohloff, K. (Eds.). (2016). Financial Cryptography and Data Security. Lecture Notes in Computer Science.

[25]   BitFury Group. (2015). Proof of Stake versus Proof of Work. White Paper.

[26]   Weking, J., Mandalenakis, M., Hein, A. *et al.* (2020). The impact of block-chain technology on business models – A taxonomy and archetypal patterns. Electron Markets, 30, 285–305.

[27]   Frizzo-Barker, J., Chow-White, P. A., Adams, P. R., Mentanko, J., Ha, D. and Greenc, S. (2020). Blockchain as a disruptive technology for business: A systematic review. International Journal of Information Management, 51, 102029.

Chapter 4

A deep dive into Hyperledger

Swathi Punathumkandi[1], Venkatesan Meenakshi Sundaram[1] and Panneer Prabhavathy[2]

Hyperledger is an open-source, network-oriented effort made to propel cross-industry blockchain developments. It is a worldwide facilitated exertion remembering pioneers for banking, cash, Internet of Things, manufacturing, supply chains, and advancement. The Linux Foundation has Hyperledger under the establishment. This chapter gives an elevated level overview of Hyperledger: why it was made, how it is represented, and what it would like to accomplish. The core of this chapter presents five convincing uses for big business blockchain in various ventures. It depicts how the Hyperledger guarantees the secure, progressively solid, and increasingly streamlined communication.

4.1 Hyperledger Frameworks

The Hyperledger methodology empowers the reutilization of normal structure blocks [1], empowers the fast advancement of segments, and advances interoperability between ventures. Hyperledger business blockchain structures are utilized to assemble undertaking blockchains for a consortium of associations. They are unique in relation to open records such as the Bitcoin blockchain and Ethereum. Hyperledger broods and advances a scope of business in blockchain technology, including

- test applications
- distributed ledger framework
- smart contract engines
- utility libraries
- graphical interfaces
- customer libraries

Some of the important Hyperledger frameworks are shown in Figure 4.1.

[1]Department of Computer Science and Engineering, National Institute of Technology Karnataka, Mangalore, India
[2]School of Information Technology and Engineering, Vellore Institute of Technology, Vellore, India

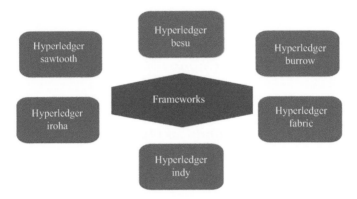

Figure 4.1   Hyperledger frameworks

4.1.1   Hyperledger Besu

Hyperledger Besu is an Ethereum client intended to be ventured amicably for both open and private permissioned use cases. It can also be run on test systems, for example, Goerli, Rinkeby, and Ropsten. Its far-reaching permissioning schemes are planned explicitly for use in a consortium domain. Hyperledger Besu incorporates a few consensus algorithms, including proof of work and proof of authority (PoA) (IBFT, IBFT 2.0, EtherHash, and Clique).

Hyperledger Besu, a Java-based Ethereum client, also known as Pantheon, is the first blockchain venture submitted to Hyperledger that can work on an open blockchain. Besu speaks to the developing enthusiasm of endeavours to manufacture both permissioned and open system use cases for their applications. Hyperledger Besu incorporates a command-line interface just as HTTP- and WebSocket-based APIs for running, observing hubs, and maintaining the Ethereum network. Hyperledger Besu does not bolster key administration inside the customer because of security concerns. Rather, you can utilize EthSigner or any Ethereum perfect wallet for overseeing private keys. EthSigner gives access to the key store and signs exchanges by means of tools such as HashiCorp Vault, and Microsoft Azure. The Besu client's APIs underpins the Ethereum functionalities, for example, keen agreement and decentralized application (DApp) advancement, organization, and operational use cases. Instruments, for example, Truffle, Remix, and web3j, empower these exercises. The customer actualizes standard JSON-RPC APIs, making reconciliation with environment tooling basic. The customer also bolsters making private, permissioned consortium systems.

The Enterprise Ethereum Alliance (EEA) was built up, particularly, to create regular interfaces among the different open and closed source extends inside Ethereum, to guarantee clients so that they do not have seller lock-in and to make standard interfaces for groups building applications. Besu makes use of venture features in arrangement with the EEA customer specification. Important features of Hyperledger Besu are depicted in Figure 4.2.

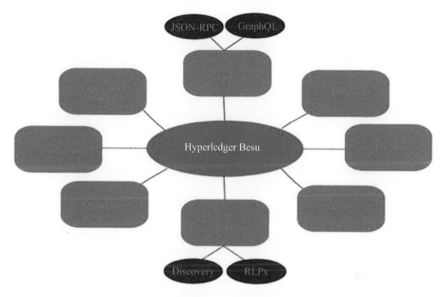

Figure 4.2   Features of Hyperledger Besu

The architecture of Besu can be explained in [2] with the help of Figure 4.3. DApp or wallet can contact with the Besu using user facing API. Hyperledger Besu gives mainnet Ethereum and EEA JSON-RPC APIs over HTTP and WebSocket conventions just as a GraphQL API. Hyperledger Besu utilizes a RocksDB key-esteem database to continue chain information locally. This information is isolated into a couple of sub-classes: Blockchain information is made out of block headers that structure the 'chain' of information that is utilized to cryptographically check blockchain state, block bodies that contain the requested transactions in each block, and exchange receipts that contain metadata identified with transaction execution, including logs.

Each block header references a world state by means of a state root hash. The world state is a mapping from addresses to accounts. Remotely possessed records contain an ether balance, while smart contract accounts also contain executable code and storage. Users can make use of Hyperledger Besu through the following link: https://https://github.com/hyperledger/besu.

4.1.2   Hyperledger Burrow

Hyperledger Burrow is facilitated by the Linux Foundation [3] and was initially planned by Monax, an open stage to manufacture, ship, and run blockchain-based applications for business systems. The processor and chipmaker Intel has likewise co-supported the task, which is as of now in the budding stage. Burrow furnishes a secluded blockchain customer with a permissioned smart agreement translator that worked to some degree to the determination of the Ethereum virtual machine (EVM). Burrow broadens past work inside the Hyperledger Project by giving an

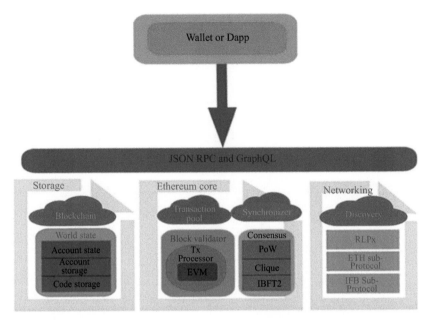

Figure 4.3   Detailed architecture of Hyperledger Besu

unequivocally deterministic smart contract centred blockchain structure to the project's general exertion. Burrows's design opens a scope of intriguing cross-venture-coordinated efforts inside the Hyperledger umbrella. Burrow's essential clients are the organizations going for esteem chain level advancement among other blockchain and shrewd agreement benefits. These clients require consents on their blockchain arrangements so as to satisfy various legitimate as well as business prerequisites for their applications. Burrow was intended to be a universally useful shrewd agreement machine and is not upgraded for the necessities of any single industry; rather Burrow has been enhanced for universally useful, cross-industry smart contract use cases. New companies to ventures are utilizing Burrow's permissioned EVM so they may use smart contract advancements from the open-source world in an increasingly secure, legitimately agreeable, and endeavour grade setting. Users can make use of Hyperledger Burrow through the following link: https://https://github.com/hyperledger/burrow.

The significant parts of Burrow are as per the following:

- smart contract application engine
- consensus engine
- gateway
- application blockchain interface

The architecture of the Burrow can be roughly sketched as shown in Figure 4.4.

4.1.3 Hyperledger Fabric

Hyperledger Fabric is an open source for enterprises. It is a permissioned distributed ledger technology (DLT), which is intended for use in big business settings, that conveys some key separating capacities over other well-known DLTs [4]. Fabric has a profoundly particular and configurable design, empowering development, flexibility and improvement for an expansive scope of industry use cases, including banking, IoT, music, cinema, healthcare, and supply chain. The fabric is permissioned, implying that the members are known to one another, and in this manner completely untrusted. This implies while the members may not completely confide in each other, a system can be worked under an administration model that is worked off of trust in members. Fabric presents a new design for transactions as execute-request approves. It tends to flexibility, adaptability, versatility, execution and privacy challenges of order-execute model by isolating the transaction flow as shown in Figure 4.5: fabric makes channels, which empower the coordination of individuals to make an alternate record of trades. This is especially noteworthy for frameworks where a couple of individuals might be contenders who need not bother with each trade. In an event that a gathering of clients makes a channel, only those individuals and no others have copies of the record for that channel. Hyperledger Fabric has an accounting system, including two sections: the world state and the exchange log. Each part has a copy of the ledger. The world state fragment shows state of the record at a given purpose of time. It is the database of the record. The transaction log part records all trades which have realized

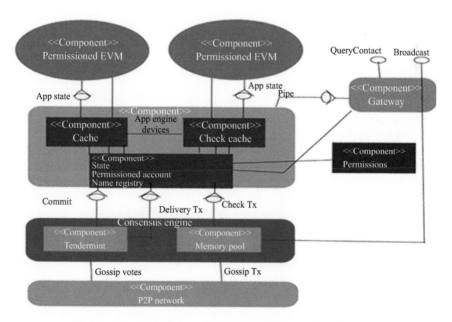

Figure 4.4   Detailed architecture of Hyperledger Burrow

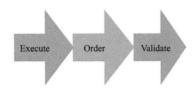

Figure 4.5   Hyperledger Fabric transaction flow

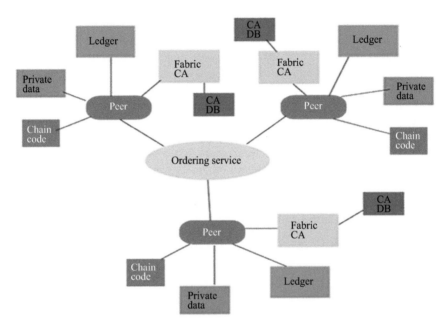

Figure 4.6   Detailed architecture of Hyperledger Fabric

the present estimation of the world state; it is the update history for the world state. The ledger, by then, is an amalgamation of the world state database and the exchange log history. The smart contracts of fabric are written in chaincode and are summoned by an application which is external to the blockchain when that application needs to interface with the record. Generally speaking, chaincode works together just with the database portion of the record, the world state, and not the trade log. Chaincode can be executed in a couple of programming vernaculars. Starting at now, Go and Node is maintained. Hyperledger Fabric architecture is depicted in Figure 4.6. To make use of fabric in your enterprise, refer to https:// https://github.com/hyperledger/fabric.

4.1.4   Hyperledger Indy

Hyperledger Indy gives tools, libraries, and reusable segments for giving advanced identities established on blockchains or other dispersed records with the goal that they are interoperable crosswise over authoritative areas, applications, and some other store-house [5]. This mix of autonomy, protection, and undeniable cases is very incredible. Think about the numerous potential advantages. Mass troves of touchy information can disappear or get futile. The financial aspects of hacking can be changed since less personally identifiable information is held by every colleague. The contending requests of saving protection and meeting guidelines can be fulfilled. People and associations can profit by more extravagant and increasingly secure cooperations. What is more, the identity ecosystem can pick up the development and dynamism of a free market. Some of the important characteristics of Indy are as follows:

- correlation,
- zero-knowledge proofs (ZKPs),
- distributed ledgers for decentralized identities,
- privacy,
- verifiable claims, and
- autonomy.

4.1.5   Hyperledger Iroha

Hyperledger Iroha is intended to be basic and simple to join into infrastructural or IoT ventures requiring conveyed record innovation. Hyperledger Iroha highlights a straightforward development, secluded, space-driven C++ plan, accentuation on customer application advancement, and another crash fault-tolerant agreement calculation, called YAC. Iroha joined Fabric and Sawtooth to turn into the third dispersed record stage under Hyperledger in October 2016. It was initially created by Soramitsu in Japan and was proposed to Hyperledger by Soramitsu, Hitachi, NTT Data, and Colu. The centre design of Hyperledger Iroha was propelled by Hyperledger Fabric. The architecture of Iroha is explained as shown in Figure 4.7. The makers of Hyperledger Iroha have accentuated the significance of this structure in satisfying the requirement for easy-to-use interfaces [5]. In doing as such, they have made a structure with many characterizing highlights and have accomplished their expressed objectives of straightforward development, an advanced C++ plan with an accentuation on portable application improvement, and another chain-based Byzantine fault-tolerant algorithm called Sumeragi. The most characterizing quality of Hyperledger Iroha is its capacity to be uninhibitedly interoperable with other Hyperledger ventures. The open-source libraries for iOS, Android, and JavaScript enable engineers to helpfully make capacities for performing regular tasks.

4.1.6   Hyperledger Sawtooth

Hyperledger Sawtooth is an undertaking blockchain stage for building distributed record applications and systems. The design targets keeping records dispersed and making smart contracts safe, especially for big business use. Sawtooth streamlines blockchain application improvement by isolating the centre framework from the application space. Application engineers can determine the business rules suitable for their application, utilizing the language of their decision, without having to know the

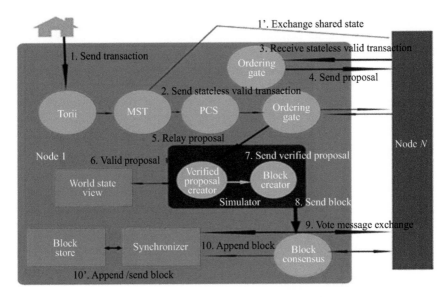

Figure 4.7   Detailed architecture of Hyperledger Iroha

basic plan of the main framework. Sawtooth is additionally profoundly measured. This particularity empowers undertakings and consortia to settle on strategy choices that they are best prepared to make. Sawtooth's centre plan enables applications to pick the exchange rules, permissioning, and consensus algorithms that help their extraordinary business needs [5].

Sawtooth makes it simple to create and send an application by giving an unmistakable detachment between the application and the main framework levels. Sawtooth gives smart contract deliberation that enables application designers to compose contract rationale in a language of their decision. An application can be a local business rationale or a smart contract virtual machine. The two sorts of utilizations can exist together on the equivalent blockchain. Sawtooth enables these plan choices to be made in the transaction handling layer, which enables numerous sorts of utilizations to exist in a similar occurrence of the blockchain. Every application characterizes the custom-exchange processors for its interesting necessities. Sawtooth gives a few model transaction families to fill in as models for low-level capacities, and for explicit applications. Transaction processor SDKs are accessible in different dialects to streamline the production of new agreement dialects, including Python, JavaScript, Go, C++, Java, and Rust. REST API improves customer advancement by adjusting a validator correspondence to standard HTTP/JSON. An example is Sawtooth supply chain. It demonstrates how to follow the provenance and other relevant data of any advantage. Inventory network gives a model application with a transaction processor, custom REST API, and web application. This model application additionally shows a decentralized answer for in-program transaction signing and delineates how to synchronize the blockchain state to a neighbourhood database for complex inquiries [6].

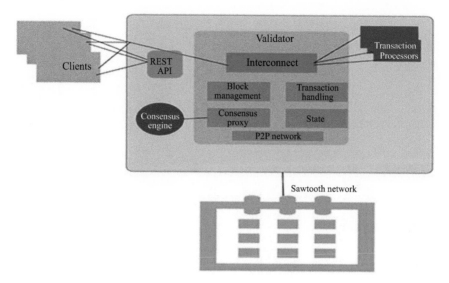

Figure 4.8   Detailed architecture of Hyperledger Sawtooth

Numerous consensus algorithms utilized in customary-reproduced databases are not intended to deal with these blockchain prerequisites. Sawtooth and proof of elapsed time (PoET) are intended for genuinely decentralized blockchain applications; that is, applications where there are numerous members in the agreement procedure that are officially and physically conveyed. PoET gives protection from awful on-screen characters and is intended to deal with the appearance and take-off of hubs in a huge system. Moreover, Sawtooth gives on-anchor administration to update the consensus, and different businesses govern the consortium consents to over the life of the system. This implies that a consortium can change consensus spontaneous utilizing exchanges as it were. Clients can even begin with an obliged consensus and later change to an agreement like PoET that bears the protected, dynamic, and adaptable qualities required by the production network.

Hyperledger Sawtooth architecture is shown in Figure 4.8.

4.1.7   Hyperledger Grid

Hyperledger Grid is a domain-specific platform for building supply-chain management solutions that incorporate appropriated record parts. This task gives a lot of particular segments for creating smart contracts and customer interfaces, including space explicit information models, smart contract business rationale, libraries, and SDKs. Hyperledger Grid is an environment of technologies, systems, and libraries that work together, giving application engineers a chance to settle on the decision regarding which segments are generally fitting for their industry or market model [5]. Hyperledger platforms are adaptable by the plan; however, in that capacity, no communication is made in the language of any business or have suppositions on how fundamental information types ought to be put away. As a

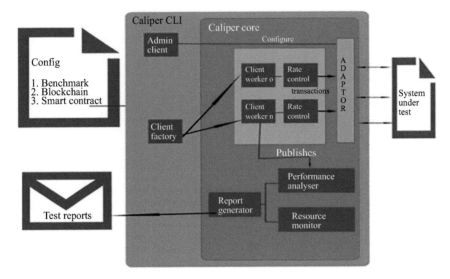

Figure 4.9   Detailed model of Hyperledger Grid

general rule, business frameworks and market models are entirely full grown, as associations have been executing electronically dependent on basic principles for a considerable length of time. The matrix will give a spot to the usage of these guidelines and standards. The detailed model of hyperledger grid is shown in Figure 4.9.

Summary of Hyperledger frameworks

- Hyperledger Besu: It is an Ethereum client intended to be venture amicable for both open and private permissioned use cases.
- Hyperledger Burrow: A blockchain client with a permissioned smart contract mediator created to some degree to the particulars of the EVM.
- Hyperledger Fabric: A platform for creating distributed record arrangements with a modularity that conveys a high level of privacy, adaptability, strength, and versatility. This empowers arrangements created with Fabric to be adjusted for any industry.
- Hyperledger Indy: A distributed record that gives tools, libraries, and reusable parts for decentralized identity.
- Hyperledger Iroha: It is intended to be basic and simple to join into infrastructural or IoT ventures requiring conveyed record innovation.
- Hyperledger Sawtooth: It is an undertaking blockchain stage for building distributed record applications and systems. The design targets keeping records dispersed and making smart contracts safe, especially for big business use.

- Hyperledger Grid: It is a domain-specific platform for building supply-chain management solutions that incorporate appropriated record parts.

4.2   Hyperledger Libraries

4.2.1   *Hyperledger Aries*

Hyperledger Aries gives a mutual [5], reusable, and interoperable toolbox intended for activities and arrangements concentrated on creating, transmitting, and putting away irrefutable computerized accreditations. It is the foundation for blockchain-established, distributed associations. This venture devours the cryptographic help given by Hyperledger Ursa, to give secure mystery the executives and decentralized key administration usefulness.

4.2.2   *Hyperledger Quilt*

Hyperledger Quilt offers interoperability between record frameworks by executing Interledger protocol (ILP), which is fundamentally a payment convention and is intended to move an incentive crosswise over frameworks – both distributed and non-distributed records. It is a basic convention that builds up a worldwide name-space for accounts, just as a convention for synchronized micro-swaps between various frameworks. Web conventions empower data to be packetized, steered, and conveyed over correspondence systems. With ILP, cash and different types of significant worth can be packetized, directed, and conveyed over payment systems and records. Hyperledger Quilt is an undertaking grade usage of the convention, created in Java, and giving libraries and reference executions of the centre Interledger parts and in-time record mixes for other Hyperledger ventures.

4.2.3   *Hyperledger Transact*

Hyperledger Transact intends [5] to lessen the improvement exertion recorded as distributed ledger software by giving a standard interface to execute smart contracts which is different from distributed ledger implementation. Hyperledger Transact adopts an extensible strategy to execute new smart contract dialects called 'smart contract engines' that executes a virtual machine or interpreter that executes smart contracts.

4.2.4   *Hyperledger Ursa*

Hyperledger Ursa is a mutual cryptographic library. It empowers usage to abstain from copying other cryptographic work and ideally increment security of the process. The library is a pick in archive (for Hyperledger and non-Hyperledger ventures) to place and utilize crypto. Hyperledger Ursa comprises sub-ventures, which are durable usage of cryptographic code or interfaces to cryptographic code.

4.3   Hyperledger Tools

4.3.1   *Hyperledger Avalon*

Hyperledger Avalon is conceived from Trusted Compute Framework which is a record-free usage of the Trusted Computing Specifications distributed by the EEA. Hyperledger Avalon is the outcome of extraordinary coordinated efforts of Hyperledger, Cloud service provider ecosystem, and EEA. This is one of the most comprehensively supported ventures to the date. The Hyperledger Avalon is intended to give the designers a chance to take profit by the computational trust and, simultaneously, alleviate its downsides. The blockchain forms and upholds the execution of arrangements and keeps up straightforwardness just as transaction auditability. In any case, the off-chain related with the principle arrangement is executing the exchanges with the assistance of trusted figure assets. Some of the features of trusted computing are multi-party commute, ZKPs, and trusted execution environment. You can use Avalon with the help of the link: https://www. hyperledger.org/projects/Avalon.

4.3.2   *Hyperledger Caliper*

Hyperledger Caliper is a blockchain benchmark apparatus or tool. It enables clients to quantify the exhibition of a blockchain execution with a lot of predefined use cases. Hyperledger Caliper will deliver reports containing various execution pointers to fill in as a source of perspective when utilizing the accompanying blockchain solutions such as Ethereum, Hyperledger Besu, Hyperledger Burrow, Hyperledger Fabric, Hyperledger Iroha, FISCO BCOS, and Hyperledger Sawtooth. The key segment in Hyperledger Caliper is the adaptation layer, which is acquainted with coordinate different blockchain solutions into the Caliper structure. A connector is implemented for each blockchain framework under test called system under test; the connector is answerable for the interpretation of Caliper NBIs into comparing blockchain convention. Caliper NBI is a collection of basic blockchain interfaces, which contains tasks to connect with backend blockchain framework.

Hyperledger Caliper will create reports containing various execution markers, for example, transactions per second, exchange idleness, and asset usage. The purpose is for Caliper results to be utilized by other Hyperledger extends as they work out their systems, and as a source of perspective in supporting the decision of a blockchain execution reasonable for a client's particular needs. You can use Caliper with the help of the link: https://www.hyperledger.org/projects/caliper.

4.3.3   *Hyperledger Cello*

Hyperledger Cello expects to bring the on-request 'as-a service' model to the blockchain environment to decrease the exertion required for making, overseeing, and using blockchains. Additionally, it can be utilized to encourage making blockchain as a service. Cello gives an operational reassure to deal with blockchain's efficiency and can run over different frameworks, e.g. virtual machine, bare metal, and different containers. Hyperledger cello is in incubation phase.

4.3.4 Hyperledger Explorer

Hyperledger Explorer is an easy to understand Web application device used to view, invoke, deploy, or query blocks exchanges and related information, network information (name, status, and hubs), chaincodes, and transactions, just as some other significant data put away in the record. Hyperledger explorer is in incubation state. Blockchain explorer gives a dashboard to survey data about blocks, transactions, hub logs, measurements, and smart contracts accessible on the system. Clients will have the option to inquiry for explicit blocks or transactions and view the total subtleties. Blockchain explorer can likewise be incorporated with any verification/approval stages (business/open source) and will be suitable functionalities dependent on the benefits accessible to the client.

4.3.5 Hyperledger Composer

A Hyperledger Composer is a broad, open-advancement toolset and system to make blockchain applications simpler. Composer aims to fasten time to esteem and make it simpler to incorporate into blockchain applications with the current business frameworks. We can utilize the composer to quickly create use cases and send a blockchain arrangement in weeks rather than months. The composer enables you to show your business about how to organize and coordinate existing frameworks and information with your blockchain applications. You can utilize a Hyperledger Composer to rapidly show your present business network, containing your current resources and the transactions identified with them; resources are tangible or impalpable merchandise, administrations, or property. As a feature of your business model, you characterize the transactions which can interface with resources. Business networks incorporate the members who interface with them, over various business systems.

The Hyperledger Composer offers a great deal of points of interest. It incorporates a quicker production of blockchain applications in simple advances, smooth, and ease displaying and testing. Composer helps the client to assemble, test, and send different choices and afterward implement the one that offers the best fit and reusability of existing applications and APIs that decrease both exertion and expenses. A Composer Playground is the electronic interface that empowers displaying the business necessities and capacities, functional testing, just as sending testing on a live blockchain. You can use a Composer with the help of the link: https://www.hyperledger.org/projects/composer. The current usage of hyperledger tools is given in Table 4.1.

4.4 Blockchain in enterprise

The year 2019 brought a flood of blockchain innovative work, with a few prominent verifications of idea or proof of concepts (PoCs) and experimental runs of

Table 4.1   Status of Hyperledger Tools

Tool	Status
Avalon	In use
Caliper	In use[a]
Cello	In use
Explorer	In use[b]
Composer	Deprecated

[a]Updations are still on.
[b]Updations are still on.
Source: Hyperledger.org.

programs over different ventures. A PoC is an early programming execution or a model intended to test the attainability and practical potential.

The pace of R&D endeavours and declarations quickened, and the expansiveness of businesses investigating blockchain extended. While the money-related segment has generally driven blockchain R&D and speculation, with ventures starting in 2016 or prior, the year 2019 saw greater movement from shipping, telecom, retail, flying, healthcare, autos, and a few different businesses. The Hyperledger fills in as a structure that unites clients, engineers, and sellers from a wide range of sectors and market spaces. Each one of these members makes them think normal: all are keen on finding out about, creating, and utilizing undertaking blockchains. While blockchain is a ground-breaking innovation, it is not one-size-fits-all. Each undertaking needs extraordinary highlights and alterations to help a blockchain accomplish its expected reason. Since various associations have various needs, there will never be one single, standard blockchain. Rather, we hope to see numerous blockchains with various highlights that give a wide scope of arrangements crosswise over numerous enterprises.

Significantly, organizations have not yet put blockchain into enormous scale generation and procedures for significant business endeavours. Like the improvement phase of numerous blockchain extends and DApps, there is a great deal of research, work, and venture yet not very many economically feasible and creation prepared arrangements, alongside a basic innovation youthfulness that hampers execution.

4.4.1   Use cases

The examples of the specialized highlights of blockchains are (i) the utilization of DLT [7] (ii) cryptographical verification, and (iii) the capacity to have smart contract rationale encoded into it. This implies that blockchains can enable different commonly untrusting clients to execute straightforwardly on a record (smart contracts self-execute exchanges) without the requirement for a confided mediator. Blockchain innovation's imaginative qualities incorporate transparency, decentralization, automation, and immutability. These segments can be applied to different enterprises, making countless use cases.

4.4.1.1 Healthcare

Enrolling and maintenance are the greatest difficulties in clinical preliminaries, and in spite of countless endeavours throughout the years, improvement remains to a great extent undiscovered. Clinical preliminary information sharing and the capacity for a look into members to encounter esteem revelation (counting individual well-being information adaptation) are a portion of the promises of blockchain for these use cases.

One of the most mainstream human services use cases for blockchain is patient data management [8]. Therapeutic records will be detached by health associations, making it hard to choose a patient's remedial history without directing their past care provider. This method can take a great deal of time and may normally achieve stumbles due to human mistake.

Identity is the most important feature of blockchain use case in medicinal services – comprehensive of identity management of people (e.g., doctor, patient, member, and supplier), unique device identifiers for restorative gadgets in the medical production network, or authoritative members or validators in a system.

Item supplies, from beginning to end-of-life, are the most predominant use case for DLT crosswise over businesses. In social insurance, medicine, clinical supplies, blood items, and therapeutic gadgets are models where blockchain is being utilized for activities, consistence, and gauging among pharmaceutical makers, blood donation centres, suppliers, drug stores, and payers.

4.4.1.2 Banking

Banks need to loan, but just to borrowers who are at great dangers [9]. This inspires the banks to assemble point-by-point, personally recognizable data from everybody who applies for a loan, for example, date of birth, yearly salary, Aadhar card, voters ID, or passport details. At last, the banks utilize this data to get to a candidate's credit assessment. Guidelines may demand that certain data is imparted to specialists, for instance, to avert illegal tax avoidance. But holding so much personal data makes each bank a succulent objective for hackers.

Rather than revealing any personal information, loan candidates can create ZKPs that their previous year income charges passed a specific limit, that they hold a substantial government ID number, and that their financial assessment met a specific edge inside the previous week. Distributed record-based identity builds up a worldwide wellspring of truth, which conveys an incentive to numerous gatherings. Candidates can give assent, and everybody can concede to when and how it was given. Banks can adjust with guidelines and show a permanent review trail. Therefore, the market can work more efficiently: banks can offer loans with certainty, while candidates can viably shield their personal information.

4.4.1.3 Supply chain management

The production network that delivers fish from sea to table is incredibly intricate and dark. It incorporates numerous members from various enterprises and administrative controls that cross national limits. That makes this store network an ideal open door for blockchain advances [10]. Oceana, an NGO, gave for securing the seas, hypothesized that a mutual stage for recognizability would improve the precision of labelling and bring down private fishing: 'In spite of imposing difficulties, fish discernibility is well inside reach. Just by monitoring where our fish originates from at each progression of the production network, we can gain ground against private fishing.'

Sensors are appended to the fish when it is caught to record information, for example, the area from which it is caught, temperature, and moistness. This information is recorded in the blockchain, alongside further occasions in the handling of the fish: possession changes, stockpiling temperature run, transport organization, etc. The record can likewise give investigation to both administrative requirement and logical examination of fish reaping and utilization.

4.4.1.4   Agriculture

The ordinary agriculture store network includes complex interconnected procedures between different partners, for example, the farmer, distributor, processing agencies, examination and insurance agencies, coordinations and transportation organizations, banks, merchants before it spans to the buyer. In this long procedure, there are a couple of difficulties [11]. Shippers think that it is difficult to follow provenance to comprehend the spot of inception and nature of the imported items. As items move between the different partners, the possession or custodian information gets hard to follow. Global merchants will not confide in unified bodies, particularly private organizations that confirm crops. Datastream between partners is successively prompting potential delay in downstream basic leadership. Blockchain can tackle these issues. Ranchers may incur extraordinary loss in agribusiness on account of some characteristic catastrophes like overwhelming downpour, wind, flood, seismic tremor, and avalanche. When the harvests get obliterated, they need to apply for the remuneration to the government through an extensive technique, and the endorsement requires a few checks. Fusing blockchain in this framework stays away from this entanglement. Moreover, customers can pay tips to the particular satisfactory farmers directly by using the data from the blockchain.

4.4.1.5   Others

Blockchain offers a wide assortment of uses in the business such as aviation, telecommunication, and IoT [12]. Blockchain has a few properties that numerous organizations need to embrace. Decentralization is essential among them. In business, there is a concentrated server which stores all the data of an organization. Any individual who needs to gain admittance to the data counsels the database in the different degrees of data. Since everything is relying upon the server, it is critical to work server constantly. There will be a bottleneck. One single server disappointment will upset the whole framework. In the blockchain, the framework works in a decentralized way. If anyone of the servers comes up short, it will not influence the working of the framework [13]. Another part of a blockchain which organizations need to receive is unchanging nature. There will be a complete adaptation of reality which anybody can check that the adjustment of information prompts the change in the hash esteem, which can recognize the altering. So nobody can alter the organization information. In other words, we can say that everybody is viewing the information, so nobody will set out to alter it. The third property of the blockchain is its cost-effectiveness. The advantages of the blockchain cause it to adjust in the business [14]. Blockchain exchanges are carefully marked utilizing the elliptic curve digital signature calculation. Exchanges spread between hubs, so their source is effectively demonstrated. The confirmation is computationally mind-boggling and comprises the essential bottleneck. By separation in concentrated databases, when an affiliation has been developed, there is no prerequisite for check of every sale that comes over it independently. The independent processing of the transaction is performing in a solitary area. Contingent upon the consensus mechanism [15], this may incorporate the objective forward and backward correspondence and oversee forks and their resulting rollback.

4.5   Blockchain in e-healthcare

Nowadays, clients expect a prompt and consistent stream of information [16]. Numerous enterprises have embraced or are starting to embrace vital advancements to ensure their clients' desire for instant data. Shockingly, the medicinal services industry has fallen behind. Heritage frameworks are difficult, slow, and frequently powerless and have a little role for the patient.

Blockchain innovation can possibly change human services, setting the patient at the focal point of the social insurance environment and expanding the protection, security, and interoperability of well-being information. The assurance of blockchain has no matter how you look at it proposals for accomplices in the medicinal services framework Profiting by this development can interface partitioned systems to deliver encounters and assess the estimation of care. In the long haul, the blockchain arrange for electronic restorative records may improve efficiencies and bolster better health results for patients. Blockchain innovation causes opportunities to lessen unusualness, to engage trustless collaboration, and make secure and immaterial information. Health and human services (HSS) pursue this rapidly creating field to recognize examples and sense zones where the help of government may be required for the advancement to comprehend its most extreme limit in social insurance. To guarantee blockchain's future, HHS should consider mapping and gathering the blockchain system, building up a blockchain structure to organize early adopters, and supporting a consortium for discourse and discovery.

4.5.1   Improve medical record access

One of the most popular therapeutic administrations use cases for blockchain shows restraint information to the executives. Remedial records will, all in all, be disengaged by medicinal workplaces, making it hard to choose a patient's restorative history without guiding their past overseer. This methodology can take a great deal of time and may frequently bring about slip-ups because of human mistake.

At present, electronic healthcare records are put away on centralized databases in which medicinal information remains to a great extent nonportable. Centralization expands the security chance impression. Additionally, concentrated databases cannot guarantee security and information trustworthiness, in any case of derecognizable proof and controlled access necessities. Incorporated healthcare data bases are legitimately a prerequisite and need in many cases hence require an additional layer of innovation to improve their versatility and security.

Created on the Ethereum blockchain, MedRec is a 'framework that organizes quiet organization, giving a straightforward and open perspective on medicinal history'. MedRec is planned to store the entirety of a patient's data in a single spot, making it less complex for patients and specialists to see. In its present plan, suppliers keep up the blockchain through the PoA system. Blockchain records can be used to give total longitudinal health records for people, giving all patients more authority over their own data through irrefutable assent. With blockchain, each patient record mirrors the most popular restorative realities from genomics information to analytic therapeutic imaging and can be dependably moved when required, with no need for a central authority.

4.5.2   Improve clinical trials

Clinical preliminary administration creates piles of information, requiring human services managers to keep solid, reliable records for peer survey, and to meet administrative prerequisites. The unsafe and capricious nature of the clinical preliminary procedure is a significant driver of expensive pharmaceutical medications. To legitimize the expenses of medication advancement, most pharmaceutical organizations plan to create 2–3 new medications for every year, except the achievement rate and long improvement courses of events with clinical preliminaries that decrease the chance of an effective item to almost zero. This enormous vulnerability converts into more significant expenses for everybody, from the examiner to the end shopper. Apart from expanded costs, researchers face difficulties of precisely recreating information, proficiently sharing information, security concerns, and patient enlistment techniques. Blockchain innovation uses a distributed computer network that empowers databases to store timestamped transaction records and archives. Every server (or hub) in the system forms and checks every datum passage, along with the transaction history, which is each transaction that recorded to the system at any time. Patients had no clue that important clinical preliminaries were in activity or that they would have profited by treatment that the preliminaries advertised. To imagine that a lot of cash and time are spent on creating drugs and practically none is spent on discovering patients for clinical preliminaries is shocking, and general society ought to be made mindful of it.

Blockchain technology will have the option to legitimately expand the amount and nature of patients enrolled for clinical preliminaries in various manners. This sort of conveyed record could enable individual patients to store their restorative information by unknown techniques along these lines making it unmistakable to preliminary enrolment specialists, who could then connect with the patients if their information meets all requirements for the clinical trial. Blockchain devices, working together with an electronic data capture, can enable clinical information to be consequently totalled, recreated, and dispersed among specialists and professionals with more prominent auditability, provenance following, and control contrasted with complex, traditional frameworks.

4.5.3   Improve drug traceability

One of the fundamental uses of instances of blockchain is sedating detectability. Medication misrepresentation is a significant issue looked by numerous pharmaceutical organizations and, as per the Health Research Funding Organization, around 30 per cent of medications sold are phoney, and the underground economy is esteemed at around 200 billion dollar every year. As indicated by another report by the World Health Organization, around 16 per cent of the fake medications contain inappropriate fixings. The primary issue with such medications is not that they are simply phoney, it is for the most part about inappropriate fixings that can place the patient's life at serious risk [17]. One explanation the Pharma business is progressing blockchain is a direct result of expanded administrative investigation because of 2012 meningitis flare-up by the medications fabricated by the New England Compounding Center. The meningitis flare-up brought about in excess of 100 deaths. So, they passed the Drug Quality Security Act (DQSA), which over a 10-year time frame expands following and security around pharmaceuticals remembering unique identifiers for every unit sold. Blockchain is a suitable innovation for the business to turn to the fact that different elements need to share a truth dependent on immutable [18] information where nobody is in charge. Blockchain wipes out the requirement for singular wholesalers to oversee huge volumes of item records and producer addresses, consenting to DQSA guidelines, while diminishing errors and giving reserve funds to the whole store network as shown in Figure 4.10.

Healthcare areas where blockchain can be applied

- **Healthcare data access control:** It guarantees to give patients progressively secure access control to oversee their health information.
- **Maintaining medical history:** It should ensure for nonstop accessibility of medicinal information to keep up the therapeutic record for better treatment and maintain a strategic distance from extra assets and expenses.
- **Drug supply chain management:** It can give secure methods for taking care of and checking the supply chain in social healthcare frameworks.
- **Billing and payers:** It can give blockchain-based healthcare payment systems which will be secure, quicker, and less complex.
- **Clinical data sharing:** It must guarantee secure medicinal information putting away and sharing among different included partners.
- **Research and clinical trials:** It may be a valuable instrument to give the safe discernibility to critical examine and clinical preliminaries.

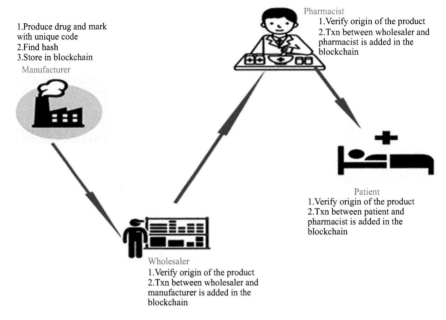

Figure 4.10   Model of drug traceability with blockchain

- **Global data sharing:** It ought to give secure medicinal services information even outside the individual nation/from anyplace on the planet at
  worldwide level.

4.6   An example of healthcare data management using IBM blockchain platform

This model tells the best way to utilize the Blockchain Solution Manager and
Blockchain Document Store [19], associated with the IBM Blockchain Platform, to
fabricate an application for the medicinal services industry. These administrations
use to oversee client access and patient therapeutic records information and make a
well-characterized progressive structure of the considerable number of partners.
The example grandstands the progression of the application from the perspective of
the administrator (admin), medical clinic administrator (hospital admin), specialist
(doctor), and patient.

   Electronic medicinal records and information is an area in genuine need of
advancement. The strategies that are presently utilized for putting away and verifying patient well-being records do not mirror the innovative progressions here
over the previous decade, and medical clinics keep on utilizing age-old data-man-
agement systems for patient data. This is somewhat because of exacting guidelines

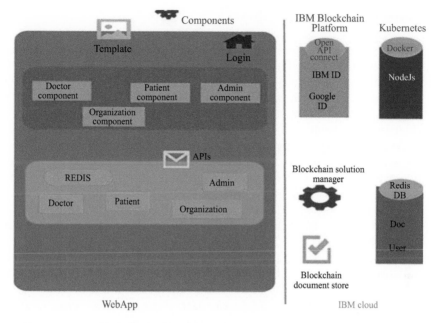

Figure 4.11   Work flow of health care data management using blockchain

around the protection and security of medicinal information, which has suppressed the utilization of current innovations that can make restorative information the board progressively straightforward and helpful for the patients and specialists. Admin is the administrator for an aggregate of emergency clinics and has the most significant level of access in the chain. They can locally available another association (clinic) to the combination and allot/de-allot hospital admin on their dashboard. Hospital admin is the administrator of a specific medical clinic that is a piece of a combination/solution. This administrator can locally avail new clients with the job of either patient or specialist, just as expel clients. The doctor is a client in the association with the fitting job who can transfer reports for patients and download and see records to which they have been allowed to access. The patient is a client in the association with the suitable job who can transfer records without anyone else, see them, see report get to logs, and furthermore oversee access to the archives on their dashboard. Initially interface the Blockchain Solution Manager and Blockchain Document Store with the IBM Blockchain Platform. Then make a Vue.js web application with various dashboards on a solitary page application, which can impart continuously with each other. Make a Node.js server that is conveyed to Kubernetes on IBM Cloud, and associated with a Redis database that runs on the IBM Cloud. Store and recover information from a Redis datastore for persistent capacity through a Node.js server. Make REST calls to outer assistance. Use JSON web token for client management. Figure 4.11 explains the work flow of healthcare data management using IBM blockchain platform.

References

[1]   IBM Corporation. hyperledger-fabricdocs documentation; 2019.

[2]   Hyperledger besu. Hyperledger; 2019. https://www.hyperledger.org/projects/besu.

[3]   Hyperledger burrow. Hyperledger; 2019. https://www.hyperledger.org/projects/burrow.

[4]   Thakkar P, Nathan S, and Viswanathan B. Performance benchmarking and optimizing hyperledger fabric blockchain platform. In: Proceedings – 26th IEEE International Symposium on Modeling, Analysis and Simulation of Computer and Telecommunication Systems, MASCOTS. Milwaukee, Wisconsin: Institute of Electrical and Electronics Engineers Inc.; 2018. p. 264–276.

[5]   Open Source Blockchain Technologies. Available from: https://www.hyperledger.org/.

[6]   Ampel B, Patton M, and Chen H. Performance modeling of hyperledger sawtooth blockchain. In: 2019 IEEE International Conference on Intelligence and Security Informatics (ISI), Shenzhen, China; 2019.

[7]   Nakamoto S. Bitcoin: A peer-to-peer electronic cash system; 2009. Available from: http://www.bitcoin.org/bitcoin.pdf.

[8]   Kuo T-T, Kim H-E, and Ohno-Machado L. Blockchain distributed ledger technologies for biomedical and health care applications Journal of the American Medical Informatics Association. 2017;24(6):1211–1220. doi: 10.1093/jamia/ocx068.

[9]   Nguyen QK. Blockchain—A financial technology for future sustainable development. In: Proceedings – 3rd International Conference on Green Technology and Sustainable Development, GTSD 2016; 2016. p. 51–54.

[10]   Apte S and Petrovsky N. Will blockchain technology revolutionize excipient supply chain management? Journal of Excipients and Food Chemicals. 2016;7(3):76–78.

[11]   Kamilaris A. The rise of the blockchain technology in agriculture and food supply chain. ResearchGate; 2018.

[12]   Alam T. Blockchain and its role in the Internet of Things (IoT). International Journal of Scientific Research in Computer Science, Engineering and Information Technology. 2019:151–157.

[13]   Wang H, Zheng Z, Xie S, *et al.* Blockchain challenges and opportunities: a survey. International Journal of Web and Grid Services. 2018;14(4):352.

[14]   Kshetri N and Voas J. Blockchain in developing countries. IT Professional. 2018;20(2):11–14.

[15]   Ben Hamida E, Leo Brousmiche K, Levard H, *et al.* Blockchain for Enterprise: Overview, Opportunities and Challenges, Blockchain for Smart Transactions—IRT SystemX, View project Kei-Léo Brousmiche; 2017. Available from: https://www.researchgate.net/publication/322078519.

[16] Dhillon V, Metcalf D, and Hooper M. Blockchain in health care. Blockchain Enabled Applications. 2017:125–138.

[17] Clauson KA, Breeden EA, Davidson C, *et al.* Leveraging blockchain technology to enhance supply chain management in healthcare. Blockchain in Healthcare Today; 2018.

[18] Swathi P, Modi C, and Patel D. Preventing Sybil attack in blockchain using distributed behavior monitoring of miners. In: 2019 10th International Conference on Computing, Communication and Networking Technologies (ICCCNT). IEEE: Kanpur; 2019. p. 1–6.

[19] Store private healthcare data off-chain and medical data management using blockchain. (2018); Medicalchain. Available from: https://medicalchain. com/en/whitepaper/.

Chapter 5

Machine learning

Deepa Chinnasamy[1] and Saraswathi Devarajan[1]

5.1 Introduction

Machine learning (ML) is a method of data analysis that automates analytical model building. Here the systems can learn from data, identify patterns and make decisions with minimal human interference. ML is an application of artificial intelligence (AI) [4,11] that provides systems the ability to automatically learn and improve without being clearly programmed. It focuses on the development of computer programs that can access data and use them in learning. The process of learning begins with observations, like direct experience, or instructions, in order to find patterns in data and make better decisions for the future.

The main aim is to let the computers to learn without human interference or assistance and modify actions accordingly. With a rising recognition that ML plays a key role in a wide range of crucial applications, like data mining, natural language processing, image recognition and expert systems, ML provides potential solutions in all these domains and many more and is set to be a support of our upcoming evolution. ML helps us in identifying patterns from the data and builds models to predict things without having any explicitly pre-programmed rules or models [8]. This process is depicted in Figure 5.1.

During 1959, the term ML was coined by Arthur Samuel. Earlier, in the traditional programming method, developers use data and some programming methodology to find the required output. In ML, the data are collected and cleaned, then models are built and final results are checked.

ML enables the analysis of massive qualities of data. It delivers faster and more accurate results in order to identify opportunities or risks; it may also require additional time and resources to train it properly. Combining machine learning with other technologies can make it even more effective in processing large volumes of information. To learn these data, there are many methods followed in ML.

ML is a tool so far to analyze, understand and identify a pattern in the data. The main idea behind ML is that the computer is trained to automate tasks [7] that

[1]Department of Computer Science, PSG College of Arts & Science, Coimbatore, Tamil Nadu, India

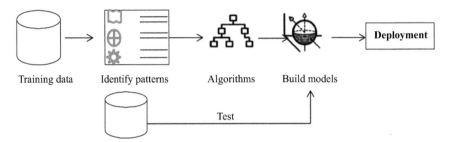

Training data   Identify patterns   Algorithms   Build models

Test

Figure 5.1   Basic execution process of machine learning [13]

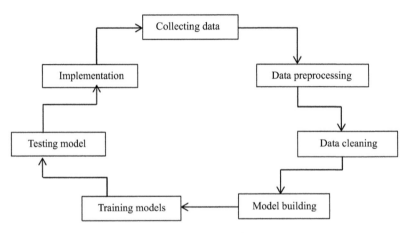

Figure 5.2   Machine learning life cycle [12]

would be impossible for a human being. The clear gap from the traditional analysis is that ML can take decisions with minimal human interference.

ML uses data as inputs to an algorithm that can understand the relationship between the input and the output. When the machine finished learning, it can predict the class of the new data point.

5.1.1   Machine learning life cycle

ML life cycle is a cyclic process that helps one to find a solution to the problem. This helps in finding new ways to apply ML methods on large, complex and expanding datasets.

ML life cycle involves seven steps in Figure 5.2, which are as follows [12]:

- Collecting data
- Data preprocessing
- Data cleaning
- Model building
- Training model

- Testing model
- Implementation

Step 1: Collecting data

The first step in the ML life cycle is collecting data, where identifying correct data for the problem is the main goal. Here data are collected from different sources that are identified and integrated to create a dataset.

Step 2: Data preprocessing

After data are collected, all the collected data are ordered in a random way. Through that, it is easy to explore and understand the characteristics, format and quality of data. This leads to a better understanding of data that leads to a better outcome.

Step 3: Data cleaning

Here the process of cleaning the data, selecting the variable to use and transforming the data in a proper format to make it more suitable for analysis is done. Data cleaning is important because all the collected data might have missing values, invalid data, noise, etc. Various filtering techniques are used for cleaning data.

Step 4: Model building

The main aim here is to build a model to analyze the data using various analytical techniques and review the outcome. It starts with different types of problems, where ML techniques such as classification, regression, cluster analysis, association are selected, and then a model is built using prepared data and evaluated.

Step 5: Training model

In this step, the model developed is trained to improve their performance for a better outcome of the problem. Datasets are used to train the model using various ML algorithms. Training a model is required so that it can understand the various patterns, rules, features, etc.

Step 6: Testing model

After the model has been trained on a given dataset, then the model is tested. The accuracy of the model is checked by providing a test dataset to it. Testing the model determines the percentage of accuracy level as per the requirement of a project or problem.

Step 7: Implementation

Implementation is the final step of the ML life cycle process in which the model is implemented in the real world. If the prepared model produces an accurate result as per the requirement with acceptable speed, then the model is deployed in the real system. But before deploying, the model will be checked whether it is improving in performance using available data or not. The implementation phase is similar to making the final report for a project.

5.1.2   Components in machine learning

All the ML algorithms are a combination of these three components which are as follows:

- *Representation*: The way of representing the information. Here the models such as decision trees, sets of rules, instances, graphical models, neural networks, support vector machines (SVMs), model ensembles are included.
- *Evaluation*: It is a way to evaluate the programs (hypotheses). Accuracy, prediction and recall, squared error, likelihood, posterior probability, cost, margin, etc. are included in the evaluation process.
- *Optimization*: The program that is generated here is known as the search process, for example, combinatorial optimization, convex optimization, constrained optimization.

5.2   Different types of learning

The following are the types of ML followed based upon the data available for every problem that has to be learned in identifying the patterns in predicting better results. These types of learning have applied to different applications. Few applications are listed in Figure 5.3 [4]:

1. Supervised learning
2. Unsupervised learning
3. Reinforcement learning

5.2.1   Supervised learning

Supervised learning is an algorithm that is learnt from sample data and associated target responses that can consist of numeric values or string labels, such as classes or tags, in order to predict the correct response later when posed with new samples. The supervised approach is similar to human learning under some supervision [10,11].

Supervised learning is categorized into two types: classification and regression [2]. Regression supports only a numeric value and classification supports for a qualitative variable such as a class or a tag. For example, a regression task determines the average prices of houses in the specific area, whereas classification-based tasks distinguish between kinds of iris flowers based on their sepal and petal measures.

Supervised learning is the most popular model for performing ML operations. It is commonly used for data where there is an accurate mapping between input–output data, in which, the dataset is labeled, meaning that the algorithm identifies the features explicitly and carries out predictions or classification accordingly. As the training period progresses, the algorithm is able to identify the relationships between the two variables such that the model can predict a new outcome.

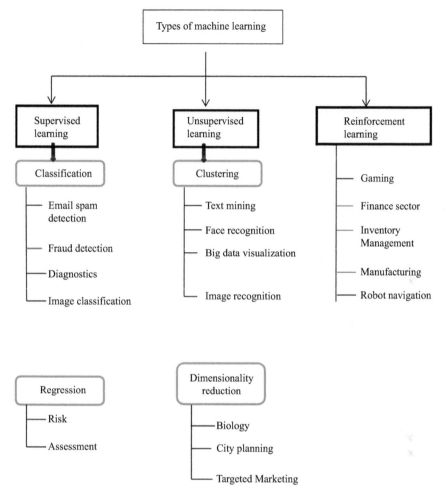

Figure 5.3   Types of machine learning with examples [15]

Supervised learning is a type of ML in which machines are trained using well "labeled" training data, and on basis of that data, machines predict the output. The labeled data mean some input data are already tagged with the correct output.

Steps involved in supervised learning:

- First, determine the type of training dataset.
- Collect/gather the labeled training data.
- Split the training dataset into training dataset, test dataset and validation dataset.
- Determine the input features of the training dataset, which should have enough knowledge so that the model can accurately predict the output.
- Determine the suitable algorithm for the model, such as SVM, decision tree.

- Execute the algorithm on the training dataset. Sometimes researchers need validation sets as the control parameters, which are the subset of training datasets.
- Evaluate the accuracy of the model by providing the test set. If the model predicts the correct output, which means our model is accurate.

5.2.1.1 Types of supervised machine learning algorithms

Supervised learning consists of many algorithms. Here we will discuss some of the popular supervised classification algorithms.

Regression

Regression algorithms are used if there is a relationship between the input variable and the output variable. It is used for the prediction of continuous variables, such as weather forecasting, market trends [5].

Classification

Classification algorithms are used when the output variable is categorical, which means that there are two classes such as yes–no, male–female, true–false. The main goal of this algorithm is to classify or categorize to which new data will fall under category.

5.2.1.2 Difference between regression and classification

The following table shows the difference between regression algorithm and classification algorithm.

Table 5.1   Differentiation between regression algorithm and classification learning [12]

Regression algorithm	Classification algorithm
The output variable must be of continuous nature or real value	The output variable must be a discrete value
The task of the regression algorithm is to map the input value (x) with the continuous output variable (y)	The task of the classification algorithm is to map the input value (x) with the discrete output variable (y)
They are used with continuous data	They are used with discrete data
It tries to find the best fit line, which can predict the output more accurately	It tries to find the decision boundary, which can divide the dataset into different classes
This algorithm can be used to solve the regression problems such as weather prediction, house price prediction	This algorithm can be used to solve classification problems such as identification of spam emails, speech recognition, identification of cancer cells

5.2.1.3 Challenges in supervised machine learning

Here, are challenges faced in supervised ML:

- Data preparation and preprocessing are always a challenge.
- Accuracy suffers when impossible, unlikely and incomplete values have been entered as training data.

- If the concerned expert is not available, then the other approach is "brute-force." It means the user needs to choose the right features (input variables) to train the machine on. It could be inaccurate.

5.2.1.4 Advantages of supervised learning
- Supervised learning allows the user to collect data or produce a data output from the previous experience.
- Helps you to optimize performance criteria using experience.
- Supervised ML helps you to solve various types of real-world computation problems.

5.2.1.5 Disadvantages of supervised learning
- The user needs to select lots of good examples from each class while you are training the classifier.
- Classifying big data can be a real challenge.
- Training for supervised learning needs a lot of computation time.

5.2.2 *Unsupervised learning*

Unsupervised learning is an ML technique, where the user does not need to train the model. Instead, the user needs to allow the model to work on its own to discover information. It mainly deals with the unlabeled data [10,11].

Unsupervised learning algorithms allow the user to perform more difficult processing tasks compared to supervised learning, although unsupervised learning can be more unpredictable when compared with other natural learning methods.

Unsupervised learning occurs when an algorithm learns from plain examples without any associated response, leaving to the algorithm to determine the data patterns on its own. This type of algorithm tends to restructure the data into something else, such as new features that may represent a class or a new series of uncorrelated values. They are fairly useful in providing the meaning of data and new useful inputs to supervised ML algorithms.

Some recommendation systems that the user finds on the web in the form of marketing automation are based on this type of learning. The recommendations are based on an estimation of what group of customers you resemble the most and then inferring your likely preferences based on that group.

Main reasons that describe the importance of unsupervised learning:

- Unsupervised learning is helpful for finding useful insights from the data.
- Unsupervised learning is much similar to human learning to think by their experiences, which makes it closer to real AI.
- Unsupervised learning works on unlabeled and uncategorized data that make unsupervised learning more important.
- In real world, users do not always have input data with the corresponding output so to solve such cases, users need unsupervised learning.

5.2.2.1   Types of unsupervised learning algorithm

Unsupervised learning consists of many algorithms. Here some of the widely used algorithms are discussed.

Clustering

Clustering is a method of grouping the objects into clusters such that objects with more similarities remain in a group and have less or no similarities with the objects of another group [3]. Cluster analysis finds the commonalities between the data objects and categorizes them as per the presence and absence of those commonalities.

Dimensionality reduction

Dimensional reduction is a process of reducing random variables by obtaining a set of principle values. The two components of dimensionality reduction are feature selection and feature extraction where a subset is found from an original set of variables that can be used to model the problem and reduce data in dimensional space, respectively. This is very helpful to reduce uncorrelated variables among the variables.

5.2.2.2   Applications of unsupervised machine learning

Some applications of unsupervised ML techniques are as follows:

- Clustering automatically split the dataset into groups based on their similarities.
- Anomaly detection can discover unusual data points in the dataset. It is useful for finding fraudulent transactions.
- Association mining identifies sets of items that often occur together in the dataset.
- Latent variable models are widely used for data preprocessing, like reducing the number of features in a dataset or decomposing the dataset into multiple components.

5.2.2.3   Disadvantages of unsupervised learning

- The user cannot get precise information regarding data sorting, and the output as data used in unsupervised learning is labeled and not known.
- Less accuracy of the results is because the input data are not known and not labeled by people in advance.
- The spectral classes do not always correspond to informational classes.
- The user needs to spend time interpreting and label the classes that follow that classification.
- Spectral properties of classes can also change over time so the user cannot have the same class information while moving from one image to another.

5.2.2.4 Difference between supervised learning and unsupervised learning

The following table shows the difference between supervised learning and unsupervised learning.

Table 5.2 Differentiation between supervised learning and unsupervised learning [12]

Supervised learning	Unsupervised learning
Supervised learning algorithms are trained using labeled data	Unsupervised learning algorithms are trained using unlabeled data
Supervised learning model takes direct feedback to check if it is predicting correct output or not	Unsupervised learning model does not take any feedback
Supervised learning model predicts the output	Unsupervised learning model finds the hidden patterns in data
In supervised learning, input data are provided to the model along with the output	In unsupervised learning, only input data are provided to the model
The goal of supervised learning is to train the model so that it can predict the output when it is given new data	The goal of unsupervised learning is to find the hidden patterns and useful insights from the unknown dataset
Supervised learning needs supervision to train the model	Unsupervised learning does not need any supervision to train the model
Supervised learning can be used for those cases where we know the input as well as corresponding outputs	Unsupervised learning can be used for those cases where we have only input data and no corresponding output data
Supervised learning model produces an accurate result	Unsupervised learning model may give less accurate result as compared to supervised learning
Supervised learning is not close to true artificial intelligence as in this, the user first trains the model for each data, and then only it can predict the correct output	Unsupervised learning is closer to the true artificial intelligence as it learns similarly as a child learns daily routine things by his experiences
It includes various algorithms such as linear regression, logistic regression, support vector machine, multi-class classification, decision tree and Bayesian logic	It includes various algorithms such as clustering, KNN and Apriori algorithm

5.2.3 Reinforcement learning

Reinforcement learning covers more areas that allow machines to interact with their dynamic environment in order to reach their goals. Through this, machines and software agents are able to evaluate the ideal activities in a specific context. With the help of this reward feedback, agents are able to learn the activities and improve them in the longer run. This simple feedback reward is known as a reinforcement signal [10,11].

It is the ability of an agent to interact with the surroundings and find out what is the best result. It follows the concept of the hit and trial method. The agent is rewarded or penalized with a point for a right or a wrong answer and, on the basis of the positive reward points, gains the model trains itself. Again, once trained it gets ready to predict the new data presented to it.

The agent in the environment is required to take actions that are based on the current state. This type of learning is different from supervised learning in the sense that the training data in the former have output mapping provided such that the model is capable of learning the correct answer, whereas, in the case of reinforcement learning, there is no answer key provided to the agent when they have to perform a particular task.

Some important phrases used in reinforcement algorithm:

- *Agent*: It is an assumed entity which performs actions in an environment to gain some reward.
- *Environment (e)*: A scenario that an agent has to face.
- *Reward (R)*: An immediate return given to an agent when he or she performs specific action or task.
- *State (s)*: State refers to the current situation returned by the environment.
- *Policy (π)*: It is a strategy that is applied by the agent to decide then extract based on the current state.
- *Value (V)*: It is expected long-term return with discount, as compared to the short-term reward.
- *Value function*: It specifies the value of a state that is the total amount of reward.
- *Model of the environment*: This mimics the behavior of the environment. It helps you to make inferences to be made and also determine how the environment will behave.
- *Model-based methods*: It is a method for solving reinforcement learning problems that use model-based methods.
- *Q value or action value (Q)*: Q Value is quite related to value. The main difference takes an extra parameter as a recent action.

Reinforcement learning judges actions based on the results they produce. It is goal oriented, and its aim is to learn sequences of actions that will lead an agent to target its goal or maximize its objective function.

Here are some examples:

- In video games, the goal is to finish the game with the most points, so each additional point obtained throughout the game will affect the agent's subsequent behavior; that is, the agent may learn that it should shoot battleships, touch coins or dodge meteors to increase its score.
- In the real world, the goal might be for a robot to travel from point A to point B, and every inch the robot is able to move closer to point B could be counted like points.

5.2.3.1   How reinforcement learning works?

Let us see some simple example which helps the user to demonstrate the reinforcement learning mechanism.

Consider the scenario of teaching new tricks to your cat:

- As cat does not understand English or any other human language, we cannot tell her directly what to do. Instead, we follow a different strategy.
- We emulate a situation, and the cat tries to respond in many different ways. If the cat's response is the desired way, we will give her fish.
- Now whenever the cat is exposed to the same situation, the cat executes a similar action with even more enthusiastically in expectation of getting more reward.
- At the same time, the cat also learns what not to do when faced with negative experiences.

5.2.3.2   Characteristics of reinforcement learning

Here are important characteristics of reinforcement learning:

- There is no supervisor, only a real number or reward signal.
- Sequential decision-making.
- Time plays a crucial role in reinforcement problems.
- Feedback is always delayed, not instantaneous.
- Agent's actions determine the subsequent data it receives.

5.2.3.3   Reinforcement learning vs. supervised learning

The following table shows the difference between reinforcement learning and supervised learning.

Table 5.3   Differentiation between reinforcement learning and supervised learning for some specific parameters [12]

Parameters	Reinforcement learning	Supervised learning
Decision style	Reinforcement learning helps you to take your decisions sequentially	In this method, a decision is made on the input given at the beginning
Works on	Works on interacting with the environment	Works on examples or given sample data
Dependency on decision	In this method learning decision is dependent. Therefore, the user should give labels to all the dependent decisions	In supervised learning, the decisions that are independent of each other, so labels are given for every decision
Best suited	It supports and works well in artificial intelligence, where human interaction is prevalent	It is widely operated with an interactive software system or applications
Example	Chess game	Object recognition

5.2.3.4   Applications of reinforcement learning

Here are some of the applications of reinforcement learning:

- Robotics for industrial automation.

- Business strategy planning.
- ML and data processing.
- It helps you to create training systems that provide custom instruction and materials according to the requirement of students.
- Aircraft control and robot motion control.

Here are prime reasons for using reinforcement learning:

- It helps user to find which situation needs an action.
- Helps user to discover which action yields the highest reward over the longer period.
- Reinforcement learning also provides the learning agent with a reward function.
- It also allows it to figure out the best method for obtaining large rewards.

5.2.3.5   Challenges of reinforcement learning

Here are the major challenges you will face while doing reinforcement earning:

- Feature/reward design which should be very involved.
- Parameters may affect the speed of learning.
- Realistic environments can have partial observance.
- Too much reinforcement may lead to an overload of states that can diminish the results.
- Realistic environments can be nonstationary.

5.3   Types of machine learning algorithms

Choosing the right ML algorithm depends on several factors such as data size, quality and diversity. Additional factors are accuracy, training time, parameters, data points and much more. Therefore, selecting the correct algorithm is both mixing of business expectation, specification, experimentation and time available.

In the following, are some best ML algorithms under each category.

5.3.1   Classification algorithms

Classification belongs to the supervised learning task that used to classify the categorical variables. Examples include spam identification, financial fraud detection.

5.3.1.1   Naïve Bayes classification

Naïve Bayes (NB) method works based on probability condition and number of counting. The model is actually a probability table that obtains updated through the training data. This algorithm uses lookup table class probabilities to predict a new observation [2].

NB classification is broken down into five parts:

Step 1: Separate by class.
Step 2: Summarize dataset.

Step 3: Summarize data by class.
Step 4: Gaussian probability density function.
Step 5: Class probabilities.

This model is useful for large datasets. This algorithm outperforms classification when compared with other classification algorithms in particular textual data analysis. It predicts probabilities for each class such as the probability that belongs to a particular class. This algorithm has the class with the highest probability that is considered as likely class. This is called **Maximum A Posteriori (MAP).**

The MAP for a hypothesis is as follows:

$$MAP(H)$$
$$= \max(P(H|E))$$
$$= \max((P(E|H) \times P(H))/P(E))$$
$$= \max(P(E|H) \times P(H))$$

$P(E)$ is evidence probability, and it is used to normalize the result. The major advantage of the NB classifier is its short computational time for training.

Types of Naïve Bayes algorithm

1. *Gaussian Naïve Bayes*

    The Gaussian NB is easiest to work because values are continuous. This NB find out mean and standard deviation from the dataset.

2. *Multinomial Naïve Bayes*

    Multinomial NB is suitable for classification, particularly for discrete values. It is one of the standard classic algorithms that are specifically used in text categorization. Each event in text classification represents the frequency of a word in a document.

3. *Bernoulli Naïve Bayes*

    Bernoulli NB is used on the data that is distributed similar to multivariate Bernoulli distributions. But Bernoulli NB is used to classify the binary value.

5.3.1.2 Nearest neighbor

The *K*-nearest-neighbors algorithm is a supervised classification algorithm [11]. It has a bunch of labeled points that are used to learn patterns. These learned patterns are used to predict the new points that have closest labeled points. The testing phase works slower and more expensive when compared with the training phase.

5.3.1.3 Support vector machine

SVM is a supervised classification algorithm used to calculate the distance between two observations [2,9]. The SVM algorithm finds decision margin that maximizes the distance between the closest members of separate classes. It facilitates modeling for data analysis through regression and classification. SVM uses a kernel mechanism for classification. This algorithm is very useful for high-dimensional space. But it takes more memory space and not suitable for larger datasets.

5.3.1.4   Decision trees

Decision tree is a supervised classification algorithm. It builds a model in the form of a tree structure. The tree consists of decision node and leaf node. A decision node has two or more branches and a leaf node represents a decision. The topmost node in a decision tree is a root node [5].

Decision trees can handle both types of data such as categorical and numerical. This algorithm is a very popular classification algorithm. But it does not handle the irrelevant data present in the dataset.

5.3.1.5   Neural networks

A neural network is the one, which is composed of neurons (units) or nodes. It consists of units, arranges in layers that convert an input vector into some output. Each unit takes as input, applies a function to it, and then passes the output on to the next layer. Weightings are calculated. From one unit to another. These weights are tuned in the training phase to adapt a neural network to the particular problem at hand.

Neural networks are a specific set of algorithms that gives new booming in ML. It has general function approximations that can be applied to almost any ML problem.

5.3.2   Regression algorithm

Regression algorithm is a supervised classification algorithm that is a subset of ML algorithms. One of the main features of supervised learning algorithms is that they model dependencies and relationships between the target output and input features to predict the value for new data.

Different types of regression algorithms are as follows.

5.3.2.1   Linear regression

Linear regression is a supervised classification algorithm. It works for continuous variable and has a constant slope output. The methodology for measuring the relationship between the two continuous variables is known as linear regression such as independent variable and dependent variable.

There are two main types:

1. Simple regression
    A linear regression line has an equation of the form $Y=mX+c$, where X is the independent variable and Y is the dependent variable. Here, m is the slope and c is the intercept.
2. Multi-variable regression

    A more complex, multi-variable linear equation might look like this, where w represents the coefficients, or weights, model will try to learn the function $f(x,y,z)=w1x+w2y+w3z$.

5.3.2.2   Logistic regression

Logistic regression is used by ML from the field of statistics. Logistic regression performs categorical classification that results in the output belonging to one of the two classes. Logistic regression has two components—hypothesis and sigmoid curve.

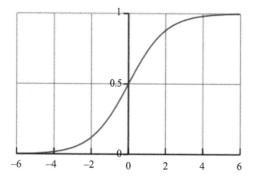

Figure 5.4 S-shaped curve [14]

The resultant likelihood of the event is based on the hypothesis. This hypothesis is fit into the log function that forms S-shaped curve called sigmoid. Through this log function, one can determine the result. The sigmoid S-shaped curve is shown in Figure 5.4.

5.3.3 Dimensionality reduction algorithm

Dimensionality reduction is one of the most imperative concepts of ML. Dimensionality reduction is the process of reducing the number of variables by some considerations from a set of variables. It consists of the most popular algorithms discussed in the following.

5.3.3.1 Principal component analysis

Principal component analysis (PCA) is the most accepted technique in multivariate analysis and dimensionality reduction [6]. PCA can be used as a preprocessing tool to reduce the dimension of a dataset that is irrelevant to the problems or uncorrelated or maximizing the difference in the variance between the variables. This PCA can be helpful in reducing the overfitting problem.

5.3.3.2 Radical basis function

A radial basis function (RBF) is a function that allocates a real value to each input from its domain, and the value produced by the RBF is always an absolute value; i.e., it is a measure of distance and cannot be negative.

Euclidean distance, the straight-line distance between two points in the Euclidean space, is typically used.

RBFs are used to approximate functions, much as neural networks act as function approximates. The following sum:

$$y(x) = \sum_{i=1}^{N} w_i \phi(\|x - x_i\|),$$

represents an RBF network. The RBFs act as activation functions. The approximant $f(x)$ is differentiable with respect to the weights W, which are learned using iterative updater methods common among neural networks.

5.3.4   Clustering algorithms

Clustering is an unsupervised learning method for finding natural groupings of observations (i.e., clusters) based on the structure within the dataset. Examples include customer segmentation, grouping similar entities in e-commerce and social network analysis.

5.3.4.1   *K*-Means algorithm

K-Means clustering is a general-purpose algorithm that makes clusters based on geometric distances (i.e., distance on a coordinate plane) between points. The clusters are grouped around centroids, causing them to be globular and have similar sizes. This is a suggested algorithm for beginners because it is simple, yet flexible enough to get reasonable results for most problems. *K*-Means clustering is a quick and efficient algorithm to define data points into categories when you have little available information about your data.

K-Means clustering is a method used for clustering analysis [3]. It aims to partition a set of observations into a number of clusters (k), resulting in the partitioning of the data into cells. It can be considered as a method of finding out which group a particular object really belongs to. This is used mainly in statistics and can be applied to almost any branch of study. For example, in marketing, it can be used to group dissimilar demographics of people into simple groups that make it easier for marketers to target. Astronomers use it to shift through large amounts of astronomical data; since they cannot analyze each and every object one by one, they need a way to statistically find points of interest for observation and investigation. The algorithm is as follows:

1. K points are placed into the object data space representing the initial group of centroids.
2.   Each object or data point is assigned to the closest k.
3.   After all objects are assigned, the positions of the k centroids are recalculated.
4.   Steps 2 and 3 are repeated until the positions of the centroids no longer move.

Strengths: *K*-Means hands down the most famous clustering algorithm because it is fast, simple and surprisingly flexible if you preprocess your data and engineer useful features.

Weaknesses: The user must mention the number of clusters, which will not always be simple to do. In addition, if the true underlying clusters in your data are not globular, then *K*-means will result in poor clusters.

5.3.4.2   DB scan algorithm

Density-based spatial clustering applications with noise (DBSCAN) is a data clustering algorithm that is commonly used in ML. Based on the set of points,

DBSCAN groups combine points that are close to each other based on a distance measurement and a minimum number of points. It also marks as outliers the points that are found in low-density regions. The DBSCAN algorithm should be used to find associations and structures in data that are hard to find manually but can be suited and useful to find patterns and predict trends. It is a density-based algorithm that makes clusters for dense regions of points.

DBSCAN is a clustering method that is used in ML to differentiate and group clusters of high density and clusters of low density. Given that **DBSCAN** is a density-based clustering algorithm, it does a great job offending as in the data that have a high density of observations, versus areas of the data that are not highly dense with observations. **DBSCAN** can sort data into clusters of varying shapes as in the following:

Step 1: Divides the dataset into *n* dimensions.

Step 2: For each point in the dataset, DBSCAN forms an *n*-dimensional shape around that data point and then counts how many data points fall within that shape.

Step 3: DBSCAN counts this shape as a cluster. DBSCAN repetitively expands the cluster, by going through each individual point within the cluster, and counting the number of other data points nearby.

Strengths: DBSCAN does not consider globular clusters, and its performance is measurable. In addition, it does not require every point to be assigned to a cluster, minimizing the noise of the clusters (this may be a weakness, depending on your use case).

Weaknesses: The user must tune the hyperparameters "epsilon" and "min_-samples," which describes the density of clusters. DBSCAN is quite sensitive to these hyperparameters.

5.3.4.3 Gaussian mixture model

For representing a normally distributed subpopulation within an overall population, *Gaussian mixture model (GMM)* is used. It does not require the data linked with the subpopulation. Therefore, the model is capable of learning subpopulations automatically. As the assignment of the population is not clear, it comes under the category of unsupervised learning.

For example, believe that you have to create a model of the human height data. The mean height of males in male distribution is $5'8''$ and for females, it is $5'4''$. We only know the height data and not the gender assignment. Distribution follows a total of two scaled and two shifted normal distributions. We make this assumption using the help of the GMM. GMM can have multiple components.

Using GMMs, we can extract valiant features from the speech data, we can also perform tracking of the objects in situation that have a number of mixture components and also the means that provides a prediction of the position of objects in a video sequence (Figure 5.5).

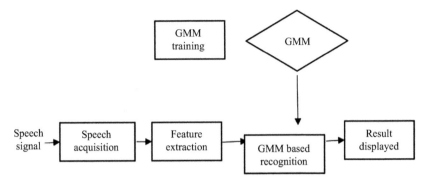

Figure 5.5   GMM working [16]

5.3.4.4   EM algorithm

The expectation–maximization (EM) algorithm is used for the model parameters to find maximum estimates when the data are incomplete, has missing data points or has unobserved (hidden) variables. It is an iterative way to approximate the maximum possibility function. While maximum likelihood estimation can spot the "best fit" model for a set of data, it does not work particularly well for incomplete datasets. The more complex EM algorithm can spot model parameters even if you have missing data. It works by selecting random values for the missing data points, and with the help of those guesses to estimate a second set of data. The new values are used to create a good guess for the first set, and the process continues until the algorithm converges on a particular fixed point. EM takes a guess at the parameters first—accounting for the missing data—then twists the model to fit the guesses and the observed data. The basic steps for the algorithm are as follows:

Step 1: First randomly, the model's parameters are identified and a probability distribution is created, which is called the "E-step" or the "expected" distribution.
Step 2: Newly observed data are given as inputs into the model.
Step 3: Probability distribution from the E-step is modified where the new data are included, which is called the "M-step."
Step 4: Steps 2–4 are repeated until stability (i.e., a distribution that does not change) is reached.

The EM algorithm always enhances a parameter's estimation through this multistep process. However, it sometimes needs a little random start to spot the best model because the algorithm can hone in on a local maximum that is not that close to the (optimal) global maxima. In other words, it can do better if you force it to restart and take that "initial guess" from Step 1 over again. From all of the possible parameters, you can then select the one with the greatest maximum likelihood.

5.3.5 *Reinforcement algorithm*

A reinforcement learning algorithm, or agent, is a study of interacting with its environment. The agent gets rewarded by performing correctly and penalties for performing incorrectly. The agent studies without involvement from a human by maximizing its reward and minimizing its penalty. Reinforcement learning is an advance to ML that is inspired by behaviorist psychology. It is much like how a child learns to perform a task. Reinforcement learning contrasts with other ML approaches in that the algorithm is not explicitly said how to perform a task but works through the problem on its own. Some of the reinforcement algorithms are as follows.

5.3.5.1 Deep *Q* networks

A deep *Q* networks (DQN) agent is value-based reinforcement learning agent that instructs a critic to calculate the return or future rewards. DQN is a variant of *Q*-learning. DQN was the first algorithm that could successfully play a wide variety of Atari games. Other algorithms at the time could perform well only at a single game but could not generalize across games. Impressively, DQN was capable of performing over the human level at a range of Atari games using only the screen pixels as input. Because it does not require any game-specific modifications to perform well at a game, DQN was heralded as a key breakthrough ahead of artificial general intelligence.

DQN overcomes unstable learning with mainly four techniques.

- Experience replay
- Target network
- Clipping rewards
- Skipping frames

5.3.5.2 Deep deterministic policy gradient

One of the challenges that the reinforcement learning community faced was figuring out how to deal with continuous action spaces. This is an essential obstacle, **since most interesting problems in robotic control, etc. come under this category.** Logically, if you discretize your continuous action space too precisely, you end up with the same curse of dimensionality problem like you had before. On the other side, a naïve discretization of the action space sends away valuable information concerning the geometry of the action domain.

Deep deterministic policy gradient is an algorithm which concurrently studies *Q*-function and a policy. It uses the off-policy data and the Bellman equation to study the *Q*-function, and uses the *Q*-function to study the policy. When there are a finite number of discrete actions, the max poses zero problem, because it can just calculate the *Q*-values for each action separately and directly compare them with others. (This also immediately gives us the action, which maximizes the *Q*-value.) But when the action space is continuous, it cannot exhaustively calculate the space, and solving the optimization problem is highly nontrivial. Using a normal optimization algorithm would make evaluating a painfully expensive subroutine. Since it would need to be run each and every time, the agent wants to decide an action in the environment, this

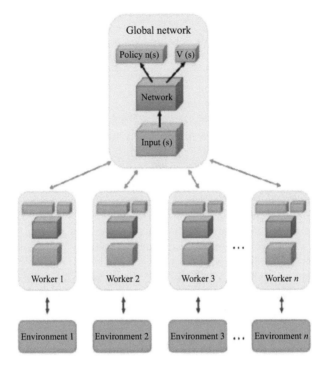

Figure 5.6   A3C algorithm flow [16]

is unacceptable. Because the action space is continuous, the function is pre-assumed to be differentiable with respect to the action argument. This allows us to set up an efficient, gradient-based learning rule for a policy that exploits that fact.

5.3.5.3 Asynchronous advantage actor critic

Asynchronous advantage actor critic (A3C) consists of multiple independent agents (networks) with their separate weights, who interact with a different copy of the environment in parallel. Thus, they can study a bigger part of the state-action space in a much shorter time. The agents (or workers) are guided in parallel and update periodically a global network, which holds shared parameters (Figure 5.6).

The updates are not happening simultaneously and that is the place where the asynchronous comes from. After each update, the agents reset their parameters to those of the global network and continue their independent exploration and training for *n* steps until they update themselves again. We see that the information flows not only from the agents to the global network but also between agents as each agent resets his weights by the global network (Figure 5.7).

Implementing the algorithm
The general outline of the code architecture is as follows:

AC_Network: This class has all the tensor flow to create the networks themselves.

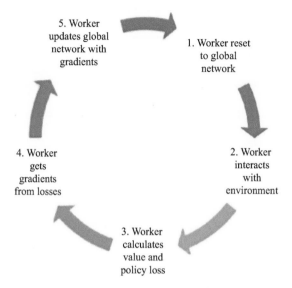

Figure 5.7   A3C algorithm implementation example [16]

Worker: This class contains a copy of AC_Network, an environment class, as well as all the logic for interacting with the environment, and updating the global network.

High-level code for creating the Worker instances and running them in parallel.

5.3.6   Machine learning in healthcare

ML is the process of guiding machines to make them recognize patterns by providing them data and an algorithm to work with the data [15]. And it has assisted a lot in the field of healthcare in a number of different ways.

Many sectors are using ML only, healthcare cannot stand behind! Google has developed an ML algorithm to find cancerous tumors, Stanford is using it to find skin cancer. Experts say the course of ML as "training" of machines, and the output that is produced is known as "model." The model is given with data, and it creates new information with whatever it had previously learned.

The three types of models used in ML are as follows:

- Classification—This model helps us to determine a category—it is one thing or another. The model is guided to categorize the dataset.
- Clustering—This model is created to identify distinctive patters in the data when there are a bunch of data available but did not have a determined outcome.
- Regression—This model is created for the need of finding value. With the help of this data, the algorithm can spot associations between any two variables and the outcome is predicted, respectively.

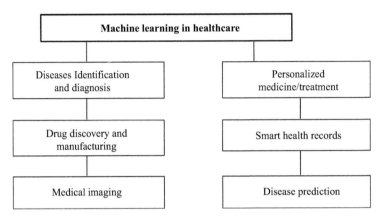

Figure 5.8   ML in healthcare industry [15]

Advancements of ML application in the healthcare industry are as follows (Figure 5.8).

5.3.6.1   Identification of diseases and diagnosis

Always identifying or diagnosing diseases manually is not an easy task, and ML plays a vital role in identifying the patient's disease, monitoring his health and suggesting needed steps to be taken in order to prevent disease. It includes minor diseases to major ones such as cancer that is tough to be identified in the early stages. For example, any type of cancer is a killer disease that leads to only death, and researchers are fighting every day to get new solutions and developments to help the people. Here ML helps the researchers in analyzing and predicting the disease.

5.3.6.2   Drug discovery and manufacturing

R&D technologies such as next-generation sequencing and precision medicine can help one to find the treatment of complex health diseases. ML algorithms like unsupervised learning can identify patterns in data without providing any predictions.

Discovering or manufacturing a new drug can be expensive and a long process because there are a number of compounds that are put to the test, and only one result can prove to be very useful. The advancements in technology like ML can lead to stimulating this process.

5.3.6.3   Medical imaging

With the help of ML techniques such as deep learning, it helps us in identifying microscopic defects in the scanned images within the patients and as a result, doctors are able to suggest a proper diagnosis. Traditional techniques like X-ray and CT scans were used to inspect minor irregularities, but with the increasing diseases, there was a need to inspect them properly and deeply. ML helps researchers to program in a way that even microscopic defects are identified in the images, which in turn help the doctors in diagnosing the disease.

5.3.6.4   Personalized medicine/treatment

With the explosion of patient data in the form of genetic information and electronic health records, now doctors are able to suggest personalized treatment to individual patients according to their exact needs. Their aim is to gain insights from huge amounts of datasets and use them to make patients healthier individually. These insights are capable enough of suggesting personalized combinations and predicting disease risk with the use of ML technologies.

5.3.6.5   Smart health records

While technology has made easy the process of data entry, there is still some time-taking process. Maintaining up-to-date health records every day is exhausting and also time-consuming. After starting such huge works, maintaining health records is another area where ML has started to develop in order to save time, effort and money. Applications like Google's Cloud Vision API and MATLAB®'s ML-based handwriting recognition technology are used for document classification methods. The goal is to provide a way to access to clinical data, modernize the workflow in the company and improve the accuracy of health information.

5.3.6.6   Predicting diseases

Various ML technologies are being used in monitoring and predicting outbreaks around the world. Scientists have access to a huge amount of data that were collected from satellites, social media platforms, websites, etc. Some ML techniques such as artificial neural networks help one to collaborate with this information and predict all data from minor diseases to severe chronic infectious diseases.

5.3.7   Advantages and disadvantages of machine learning

Nowadays, ML provides solution to problems and also benefits companies by making predictions precisely and helping them to make better decisions.

Here users will learn about the advantages and disadvantages of ML.

5.3.7.1   Advantages of machine learning

The following are the advantages of ML:

1.   Easily identifies trends and patterns

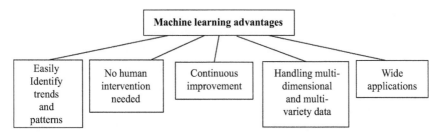

Figure 5.9   Advantages of ML[15]

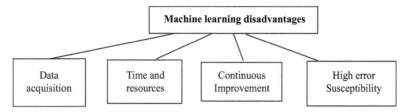

Figure 5.10   Disadvantages of ML [15]

ML can review big volumes of data and discover particular trends and patterns that would not be apparent to humans [15]. For instance, for an e-commerce website like Amazon, it serves to analyze the browsing behaviors and purchasing histories of the users to help one cater to the right products, deal and reminder relevant to them. It uses the results produced my ML to reveal relevant advertisements to them (Figure 5.9).

2. No human intervention needed (automation)

With ML, during project development each and every step does not need to be monitored. Since it has the ability to train machines the ability to learn, it lets them make predictions which help one to make decisions and also improve the algorithms on their own. A common example of this is antivirus software; they learn to filter new threats as soon as they are recognized. ML is also good at recognizing spam.

3. Continuous improvement

As ML algorithms gain experience, they keep enhancing accuracy and efficiency. This lets them provide better decisions. For example, suppose a weather forecast model needs to be designed, then the amount of data keeps increasing, and so the algorithms learn to make more precise predictions faster.

4. Handling multidimensional and multi-variety data

ML algorithms are also good at handling all types of data such as multi-dimensional and multi-variety, and they can do this in dynamic or uncertain environments.

5. Wide applications

ML applications help each and every individual, smaller to bigger organizations. For example, in a customer-oriented business, it has the capability to deliver a much more personal experience to customers and focuses the right customers in improving the business with a properly predicted strategy.

ML enters almost all the domains and directly or indirectly touches human life. They easily identify the patterns and predict the problem or give out the solutions exactly. As they get trained, the working of the ML algorithm also improves very well. Bots are much more tuned with the help of the ML algorithms and trainings.

5.3.7.2   Disadvantages of machine learning

With all those advantages to its powerfulness and popularity, ML is not perfect [15]. The following are the disadvantages of ML (Figure 5.10):

1. Data acquisition

    ML needs huge datasets to train on, and these should be inclusive or unbiased, and also of good quality. There can also be times where they must hold on for new data to be generated.

2. Time and resources

    ML needs more time to let the algorithms train and develop enough to fulfill their needs with a considerable amount of accuracy and relevancy. It also needs massive resources to function. This can mean additional requirements of machine power for you.

3. Interpretation of results

    Another major challenge is the capability to accurately predict results generated by the algorithms. You must also carefully select the algorithms for your purpose.

4. High error-susceptibility

    ML is autonomous but highly liable to errors. Suppose you train an algorithm with small datasets enough not to be inclusive. You end up with biased predictions resulting from a biased training set. This results in irrelevant advertisements being displayed to customers. In the case of ML, such blunders can start off a chain of errors that can go undetected for long periods of time. And when they do get noticed, it takes some time to recognize the source of the issue, and even longer to correct it.

    Although ML is advantageous, the amount of data that are dealt with itself a great disadvantage. Finding the right data and resources for the problem for prediction they also sometimes do not fulfill the needs. The loss of the resources, time all leads to cost problems too. Thus, these are the disadvantages of ML in the healthcare industry.

5.3.8 Limitations of ML in healthcare industry

The information explosion has produced the collection of massive amounts of data. However, there are times when using ML is just unnecessary, and can get you into difficulties.

Limitation 1—Ethics

The idea of believing data and algorithms more than our own judgment has its own pros and cons. Obviously, algorithms benefit us in many ways in almost all the domains they are used, if they are not useful then it would not be used in the first place. These algorithms make us to automate processes by making informed judgments using available data.

Limitation 2—Deterministic problems

ML is incredibly eminent for sensors and can be used to help calibrate and rectify sensors when connected to other sensors measuring environmental variables such as temperature, pressure and humidity. The correlations between these signals from the sensors can be used to write self-calibration procedures.

Limitation 3—Data

This is the most understandable limitation. If we feed a model poorly, then it will only give only poor output.

Lack of data

Many ML algorithms require a huge amount of data before they process to give useful results. A good example of this is a neural network. Neural networks are data-eating machines that require copious amounts of training datasets. The larger the architecture, the more the datasets are needed to produce viable results. Reuse of data is a bad idea, and data augmentation is useful to some extent, but having more data is always the preferred solution.

Lack of good data

The data that are of not in good quality and lack some of the good features can affect your algorithm to perform poorly, having a lack of good data can also decrease the capabilities of your model.

Limitation 4—Interpretability

Interpretability is one of the basic problems with ML. The user should know for which and why a particular algorithm is used for solving a particular problem. If that cannot be concluded then the model created will lead to bigger failures. A list of constraints that are set for proper designing is as follows:

1. Each narrow application needs to be specially trained.
2. Require a large amount of *hand-crafted, structured* training data.
3. Learning must generally be monitored: training data must be tagged.
4. Require lengthy offline/batch training.
5. Do not learn incrementally or interactively, in real time.
6. Poor learning ability, reusability of modules and integration.
7. Systems are very hard to debug.
8. Performance cannot be audited or guaranteed at the end.
9. They encode correlation, not causation or ontological relationships.
10. Do not encode entities or spatial relationships between entities.
11. Only handle very narrow aspects of natural language.
12. Not well suited for high level, symbolic reasoning or planning.

5.4 Conclusion

ML is a set of methods employed for data analysis using data learning algorithms and statistical models. Database systems use those models in order to achieve a specific task without explicit instructions, patterns and inference. ML algorithms are widely used these days in many fields. One among such field is the healthcare system. According to the problems and needs in the system, various ML techniques are implemented. It is also discussed about significance and implementation difficulties of ML in the healthcare systems, which shows how ML and healthcare systems are closely related. Algorithms are discussed on how they are handled in the healthcare systems for the betterment of the system.

References

[1]   A. Qayyum, J. Qadir, M. Bilal, and AI-Fuqaha, Secure and Robust Machine Learning For Healthcare: A Survey, Arxiv:2001.08103vl [Cs.LG] 21 Jan 2020. Https://Tinyurl.Com/FDA-AI-Diabetic-Eye.

[2]   R.P. Ram Kumar, S. Polepaka, S.F. Lazarus, and D.V. Krishna, An Insight on Machine Learning Algorithms and Its Applications, International Journal of Innovative Technology and Exploring Engineering, ISSN: 2278-3075, 2019, 8, 11S2. DOI: 10.35940/Ijitee.K1069.09811S219.

[3]   Y. Li and H. Wu, A Clustering Method Based on *K*-Means Algorithm, 2012 International Conference on Solid State Devices and Materials Science, Physics Procedia, 2012, 25, 1104–1109, https://www.researchgate.net/publication/271616608_A_Clustering_Method_Based_on_K-Means_Algorithm.

[4]   R. Cioffi, M. Travaglioni, G. Piscitellei, A. Petrilo, and F. De Felice, Artificial Intelligence and Machine Learning Applications in Smart Production: Progress, Trends, and Directions, Sustainability, 2020, 12, 492, DOI: 10.3390/Su12020492.

[5]   N. Kolla and M. Giridhar Kumar, Supervised Learning Algorithms of Machine Learning: Prediction of Brand Loyalty, International Journal Of Innovative Technology And Exploring Engineering, ISSN: 2278-3075, 2019, 8, 11.

[6]   A. Chahal and P. Gulia, Machine Learning and Deep Learning, International Journal of Innovative Technology and Exploring Engineering, ISSN: 2278-3075, 2019, 8, 12. DOI: 10.35940/Ijitee.L3550.1081219.

[7]   C.M. Bishop, Pattern Recognition and Machine Learning. Cambridge, UK: Springer, ISBN 978-0-387-31073-2, 2006.

[8]   E. Alpaydin, Introduction To Machine Learning. Bogazici University, Turkey: MIT Press, p. 9 ISBN 978-0-262-01243-0.

[9]   K. Kalpana, G. Sunil Vijaya Kumar, and K. Madhavi, Feature Selection for Machine Learning in Big Data, International Journal of Innovative Technology And Exploring Engineering, ISSN: 2278-3075, 2019, 8, 6S4. DOI: 10.359/Ijitce.F1067.0486s419.

[10] J. Brownlee, A Tour of the Most Popular Machine Learning Algorithms, 2019. https://Machinelearningmastery.Com/A-Tour-Of-Machine-Learning-Algorithms/.

[11] edX Course Book, Machine Learning Basic Concepts, 2017. https://Courses.Edx.Org/Asset-V1:Columbiax+CSMM.101x+1T2017+Type@Asset+Block@AI_Edx_Ml_5.1intro.Pdf.

[12] https://www.javatpoint.com/machine-learning

[13] https://www.guru99.com/supervised-vs-unsupervised-learning.html

[14]   https://en.wikipedia.org/wiki/Sigmoid_function
[15]   https://data-flair.training/blogs/types-of-machine-learning-algorithms/
[16]   V. Chauhan, S. Dwivedi, P. Karale, and S.M. Potdar, Speech to Text Converter Using Gaussian Mixture Model (GMM), International Research Journal of Engineering and Technology (IRJET), 2016, 3(2).

Chapter 6

Machine learning in blockchain

Kolla Bhanu Prakash[1], Vadla Pradeep Kumar[2] and Venkata Raghavendra Naga Pawan[3]

The promise and potential of blockchain to drive social impact is enormous. Blockchain will touch every significant industry which people interact with in day-to-day life. Blockchain will enable solutions that are not previously possible. Health sector recently attracted more initiatives than any other industry. Applications for blockchain in health include digital health records exchange and pharmaceutical supply chain management. In many of these areas, blockchain offers a more secure, decentralized and efficient solution than would otherwise be possible.

Blockchain and machine learning (ML) technologies are gaining strong momentum and thrust around the world. Blockchain, a disruptive technology, made its big splash with crypto currencies invention and trading. On the other hand, with predictive and descriptive algorithms, ML is making considerable waves in harnessing existing data to identify patterns and gain insights.

Congregating the two technologies can only make them super disruptive! Both have the potential to hasten data exploration and analysis as well as intensify transactions security. Additionally, distributed blockchains can be a significant and proven input for ML, which requires big datasets to make quality predictions.

It goes without saying that each technology has its degree of complexity, but both artificial intelligence (AI) and blockchain are in situations where they can benefit from each other and help one another. Both these technologies are able to effect and enact upon data in different ways as their combination makes sense, which can take the exploitation of data to new levels. At the same time, the integration of ML and AI into the blockchain, and vice versa, can enhance blockchain's underlying architecture and boost AI's potential. Additionally, blockchain can also make AI more coherent and understandable for tracing and decision-making using

[1]Department of Computer Science and Engineering, Koneru Lakshmaiah Education Foundation, Green Fields, Vaddeswaram, Andhra Pradesh, India
[2]Department of Computer Science and Engineering, BV Raju Institute of Technology, Vishnupur, Narsapur, Medak, Telangana, India
[3]Department of Computer Science and Engineering, Anurag Engineering College, Ananthagiri (V&M), Kodad, Suryapet, Telangana, India

ML techniques. Blockchain and its ledger can record all data and variables that go through a decision made under ML. The present chapter focuses on a few standard ML algorithms that are useful in supporting blockchain technology.

6.1   Introduction

ML has become a prominent research domain area in computer science where prediction is given high priority with the available data and applying efficient algorithms to process on them for good prediction results. It allows a computer to train them with specific domain dataset and perform statistical analysis and predict the output results. ML automates the decision-making based on the data inputs and processes it for further statistical analysis to provide useful insights for the users to take a practical decision.

Image recognition among social platforms is implemented in ML by integrating with other technologies. ML does text pattern matching based on the tweets made in twitter for understanding the psychology of people. ML builds highly recommended systems for selecting particular products. Simulation of the automated driverless car relies on ML to navigate faster than humans.

6.1.1   What is machine learning?

According to Tom Mitchell, the definition of ML is "The field of machine learning is concerned with the question of how to construct computer programs that automatically improve with experience." It highlights the computer program learning by its experience for automatic improvement for a better solution. ML uses computer algorithms for learning how to do a task or make predictions accurately or have some intelligent behavior. The learning is done on the basis of some observations of data, experience or instruction. Thus, the definition of Tom Mitchell matches to the general idea of ML that says about learning for doing better in future based on experience.

ML mostly works on automating the learning methods and device for better learning algorithms that work without human intervention or assistance. The prevalent paradigm is ML "Programming by Example." For example, take a specific task like spam filtering rather than coding the solution on a computer, ML can train the network to analyze the emails' metadata and filter the spam automatically with good specific examples. In general, ML is treated as a subdomain of AI. Building an expert system with an excellent knowledge is not possible without making it learning to become intelligent. Many of smart systems that recognize a language or filter the vision from good video or high-resolution images are only possible by integrating their primary task of recognition with learning, which makes their solution approach effective. Many domains share their features' similarity or applicability with ML, for example, mathematics for formulating the procedures, physics for using its basic principles like gravitation and optimization, statistics for using its basic properties of median, mode, sample size of data for interpretation and theoretical computer science like data mining that uses its exploratory data analysis. Much business solution treats the ML as predictive analytics for predicting their sales and purchases.

6.1.2   Importance of ML in blockchain

Blockchain [1] was popularized mostly in the financial industry with the usage of bitcoin. In recent years, it is merging into many sectors like the health-care industry, supply chain management, drug manufacturing and many other popular areas. The latest technology with which blockchain right now merging is ML; before knowing their integration let us have their concerns in need of others. Blockchain is mostly used for safeguarding the financial transactions/data by maintaining a decentralized digital ledger that stores all data in a highly secure manner whereas ML is known for its automation of solving problems by using statistical computing models or algorithms.

ML is popular for analyzing the patterns of a dataset and builds an efficient prediction system that takes decision automatically by processing that vast business data and provides insights for top management by using the excellent interpretation of business data with good visual graphs and interpolations. Recently advanced ML algorithms were applied to predict financial risks in insurance industries. ML runs its algorithms on vast data financial records and retrieves a different hidden pattern that provides insurance organizations to estimate the risks involved in releasing new insurance premiums accurately.

Blockchain builds the secure transactional database with specific timestamps, unalterable and permanent instances of data in a distributed ledger on different servers. Blockchain is predominantly known for using digital signature as a particular mechanism of consensus on entities of financial data. ML depends on vast quantities of data to build accurate models. The accuracy of data can be improved by collecting, organizing and auditing of it, which is the easy possible solution through blockchain.

ML and blockchain will improve each other in the following circumstances or criteria [2]:

Efficient energy consumption: Blockchain needs massive energy for processing vast data of financial transactions. ML has optimized energy algorithms by which it maximizes the power needed at every server, which acts as an intermediate node for processing those financial transaction data. It improves the transactional verification time for blockchain, and ML also directs the fastest way of processing of transactions at nearest nodes or servers and reduces the burden of storage of massive data for processing by blockchain.

Extensive data: ML works on large datasets, but for blockchain, comprehensive data processing is like a curse; it slows down its whole architecture. ML filters those unnecessary data that act as hurdles for processing by blockchain and improve its applications in more full domain areas.

Automated contracts decision-making: Business transactions are more linked with contracts that play a prominent role in improving their share values. Automating contractual decision is a critical task by blockchain. ML provides a wide range of verification learning algorithms that will verify contracts automatically from whichever location they apply without any human intervention. This automation of contractual decision-making improves the performance of blockchain in business share values and increasing value engagements.

Reducing attacks: Over 51 percent of attacks are recorded on an average blockchain node while processing data. ML can train nodes by listing various hacking scenarios that can anticipate affecting them and taking decision faster to identify the attacks and prevent them from hacking the data.

It is clear from the previous discussion that both the technologies have their significance in providing substantial benefits for various functions of the industry. ML helps in assessing, recognizing the quality of data, and blockchain improves the execution and verification of records and transactions. ML is focusing more on the automation of process while making decisions on financial transactions data, while blockchain works on improving the trustworthiness and security of transactional data.

6.1.3   Merits and demerits

ML plays its significance by automating many tasks of blockchain and supporting it in managing its functionality of securing or safeguarding the business transactions [3]. Generally, the operations of blockchain have not been accountable as they need to verify and authenticate the shared transactions data among several nodes or servers. ML makes it responsible by applying its learning algorithms or methodologies, which categorizes the type of deficiency at the node while safeguarding the data, and efficient ML algorithms can easily recover any misplacement or backtracking of those misplaced data.

Merits of ML with blockchain are as follows:

Improving data protection: Blockchain has tremendous support of standards for securing a large amount of data at different nodes and makes data accessible at any instance in encrypted way, and ML improves this data-protection ability of blockchain by adding automated nature of predicting what type of data need to be stored and processed in a chain for making as accessible as appropriate instances.

Reduce in the margin of error: ML algorithms can achieve more accuracy and reduce marginal errors while delivering the estimated output. This ability to reduce error rate enhances the functionality of blockchain in generating their results of transactional data more securely with high accuracy.

Usage of the diverse variety of data: ML works more on unstructured data for predicting the results of a system, whereas blockchain purely works on structured data for chaining the information through the specific data structure. Thus, the integration of ML with blockchain enables it to work on any variety of data and make it meaningful and secure.

Enhance the creativity of technology: ML works on the automation of processing a large number of datasets which makes blockchain free from managing intermediate agents for treating those financial data and risk involved in preparing it at a faster rate.

Demerits of ML with blockchain are as follows:

Heterogeneity of nodes: Most of the blockchain processing intermediate nodes are heterogeneous in terms of system storage and processing ability; thus, applying ML algorithms should differ their nature of processing to get efficient results.

Scalability of data: ML needs a considerable amount of datasets for processing and takes an automated decision where blockchain is rigid with providing that data as it encrypts only for that particular node, and link for data may be on the other node where further accessing of it and making it available for ML at that instance is a big question.

Decentralization of data: ML fails at certain situations for processing secure transactional data of blockchain because of its high decentralized nature of storing data and linking them for further processing.

6.2   Types of ML

6.2.1   Supervised learning

Supervised learning algorithms build a model using training dataset consisting of both input and output, a building model for the prediction. Its performance can compute with the help of test dataset. These algorithms are task driven.

The algorithms under the category are linear regression (LR), logistic regression (LogR), k-nearest neighbor (k-NN), naïve Bayes classification, decision tree (DT), support-vector machines (SVM), neural networks (NNs), etc.

6.2.2   Unsupervised learning

Unsupervised learning algorithms use dataset that includes inputs and find relative meaning in the data and collecting them as grouping or clustering data points. Unsupervised learning algorithms explore the structure of the information, extracting valuable patterns. These algorithms are data driven.

Unsupervised learning algorithms include K-means algorithm, principal component analysis, association rule, etc.

6.2.3   Reinforcement learning

Reinforcement learning is about creating a self-sustaining mechanism that develops itself based on a mixture of labeled data and incoming data that encounters within the contiguous sequences of attempts and failures.

Q-Learning algorithms, temporal difference algorithms, Monte Carlo tree search methods and asynchronous actor-critic agents are the reinforcement algorithms.

A reinforcement learning calculation, or operator, learns by collaborating with its condition. The operator gets prizes by performing effectively and punishments for performing inaccurately. The specialist takes in without mediation from a human by expanding its prize and limiting its punishment. It is a kind of unique programming that trains calculations utilizing an arrangement of remuneration and discipline.

6.3 Different ML algorithms

6.3.1 Linear regression

The relationship among the variables will use the LR model [4,5]. In this model, the value of one variable is used for computing the value of another variable. The first variable is an independent one, whereas the latter one is a dependent one. LR is used to understand the strength of the association between the dependent and independent variables, forecasting an outcome or the trend. The simplest form of an LR model in (6.1) is consisting of one dependent and another independent variable.

$$y = \alpha + \beta x + \varepsilon \tag{6.1}$$

where y is a dependent variable, x is the independent variable, α is the regression constant, β is the regression coefficient and ε is the error. The independent variable, x, also called an explanatory variable, is always a continuous variable. The dependent variable, y, is either a particular or continuous type. There could be more than one independent variable. If there is only one independent variable, such regression is considered univariate regression or simple LR, otherwise called multivariate regression.

The most popular approach for fitting a regression is the least-squares regression. In this method, the best line of the fitting is determined by the sum of the squares of the vertical deviations from each data point to the line (if precisely a point is on the matched line, then its vertical deviation is 0). There are no cancelations from positive and negative values as the differences are first squared then rounded up. For computing best fit rows, one can use ordinary least squares or partial least squares:

$$\beta = \frac{\Sigma(x - x_{\text{mean}}) \times (y - y_{\text{mean}})}{\Sigma(x - x_{\text{mean}})^2} \tag{6.2}$$

$$\alpha = y_{\text{mean}} - \beta \times x_{\text{mean}} \tag{6.3}$$

A simple LR model uses diabetes dataset [6], considering the attributes of body mass index (BMI) as predictor and outcome. Using the model, the possibility of diabetes, i.e., outcome is predicted on the basis of BMI. The model is as follows:

$$\text{Outcome} = -0.2175 + (0.01771)\text{BMI} \tag{6.4}$$

The model performance with the metric coefficient of determination is also called R square. Equation (6.5) shows the R square.

$$R \text{ square} = \left\{ \left(\frac{1}{N}\right) \times \frac{\Sigma[(x - x_{\text{mean}}) \times (y - y_{\text{mean}})]}{(\sigma_x \times \sigma_y)} \right\}^2 \tag{6.5}$$

where σ_x is the standard deviation of x, whereas σ_y is the standard deviation of y.

R square gives what proportion of the y vector prediction error removes when using the x variable with the least-squares regression. The R square for (6.4) is

0.08567. *F*-Statistic is a good indicator of whether there is an association between independent and dependent variables. *F*-Statistic is a strong measure of whether the predictor and the response variables are related. It is the division of the model mean square and the residual mean square. The *F*-statistic of the model given in (6.4) is 71.77.

The multivariable regression [5,7] is shown using (6.6), where there are single dependent and multiple independent variables:

$$y = \alpha + \beta_1 x_1 + \beta_2 x_2 + \beta_3 x_3 + \beta_4 x_4 + \cdots + \beta_n x_n + \varepsilon \qquad (6.6)$$

The example shows the following estimates occurrence of diabetes using dataset diabetes [8]. The model is as follows:

Outcome $= -0.8539 + 0.0206 \times$ pregnancies $+ 0.0059 \times$ glucose $+ (-0.0023)$ $\times$blood pressure $+ 0.0002 \times$ skin thickness $+ (-0.0002) \times$ insulin $+ 0.0132$ $\times$BMI $+ 0.1472 \times$ diabetes pedigree function $+ 0.00268$ age

$$(6.7)$$

In multiple regression, adjusted-*R*-square is considered due to the deficiency in the *R*-squared statistic. The value is 0.2959. Adjusted *R*-squared monitors the change and applies penalties for the model number of predictors. The model is over fitting if there is a significant difference between multiple *R*-square and adjusted *R*-square. Similarly, *F*-statistic is 41.29. The LR model for (6.7) is depicted in Figure 6.1.

6.3.2 *Logistic regression*

It is a model of the parametric classification. By fact, the consequence or goal attribute is dichotomous. There are only two potential types of dichotomous words. It is a special form of LR in which the focus variable is of a certain type. As a dependent variable, it uses a log of changes. LogR estimates the probability of a conditional occurrence with a logit function, a sigmoid function, being present. The

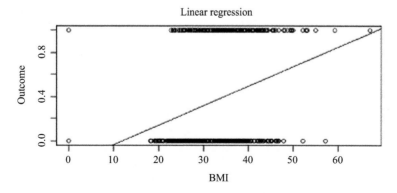

Figure 6.1   Linear regression model

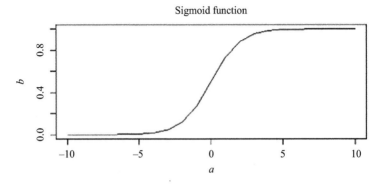

Figure 6.2   Sigmoid function for the interval −10 to +10

sigmoid function gives an *S*-form curve in the LogR. The plot for the −10 to +10 sigmoid function, also called the logit function, is seen in Figure 6.2. The logit function *s* is given in (6.9), where *y* lies between −∞ and +∞. At the squashing point, the sigmoid function goes from 0 to 1. From Figure 6.2, we have $\sigma(0) = 0.5$. If *p* is the probability of observations with a result of 1, then 1−*p* is the probability of observations with a result of 0. The odds give (6.8). The logit is the logarithm of odds shown in (6.8), and the LogR is shown in (6.9):

$$1 = \text{logit}(p) = \ln\left(\frac{p}{(1-p)}\right) \tag{6.8}$$

$$\ln\left(\frac{p}{(1-p)}\right) = \alpha + \beta x + \varepsilon \tag{6.9}$$

Using diabetes dataset [6], the LogR for the attributes BMI and outcome gives the following equation:

$$P = \frac{\exp(-3.68641 + 0.09353 \times \text{BMI})}{[1 + \exp(-3.68641 + 0.09353 \times \text{BMI})]} \tag{6.10}$$

Using (6.10), the occurrence of diabetes knows the BMI of an individual.

Properties of LogR are that Bernoulli distribution fits the dependent variable in LogR, a calculation through full likelihood and no *R* square, and system fitness is determined by concordance, *K–S* statistics.

Types of LogR:

Binary LogR: The target variable has only two possible outcomes, such as spam or not spam, cancer or no cancer.

Multinomial LogR: The target variable has more than two nominal categories, such as predicting the type of cancer.

Ordinal LogR: The target variable has more than two ordinal categories such as restaurant or product rating on a five-point scale.

1. D is dataset.
2. Find the best feature or attribute from D.
3. Split the D which contains the values of best attribute identified at step 2.
4. Make the best attribute as DT node.
5. Recursively build new decision trees using the data subset generated by step 3 to achieve point where the data cannot be further classified.
6. Class represented at the leaf node.

Figure 6.3   Decision tree algorithm

Table 6.1   Popular decision tree algorithms

CART [10]	C4.5 [11]	Random forest [12]
Recursive partition technique to create nodes	Uses information gain for selecting nodes of DT with the help of training set	Uses several separate decision trees, generated by arbitrarily chosen variables The individual trees built on an algorithm

6.3.3   Decision tree and SVM

In ML, DT is a popular algorithm for classification. A DT is a tree where each node represents a characteristic (attribute), each path (branch) renders a decision (rule), and each leaf represents an outcome (categorical or continuous value). These algorithms are supervised learning algorithms. The goal of a DT is to construct a model, which is used for the prediction of a class or a value of the target variable. The target values of the DT categorize the DT into two types: first DT based on categorical variable and the second one based on a continuous variable. The algorithm for DT is shown in Figure 6.3 (Table 6.1).

The best attribute computes entropy. DT is prone to overfitting. DT overfitting avoids DT pruning or cross-validation, using a diabetic dataset [6].

A support-vector machine (SVM) [9] supervise learning models with related learning algorithms processing classification and regression results through SVM, hyperplanes in infinite-dimensional space built to define and regress the product of linear function and squash value at [0, 1] interval in LogR. When the squash value is higher than the threshold value 0.5, the classification label is considered as 1 otherwise 0. In SVM, if the output is greater than 1, then one class label is found, and if the value is less than -1, then another class label is considered.

$$W^T x + b = 0 \tag{6.11}$$

where W is the weight vector, x is the input vector and b is the bias:

$$W^T x + b = 0 \tag{6.12}$$

A dataset containing m data points is considered, denoted as x_i each with a label y_i, which is either $+1$ or -1:

$$\text{If } W^T x + b \geq +1 \text{ then } y_i = +1$$
$$\text{If } W^T x + b \leq -1 \text{ then } y_i = -1 \tag{6.13}$$

When data are linearly separated, SVM designs are called linear SVMs, if the information is nonlinearly separated, such SVMs are called nonlinear SVMs.

The advantages of SVM are high dimensionality, memory efficiency and versatility, whereas the disadvantages are Kernel parameter selection and no direct probabilistic interpretation for group membership.

6.3.4   Naïve Bayes

In the area of ML, the naïve Bayes algorithm [9] executes classification tasks. It can classify the dataset very well even though it has big databases of issues of multiple classes and binary classifications. Naïve Bayes' primary application is text interpretation and manipulation of the natural language.

The Bayes theorem will integrate the different classification algorithms to construct a common concept in the naïve Bayes classification. The theorem functions according to the probability of the situation. Conditional probability means an event that has already happened with predetermined (based on) would occur:

$$P(A|B) = \frac{P(B|A)P(A)}{P(B)} \tag{6.14}$$

where $P(A)$ and $P(B)$ are the probabilities of observing A and B events, $P(A|B)$ is a conditional probability of an event A with conditioned event B, $P(B|A)$ is a conditional probability of an event B with conditioned event A. If an event B wants to occur, it should be dependent on an event A occurred already.

Naïve Bayes classifier considers the following:

- All dataset attributes contribute separately to the classification of the new data, although characteristics have some dependency.
- Each attribute of the dataset relates similarly to determining the classification of the new data type.
- Posterior probability has to calculate for all the qualities independently.
- Highest qualities of posterior likelihood are taken as a possible attribute and called maximum posterior.

$$MP(A) = \text{Maximum}\left(\frac{P(B|A)P(A)}{P(B)}\right) \tag{6.15}$$

The pros of naïve Bayesian classifiers are useful for continuous attributes; the model building is more accessible, faster for small- and medium-sized datasets. The cons are that it is not applicable for regression-based problems, and high independence in characteristics is not possible in real-time scenarios.

6.3.5   k-*Nearest neighbor*

The *k*-NN [9] algorithm is a simple, easy-to-implement supervised ML algorithm. It solves both the classification and regression problems. *k*-NN takes dataset *D* in parts as training and test dataset. *k*-Neighbors are chosen as a positive integer. For each data item of *n* dimensions in the test dataset, the distance between test data and each data item of training data is determined. Later, the distances are sorted in an ascending order. From the ordered data items, *k* data items are selected. Based on the voting, a class label is assigned to test data item. Functions such as Euclidean distance, Manhattan distance, Minkowski distance and Hamming distance are among the standard distance functions. The Euclidean distance function is used for continuous and categorical variables that are also associated with the Hamming distance function.

k-NN is simple to understand and implementable algorithm for nonlinear datasets with relatively high accuracy. *k*-NN suffers from expensive computation and requires high memory, and also prediction is relatively slower.

6.3.6   K-*Means*

K-Means [13] is an unsupervised clustering algorithm. It is an iterative algorithm. It partitions the dataset into *k* nonoverlapping clusters, from the dataset, *D*, with *n* data items. *K* data items, called centroids, are randomly selected from the *n* data items. The remaining data items, *n–k*, assign to *k* centroids based on least distance, i.e., nearest centroid. After an assignment, centroids are updated with mean of all assigned non-centroid data items. The process of appointment of data items to nearest centroids and computation of new centroid mean is continued until no change in the centroids.

6.3.7   *Gradient boosting algorithms—GBM, XGBoost, LightGBM, CatBoost*

In ML, various ensemble prediction models are generated for classification and regression; such models are called weak prediction models (WPMs). The WPMs are deficient of a high level of accuracy. The researchers prefer to use either feature engineering or boosting algorithms to improve the performance of the WPM. Boosting algorithms are preferred over feature engineering. The popular boosting algorithms are gradient boosting machines (GBMs) [14], XGBoost [15,16], LightGBM [16] and CatBoost [16–20] (Table 6.2).

6.4   Significance of ML in the health-care industry

The data-driven decision-making is an essential criterion of ML [21] which helps it in setting new trends and improving efficiency in research. The health-care industry uses these ML techniques for accurate diseases prediction, correct disease diagnosis and effective treatment of disease to enhance the functionality and operations of the health-care industry. The health-care industry generates vast amounts of data like

Table 6.2   Features of gradient boost algorithms

Features	GBM	XGBoost	LightGBM	CatBoost
Categorical variables processing	Handles categorical values	Cannot handle categorical values	Handles categorical values	Encoded as one-hot encoding using one_hot_max_size
Splitting criterion	Relative influence	Presorted algorithm and histogram-based algorithm	Gradient-based one-side sampling (GOSS) to filter out the data instances for finding a split value	Least-square criterion
Tree growth	Best first binary tree	Level-wise growth	Leaf-wise growth	Level-wise growth
Fastness		XGBoost is not fast as LightGBM	It is faster than LightGBM	It is slower than LightGBM
Parallel learning	Supports parallel tree building	Supports parallel tree building	Supports parallel tree building	–
Over fitting	Possible	Possible	Possible	Possible

patient's prescriptions, patient's diagnosis data and insurance information. ML algorithms effectively use these data in predicting the diseases, identifying trends in the usage of medicine, innovation in developing a new drug and performing active research in clinical trials.

6.4.1   Identifying diseases and diagnosis

ML uses sophisticated objective and automatic algorithms for analyzing multi-modal and high-dimensional biomedical data in improving the detection and diagnosis of diseases. Most of ML algorithms used for analyzing critical issues related to conditions work on maximizing its performance by considering realistic constraints and incorporate prior knowledge and uncertainty. Most of the clinical utilities are using ML tools for interpreting a large number of datasets before diagnosing the disease.

ML does manage two important roles while diagnosing diseases: (1) extracts data with specific salient features from existing raw data and (2) infers the data from using particular rules for classification of data. It uses supervised and unsupervised learning approaches for detecting the diseases. The popular method that applies for diagnosis was linear mixing of data for complete factorization, which includes principal component analysis and singular value decomposition. To improve the error correction rate in principle component analysis, the nonnegative matrix factorization algorithm uses to generate more optimal results while diagnosing the disease.

Most ML algorithms are acting as specific biomarkers for assisting clinical units in diagnosing disease [22]. One of the critical conditions is brain cancer that purely depends on magnetic resonance spectroscopy imaging scans that use metabolic markers for predicting cancer tumors using popular ML algorithm called support-vector machine for better classification. Prediction and diagnosis of heart disease have natural usage of ML algorithms. Much amount of datasets related to heart diseases are available at the University of California Irvine Machine Learning data Repository for training the algorithms, and the two popular ML algorithms called support-vector machine. Naïve Bayes proves to be efficient predictors and automates prediction system of heart disease.

Diabetes is one of the healthy and risky illnesses. Likewise, this sickness is one of the primary sources to make some other extreme disease toward death. This ailment can harm our different body parts like kidney, heart and nerves. The goal of utilizing an AI approach in this field is to identify diabetes at the beginning time and spare patients. As a characterization calculation, irregular timberland, k-NN, choice tree or innocent Bayes can utilize to build up the diabetes forecast framework. Among these, credulous Bayes outflanks different calculations regarding precision. The liver is the second most critical inside organ in our body. It assumes fundamental job indigestion.

One can assault a few liver infections like cirrhosis, incessant hepatitis and liver disease. As of late, AI and information mining will significantly identify liver infection. It is particularly provoking undertaking to foresee illness using full restorative information. Be that as it may, scientists are attempting their best to beat such issues utilizing AI ideas like order, grouping and some more. Indian Liver Patient Dataset is used for a liver infection expectation framework. This dataset contains ten factors.

On the other hand, liver issue dataset can likewise be utilized. As a classifier, Bolster vector machine can be utilized. At present, AI approaches are being utilized to distinguish and characterize tumors widely.

Additionally, profound learning assumes a critical job in malignant growth recognition. An examination indicated that in-depth knowledge lessens the level of blunder for bosom fatal growth determination. AI has demonstrated its abilities to distinguish malignant growth effectively. China analysts investigated Profound Quality: a malignancy-type classifier utilizing profound learning and physical point changes. Utilizing a profound learning approach, cancerous growth can likewise be distinguished by removing highlights from quality articulation information. Also, the convolution neural network system is applied in the malignant growth arrangement.

6.4.2   Drug discovery and manufacturing

ML algorithms have discovered their way into the field of disclosure of drugs, particularly in the starting structure, directly from the first screening of the mixes of a drug to its measured rate of achievement based on natural elements, which is primarily based on cutting edge sequencing [23]. AI is used by pharmaceutical companies in the identification and assembly phase of drugs. But this is currently limited to the use of unaided ML which can discern designs in rough details. The focus here is to establish drug accuracy fueled by unaided discovery, which enables doctors to identify components for "multifactorial" diseases. One of the key participants in the game is the MIT Clinical AI Gathering. The precision drug work [24] means that these estimates can help us explain the types of ailment and even map out suitable treatment for medical conditions such as sort 2 diabetes.

In addition to developments in research and technology, including cutting-edge sequencing and precision medications, it is often used to figure out the possible approaches to treat multifactorial diseases. Microsoft's Venture Hanover leverages ML-based technologies to build drug precision. In reality, even Google has entered the flickering wave of drug discoveries. According to the UK Illustrious Society, AI will be of enormous support in the advancement of pharmaceutical bio-production. Pharmaceutical suppliers should address the details from manufacturing processes to reduce the average time taken to produce products, while also reducing production costs. Discovery and production of drugs are very expensive and time-consuming. According to the Tufts Centre for the Research of Drug Production, a new product production usually takes more than 10 years to reach a market and costs around $2.6 billion. A drug development program seeks to identify a compound that interacts with the body's desired molecules, triggering remedy for a disease. But there is a substantial risk that the principal or beneficial drug compound could adversely react to nontargeted molecules in the body, which may cause damaging and harmful side effects.

Since pharmaceutical companies, using modern statistical developments, cannot predict the effect of a future product compound on focused and non-centered atoms, the risks of drug failure in clinical preliminaries are more significant. This condition makes the declaration of pharmaceutical goods expensive and tedious. Better prescient approaches using AI for this situation will save a lot of money. Approximately 90 percent of pharmaceutical items cannot survive the preliminary process. By mechanizing the reaction types of compound particles using AI, pharmaceuticals will boost the exposure and development of therapeutic goods and the reduction of a to-showcase incentive. As suggested by a Carnegie Mellon study, the mechanization of the drug disclosure process will minimize costs by about 70 percent.

Guaranteeing drug well-being is one of the fundamental difficulties in the medication disclosure process. Deciphering data of the known impacts of medications and foreseeing their symptoms are intricate errands. Researchers and specialists from examine organizations and pharmaceutical organizations like Roche and Pfizer have been attempting to utilize AI to get essential data from clinical information obtained from clinical preliminaries. Understanding this information with regards to sedate well-being is a functioning territory of research.

6.4.3   *Medical imaging diagnosis*

As of late, specialists have been attempting to coordinate ML and human-made brainpower in radiology. Aidoc gives programming to the radiologist to accelerate the procedure of recognition utilizing AI approaches. Their task is to investigate the therapeutic picture to offer a coherent answer for distinguishing anomalies over the body. The supervised ML is used generally in this field for therapeutic picture division where ML method is utilized. The division is the way toward distinguishing structures in a picture. For the picture division, the diagram-cut division technique is used generally. Natural Language Preparing is utilized for examination for radiology content reports. Consequently, applying AI in radiology can improve the administration of patient consideration.

For example, with the aid of ML techniques, profound research, it is currently conceivable to discover minute deformations in the patients' inside inspected pictures, and hence specialists may recommend a suitable study. Besides, techniques such as x-beam and CT scan were adequate to determine small anomalies, but there was a need to examine them properly for the increasing ailments.

For instance—ML and deep learning are both responsible for the technological progress known as PC Vision—this invention is used in the InnerEye initiative of Microsoft, which aims to create photo investigative tools. InnerEye is a research initiative that uses ML creativity to develop innovative methods for the coded, quantitative analysis of 3D radiological images. This challenge used ML to distinguish these pictures from tumors and sound life structures. They assisted with helping specialists in the field of radiotherapy and careful arranging.

6.4.4 Personalized medicine

ML for customized treatment is a hot research issue. The objective of this zone is to give better help dependent on singular well-being information with prescient examination [25]. AI computational and measurable devices are utilized to build up a customized treatment framework dependent on patients' indications and genetic information. To build up the customized treatment framework, a managed AI calculation is used. This framework is created by utilizing patient restorative data. SkinVision application is the case of customized treatment. By utilizing this application, one can check his/her skin for skin disease on his/her telephone. The customized treatment framework can decrease the expense of medicinal services.

With the blast of patient information as hereditary data and electronic well-being records, specialists can give customized treatment to singular patients as indicated by their exact needs. Their point is to pick up bits of knowledge from enormous measures of datasets and use it to make patients sound at the singular level. These bits of knowledge can recommend customized mixes and anticipate infection chance with the assistance of ML innovations.

For instance, Watson human services is one of IBM Watson's ventures that incorporate the use of AI. This is making ground-breaking assets for improving the strength of the patient. Watson human services diminished the hour of specialists that was spent on settling on treatment choices by giving them individualized treatment choices dependent on the examination of ongoing exploration, clinical practices and preliminaries. The AI-based task would now be able to offer treatment for malignant blood growth and to a lot of other diseases. Such prestigious destructive growth ability gives each patient access to the ideal choice treatment.

6.4.5   Machine-learning-based behavioral modification

Behavioral improvement [26] is a vital aspect of preventive medicine. ML advances aim to push an indent up and perform change and further affect successful patient behavioral fortifications. Somatix, for example, is an intelligence research agency focused on B2B2C that has pioneered an ML-driven technology that lately searches and perceives a range of physical and enthusiastic environments. Doctors enable one to comprehend what sort of familiar and way of life changes required for a solid body and psyche.

Human services of new companies and associations have likewise begun to apply ML applications to cultivate social alterations. Somatix, a programming stage of the knowledge analysis B2B2C, is a good example. Its ML technology uses "recognition of hand-to-mouth signs" to help people recognize and assess their actions, thereby allowing them to be open to decisions that are invigorating.

6.4.6   Smart health records

Electronic well-being records comprise whole medicinal and well-being information in a single framework to guarantee information accessibility and accessibility. ML-based electronic health record (EHR) model exchange approach applies prescient models across various EHR frameworks. Such models can be prepared to utilize datasets from one EHR and can be used to foresee a result for another context. These frameworks have heterogeneous information sources, with information that come in numerous structures—organized and unstructured, for example, pictures, content and therapeutic imaging, which is just the beginning. Putting away this information is not a worry, yet it is difficult to send this information for investigation and expectations because of conflicting arrangements. AI advancements, for example, picture preparing, optical character acknowledgement and normal language handling, can assist with changing over this information into the uniform configuration from different sources and numerous frameworks. This methodology empowers one to execute the ML show and anticipate the potential yields.

ML degree, for example, archive characterization and optical character acknowledgment can be utilized to build up a keen electronic well-being record framework. The undertaking of this application is to build up a framework that can sort quiet questions employing email or change a manual record framework into a robotized framework. This goal of this application is to assemble a safe and effectively available system. The fast development of electronic well-being records has enhanced the store of therapeutic information about patients, which is utilized for improving medicinal services. It lessens information blunders, for instance, copy data. To build up the electronic well-being recorder framework, regulated ML calculation like SVM is utilized as a classifier, or artificial NN can likewise be applied.

Although creativity has accelerated the knowledge transfer process, there are quite a few procedures that take up a substantial amount of time. Holding up current accounts of health every day is almost dull. Keeping health records in the wake of beginning these significant works is another area where AI has entered to spare time, exertion and resources. Google's Cloud Vision programming interface and the penmanship identification concept built on MATLAB®'s AI are used for database design techniques.

For example, Ciox, a European association for excellence in well-being, uses AI innovations to improve the management of data on well-being and data transfer on well-being. The aim is to promote access to health records, modernize the organization's work cycle and increase the quality of data on wellness. Ciox well-being has developed precise maps that are used to identify and extract details about well-being from various restorative documents and sum up the medical history of an individual.

Refreshing and maintaining track of medical care and the history of patient treatment regularly is a comprehensive and lengthy process. ML advances solve this problem by raising the amount of time, energy and cash contribution to the record-keeping process. Document structure approaches using VMs and optical character recognition (OCR) classification programs based on ML, such as the Google Cloud Vision programming interface, help one to organize and group knowledge about medicinal services. There are also keen well-being reports at this stage which help system experts, social security providers and patients enhance investigation, treatment delivery and general well-being.

6.4.7   Clinical trial and research

The clinical preliminary [8] might be a lot of questions that expect answers to acquire the proficiency and security of an individual biomedical or pharmaceutical. The reason for this preliminary is to concentrate on the new advancement of treatments. This clinical initial costs a ton of cash and time. Applying AI in this field has a critical effect. An ML-based framework can give continuous observing and hearty assistance.

The benefit of applying AI technique in early clinical and analysis is that it can be very well tested. Additionally, AI offers patients good health status. The use of controlled AI in social insurance will enhance the clinical trial's proficiency. Requirements for ML present an enormous degree for developing essential clinical study. Through extending quick prescient inquiry to preliminary medicinal applications, therapeutic specialists may examine an incredibly comprehensive collection of details, which would naturally minimize the costs and time needed to perform restorative analyses. McKinsey believes that several ML technologies would further boost preliminary therapeutic effectiveness, for example, by helping one to identify the optimal sample sizes for improved viability and by using EHRs to minimize chances of knowledge blunders.

Clinical preliminaries and research include a great deal of time, exertion and cash. Now and then the procedure can extend for a considerable length of time.

ML-based prescient examination that helps one to cut down the time and cash interest in clinical preliminaries however would likewise convey precise outcomes. Besides, ML advancements can be utilized to distinguish potential clinical preliminary competitors, to get their therapeutic history records, screen the applicants all through the preliminary procedure, select best testing tests, decrease information-based blunders and much more. ML apparatuses can likewise encourage remote observing by getting ongoing restorative information of patients. By nourishing the well-being experiences of patients in the cloud, ML applications will help health care clinical preliminaries (HCPs) to predict any possible dangers that may threaten the patients' energy.

6.4.8   Crowd-sourced data collection, better radiotherapy and outbreak prediction

Today, the human services area is incredibly put resources into publicly supporting medicinal information from numerous sources (versatile applications, social insurance stages and so on), obviously, with the assent of individuals. Taking into account this pool of live well-being knowledge, experts and medicine service providers will provide patients with swift and effective care (no time wasted on structured desk work). IBM has late partnered with Medtronic to gather and decode diabetes and insulin information slowly based on widely funded information. On the other hand, Apple's ResearchKit grants customers access to smart applications which use ML-based facial recognition to cure Asperger's and Parkinson's disease.

In the field of radiology, ML has ended up being monstrously useful. There are a large number of discrete variables in the restorative image inquiry that can get triggered at any abnormal minute. Calculations based on an ML are helpful here. Since ML calculations benefit from the many specific tests of knowledge, the ideal factors can be evaluated and separated all the more probable. For example, in restorative image inquiries, ML is used to classify items such as sores into various classifications—regular, rare, sore or non-sore, considerate, negative, etc. UCLH scientists use DeepMind Wellbeing from Google to develop these equations that can understand the difference between solid and carcinogenic cells, thus improving radiation therapy for harmful cells. In the area of radiology, artificial learning has proven to be incredibly beneficial. There are a plethora of discrete variables in medical image processing that can be caused at any arbitrary moment. Here, ML-based algorithms help out. Since ML algorithms learn from the many different samples of results, they can help one to classify and recognize the variables they like. In medical image processing, for example, ML is used to distinguish artifacts such as lesions into various categories—normal, pathological, lesion or non-lesion, benign, malignant, etc. UCLH researchers use DeepMind Health from Google to create algorithms that can identify the difference between healthy and cancer cells and thereby improve the radiation treatment of cancer cells.

Social insurance associations are applying ML and computer-based intelligence calculations to screen and anticipate the conceivable pestilence episodes that can take over different pieces of the world. By gathering information from

satellites, continuous reports via web-based networking media and other fundamental data from the web, these advanced instruments can anticipate scourge flare-
ups. This can be an aid particularly for underdeveloped nations that need adequate
services for social insurance. Although there are just a few instances making the
use of AI today, we may later expect dramatically enhanced and lead ML implementations in public resources [27]. Because ML is still evolving, we are in search
for some increasing astonishment that can transform human lives, deter illness and
help one to boost social security benefits by leaps and bounds. For example, bolster
vector machines and fake neural systems have predicted the jungle fever flare-up
by contemplating factors such as temperature, regular month-to-month weather and
so on. ProMED-mail, an online program, enables well-being associations to screen
illnesses and foresee infection episodes continuously. Utilizing robotized grouping
and perception, HealthMap effectively depends on ProMED to track and caution
nations about the conceivable scourge episodes.

6.5   Implementation difficulties of using ML in healthcare

The capability of ML in medicinal services is flooding, and its potential outcomes
are well past that of simply helping specialists in giving basic judgments [28]. As
per an Accenture report, development in the ML social insurance showcase is relied
upon to reach $6.6 billion by 2021, a compound yearly development pace of 40
percent. In any case, the appropriation of ML in social insurance is still in early
days, because of various difficulties blocking its force.

Privacy

Privacy, while significant in each industry, is normally authorized particularly
energetically with regards to therapeutic information. Since quiet information in
European nations is regularly not permitted to leave Europe, numerous emergency
clinics and research establishments are careful about cloud stages and like to utilize
their own servers.

For new businesses, it is difficult to gain admittance to understanding information to create items or business cases. For the most part, this is simpler for
therapeutic specialists, who can utilize standard application methodology intended
to encourage explore dependent on persistent clinical information.

Regulation

Computer-based intelligence calculations intended to be utilized in social
insurance (in Europe) must apply for CE checking. All the more explicitly, they
should be characterized by the Medical Device Directive, as clarified by Hugh
Harvey. Independents (calculations that are not incorporated into a physical therapeutic gadget) are regularly named Class II medicinal gadgets.

The General Data Protection Regulation (GDPR) orders presented in May
2018 will likewise prompt various new guidelines that should be followed and that
are, sometimes, not obvious. For instance, some level of straightforwardness in
computerized basic leadership (see beneath) will be required, yet it is difficult to

tell from the orders what level of straightforwardness will be sufficient, so we will presumably need to anticipate the main legal disputes to realize where the outskirt lies. Different issues are probably going to result from the prerequisite for educated assent. For instance, will it despite everything be conceivable to perform examine on dementia under the new guidelines, and considering a portion of the taking an interest people, it will be unable to give educated assent.

Transparency

Regardless of potential challenges in setting up parameters, straightforwardness of choice help is, obviously, foremost to restorative ML. A specialist should have the option to comprehend and clarify why a specific strategy was suggested by a calculation. This requires the improvement of progressively instinctive and straightforward expectation clarification apparatuses. There is frequently an exchange between prescient precision and model straightforwardness, particularly with the most recent age of ML strategies that utilize neural systems, which makes this issue considerably more squeezing. A fascinating perspective on straightforwardness and algorithmic basic leadership is given in a paper named *Counterfactual Explanations without Opening the Black Box: Automated Decisions and the GDPR*, which was co-composed by a legal counselor, a PC researcher and an ethicist.

Socio cultural

Specialists settle on choices dependent on learned information, past experience and instinct and critical thinking aptitudes. Getting specialists to consider proposals from a computerized framework can be troublesome. Almost certainly, a few components of ML education should be brought into therapeutic educational plans with the goal that ML is not seen as a risk to specialists, yet as a guide and enhancer of medicinal information. Truth be told, if ML is presented such that engages human specialists as opposed to dislodging them, it could save their opportunity to perform progressively significant errands or award more assets to utilize more laborers.

Engineering/technical debt

The most recent methods in AI utilizing profound neural systems have arrived at astounding execution in the last 5–7 years. Be that as it may, the tooling and foundation expected to help these strategies are as yet juvenile, and not many individuals have the vital specialized capability to manage the entire scope of information and programming designing issues. Particularly in medication, AI arrangements will regularly confront issues identified with restricted information and variable information quality. Prescient models should be re-prepared when new information comes in, watching out for changes in information age rehearses and other true issues that may make the information disseminations float after some time. In the event that few information sources are utilized to prepare models, extra sorts of "information conditions," which are only here and there archived or expressly dealt with, are presented.

In medicinal applications, move learning—utilizing a pre-prepared model and adjusting it to one's particular use case—is regularly applied, yet then a "model reliance" is presented where the hidden model should be retrained or changes its design after some time. The huge measure of "stick code" is ordinarily expected to hold an ML arrangement, together with potential model and information conditions, makes it extremely hard to perform mix tests in general framework and ensure that the arrangement is working appropriately at some random time.

An operational ML stage, for example, the one we are working at Peltarion, taking care of the whole displaying procedure, including programming conditions, information and examination, forming just as organization, can possibly explain a considerable lot of these designing and specialized obligation issues.

There is a great deal of guarantee for ML in human services; however, endeavors and advances in numerous regions should be made before AI arrangements can be conveyed in a sheltered and moral manner. Guideline, security and sociocultural angles should be tended to by society all in all; however AI programming instruments, for example, the Peltarion stage can help one to moderate a portion of the provokes identified with building and specialized obligation issues. With an operational AI stage, an AI engineer can abstain from stressing over programming library conditions, irregularities in input information handling steps and the coincidental presentation of bugs into generation code.

6.6   Applications and future scope of research

ML in medication has as of late stood out as truly newsworthy. Google has built up an ML calculation to help one to recognize harmful tumors on mammograms [29]. Stanford is utilizing a profound learning calculation to recognize skin malignant growth. An ongoing JAMA article detailed the aftereffects of a profound ML calculation that had the option to analyze diabetic retinopathy in retinal pictures. Obviously, ML places another bolt in the bunch of clinical basic leadership.

All things considered, ML suits in a few equivalent procedures to many. Calculations will provide the disciplines with reproducible or institutionalized types with a swift advantage. In comparison, those with vast image collections, such as radiology, cardiology and pathology, are solid up-and-comers. ML may be equipped to see images, discern anomalies and point to regions that need to be examined, thereby increasing the precision of each of those procedures. Long walk, ML at bedside should support the professional or internist unit. ML should deliver a target evaluation to improve performance, unwavering consistency and accuracy.

Example of sample applications of ML in healthcare can be as follows:

- *Reduce readmissions*. ML can decrease readmissions in a focused on, productive and understanding focused way. Clinicians can get day-by-day direction with respect to which patients are well on the way to be readmitted and how they may have the option to decrease that hazard.
- *Prevent hospital acquired infections (HAIs)*. Well-being frameworks can decrease HAIs, for example, central line-associated bloodstream infection (CLASBI)—40 percent of CLABSI patients bite the dust—by anticipating which patients with a focal line will build up a CLABSI. Clinicians can screen

high-hazard patients and intercede to lessen that hazard by concentrating on tolerant explicit hazard factors.

- *Reduce hospital length-of-stay (LOS)*. Well-being frameworks can diminish LOS and improve different results like patient fulfillment by recognizing patients who are probably going to have an expanded LOS and afterward guarantee that accepted procedures are followed.
- *Predict chronic disease*. ML can help clinic frameworks distinguish patients with undiscovered or misdiagnosed constant illness, anticipate the probability that patients will create ceaseless malady and present patient-explicit counteraction mediations.
- *Reduce 1-year mortality*. Well-being frameworks can decrease 1-year death rates by foreseeing the probability of death inside 1 year of release and afterward coordinate patients with suitable mediations, care suppliers and backing.
- *Predict propensity-to-pay*. Well-being frameworks can figure out who needs updates, who needs budgetary help and how the probability of installment changes after some time and after specific occasions.
- *Predict no-shows*. Well-being frameworks can make precise prescient models to evaluate, with each planned arrangement, the danger of absent, at last improving patient consideration and the effective utilization of assets.

6.7   Conclusion

ML with blockchain innovation could change the social insurance industry's IT foundation from concentrated, separated and little scope frameworks to dispersed, decentralized and overall frameworks, which could significantly improve the nature of care given and dispose of exorbitant regulatory wasteful aspects. While the way to this new worldview is laden with difficulties and vulnerability, the medicinal services industry will keep on pushing ahead by steering more ML and blockchain activities, collecting administrative help, pushing for guidelines, and in conclusion, exhibiting accomplishment in neighborhood/local endeavors. At last, the push toward esteem-based repayment and proof-based medication will fill in as the impetus to drive ML with blockchain reception in human services. For this change to happen, human services pioneers, government authorities, payers and tech trailblazers should cooperate and go up against the difficulties, a significant number of which have vexed the social insurance industry for a considerable length of time.

References

[1]   Salah, K., Rehman, MH., Nizamuddin, N. and Al-Fuqaha, A.: 'Blockchain for AI: Review and open research challenges'. IEEE Access, 2019, *7*, pp. 10127–10149.

[2]   Borad, A.: Healthcare and Machine Learning: The Future with Possibilities [online], 2017, Available from: https://www.einfochips.com/blog/healthcare-and-machine-learning-the-futurewith-possibilities (Last Accessed: 04-04-2020).

[3] Shaw, J., Rudzicz, F., Jamieson, T. and Goldfarb, A.: 'Artificial intelligence and the implementation challenge'. Journal of Medical Internet Research, 2019, *21*(7), p. 13659.

[4] Seber, G.A.F. and Lee, A.J.: "Linear regression analysis", New Jersey, Wiley Series in Probability and Statistics, 2012.

[5] Montgomery, D.C., Peck, E.A. and Vining, G.G.: "Introduction to linear regression analysis", New York, Wiley Series in Probability and Statistics, 2015.

[6] Borba, E.: Diabetes Dataset, Available from: https://www.kaggle.com/edubrq/diabetes#__sid¼js0 [online], 2018, (Last Accessed: 29-01-2020).

[7] Menon, P.: Available from: https://towardsdatascience.com/data-science-simplified-part-5- multivariate-regression-models-7684b0489015 [online], 2017, (Last Accessed: 29-01-2020).

[8] Harrer, S., Shah, P., Antony, B. and Hu, J.: 'Artificial intelligence for clinical trial design'. Trends in Pharmacological Sciences, 2019, *40*, pp. 577–591.

[9] Obulesu, O., Mahendra, M. and ThrilokReddy, M.: "Machine Learning Techniques and Tools: A Survey," 2018 International Conference on Inventive Research in Computing Applications (ICIRCA), Coimbatore, 2018, pp. 605–611.

[10] Breiman, L., Friedman, J.H., Ohlsen, R.A. and Stone, C.I.: Classification and Regression Tree, Wadsworth International Group, Belmont, CA, 1984, pp. 43–49.

[11] Quinlan, R.J.: C4. 5: Programs for Machine Learning, California, USA: Morgan Kaufmann, 1993.

[12] Breiman, L.: 'Random forests'. Machine Learning, 2001, *45*, pp. 5–32.

[13] Ayodele, T.O.: "Types of machine learning algorithms", New Advances in Machine Learning, Yagang Zhang (Eds.). IntechOpen, 2010, DOI: 10.5772/9385.

[14] Friedman, J.: 'Greedy function approximation: A gradient boosting machine'. The Annals of Statistics, 2000, *29*. 10.1214/aos/1013203451.

[15] Jidong, L. and Ran, Z., "Dynamic Weighting Multi Factor Stock Selection Strategy Based on XGboost Machine Learning Algorithm," 2018 IEEE International Conference of Safety Produce Informatization (IICSPI), Chongqing, China, 2018, pp. 868–872. doi: 10.1109/IICSPI.2018.8690416.

[16] Swalin, A.: CatBoost vs. Light GBM vs. XGBoost, Available from: https://towardsdatascience.com/catboost-vs-light-gbm-vs-xgboost-5f93620723db [online], 2018, (Last Accessed: 13-04-2020).

[17] Ershov, V.: Available from: https://devblogs.nvidia.com/author/vershov/ [online], 2018, (Last Accessed: 12-12-2019).

[18] Ray, S.: CatBoost: A Machine Learning Library to Handle Categorical (CAT) Data Automatically, [online], 2017, Available from: https://www.analyticsvidhya.com/blog/2017/08/catboostautomated-categorical-data/ (Last Accessed: 12-12-2019).

[19] Yandex, CatBoost, Available from: https://tech.yandex.com/catboost/ [online], 2019, (Last Accessed: 12-12-2019).

[20] Prokhorenkova, L., Gusev, G, Vorobev, A, Dorogush, A.V. and Gulin, A.: "CatBoost: Unbiased Boosting With Categorical Features," Proceedings of the 32nd International Conference on Neural Information Processing Systems (NIPS'18), Samy Bengio, Hanna M. Wallach, Hugo Larochelle, Kristen Grauman, and Nicolò Cesa-Bianchi (Eds.). New York, USA: Curran Associates Inc., 2018, pp. 6639–6649.

[21] Vyas, S., Gupta, M. and Yadav, R.: "Converging Blockchain and Machine Learning for Healthcare," Amity International Conference on Artificial Intelligence (AICAI). Dubai, United Arab Emirates: IEEE, 2019, February, pp. 709–711. doi: 10.1109/AICAI.2019.8701230

[22] Erickson, B.J., Korfiatis, P., Akkus, Z. and Kline, T.L.: 'Machine learning for medical imaging'. RadioGraphics, 2017, *37*(2), pp. 505–515.

[23] Vamathevan, J., Clark, D., Czodrowski, P., *et al.*: 'Applications of machine learning in drug discovery and development'. Nature Reviews Drug Discovery, 2019, *18*(6), pp. 463–477.

[24] Sikora, S., Hurley, B. and Tharakan, A.G.: Intelligent Drug Discovery, Available from: https://www2.deloitte.com/content/dam/insights/us/articles/32961_intelligent-drug-discovery/DI_Intelligent-Drug-Discovery.pdf [online], 2019, (Last Accessed: 04-04-2020).

[25] Emmert-Streib, F. and Dehmer, M.: 'A machine learning perspective on Personalized Medicine: An automised, comprehensive knowledge base with ontology for pattern recognition'. Machine Learning and Knowledge Extraction, 2019, *1*(1), pp. 149–156.

[26] Srividya, M., Mohanavalli, S. and Bhalaji, N.: 'Behavioral modeling for mental health using machine learning algorithms'. Journal of Medical Systems, 2018, *42*(5), p. 88.

[27] Müller, M.M. and Salathé, M.: 'Crowdbreaks: Tracking health trends using public social media data and crowdsourcing'. Frontiers in Public Health, 2019, *7*, p. 81.

[28] Huss, M.: Challenges Implementing AI in HealthCare, Available from: https://peltarion.com/blog/datascience/challenges-of-implementing-ai-in-healthcare, [online], 2018, (Last Accessed: 04-04-2020).

[29] Titenok, Y.: How Block Chain and AI Integration is Changing the Business, Available from: https://sloboda-studio.com/blog/how-blockchain-and-ai-integration-is-changing-business [online], 2020, (Last Accessed: 04-04-2020).

Chapter 7

Framework for approaching blockchain in healthcare using machine learning

Vinolyn Vijaykumar[1], Indrakumari Ranganathan[2] and Lucia Agnes Beena Thomas[3]

Artificial intelligence (AI) acts an integral portion of computer technology segment which underscores the pattern of intellectual machineries that exert, contemplate and react similar to humans. It is the concept and exercise of building machineries that are adept of accomplishing chores which appear to necessitate acumen. It comprises semantic networks, machine learning (ML) and deep learning perceptions. On the other hand, the blockchain permits digital data to be distributed, but not plagiarized, and it is an emerging technology which emphasizes on interoperability. It is an open structure with chunks of data associated conjointly that encompass citations to the leading block. It is a distributed and decentralized system like an uncluttered journal that accumulates an archive of possessions and dealings in a peer-to-peer system. Blockchain and fusion of ML into conventional merchandizes and its correlated amenities can produce ample prospects for establishments. This chapter explores the abilities predictable at the integration of ML and blockchain, in particular in the field of healthcare and to examine about the typical descriptions, advantages and trials of this coalition.

7.1 Introduction

In a digital ecosystem, technological development is evolving and transitioning in a swift stride, in which the yearly forecasts of developments can appear outdated even before they could be published as an article. As expertise progresses, it empowers even quicker transformation and progression, instigating an increase in the gradation of alteration, until ultimately, it becomes rampant. Business establishments and persons who do not preserve few of the foremost technological developments may be left outdated. Comprehending the vital developments will

[1]Department of Computer Applications, Alpha Arts and Science College, Chennai, India
[2]School of Computing Science and Engineering, Galgotias University, Greater Noida, India
[3]Department of Information Technology, St. Joseph's College, Tiruchirappalli, India

permit individuals and industries to formulate and sense the prospects. In this chapter, we discuss about the usage of two imminent technologies, viz., ML and blockchain, in the arena of healthcare.

7.1.1   Introduction to machine learning

ML is an applied sector of AI that offers devices the capability to mechanically acquire knowledge and progress from practice without programming obviously. This type of learning is not an easy process. As the algorithms consume training data, ML is then possible to produce more precise models based on that data. The system of acquisition starts with the examinations or statistics, such as specimens, direct involvement or training, so as to search for regularities in information and produce improved conclusions in the time to come based on the specimens that are offered. The prime intention is to let the computers acquire robotically, without human interference or aid and fine-tune activities consequently [1].

7.1.2   Introduction to blockchain

Blockchain can be thought of an arrangement in blocks, that grasps a comprehensive list of business records such as traditional public ledger. Blockchain assists as an unassailable ledger that permits transactions to materialize in a distributed way. Applications based on blockchain are emerging, scaling innumerable sectors, including fiscal services, Internet of Things (IoT), reputation system and the like [2]. A decentralized database that is unswervingly updated recurrently enables various advantages to the healthcare sector. These compensations become particularly vital, when various parties want access to the similar data. Therapeutic treatment procedures, as an example in the zone of aged care or enduring diseases, are preordained arenas of application where blockchain expertise can create additional value. A diversity of involved people (e.g., therapists, hospitals, medical specialists and general practitioners) and the expanse of media disturbances tangled during the course of treating a patient (e.g., alteration of communication media, several therapeutic fitness records and mismatched IT-related interfaces) can pave way to intensive resource authentication, time-consuming and statistics progressions for all health shareholders involved [3].

Since ML necessitates a vast amount of details and blockchain is similar to an archive of data, the incorporation of the two technologies can bring in immense opportunities in the growing technological world. Being a digital distributed ledger, blockchain can manage almost any type of transaction in existence, especially in the health sector.

7.2   The steps in machine learning

The basic steps that incorporate ML are as follows:

- Gathering data
- Data preparation
- Choosing a model

- Training
- Evaluation
- Parameter tuning
- Prediction [4]

Gathering data:

This phase is very critical as the eminence and measure of information congregated will unswervingly regulate how the prognostic model will turn out to be good. The information gathered are then organized and named as Training Data.

Data preparation:

Data preparation is the phase wherein the data is stored into an appropriate location and equipped for later usage in ML training. At this juncture, the data is primarily combined together and then the order is altered as the order of information should not disturb whatever is assimilated. The other methods of altering and manipulating like normalization, error correction happen in this phase.

Choosing a model:

The subsequent stage that trails in the sequence is selecting a prototype amongst the sundry that data scientists and researchers have formed in all these years. The perfect one is chosen that could accomplish the task.

Training:

Once the above-mentioned steps are completed, the crucial part is to determine, what is habitually measured as the core of ML called training, where the information is utilized to improve incrementally the ability of the model to foresee.

The process of training encompasses the task of initialization of few random values, say A and B of the model, to forecast the result with the acquired values then relate that with the prediction of the model and then fine-tune the values such that they are able to match the estimates that were completed prior. This procedure then reiterates and every cycle of apprising is considered as one step of the training.

Evaluation:

When the training is complete, it is verified whether it is worth, using this phase. This is the moment where the dataset that was compiled earlier comes handy. Evaluation permits the rigorous testing of the model against data that is not seen so far and used in training and is supposed to be characteristic of the working of the model in realistic world.

Parameter tuning:

After the evaluation phase is finished, any added enhancement in the training can be made possible by fine-tuning the parameters. When the training was done, some parameters were discreetly assumed. The other parameter that was included is the rate of learning that outlines how far the progress is made during each step, grounded on the evidence from the preceding training phase. These parameters have a significant part in the precision of the training model, and the duration of the training.

Prediction:

ML fundamentally uses data to respond queries. So, this phase is the concluding step where few questions are answered. This is the stage where the worth of ML is appreciated. In conclusion, the model can be used to predict the desired outcome [5].

7.3 Gathering health data

Collection of data is the method of congregating quantifiable and qualitative data on definite variables with the goal of assessing results or garnering perceptions that can be put in action. Trustworthy data assemblage necessitates a well-defined procedure to guarantee that the statistics collected is consistent, clean and reliable. It comprises making note of the objectives, finding the data necessities, concluding on a technique of collecting the data and eventually framing a plan for data collection that synthesizes the vital features of the problem. Gathering data can be considered as the significant step in cracking any supervised ML problem. The text classifier will be as beneficial as the dataset it is framed from [6].

Data quantity is advantageous in learning when it describes bias and variance trade-offs. As a cue, huge quantities of data can demonstrate beneficial to learning drives when the variability of the estimates is a problem, because the specific data used for learning profoundly impacts predictions (the overfitting problem). More data can really help because a larger number of specimens help ML algorithms to disambiguate the part of each signal picked up from data and taken into modelling the prediction.

Important points to reminisce when gathering data are as follows:

- If a public application program interface (API) is used, the restrictions of the API must be analysed before making use of them. As an example, few APIs establish a boundary on the degree at which queries can be made.
- It is better to have more training examples or samples. This will help the model to generalize effectively.
- It should be ascertained that the quantity of samples for every single class or topic is not excessively imbalanced. That is, there should be enough number of samples in each class for a vivid comparison.
- It should also be made certain that the samples effectively include the space of probable inputs, not only the usual cases [7].

The way the data is collected, procured and controlled varies and is classically not documented. To overcome this, data governance should comply with two vital requirements: the way the data is obtained and collected must be taken into consideration, and it must tackle and file any fluctuations or operations made to the data for the purpose of analysis. There must be a data-specific 'chain of custody' which must be followed to when somebody studies, processes or gathers data [8].

The blockchain is a distributed, digital archive that is helpful in recording transactions taking place in a system, protected using cryptographic expertise. Because of the unchallengeable and cryptographically substantiated security of a network of blockchain, it bids a way to rectify the difficulties presently prevailing in the data domain.

7.3.1 Influence of data assemblage in healthcare

In the healthcare segment, the unsurpassed instances of how info sketching and examination modify the world for the better improvement can be found. The usage

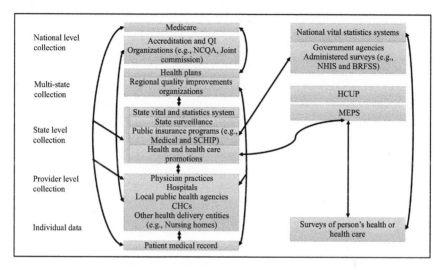

Figure 7.1   A snapshot of data flow in a complex healthcare system

of big data in medication is inspired by the requirement to resolve both local organizational problems, like plummeting assignments and intensifying returns of a health agency, and the universal issues of humankind, such as forecasting pandemics and contending prevailing disorders more resourcefully. Data assemblage in healthcare permits healthcare systems to form complete evaluation of patients, customize treatments, advance treatment procedures, progress communication between physicians and patients to facilitate improved fitness results [9].

Healthcare comprises a mixed collection of public and private data assemblage schemes, inclusive of fitness investigations, managerial enrolment and medical records, and billing records, utilized by innumerable entities, including Community Health Centres, hospitals, doctors and health plans. The data that is collected on race, ethnicity and language, to some degree, by all these entities, suggests the potential of each one to contribute statistics on patients. The course of information illustrated in Figure 7.1 does not entirely echo the complexity of the associations involved or the dissimilar data requirements within the healthcare system. Presently, disintegration of data flow arises because of mass storage space of data collection.

Not a single entity in Figure 7.1 has the ability by itself to collect data on ethnicity, race and language for the total populace of patients nor does any sole entity presently collect whole health data on distinct patients. One means to surge the efficacy of data is to assimilate them with facts from other informants. Consequently, there arises a necessity for improved amalgamation and sharing of race, language and ethnicity data inside and across healthcare units and even within a single entity if appropriate Information Technology processes do not exist [10].

7.3.2   *Recent trends in data collection*

By means of usage of smart mobile devices (e.g., smartphones and tablets) in healthcare situations has become progressively significant over the period of time. In order to overcome the downsides of conventional tools based on paper (e.g., questionnaires), mobile apps explicitly tailor-made to a definite healthcare scenario shall empower professionals from several spheres (e.g., psychology or healthcare) to organize patient data more efficiently. Based on the skills congregated from several projects apprehending mobile data collection applications in the huge scale, a number of perilous necessities have been recognized [11].

Telemedicine permits remote analyses and nursing of patients. It promises quickness, protection and dependability in recent healthcare establishments. There are numerous trials related to computerization in this genus of environment, viz., protocols, heterogeneous devices and programming interfaces; the necessity for supple, hassle-free deployment; the prerequisite for undemanding configuration, simple to achieve, accessible and, if there is a possibility, and self-adjusting systems. The concentration is on the problem of patients' essential data collection, circulation and processing. The prevailing methods grounded on manual note taking are sluggish, time-consuming and labour reserve intensive. In addition, it enforces a hindrance to real-time data access that curtails the capability of medical diagnostics and nursing. A key to mechanize this procedure from bed-side data collection to data circulation and distant access by clinical staff is invented. It is constructed on concepts of Wireless Sensor Networks and utility computing. Sensors are fitted to prevailing therapeutic devices that are interlinked to exchange amenities; these are combined to the organization's computing system infrastructure. The data becomes available from the 'cloud', from where it can be dealt with by expert systems and/or disseminated to paramedics for investigation. These know-hows offer required features for computerization in telemedicine milieu adopting the trials enumerated earlier. This involvement is 2-fold in communal and technical fields. In communal, a pioneering and least-cost solution to progress the eminence of medicinal aid distribution is demonstrated, and, in technical field, the trials of how to assimilate sensors associated with vestige medicinal devices which cloud computing services gather, process and distribute patient's crucial data are addressed [12].

7.3.3   *Healthcare datasets*

Healthcare analytics is built on data and datasets to be precise. Owing to the assortment of healthcare data sources, data calibration is a crucial support for effective and eloquent usage of the data and alliance of medical experts, insurers, care givers and government agencies. There are innumerable data sources in addition to clinical data that can be beneficial for medical analytics. These datasets include the following:

• World Health Organization
  It offers data and scrutinizes on worldwide well-being importance, including disease and health statistics. An individual page is devoted to a definite issue

and provides evidence on worldwide conditions and trend highpoints. The data comprises principal indicators, database opinions, key publications and links to related web pages on the relevant issue [13].

● Kaggle-health analytics

The dataset comprises 26 indicators like acute illness, chronic illness, immunization, mortality and others. These indicators, in turn, have sub-categories which encompass all the attributes. The investigation was conducted in Empowered Action Group states Uttarakhand, Bihar, Rajasthan, Uttar Pradesh, Jharkhand, Chhattisgarh, Odisha, Assam and Madhya Pradesh. This dataset incorporates 21 million people and 4.32 million homes spanned across the urban and rural area of these nine states. These standards would aid in improved and complete understanding and appropriate observing of several factors on well-being and fitness of populace, predominantly on Child and Reproductive Health.

● Heart-disease dataset

This dataset encompasses 76 characteristics, but all the published researches mention using a subsection of 14 of them. To be precise, the Cleveland database is the solitary one that has been utilized by ML scientists. The 'goal' field denotes to the existence of cardiovascular disease in the sick. It is numeral valued from 0 (denoting absence) to 4. Experimentations with the Cleveland database have been engrossed on merely trying to discern presence (values of 1, 2, 3 or 4) from absence (i.e., value 0) [13,14].

7.4 Data preparation

Data preparation is the procedure of sorting and converting raw data preceding to processing and analysis. It is an essential step preceding to processing and every so often comprises reformatting data, formulating alterations to data and the merging of datasets to enhance data. Data preparation is a prolonged responsibility for data specialists or commercial users, but it is indispensable as a criterion to place data in appropriate context in order to crack it into perceptions and eradicate unfairness ensuing from substandard data eminence. For example, the data preparation procedure usually embraces regulating data formats, elevating source data and/or eradicating outliers [15].

The eight rudimentary practices that make the data better are articulating the problem initially, establishing data collection mechanisms, formatting data to craft it unswerving, condensing data, comprehensive data cleaning, decomposing data, rescaling data and discretizing data. The steps in preparing the data are illustrated in Figure 7.2 [16].

7.4.1 Benefits of data preparation and the cloud

The effective, precise professional choices can only be formulated with superior data. Data preparation assists in the following:

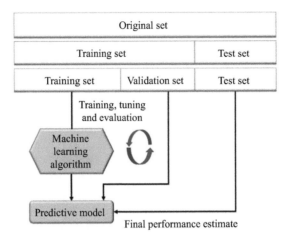

Figure 7.2   Steps in data preparation

- Resolve errors swiftly—Data preparation aids to detect errors before processing. After data have been detached from its prime source, it will become extremely tough to comprehend and correct these errors.
- Fabricate good-quality data—Sorting and reformatting datasets certifies that all the data which are used in analysis will be of great quality.
- Formulate improved commercial conclusions—Best quality data that can be treated and analysed more rapidly and competently paves way to more efficient, timely and improved commercial conclusions. Furthermore, as data and data processes advance towards the cloud, data preparation too transcends with it for even superior detriments, such as
  - Exceptional scalability—Cloud data preparation grows at the stride of the commercial business. Enterprises need not be burdened about the fundamental infrastructure or attempt to anticipate their progressions.
  - Impending proof—Cloud data preparation can upgrade mechanically so that novel competences or problematic fixes can be rectified as soon as they are published. This permits establishments to stay forward of the revolution curve without disruptions and additional outlays.
  - Augmented data usage and association—Doing data preparation in the cloud entails it is always accessible, does not necessitate any mechanical connection and enables teams to work together on the issue for faster outcomes. Furthermore, a reliable, cloud-native data preparation device will give added benefits (like an instinctive and easy to use graphical user interface (GUI)) for simpler and more resourceful preparation [15].

7.4.2   Data preparation steps

DATA preparation (or data pre-processing) is the chief phase of data processing applications, including data mining, ML, evidence extraction, data warehousing and pattern recognition. Industrial practice designates that more than 80% of the data mining job focuses on data preparation. Undeniably, once the data is suitably organized, the extracted results are more precise and consistent. This necessitates that data preparation is also a crucial step for supplementary data processing applications.

It can be classified into three main categories: discretization, feature selection and web intelligence.

- Discretization

    Discretization is an essential pre-processing phase for several ML and data mining missions. It is the method of changing continuous features of a dataset into distinct ones, so that they can be preserved as minor features by various ML algorithms.
- Feature selection

    Feature selection is a significant fragment of data preparation. It empowers both cost-effective analysts to be constructed and an enhanced understanding of the primary course that creates the data.
- Web intelligence

As the web has developed to a larger, decentralized data repository, it is effortless currently to access a huge number of data sources [17].

The notion of e-Health is very crucial currently. It can have diverse meanings and explanations, either healthcare and electronic medical records (EMR), or clinical informatics, to Telemedicine. It is the practice of healthcare which is distributed or improved through the internet and associated skills. The reputation of e-Health lies within its capacity to entail patients, around the world, an entree to their medicinal data and an actual monitoring of their fitness with the progress of IoT and associated items. It has a massive effect on diverse facets of life, and studies need to implemented in order to get the superlative results [1]. mHealth, or mobile Health, which is gaining more popularity, is a form of e-Health that can be employed in nursing patients, and steering study along with clinical education and preserving community health by tracing diseases [2]. Moreover, it progresses the interaction between patients and healthcare specialists. Thus, there is effectiveness in medications and health monitoring, broader access to therapeutic care and a reduced amount of pressure on community healthcare funds. That is why sustaining the access safety to the medicinal data that is shared in this domain is of greater interest. Blockchain is an evolving technology, initially acquainted with bitcoin [3], the renowned cryptocurrency. Earlier, it was an answer for dual expenditure and only employed as a fiscal application. But it turns out that blockchain technology can have countless other applications, and it might be the eventual key for the problems that are tackled today in e-Health and the IoT. In fact, blockchain is a distributed, peer-to-peer expertise where no tertiary parties are required.

Data pre-processing

Getting back to the dataset, at this step, the data gathered is scrutinized in terms of its essentiality, diversity and representativity for the AI project. Pre-processing includes choice of the accurate data from the comprehensive dataset and

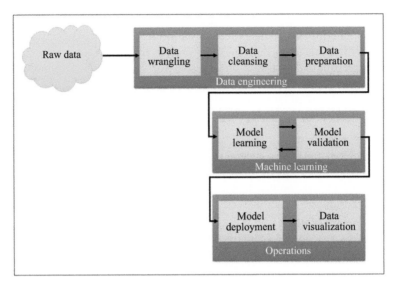

Figure 7.3   Data pre-processing

constructing a training set as shown in Figure 7.3. The process of placing together the data in this ideal format is called as Feature Transformation.

1. Format: Sales data available in various files has to be collated. For example, the total sales amount may be represented in appropriate currency format in the corresponding country need to the formatted in a single format for processing.
2. Data cleaning: During this process, the unnecessary data, blank fields are to be dealt with care and necessary data is to be supplied.
3. Feature extraction: Feature extraction involves the selection of important attributes for the accurate prediction. It also results in higher computational speed and usage of less memory [18].

7.5   Choosing a model

A model is something that is fashioned by the training process. These are primarily the ML algorithms. Some examples are linear regression, logistic regression, decision tree model, random forest, support vector machines (SVMs), Naïve Bayes, *k*-nearest neighbours (*k*NN) and *K*-means. Any of these algorithms can be used for forecasting.

7.5.1   Types of machine learning algorithms

7.5.1.1   Supervised learning

This algorithm involves a dependent variable (or target variable) which is to be forecasted from a particular set of independent variables. A function is framed using the dependent and independent variables to get the desired output for the given inputs. The model is trained till the desired accuracy level is attained. The popular supervised learning algorithms are regression, random forest, decision tree, logistic regression and *k*NN.

7.5.1.2 Unsupervised learning

The unsupervised learning does not require dependent or independent variables for forecasting. This algorithm is mainly used for categorizing the dataset into different groups. For example, dividing customers into different groups based on their interest. The most used unsupervised algorithms are *K*-means and Apriori algorithms.

7.5.1.3 Reinforcement learning

This type of algorithms is used to train the model to make accurate decisions. The model is opened to an atmosphere, where it can learn concepts by trial and error technique. The trials help the model to make accurate decisions for the given problem. The Markov decision process is a common example of reinforcement learning [19].

7.5.2 Most familiar machine learning algorithms

The generally used ML algorithms are listed in the following. They can be useful to virtually any problem:

1. Linear regression
2. Logistic regression
3. Decision tree
4. Support vector machine
5. Naïve Bayes
6. *k*-Nearest neighbours
7. *K*-Means
8. Random forest
9. Dimensionality reduction algorithms
10. Gradient boosting algorithms

7.5.2.1 Linear regression

This method is applied to analyse actual values depending on the continuous variables. A best line (regression line) is fit by the function that represents the association between dependent and independent variables. It is given by a linear equation $A = x \times B + y$ where A is a dependent variable, x is the slope, B is an independent variable, and y is an intercept. x and y are decided by using the sum of square minimization method between data points and regression line.

The two different forms of linear regression are simple linear regression and multiple linear regression. Simple linear regression is applied when there is only one independent variable. Multiple linear regression is applied when there are more than one independent variables.

7.5.2.2   Logistic regression

It is a type of classification algorithm applied to assess discrete values considering the predefined set of independent variables(s). It predicts the prospect of occurrence of an unlikely event by fitting suitable data to a logit function. Hence it is called as logistic regression. Its output values are between 0 and 1.

7.5.2.3   Decision tree

It is another type of model suitable for classification. Extraordinarily, this mechanism is used for both categorical and continuous dependent variables. Applying the independent variable, the dataset is divided into different clusters using the methods such as information gain, chi-square, gini and entropy.

7.5.2.4   Support vector machine

In this classification method, the data is categorized into different groups using the training data. Once a new input is given, referring the trained data the output category is given by SVM.

7.5.2.5   Naïve Bayes

This classification procedure is built on Bayes' theorem. Naïve Bayes classifier assumes that the existence of a particular feature in a category does not depend on any other feature. Naïve Bayesian model can be built easily even for very huge datasets. Added to its simplicity, Naïve Bayes is one of the best classification methods.

7.5.2.6   *k*-Nearest neighbours

Regression and classification problems can be solved by *k*NN. But Industries mostly apply *k*NN for classification problems. This procedure classifies the new class based on the *k*-neighbour characteristics using distance measure. The distance measure may be Manhattan, Euclidean or Hamming distance. In this, Hamming distance is used for categorical variables. When K value is 1, it is allocated to class which is its nearest neighbour.

7.5.2.7   *K*-Means

This unsupervised algorithm solves the clustering problem. This method classifies a given dataset into k different clusters named as centroids. New centroid is formed based on the existing members by applying distance mechanism. The iteration continues till a convergence occurs.

7.5.2.8   Random forest

Random forest contains a group of decision trees. Hence it is called as forest. Here each decision tree deals with a particular categorization. In order to assign a new object to a tree based on certain characteristics, the vote will be received from other trees in the forest and the tree with the higher vote is accepted by the forest.

If there are N cases in the training set, at each N case, m attributes of M total input variables reselected for creating different decision trees. Each tree grows as the new cases are added. There is no trimming.

7.5.2.9 Dimensionality reduction algorithms

In recent times, a huge volume of data is generated for corporate and any institutions. Using the whole data may decrease the performance of the algorithms. Dimensionality reduction algorithms can be applied to choose the needed features for prediction at the same time, leading to better performance. Few such algorithms are given later.

7.5.2.10 Gradient boosting algorithms

This is most appropriate for a huge volume of data for high performance predictions. This algorithm makes the weak predictors to group together to form a better predictor. This improves the performance of the algorithm.

7.5.2.11 XGBoost

It is a traditional gradient boosting algorithm (GBA), applicable in a decisive choice where winning or losing becomes the argument. It contains linear and tree learning model, which enables it with superior prediction that gives high accuracy. It is almost ten times faster than other GBAs.

7.5.2.12 LightGBM

It is a tree-based learning algorithm that performs faster, requires less memory and gives improved accuracy. This algorithm can be applied for large data as it supports GPU and parallel learning.

7.5.2.13 CatBoost

Yandex researchers developed CatBoost. It is an open-source GBA applied on decision trees. It can be easily incorporated with deep learning frameworks like Apple's Core ML and Google's TensorFlow. It requires less training time and can act on a variety of data formats [19].

7.5.3 Need for models in healthcare using blockchain

The decentralization with security and pseudo-anonymous transactions, immutability make blockchain suitable for healthcare. Healthcare ecosystem requires massive exchange of data through Electronic Medical Records between the hospitals, Test centres and insurance organizations. For smooth communication, data interoperability must be ensured. Enhancing the interoperability using blockchain technology is elaborated in the following section.

7.5.3.1 Description of healthcare interoperability

Healthcare interoperability involves utilization and interchange of information among the collaborators. This can be achieved in three levels starting from the lowest to the highest reliability.

1. Initial interoperability helps the recipient to use the data without any alteration during data exchanges between healthcare systems.
2. Architectural interoperability level clinical data is well formatted using a pre-defined format. Hence the recipient can directly use the data for interpretation.
3. Syntactic interoperability that ensures both the structure and meaning of the data is preserved during interpretation.

The previous hierarchy has to be followed for effective communication with needed safety, cost-effectiveness and quality. It is possible to apply syntactic interoperability only when initial and architectural interoperabilities are attained. This requires fundamental clinical domain knowledge. The Health Level Seven International organization shaped the Fast Healthcare Interoperability Resources (FHIR) as a sketch standard API for clinical data exchange. FHIR shares only precise and explicit information to improve the effectiveness of information exchange. Any recent healthcare app should follow the standards prescribed by FHIR.

Recent healthcare approach: Patient-focused care

Patient-focused care is followed recently. In this approach patients have the access to the medical records which avoids communication delays. The patients are notified with real-time data are updated through healthcare apps. Hence, the patients are aware of the report as and when the analysis is done [20].

7.6   Training

Training ML involves ML algorithms and datasets from which the learning process occurs to construct a model to achieve the target attribute. The algorithms mine the patterns in the given dataset that links the input data to the target and produces the output, an ML model that captures these patterns. Prediction can be done with the new dataset for which the target is unknown. To train the ML model, the following specifications are required:

1. input dataset,
2. data attribute name,
3. data transformation directions and
4. training parameters.

Based on the target, the ML process selects the correct learning algorithm [21]. The modelling process is shown in Figure 7.4. The process involves predicting the labels from the given features, tuning it for the business requirement and finally validating the data. The output obtained is used for inference, which predicts the new dataset.

7.6.1   The purpose of train/test sets

The performance of the ML model depends upon the train and test dataset which makes the ML algorithm to work efficiently. The trained model using the input

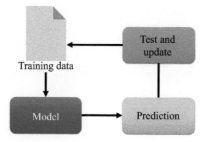

Figure 7.4 Training a model

dataset is compared with the output values of the test set to figure out a performance measure for the model on the test dataset. The efficiency of the prediction is the

'The skill of the procedure on the test set'

to

'The skill of the procedure on unseen data'.

The accuracy of the prediction depends on the following factors:

1. The algorithm must be strong to predict the output close to the expected output from unseen data.
2. The performance measures decide the accuracy of the prediction.
3. Data preparation is also playing a vital role in the prediction process. If the prediction to be returned to its original scale, the process can be reversed if the data is prepared well.
4. The programming language and complexity of the algorithm must be sensible.

The prediction procedure gives different results every time. The output is uncertain, which depends on how well the procedure is executed and makes a handshake with other algorithms. Often, it is preferred to use k-fold cross-validation as an alternative [22]. The training and test dataset should be separated as elucidated in Figure 7.5.

The training set is used to build the models whereas the test sets are kept separately to appraise the models. The processes are as follows:

1. The data should divide as a test and training set before doing any operation to estimate the performance of the model.
2. After the dividing of the dataset, the test set should not be considered until the model is finalized.

After this procedure, there may be a chance for overfitting, which occurs in the circumstance where the performance of the training data is best and the test data becomes worst [23].

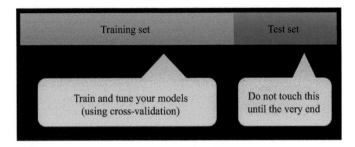

Figure 7.5   Splitting of data set

7.6.2   Blockchain for privacy in healthcare

Blockchain is becoming the primary security choice for securing healthcare data. Blockchain is based on a distributed online database, contains blocks that are linked with each other. Each block is having a timestamp of its production, hash of the preceding block and transaction data related to the application, for instance, healthcare data. A new block is created when a new healthcare data arrives and circulated to all peers in the patient network. The new block should get the majority from peers to be added to the chain. If the block has not got the majority, then a fork is created in the chain and the block is added to that and designated as an orphan and not allowed to participate in the main chain. Once a block is added to the chain, it cannot be altered without changing all subsequent blocks. The sensitive data are encrypted before the block is added to the chain [24].

7.6.3   Quantum of training data requirements

The data required for ML applications depends on the complexity of the problem and the learning algorithm. The performance of the algorithm depends on the scalability of the data so it is necessary to analyse the requirement of data for a specific algorithm. Statistical methods are available to predict the required sample size. Non-linear algorithms are non-parametric and flexible and considered influential ML algorithms as they have the capacity of learning complex non-linear relationships between input and output features. They can figure out the required parameter to model a problem along with their values. Deep learning, a branch of ML, uses non-linear algorithms to enhance the performance. Artificial neural networks and random forest are based on non-linear algorithms, proving their efficiency in many applications. A learning curve graph is useful to study how the size of the data affects the model for a specific problem. From this graph, it can be predicted how much data can be required to construct a skilful model [25].

7.7   Evaluation

Evaluation is a method of assessing excellence using some criteria governed by some set of rules. Performance evaluation is an important feature of ML. Figure 7.6 depicts

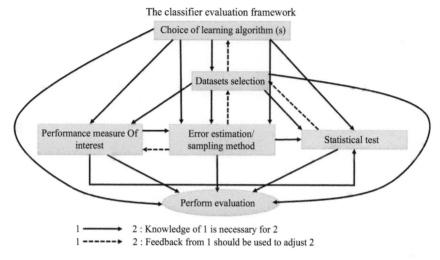

The classifier evaluation framework

1 ──────▶ 2 : Knowledge of 1 is necessary for 2
1 ------▶ 2 : Feedback from 1 should be used to adjust 2

Figure 7.6 The main steps of evaluation

the process in classifier evaluation and their steps. Every step of this algorithm, the performance, re-sampling techniques and the statistical tests are assessed. The choice made at one step will affect other steps as they are interdependent [25].

7.7.1 Evaluation metrics

Different evaluation metrics apply to various tasks such as regression, classification, clustering, ranking and topic modelling, and it falls under supervised learning. Metrics like precision-recall are well suited for multi-tasking ML algorithms. Metrics are classified into two categories: classification and regression metrics.

The different types of evaluation metrics are as follows:

- classification accuracy,
- logarithmic loss,
- confusion matrix,
- area under curve,
- F1 score,
- mean absolute error (MAE),
- mean squared error (MSE).

7.7.2 Evaluation metrics and assessment of machine learning algorithms in healthcare

The efficiency of the algorithm is directly connected with the performance measurements. If the ML algorithm deals with classification, that is, if it predicts the health condition or any health-related outcome, then they are evaluated with the area under curve or confusion matrix. If a model deals with the regression that is predicting an outcome using continuous variables, then MSE [26], MAE or the coefficient of determination methods are used. Readers with advanced statistical knowledge will recognize significant corollaries to a classical statistical approach [27].

Experiments are conducted to evaluate the performance of the blockchain system. Some of the metrics that are considered are as follows:

- transactions per network data,
- transactions per second,
- transactions per disk I/O,
- transactions per memory second,
- transactions per CPU.

7.8   Parameter tuning

To control certain procedures of the training process, some parameters are used in ML algorithms. The training model handles three categories of data: the input data, the parameters and the hyper-parameters. The input data is a collection of data from individual records that holds the essential features required for the ML problem. The data is utilized to configure the model to predict accurately. The parameters are used as a variable that is used to adjust the data to produce accurate output. The hyper-parameters are variables that govern the training process. For instance, part of setting up a deep neural network decides the number of layers between the input and the output layer. The difference between the parameter and hyper-parameter is that the parameter is not constant whereas hyper-parameter is not constant.

7.9   Predictive analytics

Predictive analytics is being widely used in analytics and statistical techniques that predict the future by analysing the present data using models. The score from the model determines the accuracy of the occurrence of an event. If the score is high then the chance of occurrence is high whereas if the score is less, then the chance of occurrence is less. Historical data is utilized by these models to make intelligent business decisions along with the risk and opportunities. The predictive analysis process is represented in the following (Figure 7.7):

1. predictions and modelling
2. predictive modelling
3. statistics, ML
4. data analysis
5. data collection
6. requirement analysis

7.9.1   *Requirement collection*

To construct a predictive model, it is needed to know the aim of the prediction. For example, a pharmaceutical company is intended to forecast the sale of medicine to

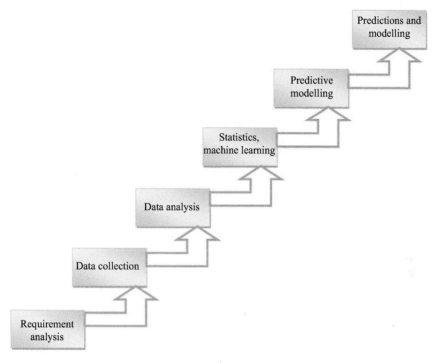

Figure 7.7   Predictive analytics process

avoid the expiry of medicines. In this scenario, the data analyst must collect data from the client to develop a predictive model.

7.9.2   Data collection

Once the requirement is finalized, the data analyst collects data, either in structured or in an unstructured format from various sources to develop a predictive model.

7.9.3   Data analysis and massaging

A data analyst collects data and pre-processes it to develop the model. The efficiency of a predictive model mainly depends on the quality of the data. This phase is also known as data massaging or munging.

7.9.4   Statistics, machine learning

The predictive analytics process uses various statistical and ML techniques. Regression and probability are the popular techniques used in the analytics process. ML tools like SVMs, decision trees and artificial neural networks are used for predictive analytics tasks. Predictive analytics models highly depend on ML and statistical techniques.

7.9.5   Predictive modelling

A working model is a prototype, developed using ML and statistical techniques with a dummy dataset. The developed prototype is tested to ensure the accuracy of the model, if the prototype is successful then the model is said to be fit. This prototype is extended to the original dataset.

7.9.6   Prediction and monitoring

After the successful development of the model, it is deployed at the client's side to predict and make decisions. The operation of the model is monitored consistently to ensure whether it is producing an accurate result or not.

Some opportunities in the predictive field are listed as follows:

- detecting fraud [28],
- reduction of risk [29],
- marketing campaign optimization [30],
- operation improvement [31],
- clinical decision support system [32].

7.10   Benefits of integrating machine learning and blockchain

Blockchain is attracting many research areas that create an idea to integrate this technology with other emerging technologies like data, the IoT and ML. The objective of blockchain is to maintain the privacy of the records and to authenticate access while ML is concerned with identifying patterns in the data stream for efficient decision-making. These two evolving technologies have prospects to be used in the healthcare industry as the privacy and security of the data is essential here. So, the merger of ML and blockchain would create a revolution in the healthcare industry.

Enhancing the operational efficiency in healthcare industry applies predictive analytics to enhance the planning and execution process of resource utilization, care delivery process, patient admittance, staff schedules and discharge. If prediction is implemented, the healthcare providers can foresee an improvement in patient access, their expenditure and increased asset utilization.

It is believed that the predictive analytics has the power to change the healthcare industry. Its benefits not only range from the efficiency and quality of patient care but also extended to healthcare staff and organizations. The Society of Actuaries has conducted a survey from more than 200 health providers and payers and inferred that 93% suggested that the predictive analytics is vital for their business. The survey reports the following outcomes:

- The data collection methods increase security for about 20%.
- Expertise needed by the organization is about 18%.
- Data visualization method represents the prediction in pictorial form (17%).

Predictive analytics is playing a vital role in the personal medicine; it allows prognostic analytics and big data to diagnose the disease without the need of familiarization. Few medicines will work for some patients but not for others as people are unique by their DNA. It is not possible for a doctor to manually analyse the patient details; in this case, predictive analysis permits the doctor to uncover the hidden patterns, correlations and insights from the health dataset of the patient.

Predictive analysis also advices the risk of death during surgery by analysing the patient's survival condition, past and present medical history and drug prescription. For, instance, a statistical tool can detect the patient health data and can predict the possibility of like age, medication adherence, chronic illnesses and past patterns of care.

Healthcare data from pharmaceutical sector can be collected and the pharmacy companies can predict the clusters of diseases and can concentrate on supply chain to target demand. Epidemiological studies use statistics to predict the illness for people at risk [33].

7.11   Conclusion

Blockchain and ML are the two technologies that have the potential to revolutionize many industry sectors. It could be predicted that the synergy of these two technologies would have greater benefits. The fusion of ML and blockchain will bring growth in diverse domains and has many potential applications. The idea of their combination is so powerful that it has recently attracted many researchers and organizations. Initially, ML and blockchain appear to be poles apart, but at the same time, they complement each other. They have applications in fields such as finance, medical, public service, security, banking and IoT. The future of this integration is a decentralized system of operations, where machines could interact in a better way with better modelling of human activities.

References

[1]   Frameworks for Approaching the Machine Learning Process, https://www.kdnuggets.com/2018/05/general-approaches-machine-learning-process.html, Accessed on May 12, 2020.

[2]   Z. Zheng, S. Xie, H. Dai, X. Chen, and H. Wang, "An Overview of Blockchain Technology: Architecture, Consensus, and Future Trends," 2017 IEEE International Congress on Big Data (BigData Congress), Honolulu, HI, 2017, pp. 557–564, doi: 10.1109/BigDataCongress.2017.85.

[3]   M. Mettler, "Blockchain Technology in Healthcare: The Revolution Starts Here," 2016 IEEE 18th International Conference on e-Health Networking, Applications and Services (Healthcom), Munich, 2016, pp. 1–3, doi: 10.1109/HealthCom.2016.7749510.

[4]   The 7 Steps of Machine Learning, https://towardsdatascience.com/the-7-steps-of-machine-learning-2877d7e5548e, Updated on September 1, 2017.

[5]   The Seven Steps of Machine Learning, https://www.techleer.com/articles/ 379-the-seven-steps-of-machine-learning/, Updated on October 24, 2017.

[6]   Gather Data (2018) https://developers.google.com/machine-learning/guides/ text-classification/step-1, Accessed on May 13, 2020.

[7]   J. P. Mueller and L. Massaron, Gathering and Cleaning Data for Machine Learning,   https://www.dummies.com/programming/big-data/data-science/ gathering-cleaning-data-machine-learning/, Accessed on May 13, 2020.

[8]   How Blockchain Technology is Making Data Collection Auditable and Transparent,   https://medium.com/swipecrypto/how-blockchain-technology-is-making-data-collection-auditable-and-transparent-e40a27c03c89, Updated on August 21, 2018.

[9]   The Importance of Data Collection in Healthcare, https://www.sam-solu-tions.com/blog/the-importance-of-data-collection-in-healthcare/,   Updated on April 2, 2019.

[10]   Race, Ethnicity, and Language Data: Standardization for Health Care Quality Improvement, https://www.ahrq.gov/research/findings/final-reports/ iomracereport/reldata5.html, Accessed on May 13, 2020.

[11]   J. Schobel, R. Pryss, M. Schickler, and M. Reichert, "Towards Flexible Mobile Data Collection in Healthcare," 2016 IEEE 29th International Symposium on Computer-Based Medical Systems (CBMS), Dublin, 2016, pp. 181–182, doi: 10.1109/CBMS.2016.43.

[12]   C. O. Rolim, F. L. Koch, C. B. Westphall, J. Werner, A. Fracalossi, and G. S. Salvador, "A Cloud Computing Solution for Patient's Data Collection in Health Care Institutions," 2010 Second International Conference on eHealth, Telemedicine, and Social Medicine, St. Maarten, Netherlands Antilles: IEEE; 2010, pp. 95–99, doi: 10.1109/eTELEMED.2010.19.

[13]   R. Sagar, 11 Open Source Datasets That Can be Used for Health Science Projects, 2019. https://analyticsindiamag.com/11-open-source-datasets-that-can-be-used-for-health-science-projects/, Accessed on May 14, 2020.

[14]   10 Best Healthcare Data Sets (Examples), https://archer-soft.com/blog/10-best-healthcare-data-sets-examples, Accessed on May 14, 2020.

[15]   What is Data Preparation?, https://www.talend.com/resources/what-is-data-preparation, Accessed on May 15, 2020.

[16]   Preparing Your Dataset for Machine Learning, https://www.altexsoft.com/ blog/datascience/preparing-your-dataset-for-machine-learning-8-basic-tech-niques-that-make-your-data-better/, Updated on June 16, 2017.

[17]   C. Zhang, Q. Yang, and B. Liu. (2005). Guest Editors' Introduction: Special Section on Intelligent Data Preparation. IEEE Transactions on Knowledge and Data Engineering, 17(9), 1163–1165. doi:10.1109/tkde.2005.146.

[18]   How to Build a Data Set for Your Machine Learning Project, https:// towardsdatascience.com/how-to-build-a-data-set-for-your-machine-learn-ing-project-5b3b871881ac, Updated on February 14, 2019.

[19]   Commonly Used Machine Learning Algorithms, https://www.analytics vidhya.com/blog/2017/09/common-machine-learning-algorithms/, Updated on September 9, 2017.

[20] P. Zhang, M. A. Walker, J. White, D. C. Schmidt, and G. Lenz, "Metrics for Assessing Blockchain-Based Healthcare Decentralized Apps," 2017 IEEE 19th International Conference on e-Health Networking, Applications and Services (Healthcom), Dalian, 2017, pp. 1–4, doi: 10.1109/HealthCom.2017. 8210842.

[21] Amazon Machine Learning, Developer's Guide, https://docs.aws.amazon. com/machine-learning/latest/dg/training-process. html, Accessed on May 16, 2020.

[22] How to Train a Final Machine Learning Model, https://machinelearningmas-tery.com/train-final-machine-learning-model/, Updated on March 17, 2017.

[23] Model Training, https://elitedatascience.com/model-training, Accessed on May 16, 2020.

[24] C. Esposito, A. De Santis, G. Tortora, H. Chang, and K.-K. R. Choo. (2018). Blockchain: A Panacea for Healthcare Cloud-Based Data Security and Privacy? IEEE Cloud Computing, 5(1), 31–37. doi:10.1109/mcc.2018.011791712.

[25] How Much Training Data is Required for Machine Learning? https:// machinelearningmastery.com/much-training-data-required-machine-learning/, Updated on July 24, 2017.

[26] What is Mean Squared Error, Mean Absolute Error, Root Mean, https:// www.studytonight.com/post/what-is-mean-squared-error-mean-absolute-error-root-mean-squared-error-and-r-squared, Retrieved June 22, 2020.

[27] G. S. Handelma, H. K. Kok, R. V. Chandra, *et al.* (2019). Peering into the Black Box of Artificial Intelligence: Evaluation Metrics of Machine Learning Methods. American Journal of Roentgenology, 212, 38–43. doi:10. 2214/ajr.18.20224.

[28] M. Nigrini, 2011, "Forensic Analytics: Methods and Techniques for Forensic Accounting Investigations", John Willey and Sons Ltd.

[29] M. Schiff, 2012, "BI Experts: Why Predictive Analytics Will Continue to Grow", The Data Warehouse Institute.

[30] F. Reichheld and P. Schefter, 2000, "The Economics of E-Loyalty", Harvard Business School Working Knowledge. Retrieved 2018.

[31] V. Dhar. (2001). Predictions in Financial Markets: The Case of Small Disjuncts. ACM Transaction on Intelligent Systems and Technology, 2(3).

[32] J. Osheroff, J. Teich, B. Middleton, E. Steen, A. Wright, and D. Detmer. (2007). A Roadmap for National Action on Clinical Decision Support. JAMIA: A Scholarly Journal of Informatics in Health and Biomedicine, 14(2), 141–145.

[33] N. Rifi, E. Rachkidi, N. Agoulmine, and N. C. Taher, "Towards Using Blockchain Technology for eHealth Data Access Management," 2017 Fourth International Conference on Advances in Biomedical Engineering (ICABME), Beirut, 2017, pp. 1–4, doi: 10.1109/ICABME.2017.8167555.

Chapter 8

Reforming the traditional business network

K.P. Arjun[1], N.M. Sreenarayanan[1], K. Sampath Kumar[1] and R. Viswanathan[1]

Today the use of internet provides so much information and knowledge related to healthcare sector that everyone gets gradually forced to use it. This scenario not only saves our time but also saves a large amount of money that many would otherwise spend for physical visit into the hospitals and clinics. Today peoples have already got used to the large number of electronic healthcare methods. It is quite interesting about how fast the healthcare industry is growing with the use of advanced technologies. In the field of healthcare, organizations are utilizing emerging technologies, mainly machine learning (ML) and deep learning. Artificial intelligence (AI) and blockchain could turn to establish something exponential in this area. It is clear that the ML and AI applications widely enhance the easiness, accuracy and speed of the diagnosis. The AI tools and algorithms help in analyzing the information more deeply and quickly with high accuracy; hence, the doctors are to be more precise with the diagnosis. Many areas such as image processing, X-ray analysis, bone age calculations and radiology are enhanced by the applications of AI. The blockchain technology is a real timestamped series of the immutable files and records of the data that would be managed by a group of computers that do not belong to any single entity. Storing and retrieving medical and healthcare sector data are more secure with the blockchain. The blockchain tools and applications help in ensuring the global integrity of the medical records. Each and every day the business industries, especially medical and healthcare sectors, are enhanced by the immense usage of adaptive technologies, and also they are establishing well-defined networks across all the interacting participants.

8.1   Introduction

AI, a use of man-made brainpower, centers around creating computer programs that can get to information and learn to take decisions alone. It gives systems the

[1]School of Computing Science and Engineering, Galgotias University, Greater Noida, India

capacity to learn without being unequivocally programmed [1,2]. Its essential objective is to build strong algorithms which can get input information and utilize statistical examination for predicting and error-free outputs. Numerous choices made by AIs can be in some cases difficult for people to comprehend. Building an AI framework with algorithms working in an encrypted state is as yet a major test for AI and its related application developers. AI has bounty to actualize as far as security is concerned. A part of the procedure that includes unencrypted information may introduce a few security risks, yet blockchain databases hold data in an encrypted structure as it is. Now decisions are recorded on a blockchain based on information-point-by-information-point structure; they can without much of a stretch be inspected with the confirmation that nobody has tempered the records.

Trust is significant when handling payments, particularly in a framework like our own that looks to support positive interest by means of motivating forces. Blockchain is a distributed electronic database that is shared between all individuals over a system, and its substance is kept indistinguishable between various individuals and updated at the same time. The three mainstays of blockchain innovation are decentralization, immutability and transparency. Blockchain can encourage disseminated and decentralized AI algorithm and increment their accuracy, trustworthiness, reliability and so on. A distributed ledger, blockchain can oversee practically any kind of exchange in presence. This is the essential purpose for its quickly developing popularity and power.

A blockchain [3,4] is exceptionally transparent as anything based on the blockchain can be seen by everybody, and every member on the network is responsible for their activities. In our structure, models can be refreshed on-chain, which means inside the blockchain system, for an exchange expense or utilized for inference off-chain, locally on the person's gadget, with no exchange costs. It is a decentralized open record that comprises a chain of blocks. The blocks on a blockchain are associated utilizing cryptographic standards. Blocks contain the digital form of data that store insights concerning exchanges, for example, date, time and the cash required for any recent buy. It is a time-period-stamped arrangement of an immutable collection of information that is overseen by a cluster of nodes which are not overseen by a single element. It has two significant advantages: first, it provides security and protection with the assistance of cutting-edge cryptographic tool, and second, it provides distributed autonomous functionalities with the assistance of smart contract. Smart contracts are unmodifiable and assessed by numerous machines, assisting with guarantee that the model does what it determines to do. The unchanging nature and permanent contract of smart agreements likewise permit us to dependably compute and deliver rewards for good information commitments. In our system, we put these open models into smart contract and code on a blockchain that guarantees that the determinations of settled upon terms are maintained.

8.2   Artificial intelligence in healthcare

The sophistication and growth of healthcare data imply that AI [5,6] is becoming rapidly implemented in the area. Payers and care providers, and life sciences companies are already employing various types of AI. The key classes of utilizations include determination and treatment proposals, quiet commitment and adherence, and regulatory activities. Throughout the healthcare sector, the effect of AI is changing treatment delivery through natural language processing and ML. As is the case for many sectors, these innovations are projected to continue to develop at a steady rate over the next few years. As AI discovers its way into everything from our cell phones to the flexibly chain, applications in medicinal services, its potential in healthcare services may involve activities that vary from easy to complex—everything from answering the phone to analyzing medical history and patterns and the monitoring of public health, developing medicinal medications and tools, interpreting radiology scans, creating clinical diagnosis and treatment decisions and even talking to patients.

8.2.1   Artificial intelligence doctors

In the analysis report of Healthcare Finance research study, it is mentioned that previously AI in the healthcare sector impacted low-skilled office tasks, such as processing data, and now that the increasing power of AI is affecting white-collar jobs. The programmers in the era of AI, the highly skilled professionals, are concerned of being displaced, and the transition so far seems to be occurring in a way that considers AI [7] to be more of a challenge than a resource. It is anticipated that the proliferation of new AI development firms will become a crucial factor in helping medical professionals save lives over the next 5–7 years. AI could be present in the operating area, delivering clinical laboratory facilities to identify energy disease origins that have never occurred before. Healthcare AI may operate with great accuracy and provide cost-effective treatment on a large scale. Watson's IBM diagnoses cardiovascular disease more effectively than cardiologists do. Chatbots give professional support to the United Kingdom National Health Service instead of nurses. Smartphone applications are already identifying skin cancer with great precision. Algorithms classify eye disorders as well as qualified doctors. Others expect that 90 percent of hospitals will be served by medical AI, which would eliminate as many as 80 percent of what physicians are actually doing. But in order for this to happen, the healthcare system will have to overcome the distrust of patients with AI.

AI would instantly allow patients to detect illness symptoms remotely before contacting the doctor. The AI system has the task of interpreting the disease pattern and decoding system details, and then communicating health issues to patients and professional doctors, since patients feel that their treatment requirements are special and that technologies cannot be properly handled. In order to understand the multiple benefits and cost reductions that medical AI has provided, treatment professionals need to find solutions to resolve such concerns. AI algorithms [8] appear to depend mainly on the quantity and quality of the data. In order to achieve more accurate and effective results from AIs, data must be collected by humans and analyzed and examined manually. Whether we put it more simply, we need to tell them to do it, so they will do it frequently. For certain nations, AI is built into specialized computational methods to support doctors in hospitals to detect cancer and other diseases. Figure 8.1 represents the human doctors replaced by AI-enabled robots in future.

We have to go through research studies that often take a long time and cost a lot to create a drug. The AI-compatible software will, however, render this phase quicker. AI is used to check current drugs that can be improved to battle diseases. Medical tracking using AI technologies can be used in the technologies added to smartwatch, where this smartwatch can track the heart rate and consumer level of operation. The smartwatch can track user habits with data that can be a source for doctors when the patient is sick. AI-designed machines can be used to remove lower back pressure or sciatica discomfort problems and even instruct the patient over the use of the right office chair for back pain, acupuncture, stretches and yoga tips. Only two drugs have been identified for use in the AI program that can reduce Ebola infectivity in just one day. The use of AI to detect cancer patients is to gain details on a piece of DNA. AI may conduct a body scan to identify cancers and disorders that anyone might have on the basis of their genetics.

8.2.2   AI—robot treatment

AI could even evaluate vast amounts of data and turn this information into functional tools that can help both physicians and patients. Increasing the introduction of AI into day-to-day medical systems may increase the quality of therapies and decrease rising costs in different ways. AI-controlled robotic systems [9] may increase the role of physicians, surgeons or nurses. AI eliminates problems and

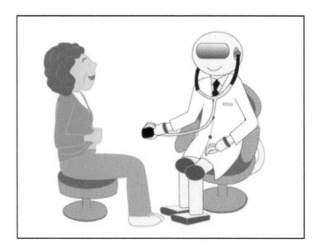

Figure 8.1   Human doctor replaced by artificial intelligence Robots

mistakes that arise during operation and initiates the hospital stay to be shorter. Robots that have been fitted with AI technologies will evaluate someone's messy report details prior to the procedure.

Robotic surgery is rapidly adopted by hospitals and clinics in the United States and Europe and used in the treatment of a wide variety of conditions. Robotic surgery, or robotic-assisted surgery, enables doctors to conduct certain forms of complicated operations with greater accuracy, versatility and power than is achievable using traditional techniques. Surgeons who employ a robotic device say that with certain operations, it increases precision, durability and stability during activity and helps them to clearly see the site relative to conventional techniques. The most commonly employed commercial robotic surgery device involves a video arm and mechanical arms with medical tools connected to them. The AI regulates the arms while positioned at the operating room.

One of the main possible advantages of AI [10] is to help people remain well enough that they do not need a doctor, or at least not as much. Figure 8.2 shows the QTrobot from LuxAI which is designed to help children with autism learn to interact with humans. The usage of AI and the Internet of Medical Things in customer health applications is benefiting people. Designers aim to build a fully autonomous diagnostician by means of robotics, thus encouraging the transfer of skills from the human doctor to the treatment machine. Robots can serve as an intermediary between a doctor and a patient where they can conduct diagnosis and care procedures, minimize human interaction and reduce the possibility of spreading infection during the coronavirus pandemic. Using these surgical procedures, surgeons may conduct difficult and complex surgeries that may have been hard or impossible with other procedures. AI is being more advanced in performing everything humans do, but more effectively, more easily and at a lower expense. Both AI and robotics are enormously promising in healthcare. During the

Figure 8.2   The QTrobot helping children with autism learn to interact with humans

procedure, the robot can lead and direct the surgeon. The usage of this robot will also create new surgical procedures from data from previous operations to speed up and simplify the procedure method. Robotic surgery also makes minimally invasive surgery feasible. The benefits of minimally invasive surgery include fewer risks, such as surgical site diseases, less suffering and loss of blood, faster regeneration and less visible marks.

The conference, hosted by Abu Dhabi-based TRENDS Research & Advisory, brought together global leaders to address the role of AI, ML, big data and other technology in the ongoing battle against COVID-19, which has infected more than 7.55 million people and killed more than 423,000 people worldwide. Robotic nurses have been created by a variety of companies and start-ups. An example is Molly, created by Sense. This robotic nurse helps nurses to screen and track the condition of the patient. Robots, artificial speakers (smart speakers such as Siri or Alexa) and AI may help offer solution to a patient's concern, says the NHS study.

8.2.3   AR/VR treatment

Augmented reality (AR) [11] is one of the newest technologies on the way to a range of industries, including gaming, medical, automobile and shopping. Since the 1960s, AR technology has been in progress. Two popular AI technologies are VR (virtual reality) and AR. When properly utilized, these tools can assist with effective treatment and enhanced care for patients, among several other benefits. In so many ways, AR is a combination of VR, imposed on real life. Such simulated contents are normally in the form of digital imagery or sound, commonly used in 3D models or videos. As data access technologies are now very sophisticated, the next move is to offer real-time, life-saving patient knowledge to surgeons that they can use in easy or complicated operations. Before utilizing AR, these surgeons used to use a portable scanner to identify major blood vessels around the injury, but now AR technology lets them detect the major blood vessels clearly and accurately by showing them in a three-dimensional simulated image. Figure 8.3 shows a group of doctors conducting surgery with the help of VR.

AR [12] will not only be used to undertake accurate and low-risk operation but can also enable doctors save time in the case of an emergency operation. Instead of searching for documents or online medical reports, surgeons may view all of this information on their AR monitor in a matter of seconds. For the people who come to the hospital for a basic treatment, nurses may use AR to locate the veins better. AccuVein is an AR start-up that utilizes a portable device and then projects across the skin of the patient and lets nurses assess where the veins are. AR works with the use of a variety of instruments, such as cameras, computer hardware or display screens. Surgeons will be able to visualize bones, muscles and internal organs without even having to cut open a body. It will also help them decide precisely when to make injections and incisions, which could be used to show life-saving details for patients and first aid during a medical emergency. Figure 8.3 shows a group of doctors conducting surgery with the help of VR.

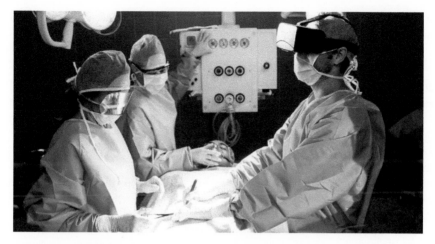

Figure 8.3   Doctors are conducting operation with help of virtual reality

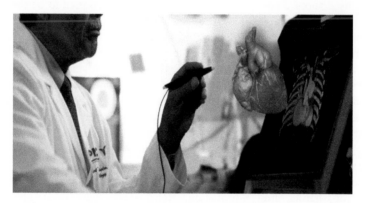

Figure 8.4   A doctor analyzing the human heart through augmented reality

There are many examples of how AR [13] can support surgeons in the process of procedures. If surgeons are doing a small operation or operating on a life-long tumor, AR will help save the lives of the patients, and we have just started to see how important this tool is to surgeons. AR often helps doctors to properly recognize and correctly interpret the signs of their patients. Patients sometimes fail to correctly explain their symptoms to clinicians, but with AR, patients can properly define their symptoms. Throughout hospitals, including Imperial College and St. Mary's Hospital in London, physicians and clinicians have also been using Microsoft's HoloLens AR glasses during multiple surgeries to treat people who have sustained severe injuries. Figure 8.4 shows a doctor analyzing the human heart through AR. AR would enable surgeons to accurately research the anatomy of their patients by inserting their magnetic resonance imaging (MRI) data and computed tomography (CT) scans into the AR headset and overlaying detailed patient anatomy on the top of their body before they finally conduct surgery. Figures 8.3 and 8.4 show how AR and VR are helping doctors.

8.2.4 Non-adherence to prescriptions

Patients who diligently [14] observe the schedule of drugs as indicated is called medication adherence. In the event where the patient refuses to comply or conform to the drug plan, it would be the case of medication non-adherence, shown in Figure 8.5. The main reasons behind medication non-adherence are the absent mindedness of larger parts of patients. The next is that the expense of the medications can discourage the patients to reestablish the remedy. Regimen multifaceted nature carries a wide explanation too, and a lot of individuals likewise identify the reactions of the medications as a purpose behind non-adherence. Many uncertainties about the medication itself or the need to take it prompt them not adhering to it.

Poor adherence to prescription medications, particularly in patients with chronic diseases, is a major challenge for both clinicians and patients. Half of the 3.2 billion prescription drugs given annually in the United States are not consumed as guided by doctors. Poor adherence to medications is reported to be the source between 33 and 69 percent of medical-related patient admissions in the United States, contributing to nearly 125,000 deaths each year.

The blockchain technologies are used to reward patients with crypto tokens so that they take their drug as ordered any time [15]. Gained tokens can then be used to reduce co-payments or their health insurance costs. The virtual assistant prompts patients to affirm that they have taken their drugs as indicated. This patient-reported knowledge is maintained in a safe blockchain-based Hyperledger system and is only exchanged with doctors, hospitals, medication suppliers and healthcare providers after agreement. Access to exact and finish drug narratives across medicinal services foundations empowers successful patient consideration. Narratives across medicinal services establishments at present depend on incorporated frameworks for sharing drug information. Nonetheless, there is an absence of

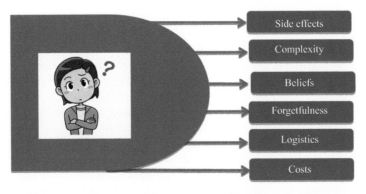

Figure 8.5   The main reasons of non-adherence of medication

productive components to guarantee that medicine narratives moved starting with one foundation then onto the next are precise, secure and reliable.

8.3   Blockchain in healthcare

Blockchain technology [16] has the power to change healthcare services, put the consumer at the forefront of the healthcare environment and improve medical data protection, safety and information sharing. Blockchain infrastructure provides a digital archive of transfers or transactions digitally. By rendering electronic medical records more effective, disintermediate and safer, this development may offer a new paradigm for health information exchanges. This new, rapidly evolving field provides fertile ground for experimentation, investment and proof-of-concept testing, although it is not a panacea. Blockchain technologies will help make the transition from organization-driven interoperability to patient-centered interoperability feasible. Blockchain technology enables patients to grant access guidelines for their medical records, enabling different researchers, for example, to view portions of their records within a limited time span. Patients can connect to other hospitals with blockchain technology and collect their medical data automatically.

Maintaining our significant health data secured [17] is currently the most popular healthcare blockchain application, which is not surprising at all. In the healthcare industry, security is a major issue. The data attacks revealed more than 176 million medical details in between 2009 and 2017. The attackers stole credit cards and financial documents, as well as details of health and biological testing. The capacity of blockchain to create an incorruptible, immutable and open database of all patient details renders it a platform fertile for safety applications. Moreover, although blockchain is open, it is also confidential, concealing any individual's identification with complicated and protected codes that can safeguard the security of medical details. The open aspect of the system often helps patients, physicians and healthcare professionals to easily and safely access the same details.

8.3.1   Blockchain in healthcare

Blockchain, the innovation hidden behind the blast in digital currency, is presently being considered for an increasingly important use for our clinical and healthcare facilities. Effectively, a considerable lot of our clinical records sit in the cloud, put there by specialists' workplaces and medical clinics—saving money on information execution costs, giving fast access, and in any other events, saving lives. Blockchain could rehash the manner in which patient's electronic healthcare records are shared and put away by giving more secure instruments to well-being data exchange of clinical information in the human services industry, by making sure about it over a decentralized distributed system.

Blockchain's open access would empower changes to a person's electronic health record (EHR) [18] (new imaging, methodology, labs) to be refreshed continuously on an EHR blockchain and immediately accessible to parties engaged with a person's consideration (social insurance suppliers, drug stores, insurance agencies, the patient). Blockchain additionally is intended to include security through its encryption. The conveyance of patients' healthcare records through a blockchain would be finished on a characterized approval premise. In spite of the administrative difficulties of managing tolerant information, blockchain's capacity to oversee information that is both carefully designed and mysterious makes it the best answers for fix human services' interoperability issues, as indicated by Shada Alsalamah, a meeting researcher in MIT's Media Lab.

Figure 8.6 shows the communication of medical records with different parties involved in the healthcare area. When discussing blockchain in healthcare, one of the applications that gets the most publicity is the formation of decentralized patient-controlled healthcare records. Blockchain innovation can significantly change healthcare IT to improve things. Lamentably, with the present promotion, blockchain is utilized and mishandled as a panacea for some of the issues of present-day medicinal IT services, to be specific interoperability and secure capacity. Blockchain will not settle those issues, which lead us to disappointment and dissatisfaction. MedRec, one model utilizing blockchains, is expected to improve electronic clinical records and permit patients' records to be obtained safely by any supplier who needs it illuminating the exercise in futility, cash and duplication in systems, disarray and once in a while even hazardous issues of records being circulated across a wide range of offices and suppliers.

8.3.2   Medical credential tracking

Blockchain is an innovation that stores information on a large number of servers permitting anyone on the network to exchange information [19]. This supports one

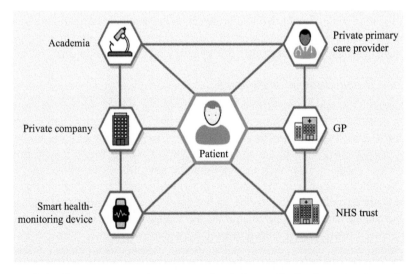

Figure 8.6   Communication between medical data with third parties through blockchain

to make correspondence arrangements that could encourage healthcare information sharing. Blockchain is a public ledger, which can be straightforwardly shared among dissimilar clients to make an immutable record of exchanges, each transaction timestamped and connected to the earlier exchange. The collection of exchanges turns into another block in the chain attached to the following block by a unique secure code. People would be conceded to get to it, and once information is entered, it cannot be eradicated. While certainly feasible, the blockchain is incredibly hard to be hacked. To control this sort of information framework, one would need to get to each and every system on the network. The suppliers apparently would keep up the control of their own information by keeping the private key, offering access to their credentials as they decide to medical clinics, insurers or information archives by means of the public key. Figure 8.7 shows some of the benefits of blockchain in medical data.

8.3.3   Drug trials

In the clinical trials in which a patient needs to get himself/herself enlisted for a clinical trial procedure, he/she needs to complete all the recommended tests once more, regardless of whether the equivalent were led quite recently. Figure 8.8 shows the blockchain-based clinical trials in the future.

Blockchains can address most of these issues directly, for example,

- Clinical data security: The capacity to follow each record and change over multiple nodes in a system.
- Immutable transaction ledger: The Federal Drug Administration (FDA) requires provable information, and blockchain records can give unchanging verification to records.
- Historical data: Having the option to follow each change, who made it, and when it was made is pivotal for clinical trials. A blockchain can make it one stride further by keeping this information in a similar spot.

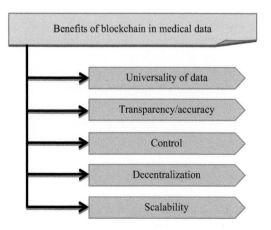

Figure 8.7   Benefits of blockchain in medical data

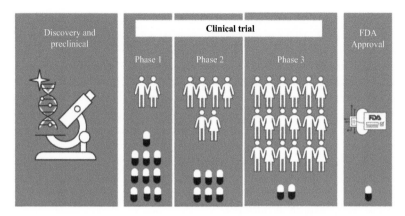

Figure 8.8   The future of blockchain-based clinical trails

- Interoperability: Exchanging data between nodes, telephones, systems, servers and others without depending on email or different techniques is pivotal for information trustworthiness.

Pharmaceutical organizations and research foundations [20] are feeling the strain to decrease the time, money and other asset costs related with directing clinical trials. Due to the development of applications of newer technologies, for example, AI, robotic process automation (RPA) and blockchain and other distributed ledger technologies, many see another way to increase productive and powerful procedures that can address the difficulties faced today. The quality of clinical research is sabotaged by extreme unfortunate behaviors, mistakes, and misrepresentations, which are unfavorable to the trust it ought to excite. In this point of view, we show how blockchains may follow and control the procedures of clinical trials to forestall these issues or if nothing else discourage them since they would get detectable and turned away.

On the basis of secure exchanges between partners organizing clinical trials, an ongoing report proposes that blockchain innovation could be a great solution. The evaluation of the estimation of blockchain innovation to the life sciences area will be somewhere between $3 billion and $5.6 billion by 2025, with the previous estimate created by PreScouter, a Chicago-based research intelligence organization. Triall unites a consortium of clinical trial specialists and blockchain engineers, which was established to handle a portion of the persevering issues that make clinical trial tasks excessively perplexing, lengthy and resource-inefficient.

8.4   Linear algebra in ML

The ideas of linear algebra (LA) are pivotal for identifying the hypothesis behind ML, especially for deep learning. They give us better instinct for how calculations exactly work in the engine, which empowers us to settle on better choices.

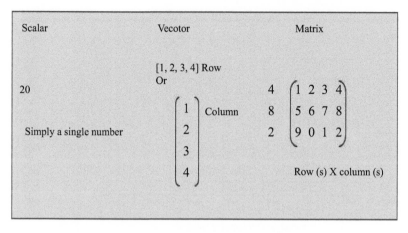

Figure 8.9   Linear algebra variables

The idea of LA is a part of arithmetic that lets us briefly portray the coordinates and interactions of planes in higher dimensions and perform procedures on them. LA manages linear equations and linear functions which are represented through networks and vectors. Generally, LA makes us comprehend geometric terms, for example, planes, in higher dimensions, and perform mathematical procedure on them. By definition, variable-based math manages scalars (one-dimensional elements), yet LA has vectors and matrices shown in Figure 8.9 (substances which have at least two-dimensional parts) to manage linear equations and functions. LA can likewise be called the extended version of algebra. Then, on the off chance that we may truly need to be an expert in this field, we should ace the parts of LA that are well significant for ML. In LA, data or information is represented by linear equations [1], which are then introduced as matrices and vectors. Accordingly, we are for most part managing matrices and vectors instead of scalars. At the same point, when we have the correct libraries, as NumPy, at our disposal, we can compute complex framework multiplication effectively works with only a few lines of code.

8.4.1   Dataset and data files

An informational collection is an assortment of data or information, simply dataset. On account of plain data or information, an informational index compares to at least single-database tables, where each single section of a table represents a specific variable, and each row relates to a given record of the knowledge collection being referred to those in Figure 8.10. ML methods learn from various examples. It is critical to have great control over data or information and the different kinds of phrasings utilized while depicting information. In this exact area, we will get familiar with the various phrasings utilized efficiently in ML when it is referring to information.

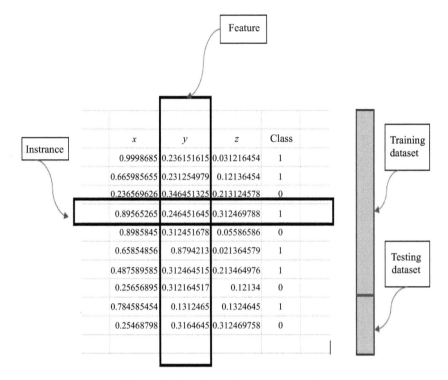

Figure 8.10   Example of dataset tables

This information is in fact a matrix (table of content): a key data pattern in LA. If we divide the information into different sources of information and fit a directed "supervised ML model," for example, the estimations and the flower species, we have a vector (Y) and a framework (X). This is another key information pattern in LA.

All lines are in the same length, for example, a similar number of sections; in this way, the information are vectorized, where columns may be given to a method or model each in turn or in clusters, and the system can be pre-arranged to anticipate lines of a fixed size.

8.4.2   *Images and photographs*

A photograph is another case of a table of content from LA. We are increasingly used to working with pictures or photos in computer vision applications. Each picture that we process is itself a table model with a width and stature and 1-pixel esteem in every cell for highly contrasting pictures or 3-pixel esteems in every cell for a shaded picture. Procedures on the picture, for example, trimming, scaling, shearing, cropping, are totally described utilizing the documentation and activities of LA.

1	red
2	green
3	blue
4	yellow
5	magenta

It may encoded as:

1	red, green, blue, yellow, magenta
2	1, 0, 0, 0, 0
3	0, 1, 0, 0, 0
4	0, 0, 1, 0, 0
5	0, 0, 0, 1, 0
6	0, 0, 0, 0, 1

Figure 8.11   Example of one-hot encoding

Cropping intends to remove undesirable territories from a picture. This procedure is one of the most essential photograph control forms. This procedure is undertaken to remove an undesirable subject or immaterial detail from a photograph, change its perspective proportion or to improve the general composition.

8.4.3   One-hot encoding

One-hot encoding: It is a procedure by which categorical variables are changed over into a structure that could be given to ML calculations to make a superior showing in forecast. To demonstrate categorical variables, we utilize one-hot encoding. This sort of categorical variable binary representation is called one-hot, in light of the fact that each line has one component with an estimation of 1 and different highlights with an estimation of 0.

Far and wide we work with categorical data in AI. Maybe the class marks for classification issues or maybe categorical input factors. It is not unexpected to encode variables to shape them simpler to deal with and understood by certain methods. One-hot encoding is the place where a matrix is created to deal with the variable with one section for every classification and a column for every model in the information set. A check is included in the segment for the categorical-value for a given set, and a zero-value is mapped [2] to every single other segment.

For example, the color variable with the five rows showed in Figure 8.11.

Each line is encoded as paired vector, a vector with 0 or 1 value, and this is a case of a sparse-representation, an entire subfield of LA. This technique has the following advantages:

- deciding the state has a low and steady expense of getting to one flip-flop;
- changing the state has the consistent expense of getting to two flip-flops;
- simple to plan and adjust and
- simple to distinguish illegal states.

And the disadvantage is as follows:

- Requires more flip-flops than different encodings, making it unrealistic for PAL gadgets, and a large number of the states are illegal.

8.4.4   Applications

LA can be utilized to process information to achieve tasks such as edge discovery, obscuring, graphical transformations, face transforming, object location and following, sound and picture compression, signal processing and damnation part of different undertakings. LA functions as a calculation motor in ML.

8.4.4.1   Clinical trial design

The clinical preliminary is a primary mainstay of the pharmaceutical medication revelation process. Basically, clinical preliminaries are inquiring about examinations which try to decide whether a clinical treatment or device is protected and viable for people. While the pharmaceutical medication industry has encountered a few changes, it stays a gainful market.

Clinical trial design [3]: Companies are creating ML calculations to assist scientists with overseeing clinical preliminary work processes.

Clinical trial optimization: Companies are creating ML models to anticipate which patients are in danger of dropping out of clinical preliminaries to forestall dangers to preliminary legitimacy.

Most of the ML use cases and developing advancements for clinical preliminaries seem to revolve around three essential applications:

- *Patient recruitment:* Companies are creating programming stages to more readily coordinate patients to clinical preliminaries depending on indicated measures.
- *Clinical trial design:* Companies are creating ML calculations to assist scientists with overseeing clinical preliminary work processes.
- *Clinical trial optimization:* Companies are creating ML models to anticipate which patients are in danger of dropping out of clinical preliminaries to forestall dangers to trial validity.

There is likewise the chance of clinical research as a consideration choice. Envision a patient in future that enters a center and the doctors are attempting to analyze an up-to-this-point undefined condition. The doctors are probably going to run a progression of tests on the patient. In the interim, the calculations recommend that the condition might be an uncommon illness for which effective treatment alternatives do not yet exist, yet there are clinical preliminaries. The doctor would have the choice to take an advantage of the clinical research foundation to additionally screen and treat the patient.

Thus, this has achieved a few things. It has helped the doctors combine the gigantic measure of information available to them, decreasing the patient's expense for screening and diagnostics since the conventions regularly take into consideration backers to support the screening.

8.4.4.2   Medical imagery

Clinical imaging refers to methods and procedures used to make pictures of different parts of the human body for symptomatic and asymptomatic treatment purposes with advanced equipment. The term "clinical imaging" [4] incorporates different radiological imaging procedures, for example, X-beam radiography, ultrasound, MRI and nuclear medicine. ML is a method for perceiving patterns that can be applied to clinical images. ML ordinarily starts with the ML calculation framework; processing the picture includes those that are accepted to be of significance in making the prediction or analysis of interest.

The uses of ML in healthcare include mainly digital diagnosis. ML can recognize the patterns of specific sicknesses inside patient electronic healthcare records and illuminate clinicians regarding any anomalies. To exhibit how ML can give a clinical determination, we will walk you through a step-by-step case of how the innovation can be utilized to recognize and analyze cancer or tumor diagnose:

1. dividing the data set
2. defining the metrics
3. evaluating the models
4. creating a neural network model
5. evaluating output quality
6. visualizing the decision boundaries
7. final prediction

However, so as to trust in the models, we have to additionally test them with new data and ensure that they are as yet prompting excellent outcomes.

8.4.4.3   Treatment planning for nuclear medicine

Nuclear medicines are the utilization of radioactive materials in diagnostic or remedial systems, most remarkably medicines for different types of cancer growth. Nuclear medicine imaging utilizes limited quantities of radioactive particles considered radiotracers that are commonly infused into blood system, swallowed or breathed in through nose. The tracer effectively goes through the zone where inspected and emits vitality as radio beams such as "gamma" beams which can recognized by a unique camera and a computer to make clear pictures of within human body. Special atomic medication imaging gives exceptional data that frequently cannot be obtained utilizing other strategies and offers the chances to recognize illness in its very most punctual states.

Radiotracers are particles connected to a limited quantity of radioactive substances that can be distinguished on positron emission tomography (PET) [5] output. Radiotracers gather in the tumors or may be in the regions of inflammation. They can likewise tie up to explicit different proteins in human body. In this field, most ordinarily utilized radiotracer is "F-18 fluorodeoxyglucose," or "FDG," a particle like glucose. Malignant human cells are all the more metabolically dynamic and ingest glucose at a big rate. This higher rate can be identified on PET sweeps. This permits doctor to distinguish disease before it might be seen on other imaging tests. FDG is only one of the numerous radiotracers being used or being developed. Doctors effectively utilize the nuclear medicine imaging strategies to picture and analyze the function and model of an organ, bone, tissue or internal framework inside the body. Atomic medications are utilized to

- detect coronary artery disease;
- visualize internal heart blood flow;
- identify heart transplant rejection;
- scan and visualize lungs for respiratory problems and internal blood flow systems;
- check metastatic bone disease;
- check painful prosthetic joints;
- detect the early onset of Alzheimer's disease;
- identify abnormal function or inflammation of the gallbladder;
- assess postoperative medical complications of gallbladder surgery;
- check fever of unknown source and
- check lymphedema.

8.5   New medical imaging modalities

The usage of imaging pre-techniques in clinical radiation is expanding with novel mechanical advances in clinical sciences. The range of a wide scope of imaging modalities is the major specialty of nuclear medicine, MRI and ultrasound, PET, medical radiation, angiography and CT scanners. These are helpful for patient monitoring, with respect to the advancement of the disease condition, which has just been analyzed, or potentially is experiencing a treatment idea.

8.5.1   Multivalued data images

We know about grayscale picture where an estimated single pixel at any picture point can be represented by a single-valued function inside the scope of 0–255 out of an 8-bit framework. Operating at a black and bright intensity picture, the visual boost covers the whole bandwidth capacity of the noticeable range running from 0.4 to 0.7 μm. The intensity model in a picture relies upon the properties of the sensors and estimating gadgets utilized in imaging the item where distinctive physical properties of article contribute diversely while creating intensity map of the item. Such images are normally represented multivalued function that implies that more than single estimations are created at the item point.

Categories of multivalued images can be grouped into the following two points:

- Multispectral: Measurements relate to various spectral groups of frequencies of electromagnetic waves. Color IP is the most widely recognized case of multispectral pictures.
- Multimodal: Measuring diverse physical properties of an article utilizing various sensors, for instance, CT scan, ultrasonography, MRI, single photon emission CT, PET and so on.

8.5.2 *Phase contrast magnetic resonance angiography (MRA)*

Phase contrast (PC)-MRA is a particular kind of MRI utilized principally to decide stream speeds. PC-MRA [6] can be viewed as a strategy for magnetic resonance velocimetry. It additionally gives a strategy for magnetic resonance angiography. PC-MRA utilizes the stage shifts acquainted with cores with movement within the sight of an attractive field inclination. A bipolar attractive field inclination will initiate a stage move to cores moving along the slope reliant on the speed, just as increasing speed and higher request movement terms. Increasingly mind-boggling slope waveforms empower affectability to explicit movement terms, for example, speed or quickening. By developing a picture in which the force is corresponding to the stage move of the cores, it is conceivable to make an angiographic picture identified with the stream properties of blood (or different fluids, for example, cerebrospinal liquid). The PC-MRA is an incredible procedure and takes into consideration the encoding of stream in one or numerous ways so that the speed affectability can be picked relying upon the vessel of intrigue. This strategy additionally takes into consideration the evaluation of stream speed and stream rate, which is not commonly accessible with other angiographic strategies.

The phase effects for fixed and moving spins exposed to a couple of bipolar slopes are represented in the diagram. A fixed turn exposed to such an inclination pair will encounter no net phase change, yet a moving spin has a net phase shift corresponding to its speed. Two spins streaming at a similar speed however in inverse ways will have equivalent yet inverse phase shifts shown in Figure 8.12. While estimating changes in the phase, along these lines, velocity can be registered.

The most generally utilized applications today are as follows:

- two-dimensional mode to create a vascular scout image prior to performing a non-PC-MRA technique;
- cine mode for qualitative or quantitative cerebrospinal fluid (CSF) flow calculation;
- two-dimensional or three-dimensional mode for intracranial MR venography and
- three-dimensional MR angiogram for niche applications.

8.5.3 *Diffusion tensor MRI*

DTI (diffusion tensor imaging) is a magnetic reverberation imaging strategy that empowers the estimation of the limited dispersion of water in tissue so as to deliver neural tract pictures as opposed to utilizing this information exclusively to allocate differentiation or hues to pixels in a valid cross-sectional picture. It permits the basic mapping of the diffusion procedure of atoms, essentially water, in organic tissues. Subatomic dispersion in tissues is not free, yet reflects interactions on numerous impediments, for example, macromolecules, fibers and membranes. Pure water particle dispersion examples can in this way uncover microscopic concerning tissue design, either ordinary or in an ailing state. An exceptional sort of diffusion weighted imaging (DWI), diffusion tensor imaging (DTI) [7], has been utilized

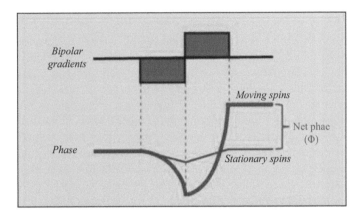

Figure 8.12   Phase contrast MRA

widely to delineate the issues of tractography in the brain. Diffusion MRI system of the brain was found to have quick utility for the assessment of suspected intense ischemic brain stroke. Since that time, enormous basic strides forward in the innovation of diffusion imaging model have extraordinarily improved picture strength and empowered numerous new medical or clinical applications. These incorporate the determination of the intracranial pyogenic contaminations, masses, injury and various vasogenic-versus-cytotoxic edemas. Moreover, the appearance of DTI and special fiber tractography has opened a totally new non-invasive window on the bright white issue network of the human brain. DTI and fiber tractography have just propelled the logical comprehension of numerous neurologic as well as psychiatric issues and have been efficiently applied medically for the mapping of expressive white issue tracts before the intracranial mass resections.

The major applications of DTI are as follows:

- efficient tract-specific localization of white matter lesions;
- specific localization of tumors in the relation to the different white matter tracts (deflection, infiltration, edema, destruction);
- localization of the major white matter tracts for the neurosurgical planning and
- evaluation of the white matter growth or maturation.

8.5.4   Federated tensor factorization

The federated tensor factorization is for computational phenotyping [8]; utilizing this technique, the various emergency clinics iteratively improve tensors and move secure summed up data to a local server, and the local server totals the data to produce various phenotypes. Tensor factorization models offer a successful way to deal with and convert huge electronic medical health data records into important clinical ideas for data analysis. These models seek a lot of differing tests to avoid unwanted population predisposition. An open test is the manner by which to determine phenotypes together over numerous medical clinics, in which the

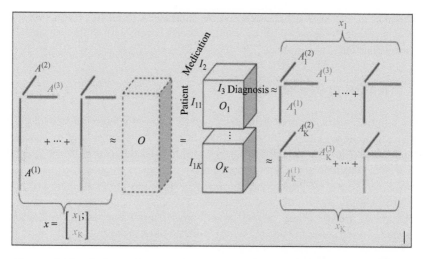

Figure 8.13   Federated tensor factorization for computational phenotyping

patient-level information sharing is absurd (e.g., because of institutional strategies). This will build up a novel method for empowering combined tensor factorization track for the computational phenotyping shown in Figure 8.13 without local sharing of patient-level information. Created secure information harmonization and its federated computation procedures depend on exchanging course technique for multipliers alternating direction method of multipliers (ADMM). Utilizing this technique, the numerous emergency clinics iteratively update the tensors and move secure summed up data to a focal server, and server totals the data and to produce phenotypes.

In federated technique, the hospitals/clinics perform the greater part of calculations, and a semi-believed server bolsters the medical clinic by collecting results from hospitals/clinics. The hospitals request a specific type of summed up tolerant data (not persistent-level information) at any rate for refreshing tensor. A test of the tensor factorization is the summed-up data that can unveil the patient-level information. For instance, a target capacity of tensor factorization is $\|X-O\|^2$, where X is a tensor to be assessed utilizing a watched tensor O. Since the target work is not directly detachable over hospitals, tensor factorization for every emergency clinic unavoidably requests the other quiet-level information. Hence, hospitals should share summed up data that does not uncover the patient-level information, yet rather contains precise phenotypes from the patient-level information.

Current methodologies for making an interpretation of EHR information into helpful phenotypes are commonly moderate, physically serious and restricted in scope. Conquering a few weaknesses of the past strategies, tensor factorization techniques have demonstrated incredible potential in finding important phenotypes from complexed and heterogeneous medical health records. On account of inspecting mistake, noise in the summed-up data can increment with little patient populations. Exactness at that point can be diminished or shaky. In this way, we have to guarantee the strength of rundown data even with little estimated or unevenly distributed examples.

8.6   Medical appliance of norms

Every single clinical device, from computerized thermometers to nebulizers to imaging equipment and all other clinical devices, will be administered by standards and guidelines [9]. The guidelines determining clinical devices as drugs cover all instruments, appliance, apparatus or embeds utilized for analysis, prevention, observing, treatment or lightening of disease or disorder, injury or handicap, control of origination and life-support hardware.

Exercises include drugs, antibodies and other natural items, and clinical devices include in vitro diagnostics with four work streams/groups:

- technologies, standards and norms;
- safety and vigilance;
- regulatory systems strengthening and
- prequalification of medicines, vaccines and IVDs.

8.6.1   Significance of medical devices

Clinical devices are important for protected and powerful prevention, analysis, treatment and rehabilitation of sickness and disease. In the field of hospitals, the clinical equipment are assumed to have an imperative role in the medical diagnosis, observation and proper treatment of various types of medical issues. These devices are intended to keep up thorough security standards so as to guarantee the highest safety of patients, and nonusage of these clinical/medical instruments could essentially pull down the clinical business and become a higher detrimental to the lives of billions of individuals around the world. Along these lines, it is highly basic that the equipment should be appropriately taken into consideration to ensure the usefulness and their unwavering quality. Clinical equipment is grouped into five unique classifications: diagnostic, monitors, support, therapeutic and clinical lab.

The diagnostic systems are utilized to decide the major identity of a potential ailment/issue and may incorporate devices such as X-ray devices, ultrasound, PET, CT and MRI scanners. Therapeutic devices are generally used to help the patients during their stay in the hospital and after various surgeries which incorporate infusion pump, LASIK surgical machines and medical lasers. Regardless of the sort of clinical equipment utilized, it is exceptionally significant that they ought to be appropriately kept up to convey longer services and to keep away from the spread of diseases. Obviously, some clinical equipment is expendable, for example, needles and gloves; however, it is not wise to discard costly devices between uses. There are different manners by which we could guarantee the usefulness of these devices. To begin with, on the off chance that we are utilizing reusable home clinical devices, we could clean them after each use with cotton soaked in scouring alcohol. After this procedure, place the debased device in an ultrasound shower that is loaded up with disinfectant solution for 15 min.

8.6.2   Medical device safety

Medical safety is described as the safety with respect to the clinical devices, diseases and human services of the unhealthy patients. Clinical safety is a wide term that can be utilized for hospital safety, medical device safety, drug safety and numerous others which go under clinical safety. The basic design and manufacturing standards are listed here, which are highly applicable to clinical equipment and IVD clinical devices.

- Medical equipment and IVD medical devices ought to accomplish the device performance proposed by their manufacturer and ought to be planned and fabricated so that, during expected states of utilization, they are reasonable for their proposed reason. They ought to be safe and proceed as proposed, ought to have dangers that are satisfactory when it weighed against the advantages to the medical patient and should not bargain the condition or the safety of patients.
- Producers ought to build up, implement, record and keep up a high-risk management framework to guarantee the continuous high quality, and safety and then execute the medical gadget. The risk-management ought to be comprehended as continuous procedure all through the whole cycle of a clinical device and the IVD medical equipment, requiring customary precise updating.
- Risk-control estimates embraced by the manufacturers for plan and production of the medical gadgets and IVD medical equipment ought to comply with safety standards, assessing the by and large recognized best in class. At the point when risk minimization is needed, manufacturers would control chances so the leftover risk related with each danger just as the general lingering risk can make a decision satisfactory.
- The manufacturer ought to inform the clients regarding any significant residual risks.
- All known clinical risks and predictable dangers, and any unpredictable reactions, ought to be limited and need to be satisfactory when it weighed against the assessed benefits emerging from the accomplished performance of the equipment during planned states of utilization considering the for the most part recognized cutting edge.
- Appropriately lessen the dangers identified with the highlights of medical equipment and IVD medical equipment and environment in which the medical equipment and IVD medical equipment are expected to be utilized.

8.6.3   Global Harmonization Task Force

The GHTF (Global Harmonization Task Force) is a group of delegates such as national medical equipment administrative specialists and the individuals from the medical equipment industry whose objective is the normalization of medical equipment guideline across the entire world. The GHTF additionally promotes technological development and encourages worldwide exchange. The essential methods are the ones by which their objectives are cultivated through the distribution as well as dispersal of harmonized direction proceedings for fundamental administrative practices. The GHTF was established in 1993 by the administrations and different industry representatives of Japan, Canada, Australia, the European Union and the United States. The motivation behind the task force is to support the union in principles and administrative practices identified with the safety, performance, lifetime and quality of medical devices. The task force also advances technical and mechanical development and encourages worldwide exchange. The essential method by which its objectives are accomplished is operated by means of the distribution, and scattering of harmonized direction records for fundamental administrative practices. This will help the developing countries to provide well-defined medical establishments for the patients.

Most advanced developing nations have insufficient national strategies and guidelines covering clinical/medical devices. WHO, in a joint effort with GHTF, could encourage access for advancing and developing nations (both those bringing in and those wishing to produce) to

- data on the major administrative frameworks for medical equipment;
- device approvals and innovation appraisal from exceptionally managed markets;
- appropriation of a solitary medical equipment classification;
- creative innovation propels and
- systems for post-market surveillance and vigilance.

8.6.4 Classification of medical devices

The FDA groups medical equipment into three principle categories: Classes I, II and III. The task of classification of equipment depends upon the level of risk [10] that is related with the equipment.

There are three classes of devices:

- Class I: These devices are generally safe. The Class I devices are considered as the most minimal degree of risk of every clinical device and are along these lines required to conform to the less degree of administrative level control. Examples are bandages, soft handheld surgical instruments, dental floss and enemas and nonelectric light wheelchairs.
- Class II: These devices are intermediate-risk medical devices. These devices are more complicated than Class I devices. These devices are likewise considered a marginally higher degree of risk than Class I devices and therefore require increasingly severe administrative controls to give confirmation of their adequacy and device safety; 43 percent of the medical equipment fall under this class. Most medical devices are viewed as Class II devices. Instances of Class II devices incorporate powered wheelchairs and some of the types of pregnancy test packs.

- Class III: These devices are the high-risk ones that are critical to health or sustaining life. They are likewise considered the highest risk and along these lines require well progressively severe administrative helps and controls to give confirmation of their adequacy and safety. Examples of Class III devices include implantable heart pacemakers and breast inserts.

There are various factors that decide how a medical device is characterized; these factors include the following:

- The span of time for which the medical device will be used.
- If the medical device is surgically invasive or not.
- If the medical device is active or surgically implantable.
- If the medical device contains medicinal substances.

References

[1] Joshi, A. V. (2020). Machine Learning and Artificial Intelligence. Springer.

[2] Ma, Y., Wang, Z., Yang, H. and Yang, L. (2020). Artificial intelligence applications in the development of autonomous vehicles: A survey. IEEE/CAA Journal of Automatica Sinica, 7(2), 315–329.

[3] Khan, M. A. and Salah, K. (2018). IoT security: Review, blockchain solutions, and open challenges. Future Generation Computer Systems, 82, 395–411.

[4] Kshetri, N. (2017). Blockchain's roles in strengthening cyber security and protecting privacy. Telecommunications Policy, 41(10), 1027–1038.

[5] Le Nguyen, T. and Do, T. T. H. (2019). "Artificial intelligence in healthcare: A new technology benefit for both patients and doctors," 2019 Portland International Conference on Management of Engineering and Technology (PICMET), Portland, OR, USA, pp. 1–15, doi: 10.23919/PICMET.2019.8893884.

[6] Arjun, K. P. and Kumar, K. S. (2020). Machine learning – A neoteric medicine to healthcare. International Journal on Emerging Technologies, 11(3), 195–201.

[7] Amisha, M. P, Pathania, M. and Rathaur, V. K. (2019). Overview of artificial intelligence in medicine. Journal of Family Medicine and Primary Care, 8(7), 2328–2331. doi:10.4103/jfmpc.jfmpc_440_19.

[8] Smith, J. (2020). Can Artificial Intelligence Replace the Role of Doctors? ReadWrite.

[9] Bhandari, M., Zeffiro, T. and Reddiboina, M. (2020). Artificial intelligence and robotic surgery: Current perspective and future directions. Current Opinion in Urology, 30(1), 48–54.

[10] Fiske, A., Henningsen, P. and Buyx, A. (2019). Your robot therapist will see you now: ethical implications of embodied artificial intelligence in psychiatry, psychology, and psychotherapy. Journal of Medical Internet Research, 21(5), e13216.

[11] Cipresso, P., Giglioli, I. A. C., Raya, M. A. and Riva, G. (2018). The past, present, and future of virtual and augmented reality research: A network and cluster analysis of the literature. Frontiers in Psychology, 9, 2086. Published 2018 Nov 6. doi:10.3389/fpsyg.2018.02086.

[12] Li, X., Xu, B., Teng, Y., Ren, Y. and Hu, Z. (2014). "Comparative research of AR and VR technology based on user experience," 2014 International Conference on Management Science & Engineering 21st Annual Conference Proceedings, Helsinki, pp. 1820–1827.

[13] Nayyar, A., Mahapatra, B., Le, D.-N. and Suseendran, G. (2018). Virtual reality (VR) & augmented reality (AR) technologies for tourism and hospitality industry. International Journal of Engineering and Technology (UAE). 7. 10.14419/ijet.v7i2.21.11858.

[14] Kleinsinger, F. (2018). The unmet challenge of medication nonadherence. The Permanente Journal, 22, 18–33. doi:10.7812/TPP/18-033.

[15] Labovitz, D. L., Shafner, L., Reyes Gil, M., Virmani, D. and Hanina, A. (2017). Using artificial intelligence to reduce the risk of nonadherence in patients on anticoagulation therapy. Stroke, 48(5), 1416–1419.

[16] Hussien, H. M., Yasin, S. M., Udzir, S. N. I., *et al.* (2019). A systematic review for enabling of develop a blockchain technology in healthcare application: Taxonomy, substantially analysis, motivations, challenges, recommendations and future direction. Journal of Medical Systems, 43, 320.

[17] McGhin, T., Raymond Choo, K.-K., Liu, C. Z. and He, D. (2019). Blockchain in healthcare applications: Research challenges and opportunities. Journal of Network and Computer Applications.

[18] Pirtle, C. and Ehrenfeld, J. (2018). Blockchain for healthcare: The next generation of medical records? Journal of Medical Systems, 42, 172.

[19] Hardin, T. and Kotz, D. (2019). "Blockchain in health data systems: A survey," 2019 Sixth International Conference on Internet of Things: Systems, Management and Security (IOTSMS), Granada, Spain, pp. 490–497.

[20] Benchoufi, M. and Ravaud, P. Blockchain technology for improving clinical research quality. Trials, 18, 335.

Chapter 9

Healthcare analytics

Yogesh Sharma[1], Balusamy Balamurugan[2] and Sreeji[2]

Healthcare is becoming very complex day by day. The data produced by healthcare is so complex that someday it would become difficult to maintain the quality of the healthcare data. A large amount of data is produced by hospitals and other medical institutes, and it is becoming difficult to find what exactly is needed. The healthcare analysis is not only helpful for patients but also for the hospitals which take care of the patients pre- and post-hospitalization. Managing healthcare data also enhances the involvement of patients with the predictive modelling and analysis based on the healthcare data. There are many sources from where a lot of healthcare data can be collected such as electronic medical records (EMR), pathology labs, immunization programs and different surveys in medical camps. These sources give data in multiple formats; so analysing the healthcare data becomes much more complex and difficult. Many different organizations manage their healthcare data using different technologies. In this chapter, we would be discussing various emerging technologies for the healthcare analytics. We would also be discussing various software which help in analysing the healthcare data and the challenges associated with the healthcare analytics.

9.1 Introduction

With healthcare analytics, the data is becoming more accessible than before [1]. The healthcare sector is growing day by day and is proving to be a flourishing sector in the economy of any country [2]. With the emergence of healthcare data, many challenges come across with the complex and poor-quality data, ineffi-ciencies, etc. [3]. In 2011, Peter Sondegaard, the Senior Vice President and Global Head of Research for Gartner, stated that "Information is the oil of the 21st century and analytics is the combustion engine." So, we should first focus on what is analytics and why it is important to the twenty-first century healthcare. The Institute of Medicine (IOM) in its 2012 report titled *Best Care at Lower Cost: The*

[1]Computer Science & Engineering Department, Maharaja Agrasen Institute of Technology, Affiliated to G.G.S.I.P University, Delhi, India
[2]School of Computing Science and Engineering, Galgotias University, Greater Noida, India

Path to Continuously Learning Healthcare in America stated that "Americans Healthcare system has become far too complex and costly to continue business as usual." Prevalent inadequacies and incapability to achieve a quick and deep clinical knowledge base and a reward system poorly focused on key patient needs all hamper improvements in the safety and quality of care and threaten the nation's economic stability and global competitiveness. In order to achieve a higher quality of care at much lower cost, we need important commitments for the motivations for culture and leadership that stand in nonstop learning. As the lessons from the research and each care experience are systematically captured, assessed and translated into reliable care, a learning healthcare system is defined as a system designed to generate and apply the best evidence for the collaborative healthcare choices of each patient and provider to drive the process of discovery as a natural outgrowth of patient care and to ensure innovation, quality, safety and values in the healthcare [4].

If we consider the various information systems like hospitals where we have electronic healthcare system as well as specialized departmental systems for laboratory diagnostic imaging, pharmacy, nutrition services, billing, anatomic pathology and so on, each of these systems is designed and intended for clinical use. In another word, for patient care and so they capture specific data about the patient. However, none of the systems have a complete set of data for individual patient or for group of patients, so all patients who were admitted in January with a certain diagnosis that can be used for analysis and reporting. Obtaining deep insight into what is happening with individual patients as well as across groups of patients requires aggregating data together from many systems and performing statistical analysis of this aggregated data. In contrast to the various clinical systems discussed earlier, a clinical data warehouse brings together the data for a patient into a single coordinated location, and this location is used for analysis and reporting purpose. This is accomplished through a process known as extraction transform and load shown in Figure 9.1, which retrieves data from various clinical systems and synchronizes the formats.

A process called transformation cleans up the data and then inputs it into the database of the clinical data warehouse. The transformation process is especially important as data can be stored in a variety of forms across systems, for example, a laboratory system might use the letters M, F, or you for patient gender male/female or unknown while the radiology information system might use one, two, or nine instead. However, they must match the designations used in the clinical data warehouse and the process of converting them to match is called transformation [5]. Another, important step is to ensure that all of a patient record from various systems are linked together. This typically requires a master patient index sometimes called a master person index to link a patient's various identifiers across systems [6].

The architecture that can be roughly sketched consists of a bottom sensor layer, a middle network layer, and a top application layer. As one of the primary information-acquiring means at the bottom layer of the tags has found increasingly widespread applications in various business areas, with the expectation that the use

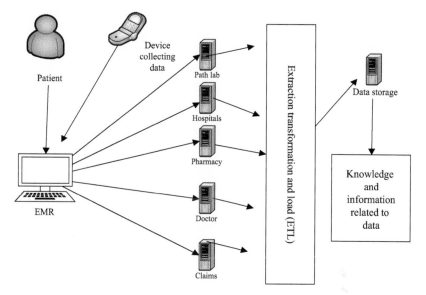

Figure 9.1   Extraction, transformation, and load (ETL) process

of radio frequency identification (RFID) tags will eventually replace the existing bar codes in all business areas.

9.2   Analytics

The term analytics has been used in a variety of ways and with different meanings. In fact, Gartner (https://www.gartner.com/en/information-technology/glossary/analytics, 2020) stated that "analytics has emerged as a catch-all term for a variety of different business intelligence BI and application related initiatives" Analytics according to the National Institute of Science and Technology (NIST) Big Data, 2015 can be defined as the finding of meaningful patterns in a given data and is one of the major steps in the life cycle of a useful data that consists of a collection of raw data, preparing the data for finding information and the analysis of the patterns to produce knowledge, and actions to produce useful values.

As shown in Figure 9.2 analytics is the complete process of a collection of data, data extraction, transformation, analysis, interpretation, and reporting. It includes statistical analysis as one of the steps further. The NIST has also specified that "analytics can also be used in referring to the methods used, with their implementation tools and the results of the tools as interpreted by the practitioner" The analytics process is the synthesis of knowledge from information. IBM, in 2013, categorized analytics into three types [7]:

1.   Descriptive: It uses business intelligence (BI) and data mining, as to ask, what has happened?

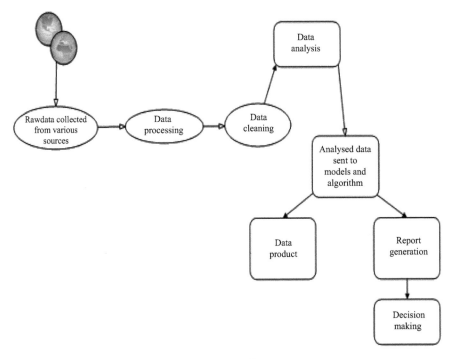

Figure 9.2   Data analytics process

2. Predictive: It uses the statistical models and forecast, as to ask, what could happen?
3. Prescriptive: It uses optimization and simulation to ask, what should we do?

To these three types, Gartner has added the fourth type, diagnostic analytics: which they define as a form of advanced analytics that examines data or the content to answer the questions, why did it happen? [8] Figure 9.3 shows the simplest type of analytics. Starts at the lower level the descriptive analytics, whereas diagnostic analytics are more valuable to the institution but also more difficult to perform. Even more difficult and also more valuable are predictive analytics. Finally, the most difficult and also the most valuable are prescriptive analytics. Let us look at each of these now.

9.2.1   Descriptive analytics

These are the simplest type of analytics and simply describe the data [9]. Common statistics are used such as the number of laboratory tests, the average age of the patient, or the average length of stay in the hospital for patient with a particular diagnosis. Descriptive analytics are often presented as pie charts or column charts, tables, or written narratives [10]. Gartner defines "diagnostic" as a form of advanced analytics that examines data or content to answer the question "why did it

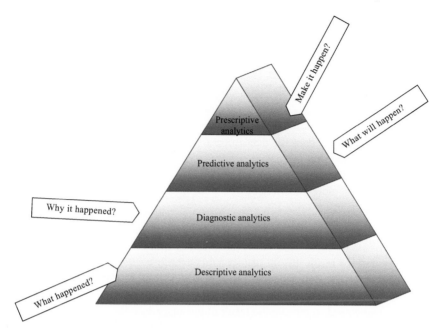

Figure 9.3   Types of analytics

happen?" Tools used for diagnostic analytics include drill down techniques, data discovery, and correlations [11].

9.2.2   Predictive analytics

The predictive analytics have the four attributes. The first one is emphasis on prediction rather than description classifying or clustering. The second attribute is a rapid analysis often in hours or days. The third attribute is an emphasis on the business relevance of the resulting insights. Finally, the fourth attribute is an emphasis on ease of use, thus making the tools accessible to business users. In other words, these tools should be available to the clinical staff to use. However, it is important to know that the predictive analysis would not go to tell the user what is going to happen in near future [12] rather the predictive analysis could only forecast about what might happen in near future with the sense of probability. This brings us to the highest level of analytics which is perspective analysis.

9.2.3   Perspective analysis

The perspective analysis can be defined as a form of advanced analytics that examines data or content to answer the question "what should be done or what can we do?" to make something happen and is characterized by techniques such as graph analysis, simulations, complex event processing, neural networks, recommendation engines, heuristics, and machine learning. Now let us look at the steps and data analysis in more detail.

Data analytics involves a sequence of steps:

1. Identify the problem.
2. Identify what data is needed and where those data are located.
3. Develop a plan for analysis and a plan for retrieval.
4. Extract the data.
5. Check clean and prepare the data for analysis.
6. Analysis and interpret the data.
7. Visualize the data.
8. Disseminate the new knowledge.
9. Implement the knowledge into the organization.

Now the first steps would be to define the problem to be studied or in business terms identify the business case. Now, the question arises, why is this important to study? How will the result impact patient care or the institution? So, the user must have a clearly stated problem or the question to guide the rest of the process. The user must also need to identify the stakeholders, who have direct interest in this problem and who need to receive the result of the analysis at the end of the process.

Next the data needed for the analysis need to be identified – where are the data elements located in what system or systems and what database tables, who is the contact person for each system who will be responsible for retrieving the data, is there a clinical data warehouse. If not, then the required data elements may be stored in different systems requiring multiple extractions steps a plan for retrieving from the various systems along with a plan for checking all the data required were actually retrieved should be developed. There needs to be some way to determine how many records are expected and then actually retrieved. This may involve cross-checking against other systems. This step requires the participation of the individual who normally perform data retrieval from the systems involved. An analysis plan needs to be developed that a statistician should be consulted, and questions to be addressed here include what is the population, what size does this sample need to be, what statistical test should be performed.

The next step is the actual extraction of the data from the system or systems involved. After the data are retrieved, the data need to be checked for completeness, is the set of data complete, where all the records that should be retrieved are actually retrieved at a minimum descriptive statistic such that counts must be performed at this step. At this point, changes to the extraction plan may be needed and another extraction from the source systems may need to take place.

Once a complete set of records is extracted from the source systems, errors in the record need to be identified and corrected and all the data have errors such as transpose letters and name sand incorrect values. Decisions must be made about how to handle empty fields. Next, data must be synchronized and transformed. For example, patients' gender in one system in the hospital may be stored as M, F, U while another system might use 1, 2, 9. One set of values must be changed so that all the records are using the same values.

After, necessary transformation steps have been completed that data is then imported into the destination system where the actual data analysis and reporting will take place. This may be a system as complex as a clinical data warehouse or a simple as a desktop computer. The data are now in the system where the analysis will be run and it should be a complete set of data. It should be checked that everything is ready for the analysis and did we get what was needed, check and verify this against the analysis plan that was developed in step 3 and that we get everything to address the problem that was identified in step 1.

Now, we are ready to do the actual analysis, to execute the analysis plan that was developed earlier. Perform the statistical analysis and enlists the assistance of the statistician to confirm the interpretations and conclusion of the analysis. Now, the system will be able to communicate the results of the analysis and how the results address the problem from step 1. This communication must be very clear and rapidly understandable to the decision-making in the institution.

So, selecting an appropriate representation for your finding is essential. Choose a visualization that is appropriate for the type of data; for example, categorical data can be represented with column or bar charts, tables, and pivot tables, while quantitative data can be shown with histograms or wide variety of other types of graphics such as scattered plots and Starr plots. Some common tools are Tableau and Microsoft Excel chart function. Once the analysis interpretation and visualizations are complete, a report must be developed. It might be a formal written document, an E-mail, or a presentation regardless of the delivery method. The report needs to clearly state the original problem. The process was used to address the problem and then the result of the analysis along with the supporting visualization. This represents new knowledge and needs to be distributed to the stake holders that were identified in step 1. Finally, the new knowledge needs to be implemented to address the original problem. This will require the participation of the stake holders.

9.3   Emerging technologies in healthcare analytics

Reference [13] has discussed about the three important emerging technologies in the healthcare analytics. The RFID and global positioning systems were discussed as the technologies that can be useful in decreasing the cost of the healthcare analytics, but it was also mentioned that the implementation of these two technologies requires significant amount during their initial set-up. But the third technology is nanotechnology. The technology is however an initial phase of its use in various healthcare systems, but the nanotechnology has transformed both the distribution of medicine and helps into setting-up of the hospital management.

Dr P. Bakker, a Medical Oncologist of Academic Medical Centre, Amsterdam, said their institute is very much interested in improving the patient's logistics and patient's safety. The institute has applied new technologies in order to improve the organizational issues and cultural issues using ITs. The institute has used the solution as RFID. An RFID tag is a small chip with an antenna, so small that it would fit in a wrist band. An RFID tag can be monitored with a transceiver. Every movement of the RFID tag passing the transceiver will be recorded. Thus, complex logistics processes of any kind can be closely monitored.

RFID might bring many improvements in the healthcare analytics. A medical centre in Amsterdam carried out a pilot project using the RFID technology [14]. The pilot project gives the insight in how processes are going and also how the quality data can improve the processes. The main objective of this pilot project was to look at the possibility of even further improvement and safety of the transfusion scene using the RFID techniques. One of the most important things was to be able to check if the right patient is getting the right product and besides that the storage condition of the project if it is in the clinical world concerning the temperature to place and the right time for the transfusion to the patients. The RFID tag ("RFID-Tag." Behance. Retrieved 15 July 2018) provides quality information on the whereabouts of the patients, employees, blood products and disposables. People's movement can be monitored not only just to locate personals but also to check on waiting times for a patient or to find out if a patient is actually the right patient for the planned surgery. Also, one can keep a close eye on logistics of blood and blood-related products. The tags are not only used to check the movements of the actual bags but are also part of the quality control cycle. They are able to store the information on location and temperature of the blood product.

There are some other interesting technologies in the healthcare analytics like big data, Internet of Things (IoT), and artificial intelligence (AI).

9.3.1   Big data technology in healthcare analytics

Healthcare generates an enormous amount of data which include laboratory test reports, imaging test such as X-rays, CT scans, financial documents, previous medication given to the patient, previous medical history, last appointments. All these data constitute a huge amount of data when several patients come under a single hospital or healthcare centre. The data used in healthcare sector is expanding at a very high speed. However, a huge amount of healthcare data is suffering from some challenges such as security of the patient's data, privacy of the patient's data, accessing of data, and how this data can be accessed outside the healthcare delivery facilities in which the healthcare data is stored. In addition to this, the storage capacity of big data and the type of solution given by the big data will be more efficient as compared to the traditional storage methods [15,16].

Big data analytics can give significant results with the improvement of patient's health with the reduction in the cost of medical expenses incurred during the treatment of patient and build a strong relationship with healthcare provider [17,18]. The big data analytics can give a better solution for the hospitals and other clinical staff based on the medical history of the patient [19]. Thus, the healthcare providers could give better care before the condition of the patient deteriorates [20].

Thus, by now we know that data analytics play an important role in providing insight into the future. Success of an organization despite the use and display of healthcare data analytics confusion exists in more than half of the healthcare providers on how much and what kind of data is needed in order to generate actionable insights from their information. In order for healthcare organizations to successfully present and make use of big data analytics, these organizations would have to look for other metrics and site on its use; hence only an organization would have to secure executive support for a special program.

Bioinformatics in healthcare also holds an increasingly important role as the use of big data analytics [21] expands consumers and physicians' relationship and is further defined by collection and filtering of statistical data. With the use of big data in healthcare, the healthcare providers go to build a sense of trust with their patients in order to shape the quality of the care given by the provider [22]. The term of transparency can be defined by the healthcare providers which might change the culture of the physicians.

9.3.2   Internet of Things in healthcare analytics

The IoT is influencing our lifestyle from the way we react to the way we behave. From air conditioners that can be controlled with the smart phone of any user to smart cars for providing the shortest routes or can be smart watch we can be used for tracking the daily activity of a person. IoT is a giant network with the connected devices [23]. These devices gather and share the data about how they are used and the environment in which they are operated [24]. All this is done by the sensors, which are embedded in every physical device be it a mobile phone or any electrical appliances, the bar code sensors, traffic lights, and almost everything that can come across in day-to-day life. These sensors continuously emit the data about the working state of the devices. The question may come across how the sensors could share this much amount of huge amount of data and how the data can be put to the benefits. The IoT provides a common platform for all these devices to dump their data and with a common language, all the devices communicate with each other. Data is emitted from various sources and sent to the IoT platform security. The IoT platform integrates the collected data from various sources and further analytics is performed on the collected data, and the valuable information will be extracted as per the requirement [25]. Finally, the result will get shared with other devices for better user experience automation and improves the efficiencies.

These wearable devices can be connected to the patient, which helps in recording the health patterns of the patient. The remote monitoring of the patient is much easier with the use of the IoT devices [26]. This means that the patient and the doctors are connected with each other throughout the day. The remote monitoring of the patient has also reduced the hospitalization of the patient and prevents re-admissions. Thus, the IoT has shown a huge impression in reducing the cost significantly while improving the treatment outcomes for the patient. Now, we will see how the IoT devices can be helpful for patients, physician, hospitals, and for the insurance companies.

9.3.2.1   IoT for patients

The IoT device can be in various forms of a wearable device. The device can be fitness band which could be worn on the wrist of the patient or any other wireless devices which could measure the blood pressure and heart rate of the patient or even the blood sugar level of any patient. These devices can be of much help for the patient as it may alert the patient for any increase in value of calories count, blood pressure variations, or be it any appointment. Thus, the IoT devices have helped many patients specially the elderly patients living alone. The IoT device may alert the family members for any disturbance in the values of the patient which in turn can contact the concerned medical agency.

9.3.2.2   IoT for physicians

The wearable devices worn by the patient not only help the patient in maintaining his or her regular health but can also be very helpful for the clinicians. The clinicians or doctors can track the patient's health on regular basis throughout the day and in the case of any immediate medical emergencies. These wearable devices help the doctors to be more watchful for their patients and connect with them proactively. The data thus collected from the patient's wearable devices may help the doctor to identify the best possible treatment for the concerned patient. The clinicians could also take the decisions based on the data collection whether the patient needs the admission in the hospital or not.

9.3.2.3   IoT for hospitals

Not only for the patients but the IoT devices can also be very useful for the hospitals. The IoT devices are the devices that consist of sensors which can collect data and give the output. So, the devices not only be useful in tracking the patient's health but the devices can also be useful in tracking the real-time information regarding the medical equipment of the hospital [27] like monitoring equipment, oxygen pumps, and cylinders. Deploying the medical staff at various locations and if medical staff going for some testing of like corona virus at different locations can be tracked and if any help needed can be given without wasting time in finding the locations. Similarly, going near to a corona patient can be avoided using the IoT devices by monitoring the patient from a distance, thus preventing the medical staff from getting infections. IoT devices could be very useful in tracking the medicines or pharmaceuticals if coming from the authenticated supplier and monitoring the temperature and humidity levels.

9.3.2.4   IoT for insurance companies

Insurance companies can control data collected through health monitoring devices for their countersigning and claims operations. This collected data could help the insurance companies to resolve the claims and can identify the predictions for the underwriting. The IoT devices can be beneficial in keeping the transparency between the insurance company and the insured person in handing the claims efficiently [28], with correct pricing and in multiple risk assessment processes. The IoT devices help the insurance companies to get the data directly from the insured customers and keep track of their day-to-day activities and keeping them on the correct treatment plan while taking the precautionary healthy measures in maintaining their health. Thus, the claims settlement could be done in an easy and quicker mode with the help of IoT devices.

9.3.3   Artificial intelligence in healthcare

This age of technology knows no bounds. Once it was thought as a futuristic threat to humankind. AI is changing and saving the lives not intended to replace clinicians and clinical judgement. It serves the purpose to enhance and complement the very human interaction a provider and patient [29]. In healthcare, AI is changing the game with its applications and decision support image analysis and patient triage with their ability to reduce the variations and duplicate testing. Decision support systems quickly decipher a large amount of data within the electronic medical record [30]. AI technology is also taking the uncertainty out of viewing patient scans by highlighting the problem areas on the images aiding in the screening and diagnosis process [31]. AI helps with the issues of physician's burnout by collecting the patient's data through a mobile app or some text messaging chat. BOTS now ask patients a series of questions regarding their symptoms taking and does some self-diagnosis based on some guesswork [32], thus saving the time, money, and effort of both the patient and provider. The AI integration working smarter enables solutions to a variety of issues for the patients, hospitals, and the healthcare industry.

The healthcare goes digital in the form of electronic health record with the use of IoT or using any other digital device. The amount of healthcare records stored in any hospital is getting huge. The large amount of data is actually an asset to any hospital. This large amount of data can be useful in the generation of various data models and could benefit the clinical, operational, or in revenue generation. The data thus collected for any patient could be very helpful in predicting the health of the patient using the history of the patient's health, which in turn could tell when the patient requires readmission into the hospital. With the use of AI and machine learning, the diagnosis of treatment could be monitored quickly, and treatment can be done more precisely. The pattern recognition feature can be very helpful, say, for example, the treatment of the patient done on one particular disease can be recorded that how long the treatment took to make the patient better on an average [33]. This duration and data could be used in treating the patients with similar diagnosis.

The healthcare is coming from multiple sources and from different places; thus there is a need for analytics that could do the healthcare analysis in much better way. The organizations that are working on the same could survive in near future, while those are not going to survive. The healthcare analytics may improve the efficiencies and also the financial conditions of any organization.

9.3.4   Blockchain in healthcare

We heard a lot of blockchain concepts in terms of cryptocurrencies like bitcoin, but this blockchain technology has emerged to be used in other sectors also, and healthcare is one of them. Blockchain is a way of storing and sharing the data in a way that can be distributed, transparent, and temper proof. Blockchain technology can be very useful in healthcare delivery. Healthcare generates an enormous amount of data which include laboratory test reports, imaging test such as X-rays, CT scans, financial documents, previous medication given to the patient, previous medical history, and last appointments. All these data constitute a huge amount of data when several patients come under a single hospital or healthcare centre. The data used in healthcare sector is expanding at a very high speed. However, a huge amount of healthcare data is suffering from some challenges such as security and privacy of the patient's data [34,35], accessing of data, how this data can be accessed outside the healthcare delivery facilities in which the healthcare data is stored. Blockchain technology can be useful in improving this challenge. One of the big factors in healthcare today is that we need to manage a large amount of data that we can call as big data [36], and this data might impact the cost, quality, and value of the healthcare that is delivered.

Blockchain technology plays an important role. The technology ensures the integrity or redundancy of the data and that the data has not been changed or tampered from its original state or damaged due to error in the database. A blockchain technology can also be useful in the distribution of the healthcare data among different nodes in a network which uses the facilities of this data. Such factors however impact the cost, quality, and value of the data being used. Blockchain technology can be useful in security and privacy of the healthcare data as only the nodes connected in the blockchain network have the right to access the healthcare data, only after getting permission from the persons own data.

9.4   History of healthcare analytics

The healthcare industry has evolved rapidly from past decade or so. Many enterprises and multiple consumer technologies have changed many folds in past decade and are still growing at a faster pace. In ancient time the diagnosis, treatment, and medication were based upon the findings of how the person's body react to the external spurs [37]. In the 1920s, the healthcare analytics based upon the treatment given to a patient whenever he/she goes with some medical problems to the doctor, and he/she would be given some treatment after the diagnosis. After every treatment given to the patient, the doctor gets the idea of giving treatment to any other patient. The doctor keeps the record of which treatment was given to what kind of diagnosis and medication accordingly.

The healthcare experts used to record the healthcare data and analysis on papers but in 1960s/1970s, the era of computer system started and this led to change in the standardization and sharing of patient's medical record. Dr Lawrence Weed, a professor of medicine and pharmacology at Yale University, has created the first Problem Oriented Medical Record which has helped many clinicians and hospitals to view the complete medical history of the patient.

In 1965, the official electronic medical record (EMR) was created and was being used by as many as 73 hospitals (www.vertitechit.com). The healthcare technology used to be very expensive, and only few could use the resources.

In the era of the 1980s, the personal desktop system really changed the healthcare industry and now not only the hospitals but also the doctors are able to invest in the machines that have changed the face of the healthcare system. In the late 1980s, the window-based systems became dominant in the clinicians offices, but these systems were used mostly for billing and making schedules for the doctors rather than creating electronic medical records of the patient.

In the mid-1980s, the IOM has started working upon the EMR, and studies were going on to find the benefits of EMR. But the study could not be published because of several issues related with the standards, security, and cost related in adopting EMR. It happened when the health-related data was not huge in number, and it was much easier to collect, handle, and analyse data. But the health-related data kept on increasing and the system that was storing the data was not enough to handle the data and the big became *big data* which could not be stored in one or two systems but the data required clouds for storing the data, and healthcare agencies needed more space to store the data and much more strong and effective algorithm and methods for the analysis of health data. The clinical documentation done will have some improvements on the programmes that encouraged the expressive results and have also played an important role in accepting the new and improved technology.

Now every hospital and clinicians have to use electronic health records (EMR) which are not only useful for hospitals in analysing the diagnosis, treatment, and medication but also from the patient's point of view that the EMR are very useful as the patient does not need to keep the medical records while moving from one doctor to another or from one hospital to another. The patient can use the electronic medical records anywhere at any time [34].

9.5   Exploring software for healthcare analytics

The healthcare software better known as software which can be used for collection of the data is going to help the persons who manage the healthcare data that could help in the operational performance, the outcomes of the clinical processes, quality, and overall efficiency of the system which in turn could improve the healthcare services by the use of efficient healthcare analytics tools. For the successful performance and patient care improvement, the hospital must also take care of the multiple things like cost, diagnosis, and patients health records (https://www.healthit.gov). Since the healthcare data collected and gathered is very huge so for the analysis purpose, the tools and the software should be of high accuracy. The healthcare analytics software could be very helpful in handling and organizing the endless paperwork associated with the healthcare analytics. The professionals in the healthcare industry use healthcare analytics tools that are able to connect to the multiple data sources that give a steady management environment wherein all the stakeholders like patient, doctors, nurses, and other person who are involved directly or indirectly should feel safe. Some BI software can be very useful in utilizing the collected data in order to predict the number of patients expected to come in the hospital on a day-to-day basis.

There are various benefits of using the healthcare analytics software (https://www.datapine.com/).

1. The healthcare BI software could be useful in tracking various activities of the hospital and could generate the analysis based on some operative inadequacies. Appropriate corrective actions can be taken after data collection that might decrease the overall cost.
2. The data analytics when incorporated with the right analytics software not only enable the administrators to handle the difficult tasks, but these software could also help in updating the patient's healthcare record that reminds the patient to stay healthy by keeping a healthy lifestyle.
3. Often, a patient needs to consult multiple doctors for some treatment and it becomes cumbersome to carry all the documents from one doctor to another. Also, sometime doctors are very busy with their schedule, and this might cause a gap of communication between the patient and the doctor. But, by utilizing the healthcare analytics software patient current progress, health record, history of treatment can be viewed from anywhere at any time with the only requirement that is of an active Internet connection. This might reduce the hospitalization.
4. BI software in the healthcare analysis can benefit the administrators to keep track of the key performance indicators which analyses, manages, and could be beneficial to the healthcare organization to enhance the performance based on the accuracy of the data collected and analytics-based perceptions [38].

With the constant growth in the healthcare data, various healthcare industries are focusing on utilizing the healthcare BI tools that not only enable hospitals and organization to establish best of the practices of care and management but also help in building the trust of the patients with the hospitals. With the increase in the number of data sources and the kind of complexity associated with the data within the healthcare organization, there is a need of more advanced analytics tools which help in building much stronger decision analytics. There is need of more predictive modelling tools, online data visualization which helps in gaining insights related with patient care and satisfaction.

9.5.1   Anaconda

Anaconda is a platform mainly useful in data science. Anaconda mainly focuses about the features and multiple packages that help a data scientist to have a platform where the user can perform the work [39]. The Anaconda comes up with several data science packages so that the data scientist could start the work quickly and easily. There are many features which make Anaconda a platform preferable over other virtual environment managers.

Unlike any other virtual environments, there is no need to create a specific directory for setting up the environment. This allows one to activate the virtual environment anywhere on the system without any location. Another feature of Anaconda is, every time user works on Python, the Anaconda makes the latest version of the Python from the server, no matter if it is installed on the system or not. The *Conda* retrieves the correct Python packages and installs them in the environment.

Anaconda is a free and open-source distribution of Python. Anaconda is not a just Python distribution but also is a wider distribution. It is mainly focused on providing everything for data sciences and machine learning applications. It has more than 150 packages included with the Python code language. Anaconda is also an event manager. The word *Conda* is also related to Anaconda distribution and how Anaconda has its own packet manager which is Conda. Conda is a packet management system just like peep in the regular Python. The user can install packages in regular Python using pip install command, whereas in Anaconda the user will use *Conda* install.

With the installation of Anaconda, the user also gets a GUI which is called as an Anaconda navigator. With the Anaconda navigator, a user can install and update packages in environment and can also search for packages in local Anaconda and Anaconda cloud.

9.5.2 SQLite

SQLite is an embedded relational database (https://www.sqlite.org/). The SQLite does not require a dedicated database management system. In order to use the database is literally part of the code, and it is not an outside resource. The SQLite created to provide a self-contained database that was both easy to use and could travel with the program by using it and also is great because it runs on pretty much any machine with no required software. The SQLite is found to be superior to the most of the other databases even with regards to the speed. However, SQLite does underperform in some of the applications when there are multiple connections or if it is asked to perform really complicated queries (https://www.sqlite.org/). SQLite has been written to be used with any languages and all the languages follow the similar pattern like SQLite. In most of situations, there are numerous extensions for even an individual language.

The biggest advantage of SQLite is that it can step on any device; it could be a machine cell phone which still does not need any kind of configuration. The SQLite is very fast and can handle any big data centre or any powerful network. The SQLite thus can be a powerful tool in the analysis of a healthcare record. As we know the data of healthcare is increasing day by day, handling this amount of data is a huge task. The data collection and gathering is done in many formats and from various sources so in order to maintain that the data SQLite could a very good tool for maintaining the data and for the data analytics. The database in the SQLite maintains this data that could be further used by hospitals healthcare analysts. Since the data collected is in different formats so SQLite is very powerful in converting strings into integer and vice versa whenever required. The SQLite provides a good platform for data analytics where querying against the large data set (like healthcare) is involved.

9.6   Challenges with healthcare analytics

There is an increase in the demand of healthcare activities with the increase in the population and with that a numerous number of challenges get associated with the healthcare activities. The process of data collection, storage, and processing of the data become more challenging due to various factors that come with the data such as high dimensionality, irregularity, and sparsity [40].

9.6.1   High-dimensional data

It happens sometime when a patient visits to a hospital for some diagnosis. The patient is first tested on few parameters whereas if some other patients visit to some other hospitals for the same diagnosis, he/she is tested with some other parameters. So it is dependent on the disease and the diagnosis. Thus, the EMR created would be different as the data is collected from different sources. This factor causes a high dimensionality of the healthcare data.

The high dimensionality becomes more challenging with the increase in the number of parameters into the model which in turn make the model more complex [41]. The noise and sparsity are the two problems that might be associated with the high-dimensional data [42]. However, there are some methods, which are feature selection and feature extraction, with which the high dimensionality of the data could be reduced.

Feature selection is the process by which a subset of relevant features is selected for the construction of a model which can be done using three methods: filter, wrapper, and embedded [43].

Feature extraction is the process of finding the most compressed and useful set of features that enhance the efficiency and processing of the data [44]. Thus, using feature selection method, the original features are embedded into a lower dimensional space, and each dimension relates to the original feature.

9.6.2   Irregularities in data

This type of challenge defines the irregularities found in the data when the data is collected multiple times, which occurs mainly in the EMR of the patient. The EMR of the patient consists of different records collected at different times. The EMR consists of a longitude matrix of the records [45,46], in which one dimension represents the medical factors on which a patient is tested and, on the other dimension, represents the time of diagnosis [47]. Thus, the way records are made in an EMR is scattered with an uneven spaced time span. All the records are stored irregular and vary significantly. The records even vary a lot in terms of time period.

9.6.3 Missing data

It is important that whatever the value of data is extracting from the EMR, data has to be accurate. In the EMR, there could be lot of inconsistences in the data matrix and some values can also missing [48]. This happens because when a patient goes for any treatment or diagnosis, all the data collected are stored into the EMR of the patient and with time the data keep on increasing and a huge amount of data collected, which is put in some data packets, might get lost in the process. So, these missing values need to fill again with the correct values; otherwise these missing values would create problems for the patient and the process of finding value starts all over again with the rediagnosis. Hence, it is sometimes a challenge in finding the correct value of data for the patient which will also be a big challenge during the analytics process of the healthcare data.

9.7 Conclusion

The healthcare has always been an important parameter in any one's life. A decade ago, we have seen the healthcare was only present in the hardcopy with the patient or in the standalone system of a doctor or hospital. The amount of healthcare data produced in the last decade was in huge amount, and the management of such huge data is a difficult task. There are many technologies that are coming up into healthcare analytics in order to do the healthcare analysis in better ways like collecting accurate information, apply good security and privacy on the healthcare data. In this chapter, it has been discussed how the emerging technologies can be very useful in the field of healthcare analytics. The emerging technologies like IoT, Blockchain, and AI have already improved the healthcare analytics and in near future, these technologies will provide much improved results in the healthcare.

References

[1] Minas NM, Ruehle K, Goecke C, Altalib K, and Zeng F. Healthcare analytics is the future. Biol Blood Marrow Transplant [Internet]. 2019 [cited 2020 Jun 24];25(3):S273–4.

[2] Yang JJ, Li J, Mulder J, *et al.* Emerging information technologies for enhanced healthcare. Comput Ind [Internet]. 2015 [cited 2020 Jun 24];69:3–11.

[3] Cortada JW, Gordon D, and Lenihan B. IBM global business services executive report. The value of analytics in healthcare [Internet]. 2012 [cited 2020 Jun 24].

[4] Budrionis A and Bellika JG. The learning healthcare system: where are we now? A systematic review. J Biomed Inform [Internet]. 2016 [cited 2020 Jun 24];64:87–92.

[5] Homayouni H, Ghosh S, and Ray I. An approach for testing the extract-transform-load process in data warehouse systems. In: ACM International

Conference Proceeding Series [Internet]. ACM; 2018 [cited 2020 Jun 24]. p. 236–45. Available from: https://doi.org/10.1145/3216122.3216149.

[6]   Wiedemann LA. Fundamentals for building a master patient index/enterprise master patient index. J AHIMA [Internet]. 2010 [cited 2020 Jun 24].

[7]   Finch G, Davidson S, Kirschniak C, Weikersheimer M, Reese C, and Shockley R. Analytics: the speed advantage: why data-driven organizations are winning the race in today's marketplace. 2014.

[8]   Rob van der Meulen JR. Gartner says advanced analytics is a top business priority [Internet]. 2014.

[9]   Mehta A. Four types of business analytics to know [Internet]. 2017. Available from: https://www.analyticsinsight.net/four-types-of-business-analytics-to-know/.

[10]   Nishioka V and Brock TW. School discipline data indicators: a guide for districts and schools. The National Center for Education Evaluation and Regional Assistance (NCEE) conducts unbiased large-scale evaluations of education programs and practices [Internet]. ERIC; 2017 [cited 2020 Jun 24].

[11]   Arora SK. What is data analysis? Methods, techniques & tools [Internet]. 2020.

[12]   Attaran M and Attaran S. Opportunities and challenges of implementing predictive analytics for competitive advantage. Int J Bus Intell Res [Internet]. 2018 [cited 2020 Jun 24]:64–90.

[13]   McGrady E, Conger S, Blanke S, and Landry BJL. Emerging technologies in healthcare: navigating risks, evaluating rewards. Journal of Healthcare Management. 2010; 55(5):353–64.

[14]   Van der Togt R, Bakker PJM, and Jaspers MWM. A framework for performance and data quality assessment of radio frequency identification (RFID) systems in health care settings. J Biomed Inf [Internet]. 2011 [cited 2020 Jun 24];44:372–83.

[15]   Sonnati R. Improving healthcare using big data analytics. International Journal of Scientific & Technology Research 2017;6(3):142–146.

[16]   Razbonyalı C and Güvenoğlu E. Traditional data storage methods and the big data concepts. Int Res J Eng Technol [Internet]. 2016 [cited 2020 Jun 24];03(06):2556–61.

[17]   Wang L and Alexander CA. Big data analytics in healthcare systems. Int J Math Eng Manage Sci. 2019;4(1):17–26.

[18]   Raghupathi W and Raghupathi V. Big data analytics in healthcare: promise and potential. Health Inf Sci Syst. 2014;2(1):3.

[19]   Pramanik PKD, Pal S, and Mukhopadhyay M. Healthcare big data. igi-global.com [Internet]. 2018 [cited 2020 Jun 24]. p. 72–100.

[20]   Bocas J. 5 Emerging technologies that will change healthcare [Internet]. 2018.

[21]   Wang B, Li R, and Perrizo W. Big data analytics in bioinformatics and healthcare. In: Big Data Analytics in Bioinformatics and Healthcare. IGI Global; 2014. p. 1–528.

[22]   Sarkar BK. Big data for secure healthcare system: a conceptual design. Complex Intell Syst. 2017;3(2):133–51.

[23]   Srinivasan CR, Rajesh B, Saikalyan P, Premsagar K, and Yadav ES. A review on the different types of Internet of Things (IoT). J Adv Res Dyn Control Syst [Internet]. 2019 [cited 2020 Jun 24];11:154–8.

[24]   Atlam HF and Wills GB. IoT security, privacy, safety and ethics. In: Internet of Things [Internet]. Springer International Publishing; 2020 [cited 2020 Jun 24]. p. 123–49.

[25]   Gubbi J, Buyya R, Marusic S, and Palaniswami M. Internet of Things (IoT): a vision, architectural elements, and future directions. Future Gener Comput Syst [Internet]. 2013 [cited 2020 Jun 24];29(7):1645–60. Available from: www.buyya.com.

[26]   Gómez J, Oviedo B, and Zhuma E. Patient monitoring system based on Internet of Things. Procedia Comp Sci [Internet]. 2016 [cited 2020 Jun 24];83:90–7.

[27]   Gholamhosseini L, Sadoughi F, and Safaei A. Hospital real-time location system (a practical approach in healthcare): a narrative review article. Iran J Public Health [Internet]. 2019 [cited 2020 Jun 24];48:593–602.

[28]   Sayegh K and Desoky M. Blockchain Application in Insurance and Reinsurance [Internet]. France: Skema Business School; 2019 [cited 2020 Jun 24].

[29]   Peete R, Majowski K, Lauer L, and Jay A. Artificial intelligence in healthcare. In: Artificial Intelligence and Machine Learning for Business for Non-Engineers. CRC Press; 2019. p. 89–101.

[30]   Evans RS. Electronic health records: then, now, and in the future. Yearb Med Inform. 2016:S48–61.

[31]   Pesapane F, Codari M, and Sardanelli F. Artificial intelligence in medical imaging: threat or opportunity? Radiologists again at the forefront of innovation in medicine. Eur Radiol Exp. 2018;2:35.

[32]   Shifa G, Sabreen S, Bano ST, and Fakih AH. Self-diagnosis medical chat-bot using artificial intelligence. J Web Dev Web Des. 2020;3(1).

[33]   Collins AS. Chapter 41. Preventing health care-associated infections. In: Patient Safety and Quality: An Evidence-Based Handbook for Nurses. 1991; 1–29.

[34]   Sharma Y and Balamurugan B. A survey on privacy preserving methods of electronic medical record using blockchain. J Mech Continua Math Sci [Internet]. 2020 [cited 2020 Jun 8];15:32–47.

[35]   Abouelmehdi K, Beni-Hessane A, and Khaloufi H. Big healthcare data: preserving security and privacy. J Big Data. 2018;5(1).

[36]   Dash S, Shakyawar SK, Sharma M, and Kaushik S. Big data in healthcare: management, analysis and future prospects. J Big Data. 2019;6(1).

[37]   Dada M (Mac) and Chambers C. Healthcare analytics. In: International Series in Operations Research and Management Science. Springer New York LLC; 2019. p. 765–91.

[38]   Diemer S. The benefits of business intelligence in healthcare [Internet]. 2019. Available from: https://www.datapine.com/healthcare-analytics.

[39]   Weldon D. 16 top platforms for data science and machine learning [Internet]. 2019. Available from: www.information-management.com.

[40]   Lee C, Luo Z, Ngiam KY, *et al.* Big healthcare data analytics: challenges and applications. 2017. p. 11–41.

[41]   Sorzano COS, Vargas J, and Montano AP. A survey of dimensionality reduction techniques. 2014 [cited 2020 Jun 24].

[42]   Fan J, Lv J, and Qi L. Sparse high-dimensional models in economics. Annu Rev Econ. 2011;3(1):291–317.

[43]   Jović A, Brkić K, and Bogunović N. A review of feature selection methods with applications. In: 2015 38th International Convention on Information and Communication Technology, Electronics and Microelectronics, MIPRO 2015 – Proceedings. Institute of Electrical and Electronics Engineers Inc.; 2015. p. 1200–5.

[44]   Meyer-Baese A and Schmid Volker JJ. Pattern Recognition and Signal Analysis in Medical Imaging: Second Edition [Internet]. Elsevier, USA; 2014 [cited 2020 Jun 24]. p. 1–444.

[45]   Keshavjee K, Bosomworth J, Copen J, *et al.* Best practices in EMR implementation: a systematic review. AMIA Annu Symp Proc [Internet]. 2006 [cited 2020 Jun 24];2006:982.

[46]   Tamersoy A, Loukides G, Nergiz ME, Saygin Y, and Malin B. Anonymization of longitudinal electronic medical records. IEEE Trans Inf Technol Biomed. 2012;16(3):413–23.

[47]   Ismail A, Shehab A, and El-Henawy IM. Healthcare Analysis in Smart Big Data Analytics: Reviews, Challenges and Recommendations. Cham: Springer; 2019 [cited 2020 Jun 24]. p. 27–45.

[48]   Hu Z, Melton GB, Arsoniadis EG, Wang Y, Kwaan MR, and Simon GJ. Strategies for handling missing clinical data for automated surgical site infection detection from the electronic health record. J Biomed Inform [Internet]. 2017 [cited 2020 Jun 24];68:112–20.

Chapter 10

Blockchain for healthcare

Anupam Tiwari[1] and Usha Batra[1]

In 10 years the electronic medical record will be the minor player, in terms of where a person's health history lives. Most of that information will be kept on the phone or in a secure cloud, and the patient will be highly engaged with collecting, curating and sharing that data. Most doctor visits will be like calling up a YouTube meets virtual human docs and there will also be an aspect of virtual reality.

As stated by LESLIE SAXON, Professor of Medicine, Clinical Scholar, Keck School of Medicine at Southern California University

10.1 Introduction

Health data primarily constitutes of details pertaining to all kinds of health statuses and parameters of an individual or population. Additionally, this admits clinical metrics and other vital parameters to include individuals or any population environmental, socio-economic and behavioural information apposite to health and wellness. While undergoing treatment, the patient's data is in parallel collected by healthcare systems, intended to be further used for analytics to encourage, restitute and sustain good desirable health in the society. This lets in exertions to decide determinants of health as well as more direct health bettering actions.

Over last two decades now, with the proliferation of information technology (IT) in this healthcare data, a new emerging threat is being realised with concerns of security, privacy and ethical concerns of patient's data [1]. The increasing collation and indexing of such health data of patients is a major component of digital health but at the same time is also being realised as a potent threat. This threat encompasses invading privacies and life changing dynamics of patients attended to, which in most of the time is coordinated without the patient's knowledge.

The worldwide proliferation of the healthcare industry with an induction of new generation technologies has facilitated exploiting and reaping digitisation benefits, which was never before. The current healthcare industry version named

[1]Department of CSE and IT, G D Goenka University, Gurgaon, India

Health 3.0 deriving from Web 3.0 is in an expedited mode to evolve to Health 4.0. This version is likely to induct blockchain technology to draw in benefits peculiar to blockchain to include the following:

- immutability
- decentralisation
- privacy
- anonymity
- security
- consensus
- transparency

These blockchain features can facilitate intra- and inter-hospital interoperability with updated patient records set in a trusted environment with transparent documentation. Besides these, with smart contracts these advantages can be extended further for the negation of multiple middle men and agencies to bring a metamorphose change ever unthought-of.

10.1.1   Bitcoin blockchain

Blockchain, the word first arrived in the technical arena around 2009 [2] and onwards wherein it was first associated primarily as the mechanics and backbone for the well-known cryptocurrency bitcoin introduced by Satoshi Nakamoto. Blockchain refers to a combination of two words, i.e. block and chain.

10.1.2   Block

Block is basically an accumulation of transactions which are being recorded uniquely inside the block. Per se bitcoin blockchain, the size of block is around ~1 MB and houses, around 1,500 transaction on average. Each block is sealed with transactions after the consensus is attained for the network by the miners aided by proof-of-work. The bitcoin blockchain is so designed that in every approximately 10 min a new block is created. Each creation of block allows a reward to the miner who solved the proof-of-work puzzle. The reward system started with 50 bitcoins/ block in 2009, and it reduces every 4 years by half, i.e. 25 bitcoins per block in 2012, 12.5 bitcoins in 2016 and 6.25 bitcoins in 2020.

10.1.3   Chain

Subsequent to the creation of the block, a new block is created with the same method with a new nonce value found by miners, and this block is cryptographically linked with the previous block with the value of hash of previous block. Thus, the hash of the previous block is linked to the newly created block and a chain of cryptographically connected blocks starts forming which is known as blockchain.

Figure 10.1 shows one such extract of a long blockchain with three blocks. Each block besides the traditional blockchain block components is shown to have sample medical transactions.

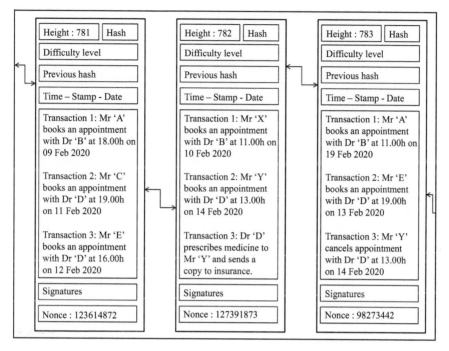

Figure 10.1   Typical blockchain schematic showing block components inside

10.2   Ethereum blockchain

Much later around late 2013, Vitalik Buterin introduced his paper on Ethereum [3] and came up with smart contracts [4] on blockchain. Smart contracts are self-executing lines of codes subject to meeting the designed terms and condition between two parties, say a buyer and a seller. The code and the agreements contained therein exist across a distributed, decentralised blockchain network.

A simple healthcare blockchain schematic for an understanding purpose is seen in Figure 10.1. The schematic shows the major components expected inside a block, healthcare per se. These would primarily constitute of any kind of transactions between the participating nodes. For example, it can be an appointment by a patient on some date time with a doctor or prescription by a doctor or an insurance claim by the patient or simply cancellation of an appointment. Now the uniqueness here involves all the participants that are digitally authenticated, which can be a permissioned blockchain and will be append-only. No transactions indexed in any block can ever be modified, i.e. they are immutable.

10.3 Contracts and healthcare: the arising need of smart contracts

Why do we at first place require any kind of 'contracts' while we discuss about healthcare and its deemed association with blockchain? While in the world today, existing traditional contracts in place are doing absolutely fine across all organisations and personnel adhering to it. But all these traditional contracts are vulnerable to different interpretations since they are written in human language which only humans can understand and interpret as they understand. What if there could have been a way out, such that the contracts become actually executable computer codes that execute all or parts of the transaction steps of a written agreement between two parties and the resultant output automatically monitors, executes and enforces a legal agreement, i.e. a definite output with no chances of wrong interpretation of any confusion? The traditional legal agreements are inherently flexible and ambiguous by virtue of interpretations of words, while code-based agreements seemingly would be highly formalised and leave minuscule space for ambiguity.

Oakhurst Dairy "Comma" case

An interesting example to quote would be the Oakhurst Dairy case at the US city of Portland. This dairy company in the US city of Portland, Maine settled a court case for $5m in the year 2018 because of a missing comma.

Few truckers of the dairy company laid claim in 2014 that they were due for unpaid overtime salaries, all because of the way commas were used in legislation regularizing the overtime payments. While the country's laws declared that overtime wasn't due for workers involved in "the canning, processing, preserving, freezing, drying, marketing, storing, packing for shipment or distribution of: 1) agricultural produce; 2) meat and fish products; and 3) perishable foods". The truckers contended to successfully debate that since there was no comma after "shipment" and before "or distribution", they were due for overtime pay.

After around 4 years in 2018, the court of appeals aligned with the drivers, and the company settled with the truckers for $5 million.

10.3.1 Smart contracts

In the year 1994, legal scholar, computer scientist and cryptographer, Nick Szabo [4], first coined the term 'smart contract' which denotes to any computerised transaction protocol that can accomplish the terms of a legal contract while in self-execution mode. This basically means subject to meeting predefined conditions equated from the legal agreement point of view, compiled in a coded computer program format, the contract will execute automatically. Once a smart contract is executed, it becomes immutable [5], i.e. there is no way it can be undone or

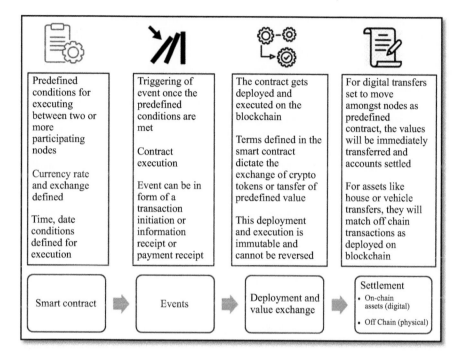

Figure 10.2 Smart contract schematic

reversed. Having been coined since 1994, a revived interest has been observed over the last decade since the inception of bitcoin cryptocurrency in around 2008.

This concept after 1994 was first kind of test bed experimented in bitcoin architecture. Small bitcoin scripts, non-turing complete [6], could be used to exchange values among user nodes, over a peer-to-peer (P2P) network where users do not need to trust each other, and there is no requirement of any third-party intervention to coordinate such transactions.

Simple schematic representation of a smart contract is seen in Figure 10.2. The following key features and characteristics of a smart contract would assist one to realise the potential and power of smart contracts which can be applied to suit in the healthcare data sector:

- All smart contracts are computers codes which are written in a language like Vyper [7], Java, Scilla [8], Lisp-Like Language or the more popular Solidity [9], which are turing complete.
- Each smart contract deployed on any blockchain like Ethereum will have a unique address.
- Smart contracts once deployed and executed cannot be reversed and are immutable.
- All smart contracts are automatically executed when predefined conditions are met. This is more like an if-then-else scenario with no space for sophisticated

variations as would typically exist in traditional contracts which lead to two different interpretations of the same sentence and meaning like the Oakhurst Dairy 'Comma' case [10] example.

- The smart contract execution and deployment speed can economise on man hours while compared to traditional legal contracts.
- Smart contracts are self-executing in nature, and there is no requirement for any arbiter or a third-party mediation to deploy or coordinate the execution. Thus, they are self-executing-self-verifying-tamper-resistant codes deployed on a blockchain.
- Smart contracts are designed as fault tolerant and execute quickly over the P2P network.
- The inviolable, self-reliant, transparent execution and deployment of smart contracts negates the possibility of bias, manipulation or error amidst participating peer nodes.
- Smart contracts though termed smart but they do not do anything intelligent on their own but do exactly what they have been coded to do. Any smart contract is only as smart as the developer has coded it. Thus, they produce the same output every time they are executed on a blockchain. This deterministic characteristic of the smart contract is a potent benefit for legal agreements and executions and permits a smart contract to be run by any participating node in a P2P network and achieve the same output.

To consider and understand an example of a smart contract in the healthcare domain, we will discuss Figure 10.3. Vide the figure, the traditional transaction flow is seen wherein everyone, including the doctor, the patient and the payee agency, has his/her manual intervention for submission, verification and validation of various documents. The sequence shown in Figure 10.3 is as follows:

- The patient checks with one doctor for an ailment prescription and advice.
- The doctor verifies the patient's claims and credentials online or on accessible database.
- The patient reports to the doctor on the day-time allotted and get the advice.
- The doctor issues the International Classification of Disease (ICD) and the current procedural terminology (CPT) code and bills the patient.
- The patient chooses to pay through the copay or deductible option as per his insurance profile and chosen choices.
- The patient gets the prescription and gets the medicine from the in-chain pharmacy.
- The doctor, in parallel, shares the CPT, ICD codes and raises the claim to the payer in digital form and also in paper form.
- The payer verifies and validates the raised claims by the doctor, checks the insurance policy of the patient and decided the final amount to be paid to pharmacy, doctor and the patient.
- All the participants get their dues and the amount claims are settled.

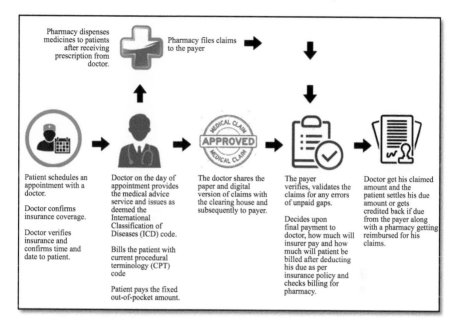

Pharmacy dispenses medicines to patients after receiving prescription from doctor.

Pharmacy files claims to the payer

Patient schedules an appointment with a doctor.

Doctor confirms insurance coverage.

Doctor verifies insurance and confirms time and date to patient.

Doctor on the day of appointment provides the medical advice service and issues as deemed the International Classification of Diseases (ICD) code.

Bills the patient with current procedural terminology (CPT) code

Patient pays the fixed out-of-pocket amount.

The doctor shares the paper and digital version of claims with the clearing house and subsequently to payer.

The payer verifies, validates the claims for any errors of unpaid gaps.

Decides upon final payment to doctor, how much will insurer pay and how much will patient be billed after deducting his due as per insurance policy and checks billing for pharmacy.

Doctor get his claimed amount and the patient settles his due amount or gets credited back if due from the payer along with a pharmacy getting reimbursed for his claims.

Figure 10.3   Traditional chain between doctor, patient and payer insurance for settling claims

Now applying the blockchain and smart contracts on the earlier-mentioned traditional sequence of settling claims, we have a chain in Figure 10.4. The sequence is briefly discussed as follows:

- The patient checks with one doctor for an ailment prescription and advice.
- The doctor verifies the patient's claims and credentials online or on accessible database.
- The patient reports to the doctor on the day-time allotted and get the advice.
- The patient's unique data and electronic medical record (EMR) hashes are stored in blockchain for anyone to verify with the patients' public key. In our case, the payer checks these credentials on the blockchain.
- The doctor pushes the data to a data storage area which is further connected with a blockchain application programming interface (API). The data hashes get stored in the blockchain vide the API.
- The payer verifies the data hashes on the blockchain tallies with what is available from the patient, doctor and pharmacy.
- The payer coordinates to arrange payments through smart contracts which verify, confirm the effected payee's credentials and deploy on the blockchain with each transaction hash after the payments have been released by the bank. The smart contracts themselves have unique addresses and once deployed, they cannot be reversed under any circumstances. This step is the major change viz-a-viz the traditional chain wherein the middlemen effect and documentation

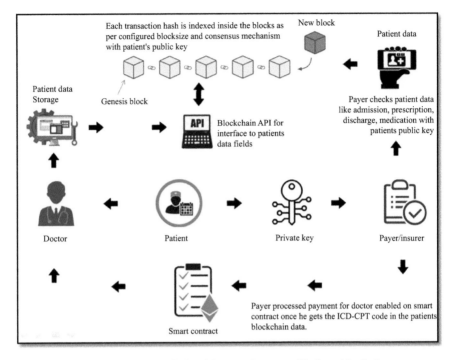

Figure 10.4   A simple healthcare chain enabled on blockchain

verification, etc. is negated leading to expedited processing and quick settlement.

• After verification, the payments as due are settled and published on the blockchain.

Before we move ahead to Ricardian contracts in Section 10.3.3, we will briefly also touch upon the concept of zero-knowledge-proof (ZKP) and healthcare.

10.3.2   Zero-knowledge-proofs and smart contracts

ZKP [11] refers to a method by which one person can prove to another person that they know a value X, without communicating any other information apart from the value X. To understand by an example, suppose a patient has to share his blood group to some doctor, so in the traditional manner he will share his health card to the doctor which will also contain his name, his citizen ID, his address, his mobile number and so many other details. These details, the doctor never wanted but the patient has to perforce share by virtue of sharing his health card information. Thus, there is an undesired sharing of information which neither of the stake holders wanted.

It is here that ZKP comes to resolve and enable the patient to just share the value, i.e. blood group to the doctor and none other information. The same can be enabled on blockchain [12] with the help of smart contracts. Notable other domain examples include zkSNARK [13], Zether [14] and Ethereum constellation [15].

10.3.3   Ricardian contracts for healthcare

The name 'Ricardian' originates from the name 'David Ricardo', a nineteenth century British economist, popular for his work in the international trade theory. Ricardian contracts [16], introduced in 1996 by Ian Grigg, refer to a method of recording a document as a legal agreement which is cryptographically signed and verified [17]. This is coordinated in a format that can be expressed and executed in software. The accrued advantage specific to Ricardian contracts is to make the format both machine readable, such that it can easily be compiled for computational purposes and also readable as an ordinary text document by lawyers and contracting parties.

Vide Article 7, mentioned at EOS GitHub repository [18], each smart contract written by any developer will be documented with a Ricardian contract, i.e. plain English equivalent of the code, expressing the exact intent of all participating parties. While smart contracts have to be written in peculiar languages like Solidity, Vyper or Java, Ricardian contract would be in plain text English explaining the exact purpose of the code lines. Few of the under development works include the following:

- *smaRT* [19]: Enables processing regulations and subsequent expression in a regulatory natural language [20] for lawyers semi-automatically, which is both human readable (in basic English) and machine readable in XML/RDF/OWL or any other language formats.
- *Common Domain Model* [21]: This model allows for a standard digital representation of events that happen during the course of life time of a legal agreement and is expressed in a machine-readable format. This ensues to enhance consistency and facilitate interoperability over legal firms and participating organisation clients.
- *Barclays template* [22]: Focus to create smart contract templates which make it easy for anyone to adopt and use.
- *Common accord* [23]: With tagline 'Bringing the world to agreement', the project focuses to make global standard codes [24] which can be exploited for automating legal documents and transactions, including contracts and legal agreements.
- *OpenBazaar*: An online shopping model which offers an absolute unique way to do shopping services [25] which does not have any middle man, and specific tasks and functions are coordinated with the Ricardian contracts.
- *Legalese* [26]: Designed to capture legal semantics and logic with computational law that implicates moving from *syntax* (i.e. the structure, form of language that lawyers use today) to *semantics* (i.e. the actual meanings attached to the words, symbols, and characters) to *pragmatics* (i.e. the context and its effect of outcomes).

Table 10.1   Ricardian vs. smart contracts

Ricardian contract	Smart contract
	Similarities
Legally executable	Legally executable
	Differences
Digitally signed and human–machine readable	Digitally signed and machine readable only
Flexible and more apt for real-world situations	Immutable once deployed in a blockchain
Pertains to recording of an agreement	Pertains to execution of an agreement
Can be modified to attain properties of smart contract	Cannot be altered to attain properties of a Ricardian contract

- *EOSIO* [27]: A blockchain platform project, currently under development, plans to enable the Ricardian contracts that can be paired with smart contracts to serve as human readable alongside machine readable.

10.3.4   Hybrid smart–Ricardian contracts

Smart contracts and the Ricardian contracts cannot be compared, notwithstanding that they share a set of commonalities; they have independent architectures and designs. While it is possible to apply a Ricardian contract as a smart contract, not all Ricardian contracts are smart contracts and at the same time, not all smart contracts can be Ricardian. The major differences are seen in Table 10.1.

Smart contracts have challenges of being neither smart nor contracts since they are basically irreversible *if-then-else* condition executions in a P2P network in a transparent and non-contradictory mode. While smart contracts can get executed automatically, a Ricardian contract focuses and records the intent of the contract and subsequently actions as deemed, irrespective it has been executed or not. Ricardian contracts are dependent upon a code by employing the hashes concerning to contract documents and are meant to be more conversant with people than machines.

While each of them, i.e. smart and Ricardian contracts have their advantages and disadvantages, the nature of evolving requirements of healthcare looks forward to a hybrid form of contracts involving both of these. So, while on one end smart contracts execute vide a code automatically subject to meeting the conditions as designed, Ricardian contracts will check, record the intent before executing and confirming a transaction to a block. A Ricardian contract commits all data from the official single contract document in a way that can be run by software and adhere to the following terms:

- contract tendered by an issuer to bearers, i.e. nodes identified on healthcare ecosystem;
- easily decipherable by people like a composed contract on paper;

- decipherable by computer programs, i.e. can be compiled and processed like a database;
- uses digital signatures;
- contains the keys-server information;
- affiliated by a unique identifier.

10.4   Applications of blockchain

Introduction of Ethereum further added value to the functionality of smart contracts into the traditional bitcoin blockchain design. It also, for the first time, added turing complete language Solidity to program smart contracts. The world of blockchain has thereafter exploded with a horde of applications in every field of banking, logistics, supply chain, land registries, inventory management, anti-money laundering tracking system, music royalties tracking, voting mechanisms, country governance and healthcare domain, to mention a few.

While the focus of this chapter will be on blockchain connected with healthcare, we will now focus on applications of blockchain in healthcare.

Blockchain can play a pivotal role in ensuring that sharing of health data is controlled with stringent access, thereby negating privacy and security threats for such health data. This can be attained by exploiting smart contracts and designing global blockchain architecture peculiar to tighten access to health data. This chapter explores the evolving healthcare industry enabled with blockchain technology, the drawbacks of previous versions and the opportunities of blockchain concepts that would aid the medical field in keeping up with Industry 4.0.

The evolution of Healthcare 1.0–4.0 is given as follows:

Healthcare 1.0: One doctor at *one hospital* can see *one patient.*

Healthcare 2.0: Multiple doctors at *multiple hospitals* can see *multiple patients'* data.

Healthcare 3.0: System accumulates the data of all patients into a single-point merged data health record and patients are given the right with whom to share data.

Healthcare 4.0: Empowerment of patient's right to be aware of his/her data enabled with new generation technologies of artificial intelligence, machine learning and blockchain.

10.5   Healthcare data

As per Seagate report [28] the worldwide data sphere, i.e. measure of new data created annually and replicated on every year, are estimated to increase by 175 zettabytes. This storage scale is primarily attributed to the 50 billion plus Internet-of-Things (IoT) devices but the astounding part is that 48% [29] of this data belongs to the aggregated data of manufacturing, financial services, media and healthcare industry combined as seen in Figure 10.5. The healthcare data

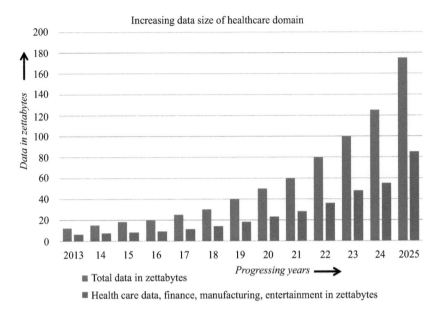

Figure 10.5   Statistics showing expected increase in data population per year

constituted from multiple resources are categorised into structured and non-structured data sets.

10.5.1   Structured data sets

Structured healthcare data set comprises distinctly defined data types whose pattern and format structures allow them to be searched in data sets without hassles. These data sets can include data like a name of the patient, his/her date of birth, blood test reports, ECG parameters or any medical test report indexed in a format and be instantly made available for search to derive useful information and analytics. Again any structured healthcare data set entry at macro level can be divided into a value and a variable name. For example, inside a patient's EMR, his weight could be mentioned as 75 kg or 165.347 lb or even 2,645.55 oz. Additionally any kind of country local name abbreviated could be used, which can make even a structured data look inconsistent and deduce false alerts. To avoid such scenarios, Logical Observation Identifiers Names and Codes (LOINC) [30] are applied across the participating nodes, i.e. hospitals, clinics and thus LOINC constitutes a database on a universally accepted standard.

10.5.2   Non-structured data sets

The unstructured healthcare data is every data, excluding that covered in structured healthcare data. Understandably, this kind of data is raw and has no standardised input formats. This can include patients' emails, recorded audio tele-conversation advises and prescriptions, X-ray images, physician-written notes or faxed/Xerox copies, emails, audio recordings or physician notes about a patient; open-source NoSQL DBMS like MongoDB, OrientDB, CouchDB are few technologies to handle unstructured data [31]. According to an estimate, more than 80% of the total healthcare data is categorised as unstructured health data [32]. While advances in health IT have expanded collection and use, the complexity of health data has hindered standardisation in the healthcare industry. As of 2013, it was estimated that approximately 60% of health data in the United States were unstructured.

10.6   Popular resources for gathering healthcare data

In a relatively better connected world today, there is no dearth of gathering of health data. Major inputs and sources of healthcare data are discussed in the following:

- *Mobile applications*: As per Statista [33], a German online portal for statistics, smart phones today count at approximately 3.5 billion among the total world population of 7.5 billion. This simply implies that the world's population owning a smart phone stands at 45.04%. With this deep penetration, the medical data gathering could not have been easier. Further to mobile phone, wearables are the new norm and are penetrating in the population at an expedited pace.
- *Customer relationship management (CRM) systems*: CRM permits medical business organisations to handle business relationships and the affiliated data information.
- *Electronic health record (EHR) systems*: It is digital record of a patient that makes information usable immediately and securely to empowered users.

10.7   Need of healthcare data

The world today has recognised that data is a colossally, unexploited valuable asset that can shift the global power around. Of this data, if we just deliberate the healthcare data of patients across the globe, what interest would it serve to benefit anyone? The need to pool in healthcare data from multiple sources assists to deduce the following advantages:

- *Cost savings as well as the ability to treat more patients*: Data statistics, prescriptions for varied symptoms, medicine treatment results and many more such vital stats are critical for practising medical professionals. This data is traditionally not available at all and practising professionals depend on publicly available unreliable data or based on some local shares and discussions among the communities. Healthcare data being made available centrally among the entire medical professionals across countries would definitely expedite the treatment and would deem a much less cost expenditure since it would be based on true data.

- *Improved health population*: Repercussion to earlier mentioned data being centrally made available to practising professionals would expedite an improved health index of population.
- *Comprehensive patient information*: Healthcare data can acquire valuable insights and trends of pandemics and diseases across nations.
- *Increased awareness among physicians*: Instead of relying on the traditional methods of healthcare data availability which is scattered in nature and has low accessibility, a common repository of healthcare data can expedite areas of research and studies among the professionals. This would facilitate increased focused research and wide awareness among practising professionals.
- *Transparency and availability of data*: Like all transactions are visible across the bitcoin blockchain by anyone, in an envisaged healthcare blockchain, the transactions peculiar to medicine, prescriptions, lab reports, diagnostics, etc. can be made easily accessible for any authorised node. This ready availability of transparent data will be a boon to practising professionals to expedite right diagnostics and prescriptions.
- *Patient profiling*: Real-time availability of patient's healthcare data, duly permissioned by patients on blockchain, to the practising medical professionals will obviously lead to expedited and timely treatment of patients.
- *Populating databases:* Analysed by artificial intelligence will be able to describe dependences between metrics and diseases.
- *Personalised medicine*: Data is the key for any practising medical professional and at the time of reporting of patient to the doctor; if the doctor has access to his complete longitudinal record, the patient will get a more personalised medicine rather than generic.

These few listed advantages go a long way to facilitate health systems make holistic views of patients, individual treatments, better communication and expedited health outcomes.

10.8   Services offered by the blockchain in healthcare

10.8.1   Data sharing and privacy issues

Hassle-free data sharing with bare thread permissions regulated by the patient is a key element in the healthcare domain. While every patient would demand and expect privacy handles to be minimally shared across, it becomes difficult to coordinate among the healthcare professionals who are more focused on their medical profession nuances. While today to make the same realise, complex and multiple proprietary software are being utilised by multiple firms, which further lead to compatibility issues in data formats sharing. However, blockchain comes as a rescue to resolve this. With the aid of smart contracts and technology inbuilt characteristics, the same can be realised with ease and no compatibility issues.

10.8.2   Longitudinal patient records and health data accuracy

Longitudinal patient records (LPR) refer basically to a 'clinical summary of a patient-based clinical experience'. LPR realises the key goal of EHR implementation which can further be exploited for evaluating and optimising healthcare improvements by medical professionals. Collecting sequences of patient history, his past disease timelines, lab reports, treatments, inpatient visits record, mobile and wearable data sets of patients and those further being deployed on blockchain will bring in transparency and immutability of records.

10.8.3   Drug track ability

The world of healthcare is debauched to a substantial extent by fake drugs supply. Today, there is no system in existence wherein a patient or any node, in the complete supply chain of medicine, can view the tracking of the medicine right from the manufacturing hub, i.e. where the medicine was manufactured. Blockchain offers this possibility of making track ability a reality. A patient or any auditing or seller agency would know in a blockchain scenario, when the medicine was manufactured, in which plant, state, country and what was the route it took to reach the last mile. This information will be available not only in real time but also in the true shared state since deployed on blockchain which is immutable relying on strong cryptography and mathematics foundations.

10.8.4   Fake medical credentials

It would be pertinent to mention that while developed nations have their systems in place to verify medical credentials of professionals in the domain, the same does not exist in the remaining nations and countries. As per [34], as many as thousands of citizens in the United Kingdom alone have bought thousands of fake medical degrees, and they are practising openly. While in this particular case, we are discussing UK citizens buying degrees from certain countries in Asia, we can imagine the plight in these nations where it is more easily coordinated. Blockchain can be a game changer in such credential validations. Universities can be tasked to put original credentials and mark sheet records on blockchain, and these can be verified by anyone without any chances of malicious appends or modifications. Across nations, side chains can further enable validation at global level.

10.8.5   Claims processing

Medical claims and the intricate procedure involved in the culmination of an insurance claim called by the patient is a challenge today, enabled further by documentation delays. Blockchain processes on a validation-based exchange, and this can be prolifically exploited to expedite medical insurance claims enabled with smart contracts. This service has been explained ahead in section with detailed schematic and use case example.

10.8.6 *Supply chain management*

Blockchain-based contracts can assist healthcare organisations in monitoring supply-demand cycles through its entire lifecycle – how is the transaction taking place, whether the contract is successful, or if there are any delays. A detailed use case of supply chain is discussed in Section 10.9.

10.8.7 *Interoperability of data among medical institutes*

In the present set-up of healthcare organisations and institutes, blockchain can easily add on to as a layer to benefit with its characteristics, easily with the use of APIs to make available EHRs accessible to deemed agencies. Thus, exploiting the blockchain characteristics will lead to an ease of interoperability and a reduction of associated burdens with data reconciliation in an expedited manner.

10.9 Medicines and supply chain tracking enabled by blockchain

As per studies in 2015 by *Organisation for Economic Cooperation and Development*, counterfeit drugs in pharmaceutical industry formed up to 3.3% of the total USD 1.1 trillion sales across globe. Undeniably with this 3.3% [35] counterfeit penetration, due healthcare in respect of effected patients will be affected. As discussed till now, blockchain can impart bare thread level permissioned powers to patients to control their respective sharing of data, whereas the same technology can be used by pharmaceuticals industry to track end-to-end supply chain of medicines.

Aided by blockchain technology, pharmaceutical industry can raise security, data provenance and integrity of its vulnerable supply chains by virtue of blockchain's inbuilt transparent, immutable and auditable characteristics. To understand it simply, we will consider the following chain of sequence:

A typical pharmaceutical chain will have stake holders, including manufacturers, logistical service providers, distributers, hospital and patient.

- First, manufacturer will manufacture drugs at his/her premises and will ensure that each medicine packed will have a unique hash code which will have all the details pertaining to origin of medicine, date-time manufactured, location of manufacturing, contact numbers, quality check details, expiry date, etc.
- Second, this hash code generated is placed in the proposed blockchain and can be accessible by anyone interested to know the details of the medicine. As it gets placed on the blockchain, it gets a unique address which can be shared across the chain for the verification or checks anytime.
- Third, subsequent to that mentioned earlier, as the medicine makes a way via distributors to destined locations, the route way details along with transportation arrangements of storage as deemed for medicine, halts en-route with date-time stamps, etc. can be recorded in the blockchain linked with the unique address mentioned at the time of first indexing.

- Fourth, as the destined locations and pharmacists receive the medicines from the distributors, they sign the receipt with their respective digital certificate. This event is again indexed in the blockchain linked to earlier unique transactions. This event can also be made to trigger notifications vide smart contracts to dependent hospitals and clinics regarding availability of the medicine. Even effected payments can be made vide smart contracts to deemed stake holders.
- Lastly, as the patient gets hold of the medicine, he can check back the entire chain with all details and verify credentials of originality of medicine.

In the previously mentioned scenario, let there be a cyber-criminal or a counterfeit medicine maker who wants to introduce his counterfeit medicine for selling to a patient. For all practical purposes, this malicious identity will not be able to do anything to blockchain being immutable. He will not be able to add or modify blockchain to include his medicine code. Now even if he makes a similar package print copying the code, the pharmacist will be able to verify by checking that this medicine is supposed to be held with some specific pharmacist as visible in chain or has already been sold. Few of the currently working and implemented projects are discussed in brief next.

TraceRx [36]: United Nation organisation uses this blockchain-based distributed ledger platform to track and monitor free drugs across the countries to resolve of theft and counterfeiting while shipment of medicines taking place. TraceRx provisions track visibility at granular level across the entire chain and P2P network to decimate supply chain breaches, bettering communication and expediting all operations.

MediLedger Network [37]: MediLedger aspires to be the industry pool effort to resolve the serialisation and counterfeit medicine problem. One of the key focuses of MediLedger to conclude in first phase of implementation is to deal with the returns issue. Per se, pharmaceutical industry statistics has revealed that while the drugs and medicines are returned back to the manufacturer (costs in USD billions) sometimes for logistics or sales reasons, 3% stock is counterfeit. To resolve this, they have identified blockchain technology to offer solutions by indexing every event to make the chain absolute transparent and auditable in true sense.

10.10   Data security concerns in EMR and healthcare domain

Health research and privacy protections of EMR data render critical and very important welfares to mankind. On one end health research data is vital for deriving benefits as seen at Section 10.7, but at the same time it is equally important to save this patients' data from cyber criminals to defend the interests of individual patients and protect their privacy from unforeseen invasions. While the IT proliferation in the health sector has just onset to say, but it has already faced many data breaches. As per Protenus 2019 [38] breach barometer, 503 healthcare data breaches occurred

Table 10.2   Year-wise data breaches of leading healthcare data companies

Name of the firm	Individual patient records breached	Year
Anthem Inc.	80 million	2015
Newkirk Products Inc.	3.5 million	2016
AccuDoc Solutions	26.5 million	2018
UnityPoint Health	14.2 million	2018
CA Department of Developmental Services	582,174	2018
Kalispell Regional Healthcare	130,000	2019
Women's Care Florida	528,000	2019
Sarrell Dental	390,000	2019
Premier Family Medical	320,000	2019
American Medical Collection Agency	20 million	2019
Inmediata Health Group	1.5 million	2019
Columbia Surgical	400,000	2019
UW Medicine	974,000	2019
Central Kansas Orthopedic Group, LLC	109,000	2020
PIH Health	199,548	2020

in the year 2019 that lead to compromise of 15 million patient records. Healthcare data breaches in last few years are shown in tabulated form in Table 10.2.

While if we see the total breaches accumulating all individual company breaches per year, the trend is seen only increasing. While IT is still to proliferate fully in the health sector, the increasing breaches present to us a fore warning for worst to arrive. The graph in Figure 10.6 shows the increasing trend per year 2009–19 wherein 3,000 plus healthcare data breaches have occurred [39].

Thus, we see a proportional increase in rising cybercrimes and data breaches in health records vs. increasing IT proliferation, and these are just the onset times. All these breaches have occurred in spite of all kinds of secured architectures in place, fully updated and functional. Table 10.2 shows major breaches which have occurred over the last 6 years. Being just the onset and times when patients are still illusive about rights of privacy and own data, it would be prudent to enable *security-by-design* right in the beginning. Blockchain technology with its inbuilt characteristics and strong rugged cryptography based consensus can offer a strong solution to the breach menace faced by the health sectors across the globe.

10.11   Choices of blockchain platforms for healthcare

When we discuss about blockchain platforms, we will not attempt and discuss to distinguish about which platform is better or which is not? Each of the blockchain platforms discussed hereafter offers unique solutions, offers different architectures and has different functional parameters in respect of their designs. To simplify with an example, the bitcoin blockchain is a cryptocurrency oriented design where the value is transferred from one account to another, but the same cannot be employed to deploy smart contracts.

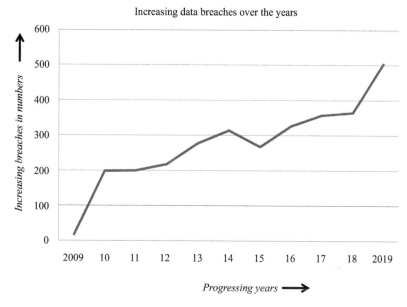

Figure 10.6 Data showing breaches per year stats

An Ethereum blockchain may deploy smart contracts but cannot transact bitcoin with its blockchain. So each of the platforms discussed ahead is not only variants from concepts originating from bitcoin blockchain but is also functionally specific to meet the demands of the healthcare in different ways. Few of the design parameters that all blockchains differ from a design perspective among each other are identified as follows:

- transactions per second (TPS)
- block size
- consensus
- encryption algorithms
- hash rate
- smart contracts deployment
- public vs. private blockchain
- block rewards
- mining and difficulty levels

It is reiterated that the above-mentioned parameters are just few among many parameters that can be tweaked and modified to give an altogether new blockchain design. Now let us discuss few of the popular and promising blockchain platforms in brief.

10.11.1 Ethereum

Ethereum [40] was introduced around late 2013 by Vitalik Buterin, a cryptocurrency programmer, and was the first platform that decoded the true potential of blockchain technology. Prior to Ethereum, all introduced blockchains were basically tweaks of bitcoin blockchain and focused on variants of bitcoin cryptocurrency.

Ethereum refers to an open-source distributed computing blockchain platform that applies the same consensus algorithm as that of bitcoin blockchain, i.e. *proof-of-work* [41]. It is the first platform that facilitated the deployment of smart contracts and fundamentally bought a revolution at the time of introduction around 2014. While bitcoin blockchain uses *Pay to script hash*, *Pay To Public Key Hash* or *Pay To Witness Public Key Hash* kind of scripts [42], Ethereum blockchain uses a proper turing complete Solidity language [9] for effecting transactions and writing smart contracts.

Ethereum has currency and has an interesting concept of gas [43], which is a kind of pricing mechanism for coordinating internal transactions. This negates spam and undesired allocation of resources on the network.

10.11.2   IBM® blockchain

The first *software-as-a-service* blockchain platform on IBM cloud is an enterprise ready private blockchain platform which is designed to ease the evolution, organisation and functioning of a decentralised, multiple institution in a multi-cloud business network. The IBM Blockchain Platform uses Hyperledger Fabric v1.4.6.

The IBM Enterprise Plan renders production ready-to-go blockchain's for organisations interested to create and join a blockchain network for running businesses. Unlike Ethereum, IBM blockchain does not have a new language on the lines of Solidity but works fine with either of Node.js, Golang or JavaScript and Java languages.

10.11.3   Hyperledger

Hyperledger [44] is the first of its kind global collaboration attempt, hosted by 'The Linux Foundation'. It refers to an umbrella of open-source communities focused to develop a suite of frameworks, libraries and tools for private blockchain deployments. Hyperledger gets together 250 member companies [45] to facilitate combined efforts for provisioning enterprise level blockchain solutions.

The most substantive difference between Hyperledger and Ethereum is the basic design, while Ethereum runs the smart contracts on the Ethereum virtual machine and Hyperledger ensues blockchain technology for enterprise grade only. The Hyperledger greenhouse facilitates formulating private blockchain projects from seed, i.e. 'Hyperledger Lab STO fruition', i.e. stable code ready for implementation and deployment. Brief details of Hyperledger projects are seen in Table 10.3.

10.11.4   Hydrachain

In a joint venture of the Ethereum project and Brainbot technologies, Hydrachain is an open-source blockchain platform [46] to support and create private/permission Blockchain networks. Hydrachain uses Python language for supporting its

Table 10.3   Hyperledger projects and libraries

Hyperledger project	Function and purpose
Fabric	Modular distributed ledger technology with privacy for business houses and enterprises
Indy	Framework for decentralised identity
Burrow	Permissible framework to support Ethereum virtual machine and WebAssembly (WASM) smart contracts
Sawtooth	Suite for deploying and running distributed ledgers
Iroha	Focuses on mobile applications
BESU	Open source java based Ethereum client
Libraries	*Function and purpose*
URSA	Shared cryptographic library for developers
ARIES	Interoperable toolkit for storing, transmitting and creating digital credentials
QUILT	Business blockchain tool for distributed ledgers
TRANSACT	Reduces efforts in coding, developing any distributed ledger software

transactions and feature functions. Hydrachain is compatible with all the contract and API level protocols in Ethereum, i.e. all the tools available in Ethereum can be utilised in Hydrachain also. Since Hydrachain is a private blockchain, the block indexing of transactions will not be based on a consensus but it will be subject to confirmation by the trusted earmarked validators.

Another interesting feature of Hydrachain is that both Serpent/Solidity language enabled smart contracts can coexist in the same chain along Python language enabled smart contracts. Another key aspect of Hydrachain is its free configurability option which provisions tailor-made block time, transaction fees, gas, etc. to fit into for any customised making. Hydrachain is perhaps the only blockchain platform that supports Dockerfile templates.

10.11.5   R3 Corda

R3 Corda [47], an enterprise level blockchain technology platform, was founded in 2014 by David E Rutter. It offers to deploy interoperable blockchain networks that interact in rigid privacy and requires two types of consensus, validity consensus and uniqueness consensus, for a transaction to get indexed inside a block. The following features are peculiar to R3 Corda:

- Leads an ecosystem of more than 300 firms working together.
- Being used in multiple domains, including healthcare, finance, insurance and other digital assets.
- XRP cryptocurrency is supported in the new R3 Corda decentralised applications (DApps).
- Can handle up to 600 TPS.
- Built specifically for financial markets though but being also tested for other domains.

- Corda is compatible with any JVM language but is written in Kotlin programming language [48].

10.11.6   MultiChain

MultiChain [49] blockchain platform facilitates business houses and organisations to build and deploy private blockchain applications with speed and is peculiar for financial transactions only. While in other blockchain platforms, the design parameters are fixed but in MultiChain blockchain platform, a single file *params.dat* holds the critical parameters which can be tweaked to suit the organisational requirements, and parameters like block incentive and transaction fees are null by default *params.dat* file that holds in configurations like

- target time for new block generation, i.e. adjusting difficulty levels for solving consensus;
- protocol of the chain;
- configure permission types;
- mining diverseness;
- mining rewards;
- block size capacity and
- meta data per transaction.

Few of the interesting unique features include the following:

- Can be used to launch tailor-made blockchain solutions.
- Launch public or private blockchains as per requirement.
- Make available chosen set of features and enhancements aimed majorly at business organisations.
- Fork of the bitcoin code base and thus have many similarities with the bitcoin documentation.

10.11.7   BigchainDB

Not exactly a blockchain platform but a blockchain database tendering decentralisation, and immutability, BigchainDB [50] has the following features:

- open source for everyone to use and deploy apps;
- each commit in the blockchain database does not need Merkle tree or sidechains for writing to block;
- no native currency;
- any asset, currency or token can be coordinated for issues;
- provisions of custom assets, transactions and permissions;
- supports both public and private networks;
- permissions can be configured at transaction levels;
- offers high TPS up to 1 million TPS, reduced latency and strong escrow functionality.

10.11.8 OpenChain

OpenChain [51] is an open-source blockchain platform, developed by CoinPrism organisation and is based on partitioned consensus wherein different sets of the data take part in different consensus protocols. Other distinguishing features include the following:

- Instantaneous confirmation of transactions.
- Nil mining fees.
- High scalability.
- *Assign aliases* to users in lieu of using base-58 or other public key address system.
- Hierarchical account system appropriating to define permissions at chosen level.
- Multiple levels of control include (a) fully open ledger which can be connected as anonymous from anywhere or (b) closed-loop ledger wherein nodes must be validated and permissioned by the validator or (c) hybrid ledger wherein the approved nodes are assigned few more rights than anonymous users in fully open ledger.
- Handle loss/theft of private keys of users wherein the affected user first informs to the company administrating the OpenChain instance followed by performing an identity check. Concomitant to this identification, the user is asked to generate fresh sets on his device.

10.11.9 Quorum blockchain platform

Quorum [52], by J.P. Morgan, is a go-Ethereum fork based smart contract and distributed ledger platform offering blockchain solutions for enterprise requirements. Other distinguishing features include the following:

- Pluggable and custom consensus *QuorumChain*, a voting-based mechanism is used in quorum blockchain.
- Focus on financial domains.
- Achieve dozens to hundreds of TPS and higher throughput relative to other decentralised blockchains.
- Support both private and public transactions.
- Being a permissioned blockchain network, it has participants only which have been pre-approved by an assigned validator mechanism.
- Introduce the concept of constellation, which refers to a mechanism for encrypting specific messages in intra-network communication.

10.11.10 EOS blockchain platform

EOS [53] is a decentralised blockchain platform planned to support DApps on the lines of Ethereum with relatively high TPS in thousands without on-chain transaction costs. Other distinguishing features include the following:

- Foremost distinguishing feature is enabling blockchain applications to scale as per requirement.
- Another big uniqueness is the implementation of Ricardian contracts, which none other platform has on date.
- EOS plans to be the first decentralised operating system to be able to support industrial scale applications.
- Absolutely no transaction fees unlike bitcoin fee or gas in other bitcoin and Ethereum blockchain.
- EOS supports up to millions of users.
- Users and participating nodes have the choice to upgrade the DApps as per their convenience of time.
- Lowest latency relative to popular blockchain platforms.
- Consensus algorithm used in EOS is distributed proof-of-stake.
- EOS attains parallel processing of smart contracts vide asynchronous communication.
- Native cryptocurrency for EOS is EOS tokens.

10.11.11   Internet-of-Things application (IOTA) blockchain platform

IoT application (IOTA) blockchain [54] is one unique platform which has been developed only for the IoT network and purposes to index and process intra IoT device transactions. It is envisaged that 40 billion plus IoT devices will be interconnected by 2025, and this huge network is what this blockchain platform focuses on. Few other distinguishing features for IOTA platform include the following:

- IOTA cryptocurrency mIOTA is used for intra transactions in the network.
- Vision to be machine-to-machine transactions platform.
- Introduce Tangle [55], a consensus-building system, wherein the IoT devices transacting on the IoT network need to verify two transactions on the network.
- Each verification requires the verifier to perform a proof-of-work associating the transactions into the Tangle ecosystem.
- Uniqueness about IOTA is that it is block less, i.e. there is no block to create and no chain to link but the transactions append to a distributed ledger.

IOTA cannot be termed an exact blockchain platform but from a healthcare ecosystem perspective, if we speak of 40 billion IoT devices by 2025, the healthcare ecosystem of devices will hold a major role among population. Thus IOTA holds immense promise to fortify and strengthen the healthcare ecosystem of medical devices and equipment.

10.12   Major healthcare blockchain use cases under development

Post 2014, after the introduction and first time realisation of Ethereum smart contracts, the blockchain ecosystem per se, healthcare domain, has been evolving at an expedited pace. Worldwide companies and researchers are currently working to realise the practical implementation and realisation of blockchain technology potential. Table 10.4 shows the major works in progress in the blockchain enabled healthcare domain.

Table 10.4 Leading project use case in blockchain-enabled healthcare

Project	Brief description
MedRec 2.0 [56]	• Time-stamped transactions are indexed in the blockchain • Focus on protecting EMRs of patients by exploiting smart contracts • Patients choose who will be able to access their data • Patients also choose to sell or share their health data to deemed buyers like research facilities and pharmacy companies
MediBloc [57]	• Personal healthcare information ecosystem, built on blockchain • Patient-centric healthcare data solution enabled on blockchain • Patient owns his or her own medical data records and not the hospital • Implements a reward system based on its cryptocurrency 'Meditoken' wherein based on set reward system the agencies involved like doctors, patients and pharmacists, etc. will be suitably rewarded with Meditokens
Medicalchain [58]	• Formulating blockchain platform to store EMR of clients and making a global register of the patients health records • Adapting its platform for applications developers and TV-medicine • Enables the patient in control of their medical data with access controls to define when, where and with whom to share the data • Doctors, patients and other stakeholders in the healthcare domain can be shared patients EHR while also protecting patient's identity from external sources
MediChain [59]	• Based on Ethereum blockchain • Enables the patients and other participating nodes in the blockchain to create custom tokens • Patients are enabled to earn money for their EMRs • Focus on high TPS to enable quick access for concerned nodes in blockchain ecosystem • Onus of permission controls lies with the patient as to whom he wants to share with and for how much time
Personal Health Record OS (phrOS) [60]	• Claimed to be the first global hospital blockchain integration project, i.e. 'global healthcare blockchain'

(Continues)

Table 10.4   (Continued)

Project	Brief description
Hashed Health [61]	• Focuses blockchain-enabled health data sharing while ensuring data privacy • Fully operational as on date and presently implemented in Taipei Medical University Hospital, Taiwan • Offers COTS technical blockchain product solutions • Focuses on reducing the cost of care and the administrative inefficiencies and human latency in work • Enables to automate multi-party smart contracts • Functioning is real-time enabled and synchronised through a distributed ledger
BurstIQ [62]	• The BurstIQ platform facilitates the guardianship of data enabled with big data while preserving exacting complaisance with HIPAA
Guardtime [63]	• Successful implementation at Estonia's healthcare systems as a first case for the company • Collaborated with Verizon Enterprise Solutions to deploy blockchain solutions based on Keyless Signature Infrastructure

10.13   Storage challenges and need for inter planetary file system (IPFS) enabled blockchain for healthcare

While we envisage blockchain-enabled solutions in healthcare to care of challenges of security and privacy, there is another challenge that will evolve further to blockchain-enabled healthcare systems, i.e. storage. Worldwide digital healthcare data is estimated to be 35 exabytes by 2025. Storage on blockchain is costly and requires immense IT infrastructure with increased storage requirements. Take, for example, the case of bitcoin blockchain, with over around 12 years of undeterred running, as on date the bitcoin blockchain size is just over 290 GB. This 290 GB basically refers to the cumulative size of blocks holding the transaction hashes. Now when we see the zettabytes of data in healthcare domain and we foresee the IT requirements, it is going to be a challenge for each participating node in the network. The high processing hardware, the amount of storage requirements for full scale nodes will be actually impossible to realise. Thus arises the need for decentralised storage and inter planetary file system (IPFS) [64] arrives as a possible solution.

10.14   IPFS

IPFS is a file sharing method among P2P networks that basically modify the conventional mode of sharing documents and files across the networks. This is attained by unequivocally distinguishing each file in a global namespace established on content addressing [65] while linking all devices on the P2P networks. Each node in IPFS is configured to store an accumulation of hashed files. Thus, the deficiencies observed in the traditionally followed client server model are negated in IPFS. The main components in IPFS file sharing protocol include the following:

- version control system
- distributed hash tables
- Merkle directed acyclic graph
- self-certifying file system
- block exchanges

10.15   Why do we need IPFS?

Bitcoin blockchain has a standard block size of approximately 1 MB, and these contain around 1,500–1,900 transaction details being coordinated from one address to other. On the other hand, if we try to impose the same kind of architecture in healthcare, huge data sets envisaged in the healthcare domain would be a challenge to reckon. Huge data sets as being discussed in the domain of healthcare of the size in zettabytes would not be apt to be indexed in blocks. Even if we increase the block size to contain the healthcare data, it would have a snowball effect into the efficiency and transaction confirmation delays. Thus, there is a need such that the blocks contain the regular hashes of the transaction and data sets are stored in a decentralised manner. This decentralised storage can be coordinated with the aid of IPFS protocol.

10.16   Blockchain and IPFS

The storing of transactions in bitcoin blockchain is designed to get committed in a final state inside block in around 10 min [66]. This committing of the transaction inside the block is further based on the configured difficulty level as gets generated as per average time of creation of blocks at every 2,016th block in cycle. The minimum 10 min the blockchain takes would not be apt in a real-time environment implementation wherein every transaction should be working in a real-time mode.

It is also realised that there are many other factors that affect these 10-min time. While the focus in this chapter is on enabling healthcare domain with blockchain, it is also at the same time realised that these transactions in bitcoin blockchain are just hashes with very miniscule bit sizes. In an envisaged scenario, real-time data of healthcare domain will be a kind of continuously populated one from various sources and be of huge sizes too.

To resolve the issue of large size data sets on blockchain, IPFS comes as a viable solution. Vide Figure 10.7, it is seen that each block has an additional attribute in the form of IPFS hash which connects the hashes of various data sets deployed on IPFS.

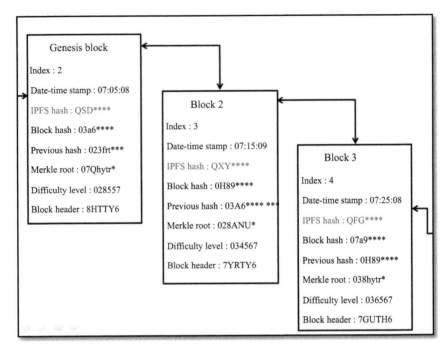

Figure 10.7   IPFS hash in blocks

Even if the blockchain is configured for hash storage only and rest for storage is enabled by exploiting cloud services, cloud API will be vulnerable. While in the case of IPFS, there will be no such issues since the storage itself is decentralised. The major advantages accrued vide IPFS association with blockchain will include the following:

- *Single-instance storage*: This refers to the negation of holding islands of data copies at various locations. IPFS, by virtue of its unique characteristics, addresses data by hashes, thus rendering integrity and distributed persistence of data.
- *File indexing, visibility and exploring*: Provisions quicker browsing of data.
- *Low bandwidth requirement*: Users can share data between each other with IPFS addressing, thus abbreviating bandwidth requirements.
- *Archiving and retrieval*: IPFS-distributed storage offers immutable and integrated data storage with offline data access.
- *Ease of distribution and accessibility*: Since IPFS is a file-distributing storage protocol, the access and secure availability comes easy for user nodes.

10.17   Challenges and roadblocks to the realisation of blockchain-enabled healthcare

Thus, as deduced by now, blockchain has a definite association ahead with the healthcare domain, but this would not be realised without a horde of challenges.

While few of the challenges with possible solutions have been discussed earlier, including big storage data sets and health insurance portability and accountability act (HIPAA) contradicts, there are multiple other challenges which are briefly discussed in the following:

- *True data sets*: Healthcare ecosystem would consist of millions of inter-connected medical machines and equipment which would be emitting real-time data of patients in a near-uninterrupted mode. These interconnected machines and equipment would be of multiple manufacturers and may not even be relating to any standard too. These would be based on variety proprietary software and firmwares which would have own sets of vulnerabilities, subject to compromise. Thus, blockchain would only be able to ensure that whatever data hashes and data are stored on it would be immutable. Data may be compromised at the origins through vulnerable device APIs.
- *Smart contracts*: Smart contracts are one of the most important blockchain features that can not only automate a lot of things and negate middlemen in the healthcare ecosystem, but also the use of smart contracts for a real-time application scenario would deem a strong stable language unlike Solidity as on date. Though Solidity, as a language, is evolving and improving fast, at the same time it has seen an extra ordinary version speed releases since its first release on 21 Aug 2015 with version 0.1.2. The language has seen 64 fresh releases since its introduction with most of them being backward incompatible.
- *Scalability*: While we envisage healthcare connected devices to billions by 2025, the sheer number of medical devices and equipment participating in the healthcare ecosystem, as part of IoT, will be a challenge to deal with. These billion plus medical devices would be required to exchange data in real time. This large scale would surely come with its own set of challenges to include storage designs, IT infrastructure, bandwidth for ensuing zettabytes of data, etc.
- *Byzantine brokers*: These brokers refer to malicious elements, who have the potential to misuse and play with decryption keys. Thus, they can create subscription corruption, message reordering and publication delay or publication corruption. The big architectural dependency on IT, more so on public key infrastructure (PKI) and digital keys infrastructure, can enable threats from such byzantine brokers that will deem extra efforts to contravene any attack endeavours.
- *Unique identification of medical devices and equipment in healthcare ecosystem*: All the participating devices will be identified by a unique set of public–private keys, and thus security by individual hospital administrators will be of preponderant importance. A simple compromise by a smart malicious cyber-criminal or a careless administrator can play mayhem in generating false and corrupted health analytic data. A need to evolve and negate out such scenarios are deemed before going live and realising a working healthcare ecosystem.

- *Throughput*: The healthcare ecosystem enabled by blockchain will heavily bank on the speed of throughputs attained to ascertain quick committing of transaction hashes in block. This would be made possible with accessibility of strong and dedicated uptime networks with huge scalability with low latency.

- *Development in isolation*: Perhaps other than technical challenges, this challenge might play a big role in expedited realisation of blockchain-enabled healthcare sector. As on date, different countries, states, IT giants and new start-ups are working in isolation unconnected with each other to prepare proprietary platforms and projects. The penultimate realisation of healthcare analytics is to acquire more specialisation in predicting root cause of diseases and pandemics to further eradicate it all together. The recent corona pandemic has clearly taught that the world cannot develop in isolation, rather it needs a global collaboration for everything. Developing something in isolation at country or company level cannot be a solution to realise long-term goals of the healthcare analytics.

- *Standardisation*: When we expect a global collaboration among countries, states and companies, the need for following a standard arises. Be it for collating formats or SI units for measurements and analytics, the need for adopting and creating standards is imminent.

- *Blockchain intersection with 'Health Insurance Portability and Accountability Act' (HIPAA)*: Till now we have discussed the accrued advantages of enabling blockchain in healthcare domain that can make a patient actually control and permit his/her data. Now we also have HIPAA [67], which makes this data sharing of the patient legally bided for use and revelation of EMRs, etc. While blockchain as a potent technology has so much to offer for healthcare domain primarily focusing on privacy and security permissions of EMRs at macro level, it just overlaps with the mandatory sharing of patient's data vide HIPAA act. So either one will make way for the healthcare, i.e. either blockchain grants macro-level permission choices to the patient or HIPAA supersedes the blockchain permissions and takes data by default. Will that be the way out? Although HIPAA, by US federal, is still not mandatory for many countries, the same is making way for evolution of similar acts across. So while researchers can keep busy with proposing new models and architectures for enabling blockchain in health-care, there is an imminent need to fine tune the two to satisfy both ends. Confidentiality, integrity and availability will be required to be fine-tuned to macro permission levels that can accomplish the HIPAA act mandate the privacy-security requirements of the EMRs of patients. So basically it entails that any blockchain project under development for imparting advantages to healthcare domain needs to be aware of the HIPAA or equivalent act as would be applicable to different countries. This would deem for a global level association of agencies resulting in tailor-made blockchain-HIPAA-enabled solutions.

10.18   Conclusion

The chapter foremost brings out in brief what blockchain technology is all about and discusses its key features. Subsequent to this, healthcare sector statistics and major healthcare data breaches over last about 5 years have been bought out. The healthcare domain encompasses not just the health data breaches but also takes into consideration all components associated with it like supply chain, medical professionals, health fake credentials and certifications, fake medicine chain. These have been discussed with possible resolves and association with blockchain technology.

Smart contracts and Ricardian contracts have been discussed in little more detail since they would be central to drawing the benefits in the healthcare ecosystem for negating middle men and implementing 'code as law'. Development per se, the domain of smart contracts is evolving, major blockchain developers and platforms like Hyperledger and Ethereum are ensuing to give it more power and speed for true realisation. However, it is felt that owing to the ambiguous and non-deterministic nature of legal agreements from an interpretation point of view, the future will bank more upon hybrid smart-Ricardian contracts, deployed on blockchain, as they attain maturity and stability.

Other than earlier mentioned various evolving and popular blockchain platforms, unique features and characteristics have also been discussed that can be associated and custom deployed with healthcare domain in future. This is followed by mentions of few projects which are already leading the way in giving out variant options of blockchain-enabled healthcare platforms. Another very important technology, which is felt to emphatically establish itself along with blockchain and healthcare together, is IPFS. The core term of reference for this IPFS too is decentralised storage. The advantages and key features of the IPFS technology have been discussed.

A brief mention about the intersection of HIPAA and blockchain has been iterated since both have a definite future role to play in healthcare sector and little contradictory aims. This is followed by challenges that need to be resolved before we attain the true realisation of the merging between blockchain and healthcare.

So, vide above we observe that we have technologies today at our doors ready to take on tasks like blockchain, IoT, expanding healthcare sector and IPFS, and the need is to expedite the developments not only in isolation but also at global level. This can only be made possible if global joint efforts are initiated to achieve and collaborate for a dream 'International Healthcare Blockchain'.

References

[1]   M. Mammadova, "The Problems of Information Security of Electronic Personal Health Data," 2015 7th International Conference on Information Technology in Medicine and Education (ITME), Huangshan, 2015, pp. 678–682, doi: 10.1109/ITME.2015.158.

[2] S. Nakamoto, (2009). Bitcoin: A Peer-to-Peer Electronic Cash System. Cryptography Mailing List at https://metzdowd.com, accessed on 21 Jan 2020.

[3] G. Wood, (2019). A Next-Generation Smart Contract and Decentralized Application Platform by Vitalik Buterin at https://ethereum.org/en/white-paper/, accessed on 29 Sept 2020

[4] S. Wang, Y. Yuan, X. Wang, J. Li, R. Qin and F. Wang, "An Overview of Smart Contract: Architecture, Applications, and Future Trends," 2018 IEEE Intelligent Vehicles Symposium (IV), Changshu, 2018, pp. 108–113, doi: 10.1109/IVS.2018.8500488.

[5] F. Hofmann, S. Wurster, E. Ron and M. Böhmecke-Schwafert, "The Immutability Concept of Blockchains and Benefits of Early Standardisation," 2017 ITU Kaleidoscope: Challenges for a Data-Driven Society (ITU K), Nanjing, 2017, pp. 1–8, doi: 10.23919/ITU-WT.2017.8247004.

[6] S. Bistarelli, I. Mercanti and F. Santini, "An Analysis of Non-standard Bitcoin Transactions," 2018 Crypto Valley Conference on Blockchain Technology (CVCBT), Aug, 2018, pp. 93–96, doi: 10.1109/CVCBT. 2018.00016.

[7] Vyper, 2019, [online] Available from: https://github.com/ethereum/vyper, accessed on 28 Sept 2020.

[8] I. Sergey, V. Nagaraj, J. Johannsen, A. Kumar, A. Trunov, and K.C.G. Hao, Safer smart contract programming with Scilla. Proc. ACM Program. Lang. 3, OOPSLA, Article 185, 2019, 30 pages. DOI: https://doi.org/10.1145/3360611.

[9] P. Hegedus, "Towards Analyzing the Complexity Landscape of Solidity Based Ethereum Smart Contracts," 2018 IEEE/ACM 1st International Workshop on Emerging Trends in Software Engineering for Blockchain (WETSEB), Gothenburg, Sweden, 2018, pp. 35–39.

[10] Oxford comma dispute is settled as Maine drivers get $5 million [online) by Daniel Victor published Feb. 9, 2018 at https://www.nytimes.com/2018/02/09/us/oxford-comma- maine.html, accessed on 23 Feb 2020.

[11] O. Goldreich, "Zero-Knowledge: Abstract of a Tutorial," The 43rd Annual IEEE Symposium on Foundations of Computer Science, Proceedings, Vancouver, BC, 2002, p. 3, doi: 10.1109/SFCS.2002.1181876.

[12] H. Al-Aswad, H. Hasan, W. Elmedany, M. Ali and C. Balakrishna, "Towards a Blockchain-Based Zero-Knowledge Model for Secure Data Sharing and Access," 2019 7th International Conference on Future Internet of Things and Cloud Workshops (FiCloudW), Istanbul, Turkey, 2019, pp. 76–81, doi: 10.1109/FiCloudW.2019.00027.

[13] R. S. Wahby, I. Tzialla, A. Shelat, J. Thaler and M. Walfish, "Doubly-Efficient zkSNARKs Without Trusted Setup," 2018 IEEE Symposium on Security and Privacy (SP), San Francisco, CA, 2018, pp. 926–943, doi: 10.1109/SP.2018.00060.

[14] B. Bünz, S. Agrawal, M. Zamani, and D. Boneh, "Zether: Towards Privacy in a Smart Contract World," Lecture Notes in Computer Science, 2020, 423–443.

[15] U. Feige, A. Fiat, and A. Shamir, Zero-knowledge proofs of identity. J. Cryptology, 1988, 1, 77–94. https://doi.org/10.1007/BF02351717.

[16] I. Grigg, "The Ricardian Contract," 2004 Proceedings, First IEEE International Workshop on Electronic Contracting, San Diego, CA, 2004, pp. 25–31, doi: 10.1109/WEC.2004.1319505.

[17] I. Grigg, "The Ricardian contract," Proceedings. First IEEE International Workshop on Electronic Contracting, San Diego, CA, USA, 2004, pp. 25–31, doi: 10.1109/WEC.2004.1319505.

[18] EOSIO Technical White Paper, Dec. 2017, [online] Available from: https://github.com/EOSIO/Documentation, accessed on 21 July 2020.

[19] smaRT [online] at https://www.smart4reg.com/, accessed on 12 March 2020.

[20] L. Theodore, J. Mooney, R. Pierangelo, and C. Mark, Disrupting Finance: FinTech and Strategy in the 21st Century, 2019. 10.1007/978-3-030-02330-0.

[21] "Ricardian contracts: A smarter way to do smart contracts?" by Jurij Lampic at https://www.schoenherr.eu/publications/publicationdetail/ricardian-contracts-a-smarter- way-to-do-smart-contracts/, accessed on 01 Oct 2020.

[22] "Barclays gets into the nuts and bolts of Smart Contract Templates" [online] by Ian Allison available at https://www.ibtimes.co.uk/barclays-gets-into-nuts-bolts- smart-contract-templates-1596874.

[23] "On the intersection of Ricardian and Smart Contracts" [online] by Ian Grigg available at https://www.iang.org/papers/intersection_ricardian_smart.html, accessed on 01 Oct 2020.

[24] "OpenBazaar contracts with CommonAccord's API design" by Dr Washington Sanchez available at https://github.com/drwasho/OB-Common-Accord, accessed on 29 July 2020.

[25] "Open bazaar tokens and Smart contracts" [online] by OpenBazaar.org available at https://openbazaar.org/blog/openbazaar-tokens-and-smart-contracts/, accessed on 20 July 2020.

[26] "Legalese, software is eating law" by at https://legalese.com/prior-art.html, accessed on 21 April 2020.

[27] "Ricardian Template Toolkit EOSIO Tools for Human readable agreement templates for smart contracts" [online] at https://eos.io/build-on-eosio/ricardian-template- toolkit/, accessed on 27 Apr 2020.

[28] "The Digitization of the World From Edge to Core" [online] by David Reinsel, available at https://www.seagate.com/files/www-content/our-story/trends/files/idc-seagate- dataage-whitepaper.pdf, accessed on 26 Sept 2020.

[29] "175 zettabytes by 2025" [online] by Tom Coughlin at https://www.forbes.com/sites/tomcoughlin/2018/11/27/175-zettabytes-by-2025/#43b8d8495459, accessed on 16 Jun 2020.

[30] G. Gilia, V. Mistretta, C. Muriana, T. Piazza and G. Vizzini, "Improving Interoperability of Clinical Documents: A Case Study of LOINC Mapping in Analysis Laboratories," 2015 International Conference on Industrial

Engineering and Systems Management (IESM), Seville, 2015, pp. 1240–1244, doi: 10.1109/IESM.2015.7380311.

[31]   B. Ristevski, and M. Chen (2018). Big Data Analytics in Medicine and Healthcare. Journal of integrative bioinformatics, 15(3), 20170030. https://doi.org/10.1515/jib-2017-0030.

[32]   "The Challenges of Unstructured Healthcare Data" [online] by Bernadette Wilson, available at https://www.carevoyance.com/blog/unstructured-data-healthcare, accessed on 28 Sept 2020.

[33]   "Global digital population as of July 2020" [online] by Published by J. Clement, available at https://www.statista.com/statistics/617136/digital-population-worldwide/, accessed on 23 Aug 2020.

[34]   "Staggering trade in fake degrees revealed" [online] by Helen Clifton, available at https://www.bbc.com/news/uk-42579634, accessed on 21 Aug 2020.

[35]   "Trade in fake goods is now 3.3% of world trade and rising" [online] by Catherine Bremer, available at https://www.oecd.org/newsroom/trade-in-fake-goods-is-now-33-of- world-trade-and-rising.htm.

[36]   "Blockchain based Pharma Supply Chain Solution for International Aid Distribution" [online] by Leeway Hertz, available at https://www.leeway-hertz.com/project/tracerx/, accessed on 21 July 2020.

[37]   "MediLedger – Blockchain solutions for pharma companies" [online] by Medi Ledger at https://www.mediledger.com/, accessed on 21 Apr 2020.

[38]   "5 Million patient records breached in 2018" [online] by Jessica Davis, available at https://healthitsecurity.com/news/15-million-patient-records-breached-in-2018-hacking-phishing-surges, accessed on 11 Jan 2020.

[39]   "Healthcare data breach statistics" [online] by HIPAA Journal at https://www.hipaajournal.com/healthcare-data-breach-statistics/, accessed on 23 Sept 2020.

[40]   R. A. Canessane, N. Srinivasan, A. Beuria, A. Singh and B. M. Kumar, "Decentralised Applications Using Ethereum Blockchain," 2019 Fifth International Conference on Science Technology Engineering and Mathematics (ICONSTEM), Chennai, India, 2019, pp. 75–79, doi: 10.1109/ICONSTEM.2019.8918887.

[41]   I. G. A. K. Gemeliarana and R. F. Sari, "Evaluation of Proof of Work (POW) Blockchains Security Network on Selfish Mining," 2018 International Seminar on Research of Information Technology and Intelligent Systems (ISRITI), Yogyakarta, Indonesia, 2018, pp. 126–130, doi: 10.1109/ISRITI.2018.8864381.

[42]   S. Bistarelli, I. Mercanti and F. Santini, "An Analysis of Non-Standard Bitcoin Transactions," 2018 Crypto Valley Conference on Blockchain Technology (CVCBT), Zug, 2018, pp. 93–96, doi: 10.1109/CVCBT.2018.00016.

[43]   L. Marchesi, M. Marchesi, G. Destefanis, G. Barabino and D. Tigano, "Design Patterns for Gas Optimisation in Ethereum," 2020 IEEE

International Workshop on Blockchain Oriented Software Engineering (IWBOSE), London, ON, Canada, 2020, pp. 9–15.

[44] J. Sousa, A. Bessani and M. Vukolic, "A Byzantine Fault-Tolerant Ordering Service for the Hyperledger Fabric Blockchain Platform," 2018 48th Annual IEEE/IFIP International Conference on Dependable Systems and Networks (DSN), Luxembourg City, 2018, pp. 51–58.

[45] "Hyperledger membership" [online] by Linux foundation projects, available at https://www.hyperledger.org/about/members, accessed on 02 May 2020.

[46] "What is HyderaChain Technology & How it Works?" at https://www.blockchain-council.org/blockchain/what-is-hyderachain-technology-how-it-works/, accessed on 03 May 2020.

[47] C. Khan, A. Lewis, E. Rutland, C. Wan, K. Rutter and C. Thompson, "A Distributed-Ledger Consortium Model for Collaborative Innovation," Computer, vol. 50, no. 9, pp. 29–37, 2017, doi: 10.1109/MC.2017.3571057.

[48] Kotlin language at https://kotlinlang.org/api/latest/jvm/stdlib/kotlin.math/-i-e-e-erem.html, accessed on 06 May 2020.

[49] A. Ismailisufi, T. Popović, N. Gligorić, S. Radonjic and S. Šandi, "A Private Blockchain Implementation Using Multichain Open Source Platform," 2020 24th International Conference on Information Technology (IT), Zabljak, Montenegro, 2020, pp. 1–4.

[50] Meet BigchainDB at https://www.bigchaindb.com/, accessed on 10 May 2020.

[51] Blockchain technology for the enterprise at https://www.openchain.org/, accessed on 01 May 2020.

[52] Evolve with quorum at https://www.goquorum.com/, accessed on 12 May 2020.

[53] EOSIO – Blockchain software architecture at https://eos.io/, accessed on 04 May 2020.

[54] B. Shabandri and P. Maheshwari, "Enhancing IoT Security and Privacy Using Distributed Ledgers With IOTA and the Tangle," 2019 6th International Conference on Signal Processing and Integrated Networks (SPIN), Noida, India, 2019, pp. 1069–1075.

[55] N. Živi, E. Kadušić and K. Kadušić, "Directed Acyclic Graph as Tangle: An IoT Alternative to Blockchains," 2019 27th Telecommunications Forum (TELFOR), Belgrade, Serbia, 2019, pp. 1–3, doi: 10.1109/TELFOR48224.2019.8971190.

[56] MedRec documentation at https://medrec.media.mit.edu/technical/, accessed on 12 May 2020.

[57] Open up infinite possibilities of healthcare data at https://medibloc.org/en, accessed on 28 Apr 2020.

[58] Medicalchain – Blockchain for electronic health records at https://medicalchain.com/en/, accessed on 29 April 2020.

[59] MediChain: A public blockchain medical information network at https://blockchainhealthcarereview.com/medichain-a-public-blockchain-medical-information-network/, accessed on 12 May 2020.

[60]   phrOS, Healthcare blockchain operating system at https://phros.io/, accessed on 12 May 2020.

[61]   Hashed Health: A platform for blockchain innovation in healthcare, accessed on 02 May 2020.

[62]   BurstIQ at https://www.burstiq.com/, accessed on 13 May 2020.

[63]   Solving real healthcare challenges with blockchain at https://guardtime.com/health, accessed on 03 May 2020.

[64]   Y. Chen, H. Li, K. Li and J. Zhang, "An Improved P2P File System Scheme Based On IPFS and Blockchain," 2017 IEEE International Conference on Big Data (Big Data), Boston, MA, 2017, pp. 2652–2657, doi: 10.1109/BigData.2017.8258226.

[65]   IPFS powers the distributed web at https://ipfs.io/, accessed on 19 May 2020.

[66]   J. Göbel and A. E. Krzesinski, "Increased Block Size and Bitcoin Blockchain Dynamics," 2017 27th International Telecommunication Networks and Applications Conference (ITNAC), Melbourne, VIC, 2017, pp. 1–6, doi: 10.1109/ATNAC.2017.8215367.

[67]   HIPAA at https://www.hhs.gov/hipaa/index.html, accessed on 10 May 2020.

Chapter 11

Improved interop blockchain applications for e-healthcare systems

Jesu Rethnam Rethna Virgil Jeny[1], Kaushik Sekaran[1] and Sai Srujan Dandyala[1]

Blockchain in healthcare plays a vital role in the form of encryption-based technology, which has been used to keep the patients' data in a secured and more distributed way. Also, the shared ledger and control access concepts in the blockchain database that leads to central authority or administration leakage. Blockchain technology in E-healthcare is also being used for digital payment systems that focus on cybersecurity, EHRs (electronic health records), patients data management, and so on. The main focus of this work has been put up in a novel patient centered framework to make the effective patient engagement, data curation, and regulated dissemination of accumulated information in a secure and interoperable environment. The framework has been designed to describe the major obstacles to the adaptation of blockchain technology in E-healthcare, such as data security, interoperability, data integrity, identity validation, and scalability. The major challenges of blockchain in E-healthcare are to validate the accuracy of data and to maintain the interoperability in the numerous medical data in the databases. Data tampering and security of E-healthcare data are being the key issues in addressing the threats in handling the healthcare-related databases. Two essential potentialities in blockchain technology are trust and traceability, which helps the generic trust problem on all public, federated, and organization levels. Data written in the blockchain cannot be updated or removed; hence blockchain technology has been opted for E-healthcare systems. Healthcare professionals have less access to the patient's medical details (data) that leads to the improper/poor diagnosis in the end results. Blockchain helps us to enable efficient sharing of healthcare data with assured data integrity and protecting patient privacy. Soon, blockchain will be greatly supported in personalized, authentic, and secure E-healthcare by combining the whole real-time clinical data of patient's health and presenting it in an up-to-date secure E-healthcare setup. Also, telemedicine and E-health are two broad areas, in which

[1]Department of Computer Science and Engineering, Vignan Institute of Technology and Science, Hyderabad, India

clinical data has been transferred to a remote specialist for expert opinion through a store-and-forward technology or online real-time clinical monitoring like tele-monitoring and telemetry. Major applications of blockchain in E-healthcare include clinical, pharmaceuticals, biomedical, HER medical, neuroscience, genomics medicine, and so on. Currently 70% of healthcare centers have been moved in the blockchain technology for data management and maintenance. In this work, both existing and modern technologies in E-healthcare have been reviewed with respect to blockchain, and the same has been described with use cases and the experimental setups. Our research in blockchain together with E-healthcare platform reviews the framework challenges and technologies to implement blockchain for E-healthcare applications.

11.1   Introduction

A blockchain is a budding list of blocks which are connected by cryptography. It is used for cryptocurrency transactions. Block stores the information about the transactions like timestamp, amount of transaction, purchase details, information about the persons involving in the cryptocurrency transaction. Also block stores a unique identity called hash. The information stored in the blocks differentiates them from other blocks. The contents in a block can be seen by anyone, but it cannot be modified. The main objective of blockchain is to permit digital information to be stored and distributed but not to get modified. Blockchain [1] is a decentralized, distributed, transparent technology for cryptocurrency. It is not controlled centrally by any entity. Public blockchains, Private blockchains, and hybrid blockchains are the three categories of blockchain networks in which public blockchain permits a person who has only an Internet connection and can do the transactions, and in private blockchain only an authorized person can involve in transactions, and hybrid is a combination of both.

A block header consists of the information like block version, timestamp, authentication information and a hash code. Block body contains the transaction information, and the number of transactions in a block depends on the size of a block (Figure 11.1).

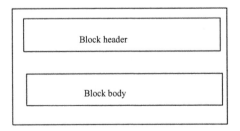

Figure 11.1   Structure of a block

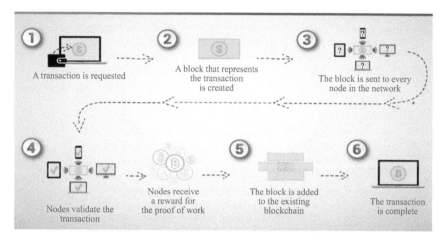

Figure 11.2 Blockchain working model

11.1.1 How blockchain is used in healthcare?

One of the major industries, which adopts blockchain, is E-healthcare. The reason behind the adoption is its decentralization (it is not permitted by a single entity to control), cryptographical storage of data (it is securable), its immutable (no one can change the data once it is stored) and it is transparent (anyone can get the access of the data) (Figure 11.2).

Blockchain permits the patients to access their medical reports from anywhere in the world, and the patients get the opinion of different doctors from other hospitals also (Figure 11.3).

Blockchain is a tool in healthcare [2] for new openings. It is used to preserve patient's personal data in a database. But there is no central level control; instead records are available in many numbers of computers and it is made available for multiple users. As the records stored in blockchain are encrypted by using cryptographic technique, data can be stored safely and the hackers can be prevented. By using secret private keys for encryption, one can avoid the possibility of thieving any data.

In blockchain, it is possible to include a new data but any of the stored data cannot be deleted. Due to this, the patent can always feel that his/her record is safe, and no one can do the modifications. Doctors while recording the data, special attention should be given and if not, it will lead to a horrible situation during the reference period.

Due to the global accessibility of records in blockchain technology, for treatment doctors can get the data very easily by anytime from anywhere in the world. Moreover, one can go with different doctors easily for their opinion about a patient.

11.1.2 Challenges in interoperability between various sections of healthcare system

As seen in our daily life, there is no authenticity from where the medicines or health products do really come from, there is no reliable information on whether a

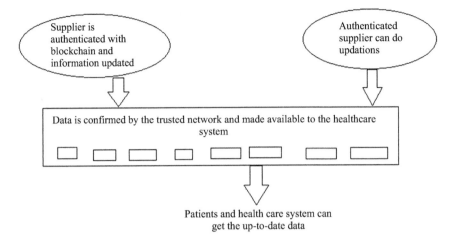

Figure 11.3   Blockchain to maintain a supplier directory

particular medicine had undergone through successful clinical trials or not. There is no communication between the hospitals at least indirectly so the information is subjected to change when the patient him/herself explains his/her health status so again a new medication with new medicines will be started when ever patients go for the sake of second opinion for a different hospital. For all these challenges, a possible solution is described in the conclusion.

11.2   Literature review

11.2.1   Electronic health records

Blockchain is an especially useful tool for generating a patient entry in online mode. Its decentralized storage, highly securable, constant procedure and right to use can be accessed from anywhere in the world. Because of this kind of road and rail network, it is not necessary for the patients to worry about the synchronization of their medical records. With the permission of patient, any doctor can do the treatment by referring the patient's record to blockchain. This methodology is updating the data in real time and reducing the processing time.

While consulting the doctor for a patient, the doctor can get the patient's blood group, his/her medical history [3] like chronic diseases, allergic reactions, etc. within few seconds of time. This information will be immensely helpful for a doctor to understand the patient's history and give a treatment very quickly.

But the data should be preserved in a predefined standardized and clear format without any confusion to the doctor who is referring to the record. One more important thing to note in the medical field has been put up here: *wrong diagnosis of disease and updating of report should not be there. If so, it will lead to a wrong treatment and make the patient in a dangerous situation.*

11.2.2 Drug tracking

Blockchain can resolve the issue of fake products. The details about the drug manufacturer, distributor, and each transaction between them are stored in block-chain. So easily and quickly tracking the authenticity, manufacturer, and distributor details can be done.

11.2.3 Blockchain in future healthcare

In the vicinity of future, IOT devices can collect the patient's information like blood pressure, temperature, pulse, heartbeats, sugar level in real time, and the same can be attached to the EHR in blockchain. This will direct the doctors to diagnose the disease more precisely and continue a treatment. By using blockchain technology [4] clinic would have been run in a cost-effective manner and can provide good services to patient without delay.

11.2.4 Blockchain and cryptocurrencies

11.2.4.1 Ethereum

Before understanding Ethereum first, let us understand how actually our data is stored on the Internet. Everything on the Internet is stored in some third-party server systems that might be Google, Yahoo, Amazon, Facebook, etc., i.e., our data is being handled by these third parties or some other middleware companies, but how long do these companies could be trusted in securing our data? Will they guarantee us that our data will not get breeched, or is the data is hack proof?

In addition, here comes the Ethereum as new technology based on blockchain technology. While bitcoin [5] is aimed only for transactions and digital currency, Ethereum is used for developing distributed applications (DApps) and replacing the Internet of third parties which store data, transactions and keep track.

Technically speaking, Ethereum is an open source, distributed blockchain-based computing platform [6]. Regarding the features of *smart contracts*, the concept of smart contracts will be discussed later in this chapter. Using Ethereum, there is a chance to recreate the Internet without the involvement of third parties. The process of elimination of the third party could be implemented using smart contracts by creating trust, and Ethereum uses consensus proof-of-work (PoW), and Ethereum provides a peer-to-peer network to eliminate the involvement of third parties.

Now let us discuss some of the features of Ethereum and then followed by how it works. First Ethereum is a decentralized system that is not controlled by any single governing body, and in today's system many or majority of the online services are centralized system which has single-point governing body or simply it is said that they are centralized system in many online services, which follow a traditional central system. Time has proved that these are highly vulnerable if this central sever goes down when there will power outages or exists central point of failure. But while coming to the case of Ethereum, it is a decentralized system in which there is no single point of failure and is highly securable and provides the trust with using blockchain technology. As discussed earlier, Ethereum being a decentralized system, there exists a peer-to-peer communication, and every single interaction will be direct between the two participants in the network, and there will be no controlling authority involved. Ethereum has its own blockchain platform simply known as Ethereum blockchain which has got its own digital asset or tokens, or digital currency known as ether (ETH). This cryptocurrency is useful in sharing the transaction fee or gas price, also to share between wallets on Ethereum blockchain [7].

Ethereum is supported by many numbers of "nodes." Nodes are the components that download the Ethereum blockchain to their computationally powered systems and completely execute or implement the consensus rules of the system by maintaining the trust and receiving the rewards (ethers) in return. Nodes not only store the transaction but also store the most recent state of the smart contract (code for business logic) within the network. So, with this, it is probable that it can also be stated, Ethereum as a "transaction-based state machine." Every state in Ethereum consists of many numbers of transactions that are grouped as a "block," and these blocks are added up to the existing Ethereum blockchain with the process of mining which is like the bitcoin blockchain [7].

11.2.4.2   Smart contracts

The word contracts will remind us regarding legal agreement; in Ethereum, smart contracts are just a piece of code, which governs the business logic of the application such as automating the transactions, and self-operating program that automatically executes the written logic when certain conditions are met. Now this eliminates the participation of third parties that are committed along with transactions in the blockchain, in which the code and the conditions are publicly available on the ledger. This will get automatically triggered when some certain conditions are met, which is to be written in the code. Regulators can watch the smart contract activity on the blockchain to evaluate the market that simultaneously maintains the privacy of individuals, and these are immutable and irreversible [7].

Ethereum runs the smart contract code when the user or another smart contract sends a message or instruction with transaction fee that is known as "Gas;" Ethereum virtual machine (EVM) compiles the smart contract on the network, and this needs a certain amount of gas. So, more machines involve running code, the higher the gas amount will be. Each basic operation on EVM costs some fixed amount of gas, and EVM basic operations are called OPCODES, so each opcode has got some fixed gas. So, gas is an abstract number that is based on the complexity of the code; the higher the complexity of the code the greater the number of opcodes is generated and the higher the gas value. For every Ethereum transaction, there are the following components (Figure 11.4):

Nonce: The total number of transactions sent by the user or sender.

GAS price: As was said it is fixed per operation. The gas price is dynamic, and it represents how much ether you are willing to pay for gas. They specify a gas price in terms of Gwei/Gas (1 Gwei equals 0.000000001 ETH) and the total fee incurred is gas_price×gas_used. The higher gas price you pay the faster the transactions are done because the gas price is the pay which goes for the miners they prioritize as per the gas_price you provided.

Gas limit: The maximum amount of gas that the sender is willing to pay for executing this transaction. This amount is set and paid up before any computation is done.

To: The address of the recipient in a contract creating a transaction, which consists of 20-byte address.

From: the address of the sender in a contract creating a transaction. Consists of 20-byte address.

Value: The amount of pay in wei to be transferred from "From" (sender) to "To" (recipient).

Data/input: It is used in contractual transactions, which contains a signature of the function and some arguments in an encoded form.

V, R, and S: It is used to generate the signature that identifies the sender of the transaction [8].

11.2.4.3   Ethereum virtual machine and DApps

Smart contracts are written in various programming languages, and Solidity is a programming language that is used to code the smart which is to be deployed on Ethereum blockchain. So, after programming, the required logic or operations can be complied with by EVMs bytecode. EVM bytecodes convert the smart contract into a series of zeros and the ones which can be read and interpreted by a network.

So, Ethereum provides a programmable blockchain. Therefore, a user or a blockchain developer can create their own distributed blockchain-based application. Now, these applications built over this are known as DApps [10]. They contain many protocols or rules that are bonded together to provide a platform for DApps. These DApps contain the smart contracts that are coded and designed by the programmer. These DApps are run upon the EVM that compiles the contract or code. Ethereum uses Keccak-256 previously known as SHA-256.

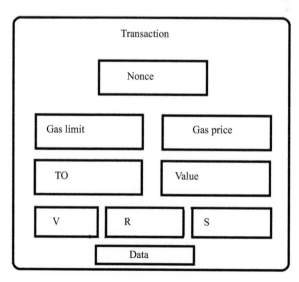

Figure 11.4   Ethereum transaction contents [9]

DApps are like typical web applications. The front end is created with the same technology as web applications. In addition, it contains a wallet that interacts with the backend blockchain. The wallet is responsible for the management of cryptographic keys and the address of blockchain.

Front End (including wallet)→Smart Contract→Blockchain [11].

11.2.4.4   SWARM

Swarm is a decentralized, permissionless communication infrastructure. It is using existing smart-contract platforms (e.g., Ethereum) to implement financial incentivization. Swarm [12] is a decentralized storage platform and provides service for content distribution, the base layer service of the Ethereum which is aimed to provide distributed, redundant storage service for DApp code, user data and state data. It also provides decentralized database services.

Swarm is designed to connect deeply to the Ethereum blockchain and an Ethereum network layer. It provides the following features like

- *Fault-tolerant*: Ensures availability of data.
- *Censorship resistant*: Stores data in no centralized manner.
- *DDoS resistant*: Distributed peer-to-peer network provides resistance towards DDoS attack.
- *Zero downtime:* Redundancy ensures continuous data delivery [12].

After uploading a document, it returns a hash thus it is used it as off chain to our DApps.

Uploading and downloading data can be done through the "swarm up" command in command line interface (CLI) on the terminal:

```
CLI Commands
$ echo "example" > sample.md
$ swarm up sample.md
```

Once the file is uploaded, you will receive a hex string that will look like this:

```
>
d1f25a870a7bb7d5d526a7623338e4d9b8399e76df8b634020d01d969584f24a
```

To download single files, use the "swarm down" command. To download single files, use the swarm down command.

```
$ swarm down bzz:/<hash>
```

11.3 Proposed method

11.3.1 EHR—architecture

This section covers the main motivation behind the explanation of Ethereum which is to develop a DApp for maintaining Electronic or digital health records. Because our aim is to construct a temper proof, secured, scalable, and confidential system for maintaining the health record digitally. To achieve this, all preliminaries are discussed in the previous section. Ethereum has been selected because of its ability to build smart contracts and develop our own programmable blockchain. Securing every file in Ethereum costs more so to minimize the dependencies and to solve the scalability problem. There is a need to consider an off-chain scaling system that "swarm" has been selected.

How the medical records are stored and secured in blockchain will be discussed here. First, for consideration of the off-chain swarm as a primary and important thing as our process starts from here. The data that is medical record is uploaded to the swarm network which then stores it into a decentralized network and returns a hash value.

This hash value will be used for storing into our DApp. By which attaining scalability and fast processing of the data are made possible. In addition, all the transactions done over this hash value are stored in blockchain which is Ethereum.

11.3.2 Smart-contract system design

System design is the most important and plays a vital role in any application building. It describes the framework of our application. This section includes the modules that are responsible for creating smart contracts and the types of users and their respective operations on the transaction and on the blockchain. The present proposed system consists of three levels where each level has its own usage and interaction to blockchain layer (Figure 11.5).

The very first level is "user-level," in which a typical user, may be a doctor, patient, lab technician, or hospital administration. At the user level, they have different roles based on different types of users; so based on their respective roles, each user will be restricted to the access of medical records and with respective roles, the transactions on the blockchain are controlled.

The different tasks based on the user role in this system are created, which read, update, delete the medical records. So as this is a DApp, a typical or traditional browser is used for communication with the system As this is a typical DApp browser or a GUI (graphical user interface) of the DApp, this GUI contains all of our prescribed system modules or functions that users can access to perform their respective operations. GUI will also be made according to the respective user role who is going to access it [13].

The next level is the "blockchain transaction level;" this layer is responsible for the whole system to be deployed on the blockchain network. By selecting Ethereum as our blockchain network, there is no need to construct or code anything

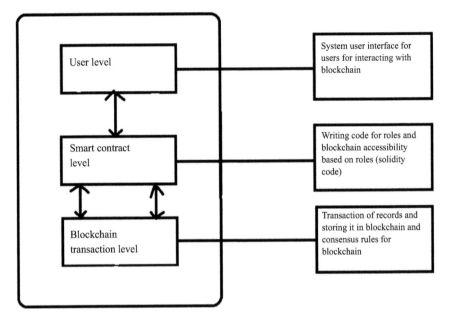

Figure 11.5   Smart-contract system architecture

at this level. Now this is the level which is responsible for communication between the user and the DApp. This layer consists of the following:

Assets: In Ethereum blockchain transactions can be updated by a user, the updating of the state of record of these transactions is known as ASSETS in Ethereum blockchain. The assets are small parts of information that the user can send to other users or can simply store it.

Consensus protocol: The Ethereum blockchain technology has got consensus PoW. Here the term consensus does mean the validation of transaction by confirming it from different nodes in the network. This consensus is the rule of governance, which is the step from which trust is gained between users. Every blockchain needs consensus to maintain the security and the data to be temper proof. So, after consensus is achieved, only the transaction is added to the block.

Network: The network here is not the Internet instead peer-to-peer communication network that is being used. In this, all the nodes are directly connected to their peers. There is no central governing node or body that controls the network. As our main intention is to create a distributed network, peer-to-peer network fits the best because there is no centralized network and all the nodes in the network are given of equal priority [13].

Now coming to transactions part, the system follows the transactions.

1. *Add records:* This creates a new patient's medical record to the DApp. This module or function contains the columns or fields like patient ID, name, and most importantly the SWARM hash. The patient's primary health records are

stored along with generated SWARM hash that contains the file uploaded and contains the lab reports if any. This module is only accessible to doctors, administrative department, except the patient.

2. *Update records:* This would update the health records of the patient; this would update the primary details of the patient but not the hash stored with it. This hash contains all the uploaded medical or health records, which are connected as off chain. This module is only accessible to doctors, administrative department, except the patient.

3. *View records:* This would let the user view the health record of a patient stored in DApp. Both patient and doctor can view the stored health records which can be done with the help of the SWARM hash code; this viewing of records can be done by an authenticating factor by the DApp. The system authentication is done with the patient's public key or public account address, and only relevant health records are only viewed to the respective patient.

4. *Delete records:* The deletion of record does mean that it is not deleted on the blockchain which would violate the main basic rule of blockchain which is immutability. Here the deletion of record means that the respective patient records are omitted by the code or smart contract. Here the user will be only doctors who will have access to the respective patient's record.

5. *Grant access:* The access should be granted or modifies through this module or functions to maintain the role with respective access to the blockchain. This is simply termed the administration module so the users here would be doctors and hospital administration.

11.3.3 Smart contract implementation

All the implementation is discussed in the previous sections about the system that is implemented with Ethereum blockchain and its respective dependencies. Now in this part, by exploring the third layer, the smart contract [14] level is derived, which is responsible for the logic and implementation of our application. As has already been discussed what is a smart contract and how essential it is to play a vital role in creating a DApp, directly jumping into the code of the smart contract would be great.

As in the earlier discussion it is said that the smart contracts are written in solidity (in our application). The basic algorithm that triggers the code or smart contract is going to be discussed. In the prescribed application, there are two smart contracts in which one is the inbuilt smart contract and for the other the code should be written as

1. Smart contract for patient records
2. Smart contract for roles

The second smart contract for roles is the built-in smart contract that constitutes a Grant Access module. The in-built smart contract means that the code for the roles and its respective access grant to the blockchain is already written in OpenZeppelin [15] smart contract. OpenZeppelin smart contracts are installed and used for easy implementation of smart contract, and OpenZeppelin ensures that the written smart contract is secured and helps you to minimize the risk that uses the battle-tested libraries for smart contracts for Ethereum in our case and also supports other blockchain platforms. It follows the most used implementations of ERC standard. OpenZeppelin makes use of the libraries that provides to create our own smart contract. Let us come to the roles of smart contract.

OpenZeppelin provides a readymade smart contract code, for that the only thing needs to do is to extend the function and to make use of it. The Asset library which is sub-library of the OpenZeppelin library consists of this role code which is responsible for granting access for different types of users, namely doctors, patients, and nurse or management administration.

The first smart contract for a patient record is written in Solidity which performs the operations on the transactions. It is purely for implementing the proposed system or framework which is to store medical records [16] on the Ethereum blockchain. The algorithm which is proposed is discussed in the following section.

Algorithm for HER

Allocate Roles:

function *Title_Roles* (New Role, New Account)

 add new role and new account in *title_roles* list

end function

Add Data:

function *Add_medical_Record* (variables which are used to modify data)

 if (role (*msg. sender*) == doctor) **then**

  add patient data to respective patient's record

 else

deny permission and Abort session

 end if

end function

Retrieve Data:

function *View_Patient_Record* (patient ID)

  if (role (*msg. sender*) == doctor) **then**

   if (*patient_id*) == true **then**

view retrieved data from given patient (ID)

    returns (patient record)

    to the doctor account that requested the retrieve operation

else return false

end if

  else

if ((role (msg. sender) == patient) **then**

 if (patient id) == true **then**

view only allowed data from given patient (ID)

 returns (patient record)

  to the patient account that requested the retrieve operation

else return false

end if

else deny the request and abort the session
   end if
end function
Update Data:
function Update medical Report (variables which are used to modify data)
  if (role (msg. sender) = = doctor) **then**
    if (ID = = patient id) **then**
     update or modify respective patient data record
     return true
    else return false
    end if
   else deny the request and abort the session
   end if
end function
Delete Data:
function Delete Patient Record (patient id)
if (role (msg. sender) == doctor) **then**
  if (ID == patient id) **then**
  delete respective patient's record
  return success
  else return fail
  end if
else Abort session
end if
end function

If observed, the earlier-written algorithm contains six functions that are *created, read, update,* and *delete* functions that perform respective operations.

The first procedure *title_role* contains two parameters which are *role_type* and *account_role* which then pushes the data into *title _roles* list. The first function is responsible for adding new doctors in the hospital and new patient which then creates an Ethereum account for every account or person added in this list. So, every account will get their own public account address which is then used to retrieve the patient's record which was discussed in earlier sections. These are further used for authenticating purpose and the *title_roles* list is further used for accessing the roles of the user in the system.

The second procedure is "add medical record" in which the parameters or the arguments are variable or memory in Solidity which consists of the patient's medical data. The users who can access this module are limited to doctors [17] and hospital administrative staff. So, the respective user role is defined by the previous function, i.e., "title role." This procedure also authenticates the doctor or users who are going to add the medical record by their public account address of doctor and not by any other person. For this, in the algorithm, it is described as "msg. sender" in Solidity programming language that validates the sender of the request in our case the sender must be the doctor. This is useful for the identification of the address of the sender, which is helpful in finding out the role of the respective account if the account is associated with the doctor role then no issues or else abort or deny the request. After the validation process, the adding of the patient's medical record is done and ends the process by saving the respective medical record.

The third procedure is "retrieve medical record," and this function can be accessed for doctors as well as patients. For this, the arguments passed will be the patient ID, with this patient the respective patient ID and the medical records are retrieved and returned to the account requested for the records. In this function, the checking of the role of the requesting account is also done because all the medical records should not be visible to the patient, and only allowed medical reports are given access to the patient where the doctor is accountable to view all the respective reports of the given patient ID.

The fourth function is "update medical report" here and the parameters passed are the data which needs to be updated along with the patient ID. This module is only for the doctors, and patients are denied to update any record; the validation process starts from the requested account if the request for updating of medical is doctor's account then continues the process for updating or stops otherwise or terminates the process and returns an denial message of the current requesting account for updating the records; then after validation the ID is checked with the patient ID to which the medical records need to be updated and return success after the modification of the patient's record.

The last procedure which is "delete record" in the above-mentioned algorithm is accessible only to the doctor's account, and the arguments or parameters passed over this function are patient ID. Here also to ensure that no third party is accessing this system validation process, which is done by verifying the role of the requested account if the account is linked to the doctor then continues the process else aborts the session; the next step is to check the ID if it is a patient ID then continues for deleting the medical records of that particular patient and returns success after deleting the record.

Now, in this section, how the overall proposed system works is discussed. First, the system is administered by the hospital management system or administration system [18] in which they define each role and the access of each role to the reports or to the blockchain. The out system mainly consists of two users' doctors and patients; these users must create the account, and the administration will map each user to a defined role, the allocation of which is done for each user. Every user will be allocated the account address and name, and all these account addresses are stored in the title_roles list. It is defined in the previous algorithm that is helpful in the validation process in further steps.

After the allocation of roles, each user will perform some transactions that are stored in the blockchain. Every user sends a request to the system which then validates the user from the title_roles list. Then the system would verify the roles of the requested account and according to the role, the data access is made, and data is viewed. After performing the functions of the transactions, these are stored in an Ethereum blockchain as discussed in the previous sections. The transactions are stored in blockchain only if the transactions from this blockchain work as a backend data storage structure for the proposed DApp browser and users can do the transaction or use this system via a web browser that is termed DApp browser. From that browser itself, a user can do all the operations and the proposed system is visible.

11.3.4   Drug traceability using blockchain

The previous section describes how blockchain is used for maintaining the patient's health record securely. Nowhere in this section any other use case of blockchain in a health record, which is drug traceability in the pharmaceutical sector, is covered. This is very important and useful in counterfeit of the medicines or drugs.

11.3.4.1   Why blockchain?

As was already discussed what is blockchain and one of its use cases also, which is not discussed anywhere in this section, and why the blockchain is used for drug traceability is a big question. By keeping in mind all the advantages of a blockchain in the medical science, the counterfeit drugs are a well-known problem, and blockchain as a technology provides a secure, transparent way of "supply chain" of any logistics in our case and the logistics are medicinal drugs, and this supply chain transparency is established from a manufacturer via wholesale and pharmacies and at the end, individual patients. This is done through means of barcodes or any auto-id technologies like RFID [19] which patients are given as a view for the entire transport system of the medicinal drug by which the patient ensures to receive the actual drugs [20]. With the use of blockchain in the "supply chain" process, it makes it much more difficult to tamper the products or to sell the products from any illegal origin. Blockchain as a platform for implementing the supply chain process enables the user to gain trust by showcasing the pedigree of the drug right from the manufacturer to the pharmacy retailer.

So, with this, it can be considered that the result of this system will allow manufacturing companies to track their products down the supply chain, and it also allows the labs to act against the counterfeit medicines as posterior of the case.

11.3.4.2   What is supply chain?

Tracking the journey of the product through various owners is generally termed a supply chain. Now, what blockchain has to do with it? The answer is, for every change of ownership, it generates a transaction that can be pushed into the block-chain network to trace back the origin of the product. Now this technique or use case has become more popular such that implementing this on blockchain-based supply chain in our medicine traceability system would make our system more feasible. There are various applications [21] on the supply chain that are seafood verification, food supply chain, coffee supply chain, automotive supply chain, and many more.

With proper implementation of supply chain management (SCM) [22], it is possible to

1. reduce or even eliminate the fraud, errors occurred in the supply chain by third parties;
2. drastically reduce the delays occurred in paperwork;
3. identify the issues at a faster rate;
4. minimize the courier or transportation costs;
5. improve management of inventory system.

In addition, with the help of blockchain, SCM will become more easy and trustable and perfectly suitable with blockchain, and it overcomes all the hurdles which SCM is facing currently. Using blockchain, implementing is possible to attain a stage where "trust" is guaranteed between the two individual parties, speeding up the slow or manual paper-based process, strengthening traceability by providing the visibility of the products along its path or route. It reduces the overall cost of the SCM, by enabling the feature of traceability, which we can also oversight on counterfeiting the products, and auditing costs are reduced and auditing process is also made simple and easy. Blockchain provides high security and transparency and also validates the authenticity of every user who accesses the blockchain network. As was discussed, Ethereum blockchain provides convenient smart contracts that can automate the process and eliminate the participation of third parties. With the help of smart contracts, supply chain stakeholders can track the products in real time. This will be discussed in our next implementation system.

11.3.4.3   Supply chain implementation

As everyone now is familiar with how Blockchain works (a key pair is generated for every user in the chain) and using Ethereum is a state-based blockchain in which the state of the transaction should be updated. It is a known fact that each participant would get their own key which has its own activity in the network; the original identity is anonymous in the blockchain. It is represented by means of this key itself. The participant here can be of anything like a device, person, or entity.

The proposed system has the following section types of actors or stakeholders who participate in the supply chain process, how they register [23] and access in the blockchain network, and at last how data entry is done with authorization, validation, and storage.

As the medicine or drug moves from manufacturer to patient, it is possessed by various owners or stakeholders, who are as follows:

1. administrator
2. manufacturers
3. wholesale retailers
4. distributor retailers
5. individual pharmacy retailers
6. patients

Each of these actors or stakeholders plays a crucial role in this system, which enters the important information about the medicine or drug and its current status on the blockchain network. As was said, each product or each medicine would have a unique digital record containing all the regarded information about the respective product [24].

Here comes the process: the first thing is each product (with respective our discussion the products are medicines or drugs) would be given or attached to a QR code or RFID, which acts as an information tag for the further process. This tag depicts the unique cryptographic ID that links physical product (medicines) to the digital ID or shows it virtually in the proposed system. Now this ID is the "assets" which are shared in the transactions in the Ethereum blockchain. This ID is shown as a part of medicines that creates a digital profile.

The stakeholders will also have their own digital profiles on the blockchain network, in which their profile views information such as how they are linked to the medicine, role of their account in supply chain, certifications, location, etc. These stakeholders would first need to get certified by the "administrator" to participate in the process of supply chain for a particular product to sustain the trust in the system. A link will be provided from medicine's profile page to stakeholder's profile page when they digitally sign on the product's profile page.

The role of an administrator who registers the actors who are involved in the supply chain and are given a unique ID (which is public account address). Upon successful registration, public and private key pair is generated for each account holder. The role of the public key that identifies the account holder is within the system network and the private key helps one to authorize the account holder or stakeholder to participate in the supply chain process and is used when ensures a transaction of the product to another account. Ensuring the transaction here means that the stakeholder allows each medicine to be digitally signed when an exchange of ownership taking place, which is added to the flow of the supply chain.

As was discussed earlier, this whole system is implemented using DApp. This acts as a user interface for the system. The full information regarding DApp was already discussed in the previous section, so the user interface or the structure of the DApp browser will be discussed, and the product's digital profile or medicine's digital profile is nothing but a DApp web page. As an actor's or a stakeholder's digital profile is also a DApp web page, there will be a customized DApp web page for every individual medicine or product which is only accessible to the specified actor and when a transaction takes place the actor profile page will be linked to the medicine's DApp web page to maintain the transparency. An authentication process is performed with actor's private key before logging into the system. The data accesses, which are given to the stakeholders, are depending upon the type of role in the supply chain process. For instance, the actor may be a patient, so should be restricted on modifying the data, and should not be given any provision for digitally signing the product as there is no use for it. So, some sets of protocols are written in the form of code and stored in the blockchain. These are known as "smart contracts", a detailed description of which is done already in the previous section regarding these. These smart contracts cannot be changed and are immutable, and the integrity within the system is maintained by using these smart contracts.

11.3.4.4   Entering data in the system

Now further inspecting how the data entry is made using the proposed system:

The first thing as said is each physical medicine is given a unique ID and obtains its own DApp web page so that all the participants or stakeholders in the supply chain process will have access directly to a medicine profile page. This is important and necessary to enable the stakeholders to further continue the process of the supply chain digitally on the blockchain.

With the help of the digital ID of the stakeholders and medicines, it is better to write a smart contract for each product in the form of rules. So only those parties who have authorized digital key would have access to the products DApp web page. The next important thing to remember, at a given point in time, is the specified medicine, owned by a single and particular stakeholder. Only this stakeholder has to be given permission to enter the data on the respective medicine's profile page and initiate the transaction to other account holders. So when the medicines are transferred from one owner to another, both the account holders or owners should digitally sign the digital contract for authenticating and validating the ownership transfer. When both the parties have signed the contract, the details regarding the transfer of ownership or the transaction will be added to the blockchain automatically. The blockchain network is responsible for timestamping the transaction, and the time is visible on the product's profile page on the DApp website. So this allows the undisputable process of the supply chain with the help of blockchain for each medicine. The system allows such that the only new owner can make an entry on the product's profile page and update the state of the medicine's journey to the patient.

In addition, in the medicine's profile page, the current stakeholder should add the description manually and some of the fields are automatically added to the system, by authenticating themselves with their given private key by the administrator. In the proposed system, there is a threshold for entering the data, and the whole description cannot be stored under the blockchain even though the cost of storing the data in the blockchain would be very costly. So there are some limitations over the consumption of data by the system. The following data fields are required to fill and store in the blockchain [25].

Here in the previous template, the stakeholders are shown in a chronological order after timestamping is done by all the stakeholders. In the previous product's profile page, the first medicine's image is shown and the medicine's ID is shown and the QR code as a unique identification is also viewed on the product's profile page and description about the medicine is also shown, which is written manually by the manufacturer of the medicine. T1, T2, ..., T5 depict the timestamp of the stakeholder after being digitally signed over the digital contract. E1, E2, ..., E5 are the entries that are made by the respective stakeholder at the point of transferring the ownership. If the patient is scanning the QR code then the page will appear with a slight modification, so that no data entry field should be accessible to the patient only the visibility of all the transactions between the stakeholders needs to be available (Figure 11.6).

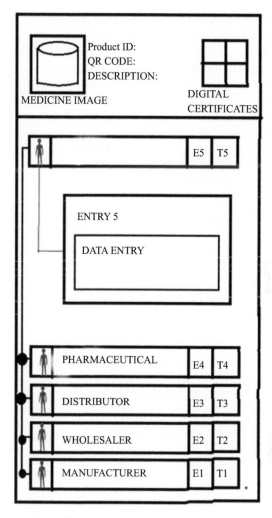

Figure 11.6   Sample template of medicine's profile page

- *Ownership of medicine*: A list of all previous owners or stakeholders of the respective medicine is made in a chronological order, each time when any transaction of ownership is done, and a new entry is created for saving the information for the current or any transaction going to occur between the current owner and new owner. Further with this implementation, enabling a controlled level of transparency between the stakeholders could be done. It is done automatically by the system.
- *Timestamping:* Whenever there is a new entry created on medicine's profile page, the system automatically saves the entry time. With this timestamping, only system is able to create the chronological order of stakeholders on the product's DApp web page or profile page.

- *Location update:* The product will be shipped to different places and different owners or stakeholders, and it is the responsibility of the current owner to write down manually the current location of the medicine. The location may be the dynamic GPS data or unique location identifier.
- *Specific data:* This field should also be written manually by the current owner of the medicine or drug. The description written in this field should be unique product-specific data, for example, the chemical formula of the data that is unique to every individual product.

11.3.4.5   Roles and data access

All the stakeholders mentioned have registered in the system via administrator and have respective unique ID on the network (Figure 11.7).

1. *Manufacturer:* The medicines that are manufactured at manufacturer's facility are entered into the blockchain by attaching a unique ID also with QR code. Key information regarding the respective medicines are to be entered into the system. A new transaction is initiated between the manufacturer and wholesale retailer. After the exchange of goods or medicines is done physically, then both the parties will be signing a digital contract, which then ensures that the transaction is recorded in the blockchain.
2. *Wholesale retailer:* The wholesale retailer accepts the goods from the manufacturer. This closes the exchange of obtaining the goods and records a new entry as a new owner of the medicines and adds description and location. Transferring the goods or medicines to the next stakeholder is a distributor retailer deal. After the exchange of goods or medicines is done physically then both the parties will be signing a digital contract which then ensures that the transaction is stored in the blockchain.
3. *Distributor retailer:* The distributor transports the medicines through many locations and at each of these locations the medicine profile page is updated by

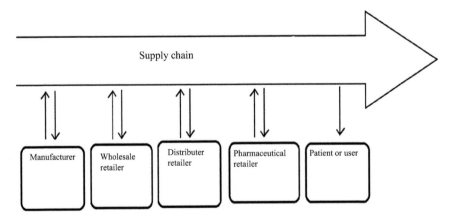

Figure 11.7   Supply chain of drug traceability

scanning the QR code of the medicines or pallet. Hence, this makes the process easier. After the exchange of goods or medicines is done physically, then both the parties will be signing a digital contract which then ensures that the transaction is stored in the blockchain.

4. *Pharmacy retailer:* The retailer accepts the medicines and updates the product's profile page by scanning the QR code on the box of the medicines and adds the descriptions of location and specific data of the medicines. After accepting the goods from distributor retailer, both the parties will be signing a digital contract which then ensures that the transaction is stored in the blockchain.

5. *Patient:* The patient then checks the whole supply chain process by scanning the QR code which is present on the medicines or on the earlier mentioned box of the medicines, which ensures the transparency of the supply chain of the medicines [26]. For patient's module, there is only viewing of all the previous transactions that are done and the write and update operations are disabled from the patient end.

11.3.5   Clinical trials using blockchain

11.3.5.1   What are clinical trials?

Clinical trials are scientific research studies conducted for finding medical, surgical, or behavioral intervention. Finding other better ways to prevent or treat disease is also exercised. These are the basic ways to find out if a new treatment, new drug, new diet, or even medical device is safe or not. It shows how safe and helpful the new experimented tests and treatments are. These clinical trials produce high-quality data for decision-making in healthcare [27].

Clinical trials follow strict scientific standards in order to protect the patients from the side effects of the newly introduced drug. Clinical trials follow four phases to approve the new drug created:

1. *First phase:* It tests an experimental drug to a small group of people to study and evaluate the possible side effects of the experimental drug on the group of people. Here it determines how the drug should be delivered.

2. *Second phase:* At this level, the trial is done on more people and ensures the effectiveness of the drug. This level or phase aims to extract data on whether the drug works in people who have a specific disease or condition.

3. *Third phase:* The numbers of participants are more as compared to previous phases. This phase compares the experimented drug with standard treatment to study safety and efficiency.

4. *Fourth phase:* In this final phase, the trials will take place in regulatory authority, which has approved the drug or vaccine, and the respective drug effectiveness and side effects are observed over a large and diverse population [28].

11.3.5.2   How blockchain is useful?

At present system, the clinical trial data can be modified or altered, and clinical trials undermine the trust and the data can also be lost accidentally or by iniquitous intent, and redundancy also occurs which may not be observed by outsiders.

Second, failing to report about all the outcomes and published analyses is not matched with the outcome, which was expected, excluding some data after studying the impact of doing. Third, data is not in a secure environment. There is a huge chance for data breach and fear for encountering fraud. With all these things, the journals and regulators have obtained no trust upon the data generated by researchers. Blockchain technology is capable of increasing the quality of the clinical trials in many numbers of ways as this is distributed ledger technology that will allow patients to store their medical reports and data in an anonymous way, and doctors or researchers could reach out the patients if the respective patient's data is suitable for conducting a clinical trial.

This blockchain also helps one to make an easier way to communicate between doctors and patients during the trial. Blockchain's biggest advantage is smart contracts that ensure traceability and transparency over the clinical trial process. As previously discussed with the help of blockchain, the process of conducting clinical trial becomes more transparent and traceable, which help journals and regulators to trust the clinical trial which is conducted and communicated over blockchain [29].

11.3.5.3 Methods for implementation of the clinical trials

It was previously discussed on the Ethereum blockchain and smart contracts about how to record transactions and the off-chain storage structures like SWARM. With the help of all the described technologies, the implementation of our proposed system for clinical trials is done as follows.

Instead of distributed storage structure like SWARM, this can also be done by using third-party tools that manage clinical trials data such as REDCap [30], OpenClinicia. The implementation part of the same procedures is followed, which is already discussed in the previous sections like storing the records in swarm that returns a hash value which is used in the transactions on an Ethereum blockchain platform. Our proposed system is based on private or permission Ethereum blockchain.

The stakeholders who can participate in this network are patients, ethics boards, funders, pharmaceuticals, researchers, regulators, publishers, medical device companies, and others. Every stakeholder is interested in assets and their outcomes. With the help of blockchain, the integration of all the stakeholders to take part and verify the transactions is done perfectly.

The proof-of-concept that is also known as proof-of-principle of the proposed system is the patients' medical record that may give or participate in the clinical trial and researchers who collect, save, and evaluate the data after clinical trials. Ethereum supports smart contracts that can be implemented using Solidity or including many other programming languages like C++, Python, Go, Java JavaScript, and Ruby.

There are two smart contracts that govern the accessibility of the clinical trial data and roles to be enrolled. First, smart contract for a patient (participant SC) controls the granting of access to queries for the oracle database, which is an off-chain resource to our implementation [31,32] (Figure 11.8).

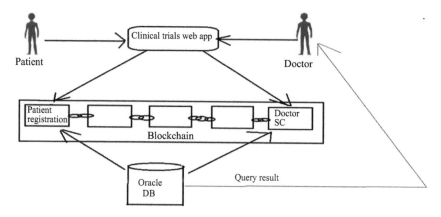

Figure 11.8   Implementation of the clinical trials

The implemented system has a GUI or a simple web application that connects the doctors and patients. The patients are registered through this web app that are saved on the backend blockchain, which creates an account in the oracle database server [33]. From this database, the doctors post the queries and get the result accordingly, and the result is also stored in the blockchain network. The DB server looks for new queries on the blockchain and results published after executing the queries on the database server.

Participant Smart Contract Algorithm:

{

MethodRegisterPatient (patient_data)

Registers a new patient for the study of clinical trails

MethodModifyAccess (patient_ID)

Modifies the patient (ID) permissions with respective to patient's ID

}

Doctor Smart Contract Algorithm:

{

MethodNewQuery (query)

A new query is submitted to the blockchain

MethodNewQueryResult (query)

A hash of the new query is recorded on the blockchain

MethodGetQuery (hash)

Waiting, queries are Retrieved from the blockchain

MethodGetUnresolvedQueries ()

Returns the total number of waiting queries from the blockchain

}

The participant smart contract contains an array in the blockchain that holds patients who are registered for the trials and the respective permissions of their data

[34]. A patient can add or register his/herself with a registered patient method and set their permission to *modifyaccess()* method.

In doctor smart contract, doctors will issue a query to the database and receive the respective result. In order to retrieve the study data, the doctors use *newquery()* method that stores the SQL query [35], and the ID (address) of the doctor is saved in the blockchain. The doctor uses the *getquery()* method for retrieving the query and its result. Using unresolved queries method increases the count of waiting queries.

As the results of the query are very huge (based on the database), it is not possible to store the results in the blockchain, so we apply a hashing algorithm like SHA-1, Keccak-256 (SHA-3), which is used to get the unique signature in further process of verification and appends it to the blockchain. The result of that query is given to doctors separately without interfering the blockchain. Also, this work could be extended for the cloud-based storage [36] and efficient blockchain management in the E-healthcare sector in the near future.

11.4   Conclusion and future scope

This chapter covers all the main use cases of blockchain in various medical sectors, now attaining the interoperability between these different sections of healthcare system that will be integrated using blockchain for the same *patient_id* is enough for the treatment of the patient, and any hospitality with the same *patient_id*, the doctor or the caretaker would able to see the whole health records as well as the respective health performance in lab tests results which is stored under the respective *patient_id*. This is how interoperability between the hospitals is achieved. This system enables a patient to retrieve his/her respective record easily that doctor needs to sign up and create an account in the blockchain network. Any records which are accessible only to doctors or lab technicians or other higher stakeholders can directly share those records with other hospital doctors or nurses or caretakers so the authenticity is maintained. This communication between hospitals is done directly with no middle person and no information are passed to the patient (if required in some cases).

The interoperable between the drug traceability and EHR as in the drug traceability of the same *product_id* can be used in EHR for a patient. The record being added to EHR for a particular patient contains certain medicines so these medicines can be linked to the *product_id* that exists in drug traceability by which consumer or patient can also verify its authenticity in transferring the drug or medicine from pharmacy to consumer retailer. After this, the same *product_id* that is mentioned in the EHR linked to *patient_id* can also be viewed by the doctors or nurses or hospital management to ensure the patient and the authenticity of medicines. Any malpractices in between the drug traceability can be caught by higher authorities, and the same information is passed to hospitals, so the doctor will not prescribe the particular medicine to any patient further.

In interoperability with clinical trials, the *patient_id* is made in EHR, and the same can be used in clinical trials, after which if the patient had gone through the clinical trial process and later he visited some other hospitals, then the same *patient_id* which he had enrolled during clinical trials could be given for the EHR. So, the information during clinical trials, which is stored under his *patient_id*, might be helpful for the doctor in treating the patient with respect to clinical trials data. The drug or medicine, which is used in the clinical trials, could be given a *product_id*, and the same could be continued for drug traceability blockchain. So, the drug manufacturer could also ensure whether the supply-chained drug has gone through successful clinical trials or not. Like this, with the help of blockchain, hospitals could create a network using simple *"ID"* whether it could be *product_id* or *patient_id*. With these ID numbers, it is possible to achieve interoperability between various sections of healthcare system.

This chapter also showcases an important application of blockchain which is supply chain and describes the methods of how the supply chain process is achieved via blockchain and how the cost is reduced by using blockchain technology. The proposed system is a proof-of-concept implementation of a blockchain for research in clinical trials. The system is applied over permissioned Ethereum blockchain in which the patients and doctors act as nodes. Patients are given the right to assign the access permission of respective data what can be viewed, and by whom, in the case of doctors' requests, the data are written into an immutable record which is blockchain. This proposed framework supports patients to take more active participation in research in clinical trials. The room for extension is very big as there is no concrete structure for authenticating patients, and the separate accounts for the rest of the stakeholders are to be created and needed to involve them in clinical trials blockchain in the form of digitally signs that are done at every stage of the clinical trial. Selecting the oracle database as an off-chain can also be changed to some other distributed file storage system like IPFS and blockchain-based SWARM and filecoin.

References

[1] Meinert E, Alturkistani A, Foley KA, *et al.* Blockchain implementation in health care: Protocol for a systematic review. JMIR Research Protocols. 2019;8(2):e10994.

[2] Griggs KN, Ossipova O, Kohlios CP, Baccarini AN, Howson EA, and Hayajneh T. Remote patient monitoring. Journal of Medical Systems. 2018;42(7):130.

[3] Leeming G, Cunningham J, and Ainsworth J. A ledger of me: Personalizing healthcare using blockchain technology. Frontiers in Medicine. 2019;6:171.

[4] Hasselgren A, Kralevska K, Gligoroski D, Pedersen SA, Faxvaag A. Blockchain in healthcare and health sciences—A scoping review. International Journal of Medical Informatics. 2020;134:104040.

[5] Nakamoto S. Bitcoin: A peer-to-peer electronic cash system. Manubot; 2019.

[6]   Wood G. Ethereum: A secure decentralised generalised transaction ledger. Ethereum project yellow paper. 2014;151:1–32.

[7]   Buterin V. Ethereum white paper, GitHub repository; 2013. [cited 02Mar2020]. p. 22. Available from: https://ethereum.org/whitepaper/.

[8]   Tam KC. Transactions in Ethereum. Medium; 2018. [cited 20Mar2020]. Available from: https://medium.com/@kctheservant/transactions-in-ethereum-e85a73068f74.

[9]   Kasireddy P. How does Ethereum work, anyway? [Internet]. Medium; 2019. [cited 14Jan2020]. Available from: https://medium.com/@preethikasireddy/how-does-ethereum-work-anyway-22d1df506369.

[10]   Johnston D, Yilmaz SO, Kandah J, *et al.* The general theory of decentralized applications, Dapps. 2014.

[11]   Voshmgir S. Token economy: How blockchains and smart contracts revolutionize the economy. BlockchainHub; 2019.

[12]   Trón V, Fischer A, Johnson N, Nagy D, and Felföldi Z. Swarm: a decentralised peer-to-peer network for messaging and storage. June, 2018. [cited 02 Mar 2020]. Available from: https://swarm-guide.readthedocs.io/en/latest/introduction.html.

[13]   Shahnaz A, Qamar U, and Khalid A. Using blockchain for electronic health records. IEEE Access. 2019;7:147782–95.

[14]   Jamil F, Hang L, Kim K, and Kim D. A novel medical blockchain model for drug supply chain integrity management in a smart hospital. Electronics. 2019;8(5):505.

[15]   Araoz M, Brener D, Giordano F, Palladino S, Paivinen T, and Gozzi A. Zeppelin os: An open-source, decentralized platform of tools and services on top of the EVM to develop and manage smart contract applications securely [Internet]; 2017. p. 13. Available from: https://zeppelinos.org.

[16]   Kaur H, Alam MA, Jameel R, Mourya AK, and Chang V. A proposed solution and future direction for blockchain-based heterogeneous medicare data in cloud environment. Journal of Medical Systems. 2018;42(8):156.

[17]   O'Donoghue O, Vazirani AA, Brindley D, and Meinert E. Design choices and trade-offs in health care blockchain implementations: Systematic review. Journal of Medical Internet Research. 2019;21(5):e12426.

[18]   Chen TS, Liu CH, Chen TL, Chen CS, Bau JG, and Lin TC. Secure dynamic access control scheme of PHR in cloud computing. Journal of Medical Systems. 2012;36(6):4005–20.

[19]   Ahuja S and Potti P. An introduction to RFID technology. Communications and Network. 2010;2(3):183–6.

[20]   Cunningham J and Ainsworth J. Enabling patient control of personal electronic health records through distributed ledger technology. Studies in Health Technology and Informatics. 2018;245:45–8.

[21]   Fan K, Wang S, Ren Y, Li H, and Yang Y. Medblock: Efficient and secure medical data sharing via blockchain. Journal of Medical Systems, 2018;42 (8):136.

[22] Hackius N and Petersen M. Blockchain in logistics and supply chain: Trick or treat? In: Digitalization in Supply Chain Management and Logistics: Smart and Digital Solutions for an Industry 4.0 Environment. Proceedings of the Hamburg International Conference of Logistics (HICL), Vol. 23. Berlin: epubli GmbH; 2017. pp. 3–18.

[23] Kish LJ and Topol EJ. Unpatients—Why patients should own their medical data. Nature Biotechnology. 2015;33(9):921.

[24] Haq I and Esuka OM. Blockchain technology in pharmaceutical industry to prevent counterfeit drugs. International Journal of Computer Applications. 2018;975:8887.

[25] Abeyratne SA and Monfared RP. Blockchain ready manufacturing supply chain using distributed ledger. International Journal of Research in Engineering and Technology. 2016;5(9):1–10.

[26] Esposito C, De Santis A, Tortora G, Chang H, and Choo KK. Blockchain: A panacea for healthcare cloud-based data security and privacy?. IEEE Cloud Computing. 2018;5(1):31–7.

[27] National Institute on Aging (US). What are clinical trials and studies? [Internet]. 2017. [cited 14Jan2020]. Available from: https://www.nia.nih.gov/health/what-are-clinical-trials-and-studies.

[28] Novartis AG. What are clinical trials? 2016. [cited 2Mar2020]. Available from: https://www.novartisclinicaltrials.com/TrialConnectWeb/whatisclinicaltrials.nov.

[29] Rohit B and Juneja M. Clinical trials on blockchain, In: PhUSE EU Connect 2019, paper TT11. pp. 1–8.

[30] Harris PA, Taylor R, Thielke R, Payne J, Gonzalez N, and Conde JG. Research electronic data capture (REDCap)—A metadata-driven methodology and workflow process for providing translational research informatics support. Journal of Biomedical Informatics. 2009;42(2):377–81.

[31] Benchoufi M and Ravaud P. Blockchain technology for improving clinical research quality. Trials. 2017;18(1):335.

[32] Maslove DM, Klein J, Brohman K, and Martin P. Using blockchain technology to manage clinical trials data: A proof-of-concept study. JMIR Medical Informatics. 2018;6(4):e11949.

[33] Guo R, Shi H, Zhao Q, and Zheng D. Secure attribute-based signature scheme with multiple authorities for blockchain in electronic health records systems. IEEE Access. 2018;6:11676–86.

[34] Zheng Z, Xie S, Dai H, Chen X, and Wang H. An overview of blockchain technology: Architecture, consensus, and future trends. In: 2017 IEEE International Congress on Big Data (BigData Congress). Honolulu, Hawaii, USA: IEEE; 2017 Jun 25. pp. 557–564.

[35] Sekaran K and Krishna PV. Big Cloud: A hybrid cloud model for secure data storage through cloud space. International Journal of Advanced Intelligence Paradigms. 2016;8(2):229–41.

[36] Sekaran K and Krishna PV. Cross region load balancing of tasks using region-based rerouting of loads in cloud computing environment. International Journal of Advanced Intelligence Paradigms. 2017;9(5–6):589–603.

Chapter 12

Blockchain: lifeline care for breast cancer patients in developing countries

Hamsagayathri Palanisamy[2], Sampath Palaniswami [1], Godlin Atlas[3], Perarasi Sambantham[2], Gayathri Rajendran[2] and Sowmiya Senthilvel[2]

Breast cancer is one of the top-positioned malignant growths among women, which is around 25% of the rest of the diseases with expected new cases gauged to across ~1,797,900 constantly 2020. The worldwide purpose behind high death rates is the absence of financially savvy procedures to detect the malignant growth at the prior stage. In this cutting-edge period, blockchain innovation turns out to be progressively pervasive in assorted fields and places its impression in a wide scope of uses in healthcare. With this novel approach, the oncology network endeavors to all the more likely to oversee and apply research to treat the human services information. Blockchain facilitates the safe transmission of patient clinical records, and additionally, it encourages analysts to open hereditary code to make development in the social insurance industry. The decentralized idea of the innovation makes a biological system of patient information that can be effectively referenced by specialists, drug specialists, medical clinics, and any other individual associated with treatment. Because of the high security arrangement, patients share their genome information to established researchers, which causes oncologists to distinguish explicit kinds of bosom malignancy effectively, and fitting medicines can be given to save the life of the patients.

The motivation behind this section is to give an outline of the blockchain innovation in the social insurance framework. This chapter covers the mechanical structure for storing and retrieving the clinical records of patients in blockchain alongside gracefully chain of the executives of medications utilizing keen

[1]Professor, Electronics and Communication Engineering, Bannari Amman Institute of Technology, Erode, India
[2]Assistant Professor, Electronics and Communication Engineering, Bannari Amman Institute of Technology, Erode, India
[3]Assistant Professor, Computer Science Engineering, School of Computing Science and Engineering, Galgotias University, Greater Noida, India

agreements. Be that as it may, blockchain is not a solution to malignant growth, yet it fills in as a potential innovative instrument to battle against bosom diseases.

12.1   Introduction

The social insurance industry is the world's biggest marketer, devouring over 10% of an entire nations output (good distribution practice (GDP)) of the most developed nations [1]. Basically, this industry incorporates speculation and commercialization of things and marketers to treat patients with therapeutics, preventive, rehabilitative, and palliative consideration. Being a mind-boggling arrangement of interconnected elements under overwhelming administrative limits, understanding information is exceptionally divided, and the expense of social insurance conveyance is constantly ascending because of inefficiencies in the framework and reliance on a few middle people.

Besides, straightforwardness in general procedure of empowering information sharing between numerous gatherings, despite the fact that as far as anyone knows beneficial to the patient, is as yet missing on full straightforwardness and control from the patient's view. Patients have shown concerned about the chance of their information being utilized by for-profit substances [2]. This has complemented a requirement for a data innovation framework that can expel the brokers and cut expenses while keeping up trust and straightforwardness. The blockchain is a continuous innovation that makes a better understanding of the difficulties of social insurance by giving decentralized trust. Blockchain-empowered decentralization vows to limit the issue of seller lock-in that has tormented the medicinal services industry. Blockchain with the utilization of artificial intelligence (AI) helps in dissecting pictures and recognizing illness getting to a greater degree reality, and information is getting always indispensable to tolerant consideration. Information can help foresee malady and guide specialists toward treatment. Additionally, it has high suggestion toward pharmaceutical gracefully chain of the board, where it guarantees full straightforwardness in the whole delivery procedure of the medications, which assists with observing work expenses and waste emanations. Thus, the blockchain helps one to analyze quicker and gives specific consideration plans to malignancy patients.

Persistent information is dispersed across various substances in the worth chain of the social insurance industry alluded to as information storehouses, and sharing of valuable data is inclined to a staggered procedure of authorization control. Along these lines, intermittently significant information is not open and accessible at the period of pressing scarcity. Blockchain can unravel this issue with well-being data trade (health information exchange (HIE)) by filling in as a reason for being confided in a decentralized database. It can empower one-stop access to the whole clinical history of a patient over all medicinal services suppliers. Access control framework constructed utilizing trust on blockchain places patients in charge of their information; they can give assent and access rights to outer gatherings like scientists to approach all or subset of their clinical records. This element fits pleasantly with the patient-driven model of social insurance where blockchain can go about as an impetus instigating trust.

The records composed on the blockchain are unchanging and cannot be adjusted or erased. This attribute of blockchain gives properties such as information trustworthiness and provenience which can be utilized to fabricate techniques to forestall medical forging and clinical fakes. For example, fake outcomes and evacuation of information in clinical preliminaries which do not line up with scientist's predisposition or financing source can be forestalled by authorizing the uprightness of information in blockchain. Likewise, it permits keeping an unchanging log of the subject's assent in a clinical preliminary. On a financial note, blockchain could spare many billions for the pharmaceutical business by defining a chain-of-authority in the flexible chain [3,4]. It is conceivable to compose custom laws and rules framing contracts on the blockchain, which are equal to certifiable agreements and can be legitimately authoritative. These agreements are alluded to as shrewd agreements. Keen agreements can be utilized in a few procedures inside medicinal services, including charging and protection which help in mechanizing the procedure and lessening the expenses. Later in the resulting areas, it describes few organizations utilizing the keen agreements to assemble arrangements. This part examines the issues in the human services environment and how the correct utilization of blockchain innovation may tackle these issues, and lastly, it is finished up with conversation on the scene of social insurance, issues in that, guarantees of the blockchain, and the condition of blockchain-based arrangements.

12.2 Blockchain

Blockchain is one of the most advertised advancements of the current day with use cases and new businesses showing up at steady pace. It is a decentralized record that utilizes calculations and solid encryption to record computerized exchanges or information in a straightforward, secure, and unknown way. By permitting advanced data to be appropriated yet not duplicated, this innovation has made the help for another type of web. The blockchain organize exists in a condition of accord, naturally taking a look at itself intermittently—for example, at regular intervals—making interims known as "squares." Each square portion consists of a hash pointer as a connection to a past square, a timestamp, and exchange information. It is regularly overseen by a "miners" which aggregately clinging to a convention for approving new squares (blocks). By structure, blockchains are naturally impervious to alteration of the information.

12.2.1 Key attributes

A key characteristic of blockchain is decentralization; no focal position controls the substance added to the blockchain. Rather, the sections in the blockchain are settled upon in a shared system utilizing different agreement conventions. Another key attribute of blockchain is persistency. It is for all intents and purposes difficult to erase passages in the wake of being acknowledged onto the blockchain because of the circulated record, stored over different hubs [6]. Besides, the chance of obscurity is an engaging trademark used in numerous blockchains. Blockchains make review and detectability conceivable by connecting another square to the past by including the hash of the last mentioned and along these lines framing a chain of squares. The exchanges in the squares are shaped in a Merkle tree [7] where each leaf esteem (exchange) can be checked to the known root. This empowers the tree structure to check the honesty of the information.

12.2.2   Kind of blockchains

There are chiefly three sorts of square chains: open, consortium, and private [6]. They have various qualities with respect to who can get to compose and read the information on the blockchain. The information in an open chain can be seen by all, and anybody can join and add to both agreement and changes, profoundly programming [6]. The open blockchain is generally utilized in digital forms of money, and the two biggest cryptographic forms of money, Bitcoin [1] and Ethereum [5] (the principle chain), are sorted as open permissionless chains. A consortium blockchain can be considered somewhat brought together, with just a set number of chosen gatherings of elements approaching perspective and take an interest in the agreement convention. In a private blockchain, the system is disseminated at this point, frequently brought together. Just some chosen hubs can take an interest in the system, and they are frequently overseen by one focal authority [6]. The discussion around the definition and the arrangement of various sorts of blockchains introduced here is progressing. As of now, there is no wide accord of which dispersing characteristics and agreement instruments are required to mark an innovation as "blockchain" [8–9].

12.2.3   Agreement instruments

A key part of blockchains is the manner in which information sections are acknowledged onto the dispersed record by a circulated accord convention approving the information passages. Proof-of-work (PoW) is the agreement convention most emphatically connected with blockchain because of its mix in Bitcoin. At the point when PoW convention applies, purported excavators are contending in settling a computational hard riddle. Utilizing extreme power, the excavators attempt to discover a hash of the proposed obstruct with a worth lower than a foreordained one. The miner who initially processes this hash esteem approves the exchanges inside the square and gets honor (1). A significant disadvantage of the PoW convention is its vitality-requesting nature when applied on a huge blockchain. This is represented by the way that the flow power devoured for Bitcoin mining is similar to the power necessities of a smaller nation [10–13]. With proof-of-stake (PoS), the determination of a favoring hub is dictated by the stake every hub has in the blockchain. For cryptographic forms of money, the stake is spoken to by the parity one has of given cash. This, be that as it may, might give an out-of-line bit of leeway to the "most extravagant" hub. To represent this, few halves and half forms of PoS have been recommended where the stake is joined with some randomization to choose the supporting hub. The second-biggest digital currency, Ethereum, is intending to move from PoW to PoS [6].

12.2.4   Shrewd agreements

Some blockchain frameworks such as Ethereum bolster savvy contracts [5]. These are self-executing authoritative understandings where pre-settled upon arrangements are formalized in the source code. Since brilliant agreements are naturally authorized depending on these pre-concurred arrangements, they work with no outsider or moderate. This capacity inside a brilliant agreement can be awoken in a blockchain exchange, and the utilization of this usefulness is by all accounts speaking to the well-being domain [5].

12.2.5   The capability of blockchain in the human services space

The human services part is an issue-driven information and work force con-centrated area where the capacity to get to, alter, and trust the information rising up out of its exercises is basic for the activities of the division overall. The event isolates the activities that are inside the social insurance division into triage, medical issue explaining, clinical dynamic, acknowledgment, and evaluation of information-based consideration, accomplishing the ideal wellbeing results depending on drawing in a multidisciplinary group of well-being faculty that applies the most proper information, innovations, and aptitudes when managing the patient. While working together with instructive establishments, the social insur-ance segment must give access to patients and give a field for preparation, so understudies can create and refine the fundamental abilities. Consequently, the instructive foundations give the division-qualified work force. While working together with foundations and organizations with an examination and building motivation, well-being establishments must help with giving access to experts, witnesses, test people, and tests.

While taking an interest in imminent clinical preliminaries, well-being orga-nizations must help with creating, arranging, leading, and detailing the trials. Consequently, the examination and building organizations give the medicinal ser-vices part refreshed information, strategies, and devices. Henceforth, the exercises of well-being establishments are firmly intertwined with foundations occupied with instructing well-being work force and in biomedical research and building. The exercises require powerful trade of assents, tolerant related information and evi-dences, and repayments forms, which successfully implies trading information across institutional outskirts. Simultaneously, well-being establishments are ordered to secure the profoundly delicate information that patients decide to impart to them. To both keep up the patient's protection and trade information with dif-ferent foundations in the social insurance biological system, get to control, prove-nience, information uprightness, and interoperability are urgent. The conventional method of accomplishing access control generally accepts trust between the pro-prietor of the information and the substances putting away them. These substances are frequently served and are completely dependent for characterizing and implementing access control strategies [14]. Interoperability is the capacity of various data frameworks, gadgets, or applications to interact, in a planned way, inside and across authoritative limits to access, trade, and helpfully use information among partners, with the objective of upgrading the strength of people and populaces. Information provenience alludes to the chronicled record of information and their birthplaces. In the well-being space information, provenience can, for instance, convey auditability and straightforwardness in electronic health record (EHR) and accomplish trust in EHR programming framework. Information respectability as a general definition given by Courtney and Ware is the information quality definition, which manages the normal nature of the information [15]. This implies how much the normal nature of the information is met or surpassed, which decides the information trustworthiness. Social insurance foundations at present experience an expanded interest of certifiable information from industry and research associations [16]. Simultaneously, unapproved sharing and profoundly exposed break-ins and theft of delicate information continually dissolve the open trust in medicinal services foundations. A third issue is misbehaviors inside the social insurance environment that abuses exactly the same trust. This is a circumstance that prescribes to reevaluate and thought of elective methodologies. With a portion of its key traits, for example, decentralization, appropriation, and information uprightness, and with no vital outsider, blockchain innovation has many engaging properties that could be used to improve and get a more significant level of interoperability, data sharing, get to control, provenience, and information respectability among the referenced partners, along these lines moving toward another foundation for building and looking after trust.

12.3   Healthcare data management

The administration of medicinal services information that incorporates capacity, get to control, and sharing of the information is a significant part of the social insurance industry [16–21]. Appropriate administration of medicinal services information improves social insurance results by permitting all-encompassing perspectives on patients, customized medications, and efficient correspondence. It is additionally basic for working human services industry cost-viably and efficiently. Be that as it may, overseeing social insurance information is a difficult assignment because of its touchy nature and ensuing trust issues. Furthermore, it is one of the principle reasons why the human services framework is disengaged—social insurance information and administrations exist in different structures in a few storehouses. This detached framework is a guilty party for a few inefficiencies in social insurance and is a significant obstacle for medicinal services inquired about. Human services experts by and large do not approach the total information of patients, in this manner, hampering the resulting analysis and treatment steps, and specialists battle to find the ideal information for their examinations, in this way, hindering social insurance exploration.

Blockchain may empower the efficient sharing of human services information while guaranteeing information honesty and securing tolerant protection. Secure, efficient, savvy, and interoperable HIE can be worked with its correct use nearby with different innovations. Besides, the reception of blockchain can push forward the development of patient-driven medicinal services model where patients control their social insurance information. The significant obstacles behind information partaking in both patient-driven and conventional models are the absence of trust and motivating forces to share. The blockchain innovation can take care of the two issues by going about as a trust layer and presenting the impetus components, for example, remunerating crypto tokens for sharing information.

Besides, blockchain can be the scaffold for the coordination of clinical gadget information and social insurance web of things; the human services and way of life information gathered by wearable gadgets can be basic for right conclusion however are underutilized since there is an absence of an appropriate path for a doctor to get to the patient-produced information. With blockchain-empowered trust and impetus structure, there is a guarantee for a worldwide HIE and a commercial center on it. Be that as it may, the absence of regular human services information guidelines can be one of the significant deterrents to defeat before the advancement of an interoperable HIE interfacing various divergent information storehouses. Notwithstanding, there is a likelihood that the impetuses presented by blockchain-based information trade may fuel the creation and the advancement of the open information norms. Blockchain-based HIE will be an intriguing use case that requires the equalization among protection, straightforwardness, and efficiency. Besides, nation-specific guidelines will be another hindrance for an HIE associating different administrative areas. Since patients have full responsibility for medicinal services information in numerous nations, blockchain empowered patient-driven human services information model can be one fitting approach to sidestep these administrative difficulties.

12.3.1 *Blockchain-based smart contracts for healthcare*

Shrewd agreements are utilized from Ethereum to make keen portrayals of existing clinical records that are stored on the system inside individual hubs. Agreements are assembled to contain record possession metadata, consents, and information honesty. Our framework's blockchain exchanges convey cryptographically marked guidelines for dealing with these properties. State-change elements of the agreement do arrangements, just by authentic exchanges upholding information shift. These guidelines can be organized to implement any arrangement of rules directing a specific clinical record as long as it very well may be computationally spoken to. For instance, an arrangement may force sending separate assent exchanges from the two patients and medicinal services experts before giving an outsider review consent. A framework dependence is planned on blockchain keen agreements for complex human services workflows. Keen agreements have been intended for clinical workflows and afterward overseeing information get to consent between various substances in the social insurance environment.

A brilliant agreement, stored on blockchain innovation, could be planned, which can have all the conditions from overseeing various authorizations to getting of information, and it tends to be seen that various partners are associated with this plan completing various exercises. It will help in making better collaboration among specialists and patients. Information approval rules are installed in keen agreements. It can likewise help in following all the exercises with interesting patient id from its starting point to its acquiescence. Various situations have been structured and clarified nearby all the capacities, and procedures are all around portrayed installed in the keen agreements. There will be no compelling reason to have a brought together substance to oversee and favor the activity as it very well may be straightforwardly overseen through the savvy contract which will altogether decrease the organization cost of overseeing process. The entirety of the clinical record information is stored in neighborhood database stockpiling to keep up the presentation and monetary feasibility, and the hash of the information is the information component of the square dedicated to the chain.

The information exchanges are marked with the proprietor's private key (patient or specialist). The square substance for the framework communicates with information possession and viewership consents shared by individuals from a distributed private system. Blockchain innovation underpins the utilization of brilliant agreements that empower us to robotize and follow certain state advances. Supplier connections are understood and logged through keen agreements on an Ethereum blockchain that partner a clinical record with review consents and information recovery directions (basically data pointers) for outside server execution to guarantee against altering, a cryptographic hash of the record is remembered for the blockchain, in this manner guaranteeing information respectability.

Suppliers can include another record related with a particular patient, and patients can permit record sharing between suppliers. Gathering new data gets a computerized warning in the two cases and can check the proposed record before the information is acknowledged or dismissed. This keeps members in the development of their records educated and locked in. This framework organizes ease of use by additionally offering an assigned agreement that totals references to all patient–supplier connections of a client, along these lines giving a solitary perspective to check for any clinical history refreshes. Open key cryptography is utilized to oversee personality confirmation and utilize a DNS-like usage that maps a previously existing and generally acknowledged type of ID, for example, name or government-managed savings number to the Ethereum address of the client. In the wake of alluding the blockchain to affirm authorizations by means of database confirmation server, a matching up calculation handles "off-chain" information trade between a patient database and a supplier database.

Diverse clinical work processes, including explicit clinical methodology, have been planned and actualized by means of blockchain savvy contract framework. These incorporate giving essential clinical solution to the treatment of complex ailments and their method like treatment technique for the medical procedure patients. The motivation behind planning these clinical savvy contracts is to encourage the patients, specialists, and the social insurance association to beat the authoritative wasteful aspects. This framework will help in clinical information recovery, investigation, and the executives of complex social insurance information and techniques.

12.3.2 The process for issuing and filling of medical prescriptions

The principle objective is to smoothen out the clinical medicine dealing with process by wiping out the long holding up time process, expelling the extortion component from the framework and lessening the blunder rate made by specialist misinterpretations. A specialist composes a solution for the patient and puts it to the patient's social insurance records by means of a brilliant agreement. The drug store at that point gets to this medicine through the shrewd agreement on the Ethereum blockchain by means of consent allowed by essential specialist and a patient. In the wake of getting to the solution, drug store at that point gives the medication along its expiry date, and measurements utilize presented on the patient social insurance records by means of brilliant agreements and afterward the medication is prepared for the assortment by the patient.

The savvy contract includes by and large sorted out medication fulfillment among specialists and medication stores. Specialists invest less occasions the energy in clarifying meds and demands or by and large talking with tranquilize stores following a patient's visit, holding up time process, expelling the misrepresentation component from the framework and decreasing the blunder rate made by specialist misinterpretations. A specialist composes a remedy for the patient and puts it to the patient's social insurance records by means of a brilliant agreement. The drug store at that point gets to this medicine through the brilliant agreement on the Ethereum blockchain by means of authorization allowed by an essential specialist and a patient.

At this stage, Drug store provides the medication along its expiry date and dose utilization and it is shared to the patient health insurance records through brilliant agreements, and afterward the medication is prepared for the assortment by the patient. The shrewd agreement includes for the most part sorted out medication fulfillment among specialists and medication stores. Specialists invest less occasions the energy in clarifying prescriptions demands or by and large talking with tranquilize stores following a patient's visit. Information stream for giving a clinical medicine includes tolerant, essential specialist, and drug store as appeared in Figure 12.1. It additionally contains the subtleties of remedy that incorporate medication id, expiry date, understanding id, and so forth.

12.3.3 Sharing laboratory test/results data

The principle objective is to share the data by means of blockchain brilliant agreements by allowing labs, specialists, crisis centers, and various accomplices to successfully access and offer a patient's helpful data among various partners as it very well may be found in Figure 12.2.

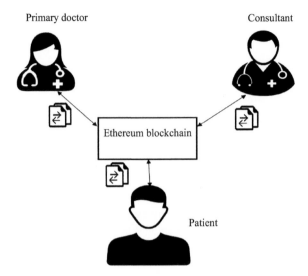

Figure 12.1   Enabling effective communication between patients and service providers

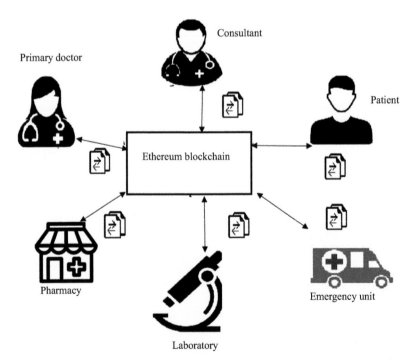

Figure 12.2   Sharing laboratory test results data

Consider a utilization situation where a patient visits a lab for a blood test. In the wake of being handled, the lab will place the outcomes into the patient records, and the patient gets these notifications by means of Ethereum blockchain, a notification that the prepared consequences of the test are available, and can pick whether to empower the lab to encode the data and put them on Ethereum blockchain. The patient awards authorization for the data to be posted on the blockchain. The pharmaceutical organization bills were prepared through smart agreements, by granting some portion of the received charge to the patient, and another segment to the labs that details the proper test results for the patient. Suppose, if a patient visits a lab for a blood test. The lab will place the outcomes into the patient records, the patient gets these notices by means of Ethereum blockchain, a notification where the consequences of the test are available, and can pick whether to empower the lab to encode the data and put them on Ethereum blockchain.

The patient awards consent for the data to be posted on the blockchain. In the event that there is a crisis with the patient or he is lethargic, the crisis division would have the option to understanding data rapidly by means of Ethereum blockchain and to give a second treatment. By permitting patient's clinical records to be posted on medicinal services blockchain, a patient abstains from conveying the consequences to the research center all alone or significant records to be faxed to various consideration suppliers. He additionally guarantees that all of his human services suppliers have the vital data to give the most ideal consideration. Research centers diminish the administrative costs of printing and mailing or faxing each test result to particular providers. Besides, labs and patients get to the medicinal services blockchain, where they may get portions from insurance firms that counsel the moved data to process claims or from pharmaceutical associations that select the data for use in examinations.

Both the primary doctor and consultant gain access to integrated remedial data on their patients at no cost, diminishing definitive work and expenses. Data to process claims or from pharmaceutical associations that select the data for use mulls over. Masters and crisis facilities gain admittance to united helpful data on their patients at no cost, diminishing definitive work and expenses.

12.3.4   Enabling effective communication between patients and service providers

In this situation, the patient presents a solicitation for an ailment as appeared in Figure 12.3. Consequently, this sends solicitation to the essential specialist through the brilliant agreement framework. Any patient data about the historical backdrop of treatment ought to be accounted for on the EHR. It is worth noting that patient record is kept up by a neighboring database where there are specific rules on who can approach the record to what degree, and these standards are administered by the brilliant agreements on Ethereum blockchain.

Another situation is where the patient presents solicitation for a specific clinical treatment. Subsequently, it sends this application to the fitting authority through the severe structure of the understanding. A specialist comprehends the

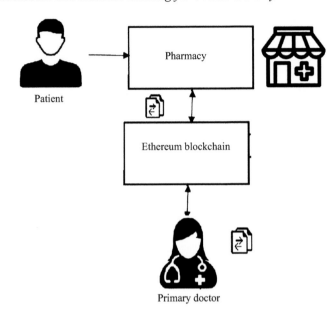

Figure 12.3   Process for issuing and filling of medical prescriptions

interest and reacts with a proposal and where patients are just exchanged for additional consideration with the authority. Any patient information with respect to the historical backdrop of treatment must be accounted for on the EHR. Note that a close by database keeps tolerant records where there are expressed rules that can move toward the record to what degree, and these rules are controlled through the learned agreements on Ethereum blockchain.

Patients looking for well-being data on a specific subject get a proposal that is unmistakably more customized than those given by a web search. Senior doctors increase another method of adapting their ability without having overbooked their calendars, while junior doctors can get to another potential patient market and fabricate their image inside their claim to fame. Facilities urge patients to get suggestions from junior specialists.

12.3.5   Smart-contracts-based clinical trials

Furnishing medication and clinical gadget makers have a less difficult and more savvy option in contrast to the present enrollment of clinical preliminaries, which frequently requires extensive costs to purchase understanding contact data from autonomous information suppliers and to execute far-reaching pull-showcasing efforts.

The primary objective is to permit clients to run clinical-preliminary-related brilliant agreements on an Ethereum system, bringing about more secure pre-scriptions and expanded open enthusiasm for clinical research [21–32]. In this procedure, we will deal with metadata, including convention enlistment, preset

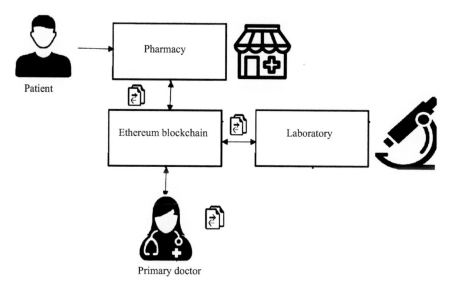

Figure 12.4   Smart contracts-based clinical trials

examination subtleties, screening, and enlistment logs by means of keen agreements.

A pharmaceutical organization searches for metadata stored on the Ethereum blockchain to distinguish potential patients for incorporation in clinical preliminaries as appeared in Figure 12.4, bringing about more secure medications and expanded open enthusiasm for clinical research. In this procedure, we will deal with metadata, including convention enlistment, preset examination subtleties, screening, and enlistment logs by means of savvy contracts. A pharmaceutical organization searches for metadata stored on the Ethereum blockchain to distinguish potential patients for consideration in clinical preliminaries. The association at that point makes an impression on choosing patients, including an application to peruse access to their clinical records and any important outcomes from the research facility study. On the off chance that the patient permits get to, a pharmaceutical organization's bill would be prepared through shrewd agreements, granting some portion of the received charge to the patient, and another segment to the labs that detailed the proper test results for the patient. Through legitimately focusing on qualifying clients, medication and clinical gadget makers will altogether diminish spending on information purchasing and showcasing endeavors. Patients, in the meantime, notwithstanding accepting payment for taking an interest in preliminaries, would access new treatment alternatives. Research facilities that were engaged with posting results would have another method of adapting their information.

Patients, then, notwithstanding accepting remuneration for contributing in preliminaries, would access new treatment alternatives. Research facilities that were engaged with posting results would have another method of adapting their information.

12.4   Healthcare data management

Pharmaceutical supplies are a significant part of clinical consideration and human services conveyance [33–42]. In this area, surveys on different inventive applications and activities in the pharmaceutical segment cover the whole range directly from the medication disclosure and clinical preliminaries for the market prologue to arrangements toward the finish of the chain such as fake medications identification and patient adherence to drug.

12.4.1   Medication revelation and pharmaceutical research

Medication revelation and research take a significant cost on the activities of any pharmaceutical organization. With expanding expenses of social insurance, along with the need to improve quicker on new therapeutic medications, it is basic that different pharmaceutical organizations find a way to work together seriously. Blockchain can empower the mechanical stage to encourage the exchange of confided data and information among different gatherings. The utilization of blockchain for vigorous computerized confirmation of intellectual property (IP) through unchanging records and time-stepping is one fitting recommendation for the joint effort. Blockchain-based arrangements can likewise give systems to share clinical and preliminary information seriously. Much under a non-shared research and medication improvement situation, blockchain gives benefits to viably following and overseeing different parts of clinical preliminaries such as informing the executives, assenting the board, following symptoms of medications utilization, and so on. Additionally, it is not remarkable for a pharmaceutical think-tank to redistribute their clinical research ventures. For this situation, blockchain could give a possible system to guarantee information honesty and legitimate result approval. In the present framework, the pharmaceutical organizations may have impetuses to distort results, for example, in revealing the reaction of new medications. With an open research environment dependent on blockchain innovation, looking into yields is straightforward, and examination yields are approved making the bogus portrayal of the outcomes difficult.

Numerous blockchain-based answers for IP of the board have been proposed in the conventional space, which can likewise be applied for the advancements in tranquilize improvement. A model, for this situation, is the aspiration to utilize blockchain-held electronic lab scratch pad arrangements from Labii [43]. Bernstein [44] gives a blockchain-based administration of advanced path with time stamping to defend needs in IP; this element can be beneficial in community-oriented pharmaceutical research. iPlexus [45] utilizes blockchain to make any unpublished and distributed information from tranquilize improvement reads promptly accessible for use. Blockchain illuminates the riddle of keeping up trust and ensuring IPs to empower such a momentous activity and system.

Blockchain likewise has use cases in the administration of the clinical preliminary procedure for pharmaceutical research. As of late, IEEE Standard Association [46] sorted out a discussion on Blockchain for Clinical Trial with the intent to utilize blockchain to cause developments in tolerant enrollment, to guarantee information honesty, and make fast advances in tranquilize improvement. Scrybe [47], a blockchain venture introduced in the discussion, empowers an efficient and believed system to assist the clinical preliminaries and research process. Of others, it permits a simple and straightforward structure for lawful and moral approvals of the preliminary procedure by the inspectors. The work in [48] shows how blockchain can be utilized to deal with the assent, information, and result from a clinical preliminary in a trustful and open way. Such developments in clinical preliminary rollout and the board are pivotal for headways in pharmaceutical research. A great deal of clinical preliminaries runs over the financial plan and courses of events. Serious sharing of clinical and preliminary information can quicken research and disclosure. Such sharing of information can be empowered with blockchain.

Further, the exploration part of pharmaceuticals is very wide that plagues the medication disclosure procedure to gadget producers and clinical preliminary results. An answer over this range is given by BlockRX [49] utilizing supposed progressed computerized record innovation (ADLT). The all-encompassing objective is to interface between the as-of-now-disengaged parties in storehouses.

12.4.2   Flexibly chain and counterfeit medications discovery

The significance of the flexibly chain in the clinical business cannot be exaggerated. Directly from the crude materials and creation to various phases of capacity and dissemination, appropriate observing and following are required to guarantee ideal and proposed use. One of the developing worries as of late is that of fake medications. There must be a system for the end clients and all the partners of the gracefully chain to check the elements of a medication. With the absence of an appropriate following component, there are sufficient feeble connections in the gracefully chain where the medication can be messed with, or a fake medication can be injected in the flexibly. To address this developing concern, new guidelines have been delivered to have all partners of the medication flexibly chain give a powerful component to track and follow the pharmaceutical supplies that go through them. Blockchain gives a consummately fitting answer for this requirement for following, where this data must be kept up in an open yet protected and carefully designed framework available to various gatherings.

Numerous arrangements have along these lines been proposed utilizing blockchain to follow the gracefully chain of pharmaceutical supplies. The MediLedger venture [50] is building an open system for the pharmaceutical flexibly chain. The system is a permissioned blockchain for the accomplices engaged with the flexibly chain of pharmaceuticals. The idea is in accordance with the track and follows guidelines. The law requires an approach to follow doctor-prescribed medications through the whole gracefully chain utilizing interoperable frameworks; MediLedger, a task propelled by pharma giants such as Pfizer and Genentech, is proposed to tackle utilizing blockchain innovation. One of the most eager undertakings in this space is Ambrosus [51] with its flagship item AMB-net, a blockchain-based Internet of Things (IoT) organized for gracefully chain focused for food and pharmaceutical businesses. On AMB-net, organizations can manufacture their custom flexibly chain arrangements. MODsense T1 from Modum [52] gives a temperature sensor to observing the conditions in the gracefully chain of pharmaceuticals, helping meet the administrative prerequisites on GDP of therapeutic items for human use. The sensor information and other computerized records are kept up utilizing a blockchain. A few other blockchain-based arrangements in the gracefully chain industry likewise list the pharmaceutical business as their essential application regions. BlockVerify [53], for instance, lists pharmaceuticals as one of the primary application regions for their flexibly chain arrangement for forestalling fakes. In the given arrangement, the historical backdrop of the products is recorded with the BlockVerify tag on a blockchain.

12.5   Challenges and future scope

In spite of the monstrous potential, there are confinements as of the present condition of the blockchain. Currently, every hub in the system forms the exchange which makes the blockchain rather moderate and unsatisfactory to deal with genuine exchanges that run in a huge number of exchanges every second. This difference features the scaling issue that blockchains need to defeat for more extensive selection over all businesses. In addition, with the development in use, the size of blockchain is expanding colossally, making it difficult for typical clients to keep its full duplicate. On a positive note, with colossal venture and research endeavors put into blockchain [32], a superior adaptable blockchain may advance later on.

Decentralization, consistency, and versatility are the three alluring properties that blockchain stages endeavor to keep up. A blockchain framework holds three properties; there will consistently be an exchange off. Platforms such as Bitcoin and Ethereum are decentralized frameworks where they give sufficient decentralization, and the consistency of information however needs versatility. Then again, Hyperledger is a case of a centralized framework which guarantees information consistency and can scale 10k exchanges every second at the expense of losing decentralization.

There are different features to the difficulties on the reception of the blockchain innovation in the medicinal services space incorporates.

12.5.1   Interoperability and integration with the legacy
systems

Human services space has countless innovations, gadgets, and segments, not overlooking the work force, which all meet up to comprehend the present needs in the space. There are enormous spaces for enhancements, with blockchain innovation giving a guarantee to conceal a portion of this room. Be that as it may, the blockchain innovation would at present be only one piece, however likely urgent, of the riddle. The blockchain innovation needs to coordinate well with existing frameworks, and the combination will be a difficult one in view of a few reasons, for example, interoperability. The fact that the medicinal services space has numerous quantities of gadgets and gadget types makes it much more difficult. Every significant gathering and partner should all meet up to utilize blockchain innovation progressively in human services. On the off chance that blockchain cannot be an impetus for this participation among partners and applicable gatherings, at that point, it most likely does not have a lot of significant worth well beyond being a basic and helpful apparatus to fathom a few issues around trust. A significant number of different issues around biological system building are there, paying little mind to the blockchain. A significant part of this conversation additionally identifies with the preparation of medicinal services IT faculty. These work forces may have been reprepared on blockchain innovation if the blockchain innovation would go into the human services space.

12.5.2 Selection and motivating forces for support

As talked about, the selection of blockchain innovation in the medicinal services space would require co-appointment and co-activity of various partners. These partners, for instance, could be the emergency clinic, gadget producers, care staff, patients, and so on. As the appropriation of blockchain innovation would require co-activity from various partners, with certain adjustments in every one of these partners present operational and plan of action, it would be normal for these partners to anticipate that some motivating force should take an interest in the change procedure. So as to deal with these desires, new plans of action must be investigated that can give reasonable motivations to all the partners. The given motivations ought to recognize the expenses and endeavors in conveying or embracing a blockchain-based advancement, alongside any basic changes in the operational model that the particular arrangement involves. The technique for blockchain-based patient information system should be considered. In this specific situation, a reasonable motivator plot must be formulated in a manageable plan of action that can be acknowledged by the patients, gadget produces, backend IT arrangement suppliers, emergency clinics, and so on. As this application is as yet developing, it would be some time before demonstrated powerful motivation models are in abundance. Meanwhile, any related danger of a specific motivator model must be thoroughly surveyed and quantified however much as could reasonably be expected.

12.5.3 Uncertain expense of activity

The significance of the flexibly chain in the clinical business cannot be exaggerated. While blockchain has promising highlights, for example, no need of focal power, straightforwardness, and moderately quick settlement of exchanges, the expense of working blockchain frameworks is not yet known. Today, a significant measure of assets in medicinal services is being spent on work force, time, and cash to assemble and deal with the current conventional data frameworks and information trades. What is more, there is an overhead of persistently refreshing the frameworks, investigating issues, performing reinforcements, agonizing over hacks, and information penetrates. The blockchain-based HIE framework could demonstrate itself to be financially savvy and more efficient contrasted with the conventional HIE framework. This, for instance, could come because of the improved security by structure. Regardless, the general cost factors engaged with a blockchain-innovation-based social insurance administrations must be vigorously evaluated in a given business and operational model of a human services association.

12.5.4   Regulation

An answer in the social insurance space needs to hold fast to a different arrangement of guidelines as the patient's well-being and even life is in question, legitimately or by implication. Further, as it concerns well-being information, the worries in regards to information protection are additionally the most noteworthy. The blockchain innovation being another mechanical arrangement is being embraced among the early clients, in which one of the difficulties stays on how the arrangements on blockchain innovation agree to existing guidelines and measures. While existing HIE frameworks have various years to develop toward meeting the administrative prerequisites, the blockchain innovation may be still in the advancement stage to find the sweet arrival spot inside the social insurance space where it can likewise enough stick to set medicinal services measures and guidelines. To accomplish this, various pilot organizations thorough test and approval of the basic mechanical pieces must be considered by the arrangement suppliers. The necessities to hold fast to guidelines could likewise be a catalyst for additional innovative progressions in the blockchain innovation.

12.5.5   Governance

The fundamental reason of the circulated idea of blockchain assists with bringing various gatherings into a believed exchange plot, without the need of any brought together specialists. Be that as it may, in the event that considers how human services associations work, there can be a few distinctive operational models. In certain operational models of blockchain-based arrangements, it may be basic to have a specific partner expecting the job of a controller to administer the general activity of the blockchain. This administering model may, for instance, be expected to meet the administrative prerequisites. It is not yet clear about how such an administration structure can be overseen appropriately in a framework with different unique gatherings. This part of administration will likewise have a connection with the expected impetus plans. In any case, as the reception of blockchain-based arrangements will advance in the medicinal services space, it would see different arrangements additionally to the prerequisites of administration.

12.5.6   Scaling

In human services as well as any industry, the fundamental blockchain organization must be versatile for effective use of any blockchain-based arrangements. All things considered, in any event in the early stage, a few arrangements in human services will utilize semi-permissioned blockchains which are adaptable and have high exchange throughput at the expense of decentralization. Notwithstanding, there will at present be a requirement for open blockchains for correspondence among permissioned blockchain systems. Furthermore, a blockchain-empowered worldwide HIE must be conceivable with exceptionally adaptable open blockchains. In current structure, open blockchain systems such as Bitcoin and Ethereum are not quick and modest enough to have any decentralized applications for a huge scope. Nonetheless, there have been a few progressing scaling endeavors, for example, lightning system, state channels, plasma chains, sharding, zk-SNARKs, and so on, and some of them are as of now being received practically speaking. Later on, all things considered, the open blockchains will be quick and modest enough for their mass appropriation.

In the most recent decade, we have watched the advancement of blockchain in three ages. Digital currencies came in the 1.0 age, which was basically structured as an elective installment framework. At that point, decentralized applications dependence on keen agreements (Dapps) spoke to the 2.0 applications giving business rationale deliberation and execution on a believed stage where well-being and security of shrewd agreements is the key issue. Savvy contracts can be approved and tried before arrangement on a live blockchain that forestalls financial misfortunes due to flaws in the code. The third era is adopting an unavoidable multidimensional strategy interfacing IoT, AI, and various parts of science. These various ages of blockchain are advancing all the while in their own pace, tending to the issues such as adaptability, security, and protection en route. In addition, ventures such as Holochain [33] and Hashgraph [34] are creating adaptable and universally useful stages for operator-driven decentralized applications; conventional blockchains are information driven making them difficult to scale.

12.6 Conclusion

Blockchain innovation can possibly take care of a few issues tormenting the social insurance industry today. As a trust arbiter, it can empower novel social insurance arrangements, and as a motivator machine, it can empower novel plans of action that may prompt another dynamic among different medicinal services partners such as patients and suppliers. A patient-driven medicinal services model and a worldwide HIE may be acknowledged by excellence of blockchain-empowered decentralized trust and motivating force structures. Also, blockchain-based decentralized system/administrations may limit merchant lock-in issues in human services. In this section, we looked into significant use instances of blockchain, for example, social insurance information of the executives, gracefully chain of the executives in the pharmaceutical business, medicine adherence, charging/claims of the board, and examination. Instances of associations creating blockchain-based applications for these utilization cases were additionally introduced. The proposed applications go from moonshot ventures attempting to construct a total decentralized medicinal services environment to specific applications, for example, information provenience, fake medications identification, and assent of the executives. In spite of the massive capability of blockchain innovation and a tremendous measure of enthusiasm around it, we found that its effect on medicinal services is insignificant, and the medicinal services are still in the good "ol" days. A large portion of the blockchain-based medicinal services arrangements are still as novel ideas carried out by whitepapers, models, or just few working items with a restricted client base. Notwithstanding, the field is advancing quickly; we foresee a significantly positive effect of blockchain in social insurance later on. Difficulties, for example, inter-operability, coordination with the current frameworks, vulnerability in cost, mechanical and selection obstruction, administrative consistence, and scaling must be effectively handled to help blockchain positively shape the medicinal services industry.

References

[1] K. Sharma, F. Rafiqui, P. Attri, and S. K. Yadav (2019). A two-tier security solution for storing data across public cloud. *Recent Pat. Comput. Sci.*, 12 (3), 191–201.

[2] K. Sharma and G. Shrivastava (2014). Public key infrastructure and trust of web based knowledge discovery. *Int. J. Eng. Sci. Manage.*, 4(1), 56–60.

[3] G. Shrivastava, P. Kumar, B. B. Gupta, S. Bala, and N. Dey (Eds.) (2018). *Handbook of Research on Network Forensics and Analysis Techniques*. IGI Global Core Reference Title in Security & Forensics.

[4] F. A. Ahmad, P. Kumar, G. Shrivastava, and M. S. Bouhlel (2018). Bitcoin: Digital decentralized cryptocurrency. In *Handbook of Research on Network Forensics and Analysis Techniques* (pp. 395–415). IGI Global Core Reference Title in Security & Forensics.

[5] S. R. Srivastava, S. Dube, G. Shrivastaya, and K. Sharma (2019). Smartphone triggered security challenges-issues, case studies and preven-tion. In *Cyber Security in Parallel and Distributed Computing: Concepts, Techniques, Applications and Case Studies*, Wiley online library (pp. 187–206).

[6] R. Amit and C. C. Zott (2015). Crafting business architecture: The antecedents of business model design. *Strateg. Entrepreneurship J.*, 9(4), 331–350. Volume 7, 2019 25705.

[7] T. Stevenson (2002). Anticipatory action learning: Conversations about the future. *Futures*, 34(5), 417–425.

[8] S. Inayatullah (2006). Anticipatory action learning: Theory and practice. *Futures*, 38(6), 656–666.

[9] D. Coghlan and T. Brannick (2010). *Doing Action Research in Your Own Organization*, 3rd ed. London, UK: Sage.

[10] P. Reason (2006). Choice and quality in action research practice. *J. Manage. Inq.*, 15(2), 187–202.

[11]   H. Tsoukas and J. Shepherd (Eds.) (2004). *Managing the Future: Foresight in the Knowledge Economy*. Hoboken, NJ, USA: Blackwell Publishing Ltd.

[12]   J. M. Ramos (2006). Dimensions in the confluence of futures studies and action research. *Futures*, 38(6), 642–655.

[13]   J. Floyd (2012). Action research and integral futures studies: A path to embodied foresight. *Foresight*, 44(10), 870–882.

[14]   A. Bryman and E. Bell (2011). *Business Research Methods*, 3rd ed. New York, NY, USA: Oxford Univ. Press.

[15]   R. K. Yin (2009). *Case Study Research: Design and Methods*, 4th ed. Newbury Park, CA, USA: Sage.

[16]   S. Nakamoto (2008) *Bitcoin: A Peer-to-Peer Electronic Cash System*. [Online]. Available: https://bitcoin.org/bitcoin.pdf.

[17]   J. Yli-Huumo, D. Ko, S. Choi, S. Parka, and K. Smolander (2016). Where is current research on blockchain technology?—A systematic review. *PLoS One*, 11(10), e0163477.

[18]   M. Vukolić (2016). The quest for scalable blockchain fabric: Proof-of-work vs. BFT replication. In *Open Problems in Network Security*, vol. 9591, J. Camenisch and D. Kesdoğan (Eds.). Cham, Switzerland: Springer.

[19]   K. Christidis and M. Devetsikiotis (2016). Blockchains and smart contracts for the Internet of Things. *IEEE Access*, 4, 2292–2303.

[20]   A. Baliga (2016). *The Blockchain Landscape*. Persistent Systems Technical support.

[21]   D. G. Sirmon, M. A. Hitt, R. D. Ireland, and B. A. Gilbert (2011). Resource orchestration to create competitive advantage: Breadth, depth, and life cycle effects. *J. Manage.*, 37(5), 1390–1412.

[22]   R. Adner and R. Kapoor (2010). Value creation in innovation ecosystems: How the structure of technological interdependence affects firm performance in new technology generations. *Strateg. Manage. J.*, 31(3), 306–333.

[23]   B. Demil and X. Lecocq (2010). Business model evolution: In search of dynamic consistency. *Long Range Plann.*, 43(2–3), 227–246.

[24]   M. Johnson, C. M. Christensen, and H. Kagermann (2008). Reinventing your business model. *Harv. Bus. Rev.*, 86(12), 50–60.

[25]   A. Osterwalder and Y. Pigneur (2010). Business model generation: A handbook for visionaries. In *Game Changers, and Challengers*. Hoboken, NJ, USA: Wiley.

[26]   H. Chesbrough (2010). Business model innovation: Opportunities and barriers. *Long Range Plann.*, 43(2–3), 354–363.

[27]   C. Zott and R. Amit (2013). The business model: A theoretically anchored robust construct for strategic analysis. *Strateg. Org.*, 11(4), 403–411.

[28]   D. Messerschmitt and C. Szyperski (2003). *Software Ecosystem: Understanding an Indispensable Technology and Industry*. Cambridge, MA, USA: MIT Press.

[29]   K. Samdanis, X. Costa-Perez, and V. Sciancalepore (2016). From network sharing to multi-tenancy: The 5G network slice broker. *IEEE Commun. Mag.*, 54(7), 32–39.

[30]   J. Wang, A. J. Conejo, C. Wang, and J. Yan (2012). Smart grids, renewable energy integration, and climate change mitigation—Future electric energy systems. *Appl. Energy*, 96, 1–484.

[31]   A. C. Pereira and F. Romero (2017). A review of the meanings and the implications of the Industry 4.0 concept. *Procedia Manuf.*, 13, 1206–1214.

[32]   J. Smit, S. Kreutzer, C. Moeller, and M. Carlberg (2016). *Policy Department A: Economic and Scientific Policy – Industry 4.0* (pp. 1–94). European Parliament, EU.

[33]   A. Wang, L. Yu, A. Mudesir, D. Zhu, B. Zhao, and T. S. Siew (2017). *5G Unlocks a World of Opportunities: Top Ten 5G Use Cases*. Shenzhen, China: Huawei Technologies Co.

[34]   DotEcon Ltd and Axon Partners Group (2018) *Study on Implications of 5G Deployment on Future Business Models*, vol. 18 (pp. 1–116). US.

[35]   P. Suthar (2017). *5G Technology Components—Building Blocks of 5G Networks*. Helsinki, Finland: Nokia.

[36]   K. Paneta (2017). *Top Trends in the Gartner Hype Cycle for Emerging Technologies*. Stamford, CT, USA: Gartner.

[37]   A. Pazaitis, P. De Filippi, and V. Kostakis (2017). Blockchain and value systems in the sharing economy: The illustrative case of Backfeed. *Technol. Forecast. Soc.*, 125, 105–115.

[38]   Ž. Turk and R. Klinc (2017). Potentials of blockchain technology for construction management. *Procedia Eng.*, 196, 638–645.

[39]   S. Huckle, R. Bhattacharya, M. White, and N. Beloff (2016). Internet of Things, blockchain and shared economy applications. *Procedia Comput. Sci.*, 58, 461–466.

[40]   P. U. Eze, T. Eziokwu, and C. R. Okpara (2017). A triplicate smart contract model using blockchain technology. *Circ. Comput. Sci.*, 1–10.

[41]   J. B. Benet (2014). *IPFS—Content Addressed, Versioned, P2P File System*. CoRR, vol. abs/1407.3.

[42]   V. Dieterich, M. Ivanovic, T. Meier, S. Zäpfel, M. Utz, and P. Sandner (2017). *Application of Blockchain Technology in the Manufacturing Industry* (pp. 1–23). Germany: Frankfurt School Blockchain Center.

[43]   2018; https://blog.labii.com/2018/03/using-blockchain-technologyinelectronic-lab-notebook-eln.html (accessed September, 2018).

[44]   2018; https://www.bernstein.io/. Bernstein – Blockchain for Intellectual Property (accessed September, 2018).

[45]   2018; https://www.innoplexus.com/life-science-ai-products-solutions-3-2/iplexus. iPlexus. (accessed September, 2018).

[46]   2018; https://blockchain.ieee.org/standards/clinicaltrials (accessed November 6, 2018).

[47]   R. R. Worley. Scrybe: A blockchain ledger for clinical trials. In IEEE Clinical Trials Forum, 2018.

[48]   M. B. Ravaud. Blockchain technology for improving clinical research quality. Trials, 2017.

[49] BlockRx: The Pharmaceutical Blockchain of Value, 2017. Retrieved from https://www.blockrx.com/white-paper/ (accessed September 2018).

[50] Building an Open Network for the Pharmaceutical Supply Chain, 2017. Retrieved from https://www.mediledger.com/ (accessed September 2018).

[51] R. Craib, G. Bradway, and X. Dunn. Ambrosus White paper, 2018. https://ambrosus.com/assets/en/Ambrosus-White-Paper.pdf. (accessed October 29, 2018).

[52] MODSense T1, 2018. Retrieved from https://modum.io/solution/products (accessed September, 2018).

[53] Blockchain Based Anti-Counterfeit Solution, 2018. Retrieved from. URL http://www.blockverify.io/ (accessed September, 2018).

Chapter 13

Machine learning for health care

B.K.S.P. Kumar Raju Alluri[1]

Machine learning (ML) is predominately being used to solve various technical and nontechnical challenges around the world. Taking the context of health care, ML took over the control and helping many practitioners for effective decision-making. Practically, this is once again proved by the researchers as they are using the ML algorithms for fast detection of COVID-19 and steps are initiated for the drug discovery of the same. In this chapter, we initially discuss the work happening in COVID-19 using ML algorithms. Then, we summarize the role of ML for analyzing and assessing various chronic diseases. Even though ML algorithms are predicting multidimensional aspects of the target disease, the experts in the field are still hesitating to use those outcomes as they lack in justification. To address this, a separate concept called explainable AI (XAI) is discussed.

Data scientists are using ML algorithms to address chronic health issues with less cost and in a more accurate way. The question is, how ML could achieve this? This will be the main motivation for the entire chapter. In a recent report of a Harvard Medical Survey, it said that nearly 5,000,000 Indians die every year due to the medical errors (Harvard, 2020). These errors are getting reduced when the same disease is analyzed with ML. There is a famous proverb, "Prevention is better than cure." According to World Health Organization, in most of the cases, chronic diseases cannot be prevented. But, the impact of them can be reduced with proper data collection and effective analysis using advanced ML algorithms. For instance, to detect lung cancer, it would cost hundreds of dollars for undergoing diagnosis and medication. Above that, if the disease is detected in the advanced stages then the probability of the cure is also very less. All these negative consequences can be reduced drastically when the usage of ML for health care is further exploited.

13.1 Machine learning pipelining

ML algorithms for any industry, including health care, follow the below process:

[1]School of Computing Science and Engineering, VIT-AP University, Amaravati, India

1. Data collection: Data is the core element of any data analytics application. The quality of the data is a dependent factor for achieving higher accuracy in predictions. Data readily may be available in the target organization or the data scientist has to take initiation to collect it through several sources. These include social media and other web locations. In the worst case, experiments or surveys need to be conducted for data collection.
2. Data storage: The collected data can be in a structured format, a semistructured or an unstructured format and saved in high-end system for analysis.
3. Descriptive statistics: Understanding the data is a driving force for applying appropriate transformations. This would in turn help the data scientist to work with suitable algorithms with appropriate parameters/hyper parameters to ensure better accuracy.
4. Preprocessing: This involves handling missing values, standardizing and normalizing the values, identifying and removing outliers, correcting any other semantic issues, etc. Most of the time, the data scientist would spend time in the preprocessing stage.
5. Build models: Choosing a right path will also save a lot of time instead of trying all the statistical and ML models. The general guidelines are, if the target dataset is small enough and the relationships among the attributes are not complex then statistical modeling would be sufficient otherwise go for machine leaning or deep learning models.
6. Evaluate the models: The data scientist should have enough mathematical background to interpret and improve the results further.

13.2 Applications of ML in health care

When the previously mentioned stages of ML are applied on the health-care data, the applications are endless and some of them are as follows:

- Reduce the risk: When a patient visited the doctor, he/she may be diagnosed with a disease and then medication is prescribed accordingly. Further, a hospital technical team can use ML capabilities to monitor the patient health status and to check whether patient is following the guidelines suggested by the doctor like in-time taking of medicine, food intake.
- Predict the disease: Sometimes, the diagnosis may be done in a wrong way and in some other cases, diagnosis may not be done at all. In any of these situations, employing ML at right time would predict the risk of the patient in getting affected with the chronic disease.
- Drug discovery: Identifying the right molecule, right protein structure and genome sequence for drug discovery is highly time consuming. But ML would make this a reality if the appropriate data is available.
- Detection of the disease: Sometimes the doctors may go wrong in detecting the disease after looking at the lab reports especially in the case of computed tomography (CT) scans and X-rays. The ML system upon extensive training can detect the chronic disease with high precision. In some cases, identifying

the exact problem is required, then the doctor has to scan patients' previous electronic health records (EHR) and identify the exact reason for those symptoms that can be done automatically using ML algorithms.

• Recommendations in medication: The doctors when entered the specific symptoms to an ML engine then it would recommend the medicines with great visual statistics based on the past success rate of similar patients when followed with the same medication.

13.3 Common machine learning approaches in machine learning

ML introduction and the frequently used algorithms are discussed in Chapter 5. In this chapter, we just brief them without going into many details.

13.3.1 Artificial neural networks

Artificial neural network (ANN) comes under black box model and currently solving many health-care problems with high accuracy. Common ANN architectures are convolution neural networks (CNNs) and recurrent neural networks (RNNs).

1. Convolution neural networks (CNNs): CNN is commonly used for image analytics as CNNs process them by preserving spatial primitives. CNN will not flatten the image as it will lead to spatial information loss. CNN uses tiny kernels to process image data (the number of kernels you choose is hyperparameter and it depends on the user) and using which the convolution layer is formed. Then this layer is further divided in a non-overlapping way to form a pooling layer. The color images are also handled in the same way, i.e., for a single-color image, we will have 3-convolution layers and 3-pooling layers—each for R, G and B, respectively.
2. Recurrent neural networks (RNNs): RNN has memory and it can take hidden layers information of the previous layer to the current layer. RNN is typically used in processing the sequence data, for which it is used in applications like, trading stocks, music analysis and speech recognition.

13.3.2 Tree-like reasoning

The problem with ANN is, they lack in justifying capabilities of the generated outcomes. This problem is addressed with tree-based algorithms like, decision tree and random forest.

We take decisions or come to conclusions in our daily life based on multiple factors. In health sector, the doctors would also follow a structured approach based on the symptoms of the patients and identify the appropriate reason(s) and cure of the disease identified. For example, to do risk analysis of COVID-19 in Indian citizens who visited foreign countries and returned to the country, the doctors can do preliminary assessment using the following if-then rules in a visual form (Figure 13.1).

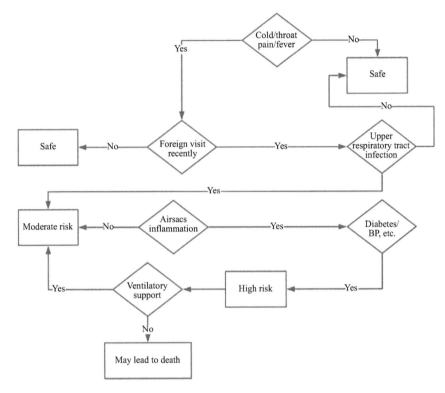

Figure 13.1   A visual representation of IF-THEN rules

Figure 13.1 is generated manually by a keen observation of the current situation in the country. But when the depth of the disease increased then the complex relationships should be embedded in the visual which is automatically constructed by the ML algorithms. An ML algorithm named, "decision tree" works to address this problem by identifying the correct split point based on the entropy or information gain. Also, during the construction of the tree, we can limit the depth and specify other constraints to avoid overfitting. An ensemble approach of decision trees is random forest that will generally perform well than individual decision tree algorithms.

But the problem with tree-based algorithms is, they may not perform well as ANN. So, the researchers around the world added interpretability to the ANN without compromising its performance and it is specifically called as XAI which will be discussed in the last section of the chapter.

13.3.3   Other common ML algorithms

Health-care problems are also commonly solved by algorithms like Naïve Bayes, support vector machines (SVMs) and regression.

- Naïve Bayes: This algorithm is based on the Bayes theorem, and it is called Naïve as it holds an assumption of equal weightage of all variables w.r.t. the class label.
- Support vector machine: This is a black box model like ANN and justifying its outcomes is highly time-consuming. Basically, it finds the maximum margin between hyperplane and data points.
- Regression algorithms: There are many types of regression algorithms like logistic, linear, lasso, ridge, polynomial and stepwise. Based on the underlying objective and dataset, we choose the right regression approach. For example, if the data has categorical class label and if we want to find a relation between ordinal feature and class label then we use ordinal logistic regression.
- By now, need for using ML in health care with basics of the algorithms is briefed, and we are now ready to understand how ML is applied to solve health-care problems.

13.4 Application of machine learning in health care

ML algorithms are extensively being applied in multiple domains. This book/ chapter particularly focuses on ML applications in health care. In the health domain, the usage of ML tremendously increased in the recent times for detecting, drug discovery, medication and monitoring of disease(s). To explain the capabilities of ML/artificial intelligence (AI) in this sector, COVID-19 is taken as a real case and later, we also discuss the work being done to detect and analyze other chronic diseases.

13.4.1 COVID-19—interpretation, detection and drug discovery using machine learning

By the time of writing this chapter, more than 19 lakh people were affected and 1 lakh deaths were recorded worldwide due to COVID-19. Mainly, all these happened because of lack of understanding about medical intricacies about the epidemic. From last few months, researchers around the globe published quality papers on COVID-19 based on which we group the work into the following three categories:

- understanding the COVID-19
- fast and accurate detection of COVID-19
- drug discovery of COVID-19

13.4.1.1 Interpretation of COVID-19

The authors in [1] used publicly available dataset from Kaggle (January 13, 2020 to February 28, 2020—1,085 reported cases, 8 selected features). Random forest (70% training and 30% testing) achieved highest receiver operating characteristic (ROC) of 0.97 and concluded that Age is the deciding factor for mortality and then appropriate time to admit in the hospital reduced the mortality rate.

In [2], to predict the confirmed, death and recovered cases of COVID-19, the authors used long short-time memory (LSTM) and GRU (gated recurrent unit) individually and also combined them. For LSTM, a 50-node architecture of 4 layers is used with a dropped rate of 0.2. While implementing GRU, similar hyperparameters of LSTM are used. Both of them when applied separately did not perform well, but hybrid approach (LSTM+GRU) achieved descent performance, especially to predict the number of confirmed cases (87%).

In a recent study [3], not only the senior aged has high risk of mortality for COVID-19, but young adults also have the same risk owing to their history of clinical reports. A hypothesis of using angiotensin-converting enzyme 2 medication to treat other chronic diseases like diabetes and hypertension would increase the complications in treating COVID-19, and this has to be confirmed with huge clinical and lab results. The authors suggested that ML algorithms can be used to detect a severity of COVID-19 based on angiotensin enzyme.

Survival-dependent factors of COVID-19 are experimented and identified that high lactic dehydrogenase (LDH) is the case of severity. The approach is tested on 400 patients and observed that fever is the most common symptom and dyspnea is the least observed symptom. For feature selection, XGBoost algorithm is used and the same algorithm is used for classification and an accuracy of 96% is noted [4].

The authors in [5] identified the capabilities of AI to assess various factors relevant to COVID-19.

1. Whether a person will be infected with corona or not based on his health condition and travel history.
2. Identify the protein structure of COVID-19 and reuse the existing drugs or develop new vaccine for it.
3. Predict the confirmed/death/recovered cases based on the rules imposed by the governments.
4. Identify the propagation of misinformation during COVID-19.
5. Prepare the countries in which pandemic has not yet spread.

Impact of quarantine during COVID-19 phase is assessed. Neural network-based reproduction number is used to assess the quarantine strength $Q(t)$ [5].

Various ML algorithms are used to predict the trend of COVID-19 in terms of deaths/confirmed/recovered cases in China and across the world. According to the prediction, the epidemic will reach its peak during the second week of April and control on the outbreak is likely to be seen in mid-June by which number of cases will cross 4 lakhs with a mortality rate of 4% across the world [6].

In [7], analytical model is proposed to predict the dynamic diffusion of the model. The novel approach over here is to simplify kappa and zeta parameters. The method has been tested on the data collected from Korea (10 days training and 10 days for testing) and an accuracy of 83% is observed. The model still needs to be validated on multiple environments and parameters need to optimize further.

The authors in [8] could gather 1,933 samples of antibody sequences and then applied various ML algorithms to identify the stable sequences that neutralize the COVID-19 (best assessment is made by XGBoost with more than 90% accuracy).

Also, their experiments resulted in 8-antibodies that can show control on COVID-19 spread.

In (Ronsivalli, 2020), the authors proposed an approach to assess the risk rate of COVID-19 to different environments using neural networks. The variables considered for this objective are as follows:

- contact among people
- density
- age
- number of public places nearby
- resident details (income, education details, etc.)

A study on psychological impact of COVID-19 on various kinds of people is done by [6]. Weibo posts (users' profile, messages and network data) during January 13, 2020 to January 26, 2020 of 17,000 users are collected to assess various cognitive and emotional indicators. The conclusions are negative emotions have increased and life satisfaction is decreased. A two-stage process is followed: (1) POS tagging and category extraction and (2) taken the base of psychological prediction model. The authors compared the impact before and after COVID-19 [6].

In [9], the authors proposed an approach to assess the rate of transmission within a city and between cities. The system suggested that quarantine and lockdown are effective measures to reduce the virus spread and for which some of the significant features selected by lasso regression are as follows:

- population density
- doctors available
- GDP per capita
- weather conditions
- distance to the red zone

These features are given as input to regression models like ordinary least squares and IV regression models and both of them achieved a descent performance [9].

Misinformation spread during COVID-19 pandemic is controlled and text to speech conversion feature is deployed as an android application (WashKaro). Broad steps are as follows (Randy *et al.*, 2020):

1. tokenization and stop words removal;
2. stemming;
3. word embeddings (word2vec, GloVe, Google Sentence encoder, term frequency-inverse document frequency (TF-IDF));
4. translator from Text 2 speech.

Based on protein structure, electrostatic features are identified to potentially help the researchers to search for therapeutic measures [10]. Lack of data is a major setback for the researchers to establish fool proof conclusions about COVID-19. To handle this, the authors suggested a mobile-based approach and it collects the following details [11]:

- location-related data;
- gender;
- age;
- travel history;
- close contact with COVID patient in past 14 days;
- any symptoms like fever, cough, headache, respiratory issues;
- dependents information.

In [12], authors proposed a Monte Carlo simulation approach to identify the incubation period w.r.t. COVID-19. The results showed that the distribution is not log normal, Weibull and Gamma distribution but the incubation period varies based on the age, i.e., age ≥ 40 requires more incubation period than expected 14 days.

13.4.1.2 Detection approaches for COVID-19 using ML algorithms

Since COVID-19 is an epidemic, timely detection would reduce the severity of it on an individual and on the society as well. Using ML, the detection of COVID-19 is observed to be faster and accurate and the quality works are summarized as follows:

As of now, detecting the COVID-19 through the regular test is time-consuming. During this process, CT of chest need to be analyzed and also epidemic severity varies from patient to patient as it involves analyses of long sequence of patterns. This is automated using CNN by considering COVID-19 pneumonia cases and non-COVID pneumonia images collected from Wuhan and Xiamen university (75% training and 25% testing) [13].

In [13], the authors confirmed that detecting COVID at early stages is very difficult and require multiple retests. The medical challenges during its detection are as follows:

- nucleic acid identification rates are high,
- nonstability of RNA,
- lack of sufficient assay kits.

It is observed that 86.2% of admitted patients have abnormal tomography images (alveolar damage with cellular fibromyxoid exudates). Authors used PyTorch to use ResNet Architecture and CNN with five output neurons (COVID, non-COVID, bacterial pneumonia, tuberculosis, normal lung) and applied Adam and SGD optimizers with different learning rates for adjusting the weights. The average accuracy of 98.7% is observed in classifying any of the five outcomes during training and testing. The limitation of the study is, patients with more than one chronic study along with COVID-19 and their impacts are not evaluated and also require the approach to be tested across different environmental conditions.

In [14], the authors proposed a scoring-based deep learning approach to detect COVID-19, and it is validated using multiple datasets and area under curve (AUC) of 95% is observed. Initially, the approach extracted ROI from tomography images using U-Net architecture and then corona-related symptoms are retrieved using

ResNet framework. Also, a visual approach is implemented for time series analysis using heat maps. The limitation with this approach is, it is not tested and compared across other pneumonias.

The authors in [15] proposed an approach to understand the pattern in genome sequence classification using ML algorithms and digital signal processing. Their experiments concluded that COVID-19 originated from bat.

In [16], the authors proposed an approach to predict the abnormalities in respiratory system using deep learning approaches and proposed respiratory simulation model (RSM) to address the lack of data and varying respiratory patterns between inner and outer classes. The RSM model follows the following steps:

1. Generated synthesized data using sine wave concept.
2. Understand the respiratory patterns in ROI (chest, abdomen and shoulder) using a depth camera.
3. Apply GRU approach with attention on the collected data.
4. Do the comparative analysis—LSTM vs GRU vs GRU-AT vs LSTM-AT and observed that GRU-AT achieved highest accuracy.

To automatically identify the COVID-19 patients for X-Ray images, the authors in [17] proposed COVIDX-Net framework and it has the following modules:

1. Rescale images (224×224) and perform one hot encoding on class labels.
2. Perform training using deep learning models.
3. Apply various tuning parameters using multiple architectures like VGG19, DenseNet201, Xception, InceptionV3, ResnetV2, MobileNetV2 and InceptionResnetV2.

   The algorithm performed well and achieved highest F1 score of 0.89 and lowest of 0.67.

ML-based severity analysis of COVID-19 is assessed using CT images (176 patients, 19 confirmed cases). Random forest is used to train the model and an accuracy of 87.7% is achieved. The results show that volume and grouped glass opacity regions are highly relevant to decide COVID-19 severity. A UAI-Discover Tool is used to analyze the CT images. The limitation of their work is, binary class label is used and requires severity analysis at multiple levels [18].

The severity of the disease is also assessed by the authors in [4] using ML algorithm XGBoost. The model considered more than 2,700 patients from January 11 to February 18. From hundreds of features, only significant features are considered:

- LDH
- lymphocyte
- high sensitivity, C-reactive protein (hsCRP)

XGBoost gave highly interpretable results and few of them are as follows:

1. LDH$<$364$\rightarrow$hsCRP !$<$41.2$\rightarrow$lymphocyte !$>$14.7$\rightarrow$leads to death
2. LDH$>$36.5$\rightarrow$leads to death

In [19], the authors collected samples from China during 20 December to 10 February, which recorded the following features: age, gender, respiratory related symptoms, gene sequences, etc., a total of 35 features were considered. Lasso feature selection approach is used and AUC of 0.8 is observed. An app is built to predict the risk of getting COVID-19 by giving significant features as input.

The authors in [20] developed an online webservice to probably detect COVID-19 at its early stages using ML algorithms The system is tested on the data collected from January 14 to February 26 (132 Training and 32 testing) by applying feature selection (lasso regression) followed by the usage of ML algorithms like logistic regression, decision tree and AdaBoost. Lasso with logistic regression achieved highest AUC, i.e., 0.9 and it considered the following input parameters: age, gender, highest temperature, heart rate, diastolic, BP, systolic, BP Platelet count, mean corpuscular hemoglobin content, basophil count, monocyte ratio and eosinophil ratio. The previous model is released as a webservice and publicly available in the following link: https://intensivecare.shinyapps.io/COVID19/.

The authors in [21] suggested to use AI capabilities for detecting COVID-19. Instead of single modality, multimodality and multitudinal data should be used for an effective discovery of COVID-19. For example, instead of relying on CT scans, the experts should also use X-rays for an effective interpretation of the patient's situation.

13.4.1.3   Drug discovery for COVID-19

It is not easy to introduce drug/vaccine for highly commutable and dynamic virus like COVID-19, but still significant efforts were being made in this direction in this short span and hopefully in the coming weeks, a drug would be available to the public and reduce its impact on the world. Some of the highly relevant works in the direction of drug discovery are briefed as follows:

An extensive analysis on drug discovery candidates were identified, i.e., poly-ADP-ribose polymerase 1 inhibitor—a non-toxic, anti-viral, inflammatory effect CVL218 is suggested experimentally by the authors in [22]. The work in (Zharoronkov *et al.*, 2020) focused on identifying the clinically approved drug like inhibitors using deep learning algorithms. An extensive set of ML algorithms were applied to generate molecular structures. Protease dataset is used and a Self-Organizing map is applied on it to generate various molecular structures in less time with cost minimization.

Residual similarity in amino acid sequences of protein structures are identified by neural networks. The proposed system by [23] achieved high performance (time and accuracy). Similar framework can be used for predicting/understanding the protein structures of COVID-19. In [24], Vaxigen ML model is proposed for drug discovery of COVID-19. The experiments identified the following relevant protein items for the drug—the adhesins identified are-s, nsp3, 3cl-pro, nsp8-10, anti-genicity proteins identified are-s, nsp3, nsp8. Among all, nsp3 protein showed to play a crucial role in preparing vaccine for COVID-19.

COVID-19 is a positive RNA virus and we need to block viral RNA synthesis. Long short-term memory is used to read SMILES finger prints and predict

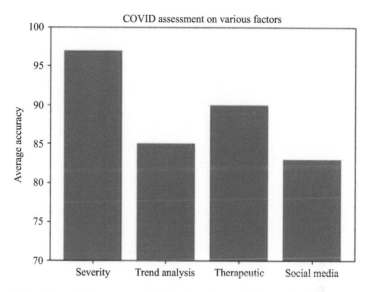

Figure 13.2   Average accuracy of ML algorithms in assessing various factors of COVID-19

IC50 molecules and then authors in [25] suggested that lower binding energies of them are probable direction for COVID-19 drug discovery. In [26], the authors used ML to identify the potential T-cell and B-cell epitopes which can be used to develop the vaccine. Also, spike protein could potentially help the process of COVID-19 drug discovery.

We divided the work on COVID-19 interpretations into four categories, and assessment is made using various ML algorithms and the average accuracy in each mode is shown in Figure 13.2. COVID-19 detection is costly and time-consuming process and to reduce this effort, ML algorithms are being used for faster and effective detection (Figure 13.3). But these approaches were yet to be scientifically proven globally as there are changes in the COVID-19 mutations from one country to the other, and lack of sufficient detailed data is the hurdle factor. We reviewed more than 57 papers and identified the dataset used for COVID-19 analysis, and it is summarized as shown in Figure 13.4.

13.4.1.4   Machine learning for chronic disease analysis

ML algorithms are applied to handle various diseases. Significant works in the recent past are briefed as follows:

Gait classification patterns are identified in cerebral palsy by applying various ML algorithms and observed that neural networks achieved an accuracy of 93% and more interpretable clinical results were observed in Decision Trees with an accuracy of 78% (Zhang *et al.*, 2020).

The authors in [27] collected the data of hundreds of patients with myocardial infarction (MI) in Czechia and Syria. The real-time data suffers with two

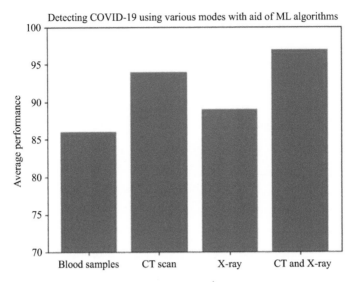

Figure 13.3   Different modes of samples used for detecting COVID-19 using ML algorithms

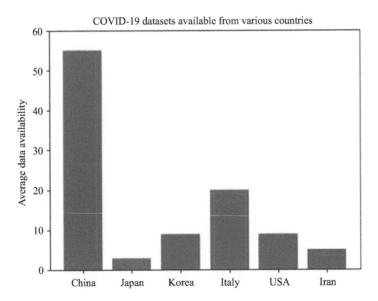

Figure 13.4   COVID-19 data availability for applying ML algorithms across various countries

problems—incomplete and imbalanced, which are solved using tree-augmented Naïve Bayes. The patients were assessed with the risk of mortality based on MI data by applying various classification algorithms.

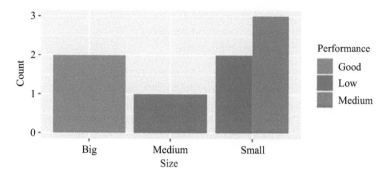

Figure 13.5   Impact of dataset size in deciding the ML algorithms performance on chronic disease analysis

In [28], the authors proposed an approach to detect posterior MI by understanding the electrical conduction changes of cardiac activity using multiscale eigen vectors. The preprocessed data is given to various classification algorithms like *K*NN and SVM (linear and radial basis function (RBF)). Even though, they have performed well on the tested datasets (PhysioNet/PTBDB diagnostic), the authors observed that the techniques could not handle class imbalance and the problem is solved using Weighted SVM and then an accuracy of 96% is observed.

The authors in [29] proposed an approach to detect abnormal mental status (AMS) patients for clinical notes through natural language processing (NLP)-based deep learning models. The clinical notes is taken from REDgp (online data entry providing system) and annotated by various clinical experts (AMS or NoN AMS). The data is given as input to TF-IDF to generate sparse feature matrix. Then CNN is applied separately with predefined word to vector or without pretraining but with word embeddings. A 5-fold cross-validation is applied to achieve AUC of 95%. The same data when evaluated to classify based on ICD codes achieved an accuracy of 81.3%.

In [30], autistic spectrum disorder (ASD) is detected using fuzzy neural networks (FNN) with rectified linear unit (ReLU) activation function, and *F*-score is used during the stage of pruning. An interesting aspect is, FNN did not perform better than the other algorithms like, multi layer perceptron (MLP) and J48 but embedded with a special feature of extracting knowledge from the given problem statement.

We summarized the ML algorithms performance of chronic disease analysis based on the dataset size. In Figure 13.5, we can observe that bigger datasets generally result in high performance. But in health care, medical practitioners are still hesitating to use these models because they lack in justification of outcomes. So, a separate concept called explainable AI (XAI) was introduced.

13.5   Breaking the blackbox of neural networks through explainable AI

Most of the ML algorithms require human effort during feature engineering. This effort is reduced by using deep learning algorithms like CNN and RNN. These architectures take raw patient data as input and use multiple nonlinear hidden layers to produce the desired outcome in several iterations.

Advantages of deep learning algorithms:

- Great learning capabilities: The distributed memory of multilayered neural networks would increase its abilities to predict on similar events based on the selected instances for training.
- Fault tolerance: The malfunction of neurons will not stop the network in evaluation of the nodes and generation of the output.
- Parallel processing abilities: Model parallelism and data parallelism are the premier reasons for using the neural networks for deep learning.
- Robust: Once the neural network is trained, the output will be generated even with certain missing information.

Disadvantages of deep learning algorithms:

- Less interpretability: The black box strategy of neural networks would make the practitioner to face difficulties in justifying the predictions.
- Infrastructure difficulties: Analyzing big data would require GPU capabilities and traditional computers would not be sufficient.

The infrastructure issues were resolved with the usage of cloud computing and high-end machines. But effective interpretability of the neural networks is still an open challenge and efforts were made in this direction to create a separate sub-domain of AI called explainable AI. Deep learning models are good at achieving performance, but they lack in explainability. The better the prediction accuracy, there is a high chance that the model gets complicated for interpretation. XAI balances these two factors, i.e., keep the model performance intact and produce interpretation of the outcomes in various forms (Figure 13.6).

XAI justifies the predictions and will not focus on revealing inner workings of the algorithms. This would further help the organizations to face unseen and unexpected situations. This field aims at improving the existing models and reveals new facts by giving appropriate explanations. The smooth integration of XAI in ML workflow is shown in Figure 13.7.

It is important to note that designing AI algorithms with justifying capabilities would lead to bias system and therefore not recommended for all contexts. XAI is highly essential in fields like health care as doctors' decision taken based on the AI system predictions should not go wrong as it costs the life of human(s). An ideal case of using XAI for health care should satisfy multiple conditions and the same is shown in Figure 13.8.

Medical data usually comes in 2D/3D/4D images and applying XAI on them involves lot of challenges as follows:

- As normal images, high-quantity medical images are not available as they are patient specific.
- High-dimensional images require more space and time for which preprocessing techniques like sampling should be used, but these sorts of approaches would alter the actual data or may not give comprehensive conclusions.

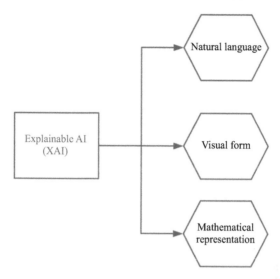

Figure 13.6   Possibilities in XAI

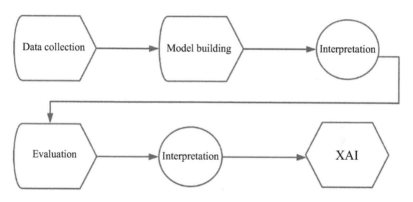

Figure 13.7   Integrating XAI in ML pipeline

- While preprocessing, the ML engineer should have complete knowledge on the medical images otherwise he/she may remove important features critical for expert personnel diagnosis.

To handle these challenges, few significant works have been published in recent years and they are briefed as follows:

The authors in [31] proposed a model agnostic approach named "Anchors." These are basically advanced if-then rules based on conditional probability. This concept is applied to interpret the outcomes of black box deep learning models. The anchors were not limited to plain text but also applied on images and for its construction, where beam search algorithm has been applied. Anchors were tested on

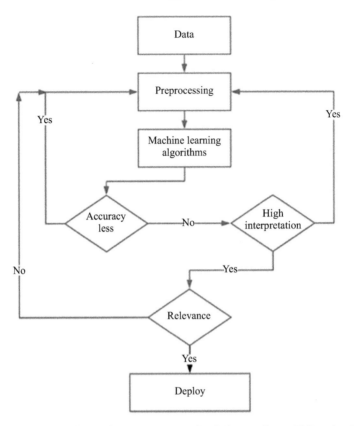

Figure 13.8   Multiple conditions to cross check for applying XAI in health care

unseen instances of three datasets and observed an average precision greater than 95%. The results were compared with linear explanatory methods like LIME and observed that the results are not consistent across instances. Anchors still suffer with potential limitations like the coverage of rare predicates and this happened because part of anchors is not guaranteed and there are high chances of generating ambiguous anchors.

In [32], the classification trees comprehensibility depends on lot of factors like size of the tree, depth of the question, branching factor and number of leaves. Multiple trees were constructed by covering multiple combinations of previously mentioned parameters and user survey with 69 people is conducted by posing tens of questions and taking responses to assess the interpretability. For every response, several parameters were recorded like time to answer, difficulty of the question and depth reached to answer. Also, the subjective differences in the answers for the same question across multiple subjects are observed. In the same direction, two new comprehensibility measures were introduced focusing on tree semantics.

Authors in [33] proposed a visual approach named RuleMatrix for improving the interpretability of the ML outcomes. As part of this, it identified significant factors utilized by the model for predictions. The approach is tested on real situation of diabetes classification and achieved a classification accuracy of 79%.

The initial efforts in interpretability of black box methods like SVM is explained with a credit score case study by [34]. The authors proposed visual and nonvisual rule-based approaches from the SVM model evaluated on the target datasets. Inverse classification and self-organization maps are suggested as alternatives to SVM rule generation.

The authors in [35] proposed a framework using which the users can select features of interest for which interpretable prediction outcomes will be generated. The approach can be integrated with image classification after the superpixels phase in intermediate layers of networks. The method is compared with locally interpretable model agnostic explanations (LIME) using real-time survey and observed that the proposed approach is far better than LIME.

In [36], a Global model agnostic approach is proposed, which is capable of giving unambiguous interpretations of black box models. The approach takes subsets of decision sets by considering user features of interest to generate customized interpretations from the model. The approach is tested on depression diagnosis dataset and compared with existing approaches like interpretable decision sets, Bayesian decision lists and identified the current approach outperformed others in terms of accuracy and running time.

Regulation by European authorities gave difficult times for the AI professionals in health care as it suggested that algorithm decisions should be verified manually and it is costly and time-consuming process [37]. Moreover, right to explain would not be practically possible in most of the black box deep learning models.

Taking the previous works as base, XAI is applied in health care and increased the transparency in decision-making thereby enhanced the reliability of the experts/management to use AI for addressing health-care issues. The authors made initial efforts in distinguishing blackbox methods interpretability and representations and then suggested the need for gray-scale approaches, i.e., interpretable model representations [38].

In [75], heat map is generated from tomography images and high-intensity regions indicate issues in the context of macromolecules. The authors considered tumor images of breast and applied multi-instance fusion approach on top of CNN. Further, they have taken similar context images and automatically identified tumor cells using super pixel maps.

The authors in [39] used neural networks to identify neural disorders and interpret them using their multistage pipeline method. The approach not only applies for identifying ROI in neurological disorders, it can be generalized for interpreting other deep learning approaches.

In [40], the authors contributed to the following:

- For detecting the brain tumors, confocal laser endomicroscopy imaging became more popular in the recent times.
- The problem with health-care images of any chronic disease is lack of annotated huge datasets especially for new epidemics. The authors proposed weakly supervised approaches which reduce the effort in manual annotation.
- This approach relies on image level annotations to perform feature localization using CNN-based multiscale activation functions that achieved an accuracy of 87%.

The authors in [41] used CNN for detecting and interpreting Alzheimer's dataset. More than 70,000 annotations were made to train the model, and it performed well on test plaque images with a precision of 74%. To increase the interpretability, they have used saliency maps.

The auto-selection of scale while using CNN would help the observer to know the process employed by the network in identifying the object. The proposed approach is tested on multiple contexts like CT and MRI segmentations [42]. The authors in [43] introduced Bayesian rule lists (BRL) for predicting the heart strokes and they proved that proposed approach achieved better performance than traditional ML algorithms. In addition to that, BRL produced highly interpretable results.

In (Ular *et al.*, 2018), the arterial spin labeling images generally have high noise that leads to low-end images and to improve the quality and interpretability, cerebral blood flow parameter is considered during the training of CNN.

The authors in [44] proposed a generalized framework for improving the statistical inference of the medical images especially, neuroscience. The framework is augmented to work in closed form with a capability of considering the null distribution during analysis.

Reference [45] used CNN to combine tomography and resonance images for pharmacokinetic model building with reduced acquisition times. The proposed approach is capable enough of understanding the relation between tomography and blood flow. The method is tested on Alzheimer's dataset and observed that acquisition times were almost reduced by 75% with improved quantification and analysis. In [46], a multimodality interpretable approach (EHR and cardiography videos) is used for risk assessment and identified significant performance improvement (AUC=0.8) in comparison with single modality (AUC=0.7).

To detect amyotrophic lateral sclerosis from electromyogram (EMG) signals, the authors in [47] have used frame single value decomposition (SVD). The method produced more interpretable results as it is based on canonical correlation analysis. Moreover, fusion techniques are applied for EMG signals classification based on the attribute distributions. The framework is applied on multiple datasets and achieved an average accuracy of 98.9%.

Unpredictability nature of epilepsy neurological disorders makes it difficult to detect. The authors in [48] have discretized and applied wavelet transformations on EEG signals. Then reduced feature matrix is processed using cross entropy ANNs.

The results are more interpretable as ANNs are trained well using Genetic and Gradient based algorithms.

In [49], the authors proposed optimal multi-basis wavelet transformations for EEG signals to make them more interpretable. Then the extracted feature map is fed as input to various kernels of SVM and observed an accuracy of 99.67%. Anatomic patterns were identified from 3D segmentations of cardiac images without changing the input space and achieved a real-time accuracy of 90% when applied on ACDC MICCAI 2017 dataset [50].

Case-based reasoning (CBR) identifies relevant old queries and solutions based on new queries. CBR approaches were not used often because the solutions provided by it are limited to the database old cases. The authors addressed the issue by focusing on visual qualitative and quantitative interpretability of CBR outcomes. The approach achieved descent accuracy and showed par performance with KNN with better interpretability [51].

The authors in [52] have used convolutional neural networks and multilayer perceptron to detect malaria infection from the images collected from Kaggle. Further, they have applied LIME for generating interpretable results.

Identifying the best classification algorithm on genome data is time-consuming but most of the times, ensemble approaches would result in better accuracies. The problem with them is, they lack in interpretability. The authors in [53] proposed a visual approach where from huge set of ensembles, only decisive factored features are identified. The selected small ensembles outperformed single classifiers and also justified the prediction outcomes.

Generally deep learning algorithms perform well with large datasets. But the authors in [54] trained the system even with smaller datasets to detect intracranial hemorrhage and achieved an average sensitivity of 95%. In addition to achieve good performance, the approach generated highly interpretable results and sheds light on the justification of the outcomes made by the black box methods.

An interpretability approach named RetainVis is proposed, which can take EHR, user and domain expert inputs and produce visual explanations particularly heart- and eye-related diseases. The approach used RNN by adding the temporal aspects to the model that would further increase the visual interactivity [55].

From the previous work, we can conclude that XAI is still at nascent stage, and it is particularly to be exploited in the health care domain.

13.6   Conclusion

Health care industry evolved at a huge pace in recent times and one of the main reasons is the usage of technology like AI. This is proved once again by a fast combat of COVID-19 in China using advanced image processing systems. Also, in a short span, researchers around the world published high-quality papers to detect and prepare drug/vaccine for COVID-19 and clinical trials for the same are in progress. From the last one decade, medical and ML fields smoothly fused to detect and analyze various diseases in a fast and effective manner. But ML usage in health care needs to be exploited further, which is possible when it has explainability (XAI) capabilities.

References

[1]   Sarkar, Jit, and Partha Chakrabarti. "A machine learning model reveals older age and delayed hospitalization as predictors of mortality in patients with COVID-19." *European PMC, medRxiv* (2020).

[2]   Bandyopadhyay, Samir Kumar, and Shawni Dutta. "Machine learning approach for confirmation of COVID-19 cases: Positive, negative, death and release." *medRxiv* (2020).

[3]   Alimadadi, Ahmad, *et al.* "Artificial intelligence and machine learning to fight COVID-19." *Physiological Genomics* 52 (2020): 200–202.

[4]   Li Yan, Hai, Tao Zhang, *et al.* "Prediction of criticality in patients with severe COVID-19 infection using three clinical features: A machine learning-based prognostic model with clinical data in Wuhan." *medRxiv* (2020).

[5]   Joseph Bullock, Alexandra Luccioni, Katherine Hoffmann Pham, Cynthia Sin Nga Lam and Miguel Luengo-Oroz. "Mapping the landscape of artificial intelligence applications against COVID-19." *arXiv preprint arXiv:2003. 11336* (2020).

[6]   Sijia Li, Yilin Wang, Jia Xue, Nan Zhao, and Tingshao Zhu, "The impact of COVID-19 epidemic declaration on psychological consequences: A study on active Weibo users." *International Journal of Environmental Research and Public Health* 17(6) (2020): 2032.

[7]   Kim, Song-Kyoo. "AAEDM: Theoretical dynamic epidemic diffusion model and COVID-19 Korea pandemic cases." *medRxiv* (2020).

[8]   Magar, Rishikesh, Prakarsh Yadav, and Amir Barati Farimani. "Potential neutralizing antibodies discovered for novel corona virus using machine learning." *arXiv preprint arXiv:2003.08447* (2020).

[9]   Qiu, Yun, Xi Chen, and Wei Shi. "Impacts of social and economic factors on the transmission of coronavirus disease (COVID-19) in China." *medRxiv* (2020).

[10]   Li, Wei. "Structurally observed electrostatic features of the COVID-19 Coronavirus-Related Experimental Structures inside Protein Data Bank: A Brief Update." *Life sciences, biophysics* (2020).

[11]   Rao, Arni SR Srinivasa, and Jose A. Vazquez. "Identification of COVID-19 can be quicker through artificial intelligence framework using a mobile phone-based survey in the populations when cities/towns are under quarantine." *Infection Control & Hospital Epidemiology* (2020): 1–18.

[12]   Han, Henry. "Estimate the incubation period of coronavirus 2019 (COVID-19)." *medRxiv* (2020).

[13]   Min Fu, Shuang-Lian Yi, Yuanfeng Zeng, *et al.* "Deep learning-based recognizing COVID-19 and other common infectious diseases of the lung by chest CT scan images." *medRxiv* (2020).

[14]   Ophir Gozes, Maayan Frid-Adar, Hayit Greenspan, *et al.* "Rapid AI development cycle for the coronavirus (COVID-19) pandemic: Initial results for automated detection & patient monitoring using deep learning CT image analysis." *Image and Video Processing (eess.IV); Computer Vision and Pattern Recognition (cs.CV); Machine Learning (cs.LG)* (2020).

[15]   Gurjit S. Randhawa, Maximillian Soltysiak, Hadi El Roz, Camila P. E. de Souza, Kathleen A. Hill, and Lila Kari. "Machine learning using intrinsic genomic signatures for rapid classification of novel pathogens: COVID-19 case study." *bioRxiv* (2020).

[16]   Yunlu Wang, Menghan Hu, Qingli Li, Xiao-Ping Zhang, Guangtao Zhai, and Nan Yao. "Abnormal respiratory patterns classifier may contribute to large-scale screening of people infected with COVID-19 in an accurate and unobtrusive manner." *arXiv preprint arXiv:2002.05534* (2020).

[17]   Hemdan, Ezz El-Din, Marwa A. Shouman, and Mohamed Esmail Karar. "COVIDX-Net: A framework of deep learning classifiers to diagnose COVID-19 in X-ray images." *arXiv preprint arXiv:2003.11055* (2020).

[18]   Zhenyu Tang, Wei Zhao, Xingzhi Xie, *et al.* "Severity assessment of coronavirus disease 2019 (COVID-19) using quantitative features from chest CT images." *arXiv preprint arXiv:2003.11988* (2020).

[19]   Zirui Meng, Minjin Wang, Huan Song, *et al.* "Development and utilization of an intelligent application for aiding COVID-19 diagnosis." *medRxiv* (2020).

[20]   Cong Feng, Zhi Huang, Lili Wang, *et al.* "A novel triage tool of artificial intelligence assisted diagnosis aid system for suspected COVID-19 pneumonia in fever clinics." (2020).

[21]   Santosh, K. C. "AI-driven tools for coronavirus outbreak: Need of active learning and cross-population train/test models on multitudinal/multimodal data." *Journal of Medical Systems* 44(5) (2020): 1–5.

[22]   Yiyue Ge, Tingzhong Tian, Suling Huang, *et al.* "A data-driven drug repositioning framework discovered a potential therapeutic agent targeting COVID-19." *bioRxiv* (2020).

[23]   Andrew W. Senior, Richard Evans, John Jumper, *et al.* "Improved protein structure prediction using potentials from deep learning." *Nature* (2020): 1–5.

[24]   Edison Ong, Mei U Wong, Anthony Huffman, and Yongqun He. "COVID-19 coronavirus vaccine design using reverse vaccinology and machine learning." *Front Immunol, bioRxiv* (2020).

[25]   Patankar, Sayalee. "Deep Learning-Based Computational Drug Discovery to Inhibit the RNA Dependent RNA Polymerase: Application to SARS-CoV and COVID-19." (2020).

[26]   Ethan Fast, and Binbin Chen. "Potential T-cell and B-cell Epitopes of 2019-nCoV." *bioRxiv* (2020).

[27]   Salman, Issam. "Heart attack mortality prediction: An application of machine learning methods." *Turkish Journal of Electrical Engineering & Computer Sciences* 27(6) (2019): 4378–4389.

[28]   Prabhakararao, Eedara, and Samarendra Dandapat. "A weighted SVM based approach for automatic detection of posterior myocardial infarction using VCG signals." *2019 National Conference on Communications (NCC)*. IEEE, 2019.

[29]   Jihad S. Obeid, Erin R. Weeda, Andrew J. Matuskowitz, *et al.* "Automated detection of altered mental status in emergency department clinical notes: A deep learning approach." *BMC Medical Informatics and Decision Making* 19 (1) (2019): 164.

[30]   Augusto Junio Guimarães, Vinicius Jonathan Silva Araujo, Vanessa Souza Araujo, Lucas De Oliveira Batista, and Paulo Vitor Campos Souza. "A hybrid model based on fuzzy rules to act on the diagnosed of autism in adults." *IFIP International Conference on Artificial Intelligence Applications and Innovations.* Springer, Cham, 2019.

[31]   Ribeiro, Marco Tulio, Sameer Singh, and Carlos Guestrin. "Anchors: High precision model-agnostic explanations." *Thirty-Second AAAI Conference on Artificial Intelligence*, 2018.

[32]   Luštrek, Mitja, Matjaž Gams, and Sanda Martinčić-Ipšić. "What makes classification trees comprehensible?" *Expert Systems with Applications* 62 (2016): 333–346.

[33]   Ming, Yao, Huamin Qu, and Enrico Bertini. "RuleMatrix: Visualizing and understanding classifiers with rules." *IEEE Transactions on Visualization and Computer Graphics* 25(1) (2018): 342–352.

[34]   David Martens, Johan Huysmans, Rudy Setiono, and Jan Vanthienen. "Rule extraction from support vector machines: An overview of issues and application in credit scoring." *Rule Extraction From Support Vector Machines*. Springer, Berlin, Heidelberg, 2008. 33–63.

[35]   Himabindu Lakkaraju, Ece Kamar, Rich Caruana, and Jure Leskovec. "Faithful and customizable explanations of black box models." *Proceedings of the 2019 AAAI/ACM Conference on AI, Ethics, and Society*, 2019.

[36]   Himabindu Lakkaraju, Ece Kamar, Rich Caruana, and Jure Leskovec. "Interpretable & explorable approximations of black box models." *arXiv preprint arXiv:1707.01154* (2017).

[37]   Wallace, Nick, and Daniel Castro. *The Impact of the EU's New Data Protection Regulation on AI*. Centre for Data Innovation, Washington, DC, USA, 2018.

[38]   Bibal, Adrien, and Benoît Frenay. "Interpretability of machine learning models and representations: An introduction. "*In 24th European Symposium on Artificial Neural Networks, Computational Intelligence and Machine Learning*, 2016. 77–82.

[39]   Xiaoxiao Li, Nicha C. Dvornek, Juntang Zhuang, Pamela Ventola, and James S. Duncan. "Brain biomarker interpretation in ASD using deep

learning and fMRI." *International Conference on Medical Image Computing and Computer-Assisted Intervention.* Springer, Cham, 2018.

[40] Mohammadhassan Izadyyazdanabadi, Evgenii Belykh, Claudio Cavallo, *et al.* "Weakly-supervised learning-based feature localization for confocal laser endomicroscopy glioma images." *International Conference on Medical Image Computing and Computer-Assisted Intervention.* Springer, Cham, 2018.

[41] Ziqi Tang, Kangway V. Chuang, Charles DeCarli, *et al.* "Interpretable classification of Alzheimer's disease pathologies with a convolutional neural network pipeline." *Nature Communications* 10(1) (2019): 1–14.

[42] Yao Qin, Konstantinos Kamnitsas, Siddharth Ancha, *et al.* "Autofocus layer for semantic segmentation." *International Conference on Medical Image Computing and Computer-Assisted Intervention.* Springer, Cham, 2018.

[43] Benjamin Letham, Cynthia Rudin, Tyler H. McCormick, and David Madigan. "Interpretable classifiers using rules and Bayesian analysis: Building a better stroke prediction model." *The Annals of Applied Statistics* 9(3) (2015): 1350–1371.

[44] Erdem Varol, Aristeidis Sotiras, Ke Zeng, and Christos Davatzikos. "Generative discriminative models for multivariate inference and statistical mapping in medical imaging." *International Conference on Medical Image Computing and Computer-Assisted Intervention.* Springer, Cham, 2018.

[45] Catherine J. Scott, Jieqing Jiao, Manuel Jorge Cardoso, and Andrew Melbourne. "Short acquisition time PET/MR pharmacokinetic modelling using CNNs." *International Conference on Medical Image Computing and Computer-Assisted Intervention.* Springer, Cham, 2018.

[46] Alvaro E. Ulloa Cerna, Marios Pattichis, *et al.* "Interpretable neural networks for predicting mortality risk using multi-modal electronic health records." *arXiv preprint arXiv:1901.08125* (2019).

[47] Anill Hazarika, Mausumi Barthakur, Lachit Dutta, and Manabendra Bhuyan. "F-SVD based algorithm for variability and stability measurement of biosignals, feature extraction and fusion for pattern recognition." *Biomedical Signal Processing and Control* 47 (2019): 26–40.

[48] Kocadagli, Ozan, and Reza Langari. "Classification of EEG signals for epileptic seizures using hybrid artificial neural networks based wavelet transforms and fuzzy relations." *Expert Systems with Applications* 88 (2017): 419–434.

[49] Zhang, Tao, Wanzhong Chen, and Mingyang Li. "Classification of inter-ictal and ictal EEGs using multi-basis MODWPT, dimensionality reduction algorithms and LS-SVM: A comparative study." *Biomedical Signal Processing and Control* 47 (2019): 240–251.

[50] Carlo Biffi, Ozan Oktay, Giacomo Tarroni, *et al.* "Learning interpretable anatomical features through deep generative models: Application to cardiac remodeling." *International Conference on Medical Image Computing and Computer-Assisted Intervention.* Springer, Cham, 2018.

[51] Jean Baptiste Lamy, Boomadevi Sekar Gilles Guezenne, Jacques Bouaud, and Brigitte Séroussi. "Explainable artificial intelligence for breast cancer: A visual case-based reasoning approach." *Artificial Intelligence in Medicine* 94 (2019): 42–53.

[52] Meske, Christian, and Enrico Bunde. "Using explainable artificial intelligence to increase trust in computer vision." *arXiv preprint arXiv:2002. 01543* (2020).

[53] G. Stiglic, M. Mertik, V. Podgorelec, and P. Kokol. "Using visual interpretation of small ensembles in microarray analysis." *19th IEEE Symposium on Computer-Based Medical Systems (CBMS'06)*. IEEE, 2006.

[54] Hyunkwang Lee, Sehyo Yune, Mohammad Mansouri, *et al.* "An explainable deep-learning algorithm for the detection of acute intracranial haemorrhage from small datasets." *Nature Biomedical Engineering* 3(3) (2019): 173.

[55] Bum Chul Kwon, Min-Je Choi, Joanne Taery, *et al.* "RetainVis: Visual analytics with interpretable and interactive recurrent neural networks on electronic medical records." *IEEE Transactions on Visualization and Computer Graphics* 25(1) (2018): 299–309.

Chapter 14

Machine learning in healthcare diagnosis

Sugumaran Muthukumarasamy[1], Ananth Kumar Tamilarasan[2], John Ayeelyan[3] and Adimoolam M.[4]

The emerging healthcare diagnosing system is the main core part of hospital management and widely used applications for diagnosing the human body, to find the disease in a mining manner by applying new technologies in image processing with machine learning (ML) intelligent system. In health diagnosing systems, the automatic processes are unimaginable, and it is reducing the time and complexity of tasks. For the automatic process of diagnosis systems, a vast number of techniques and methodologies are introduced and applied to perform the intended diagnosis tasks. ML is an inevitable tool in the medical diagnosis system, and it is the most important application of artificial intelligence (AI).

ML is an automatic self-learning system, and it has been improving from the experience of data explicitly programmed to deep analysis. The main aim of the ML system is that it allows the machine to automate the process to perform the task without any assistance. It includes human interactions in the analysis system. ML algorithms are categorized into two ways: supervised and unsupervised. The supervised learning is one in which the examples of the concern data predicts its future data, whereas the unsupervised learning is the process in which the data is trained and classified or labelled.

The medical diagnoses are carried out to predict excellent accuracy about disease identification and respecting part in the human biological system. The medical diagnosis applications are cancer cell identification, heartbeat analysis, disease identification system, nervous system diagnosis, ortho-care system, various analyses of disease identification, etc. The applications of such a diagnosis system are able to give the right solution for quick disease recovery. In the past, medical

[1]Department of Computer Science and Engineering, Pondicherry Engineering College, Puducherry, India
[2]Department of Electronics and Communication Engineering, IFET College of Engineering, Tamilnadu, India
[3]School of Computing Science and Engineering, Galgotias University, Greater Noida, India
[4]Department of Computer Science and Engineering, Saveetha University, Chennai, India

diagnoses are sampled with minimal identification due to inefficient technology and time limitation. However, nowadays, tremendous research has been proposed and carried out to give an accuracy of identification and fast recoveries in the health field.

The diagnoses of medical systems are widely applied for fast identification diseases, remedial, and risk-free treatment for indented diseases. It is also growing technology; even challenges and risks are more and more. ML algorithms are playing essential roles in medical diagnosis systems. Various researches are carrying out in the present scenario towards treating and producing more suitable in inevitable situations. In this chapter, the healthcare sector's diagnosing system is discussed, and the intended ML algorithm is identified and applied to make the diagnosis system more accurate and error-free using supervised and unsupervised ML algorithms.

14.1   Introduction

ML is used to make healthcare smarter. The subset of AI and the application of ML are enormous. It has provided endless applications in the healthcare industry. It uniquely provides to straight-line administration in healthcare. It performs the process, map, treat the diseases, and provide personalized treatments and care. Today by using ML, different types of diseases receive the predictions and diagnosing. The prediction and diagnosing diseases are cancer, breast cancer, blood pressure monitoring, heart disease analysis, prediction-based neurological diseases, etc. The different techniques are used to predict and analyse diseases. Some of the techniques are decision trees (DTs), k-means, k-nearest neighbour (k-NN), regression, random forest (RF) tree, etc. This chapter focused on the state of arts of ML in diagnosing the system: three diseases diagnosing system techniques such as heart, cancer, and neurological and finally challenges and conclusion.

14.1.1   *State of art of diagnosing system using machine learning*

AI is defined as the research of intelligent agents, and it acts intelligently as humans. Philosophical AI can be classified into a strong AI or a weak AI. Machines that act as smart are said to have weak AI, and intelligent machines can actually assume that they are said to have strong AI. In today's applications, most AI researchers are involved in using weak AI to perform specific tasks. ML techniques are often used to learn from the data and reach the weakest AI. ML incorporates scientific research of mathematical models and algorithms that can learn slowly from data and achieve desired performance in a specific task. Knowledge/rules/ findings based on ML-based data are expected to be relatively small. Therefore, ML is used for many tasks that require automation, especially in situations where people cannot configure a set of commands to perform the tasks they want. Depth of learning is a subset of ML that focuses on the provision of learning data by computational models containing multiple layers of processing. ML has categorized as follows: supervised learning, unsupervised learning, reinforcement learning semi-supervised learning, and active learning tasks. The supervised type learning maps the input data to target labels. This type of problem again classified into regression and classifications [1].

The goal of unsupervised learning is to find samples from a dataset that contains input data without target labels. Examples of unsupervised learning tasks include (1) identifying the underlying distribution of data, (2) finding natural clustering/clustering in data, and (3) reducing dimensionality. The commonly used algorithms for unsupervised learning are k-clustering, principal component analysis, hierarchical clustering, autoencoders, and parse windows for density estimation. Both semi-supervised learning and active learning deal with partially labelled conditions. With semi-supervised learning, the goals are similar to those of supervised learning. However, the methods in this category also use unlabelled data, and they attempt to improve the performance of supervised learning, using only labelled data. Active learning techniques are commonly used in situations where manual annotation of data is expensive. Active learning focuses on methods that best indicate which unlabelled data is next labelled so that way, the desired supervised learning task can be obtained with minimal labelling effort. Reinforcement practice involves how intelligent agents learn and perform actions to enhance the concept of reinforcement.

The researchers of the medical diagnosing system agree that AI and ML algorithms work well in the prediction and diagnosis of various diseases. The various patterns of diseases and techniques of prediction and diagnosed by AI and ML techniques [2] are given in Figure 14.1. Figure 14.1 describes different diseases and corresponding ML techniques for various diseases.

14.2 Heart diseases diagnosing system using machine learning

Ongoing advances in figuring and improvements in innovation have encouraged the standard assortment and capacity of clinical information that can be utilized to help clinical choices. In many nations, there is a first requirement for gathering and getting sorted outpatient information in digitized structures. At that point, the gathered information is to be broken down altogether for a clinical choice to be drawn, regardless of whether this includes conclusion, forecast, course of treatment, or sign and picture examination. The heart is a sort of solid limb where the body receives siphons blood and is the focal piece of the cardiovascular framework of the body that likewise encloses lungs. The framework of cardiovascular likewise involves a veins system, for instance, conduits, veins, and vessels. These veins convey blood everywhere throughout the body. Anomalies in ordinary bloodstream from the heart give data a few heart-related illnesses, which are usually called cardiovascular infections (CVDs).

The primary purpose of heart ailments is behind death around the world. World Health Organization reviews that 0.0186 billion all-out worldwide passings happen

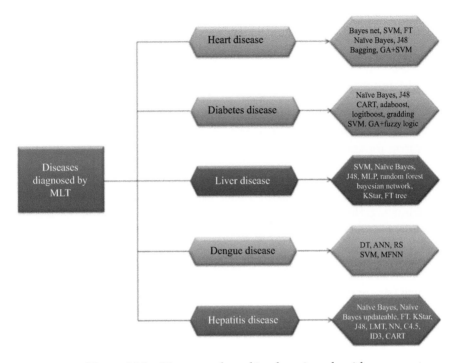

Figure 14.1   Disease and machine learning algorithm

on account of coronary failures and strokes. Over 75% of passings from CVDs happen for the most part in centre disburse and short wages homelands. As well, 85% of the passings that take place unpaid to CVDs are an effect of stroke and heart stabbing [3]. In this manner, the recognition of heart variations from the norm at the beginning period and instruments for the expectation of heart sicknesses can spare a great deal of living and assist specialists to structure a compelling treatment chart, which at last diminishes the death rate because of cardiovascular ailments. Because of the improvement of advance human services frameworks, heaps of patient information are these days accessible (e.g., Electronic Wellbeing Record System's Enormous Data) that could be utilized to structuring prescient cardiovascular illnesses mock-ups. Information mining or AI is a revelation strategy for investigating enormous information on or after a mixture of points of vision. Further, it is embodying it into valuable data. 'Information mining is a non-insignificant extraction of understood, already obscure, and possibly helpful data about information' [4]. These days, an immense measure of information relating to malady conclusion, patients, and so on are created by medicinal services ventures. Information mining gives various methods that find concealed examples or similitudes from the information. An AI calculation is proposed for the execution of a coronary illness expectation framework that is approved on two unlock the right to use coronary illness forecast datasets.

The significance and points of the utilization interest and ML-based forecasting framework and coronary illness discovery have been chattered about in a few research discoveries. The utilization of human-made consciousness in the infection identification framework, particularly the cardiovascular malady framework location, gets a better exhibition of other existing generally utilized models and introduced from American Heart Association and American College of Cardiology models in CVD identification and forecast [5]. The chance and recounted issues of contribution propelled types of the assistance of human well-being of the board framework were dissected in 2011 by Wang, Nakahira, and Zhao. The concept equally provided an examination guidance of clinical innovation on IoT [6]. Numerous kinds of well-being associated sensors and advances were investigated near them. They recognized a few issues which should be tackled. Chiuchisan and Geman in 2014 discussed the home observing framework, and the choice emotionally supportive network was plotted [7]. The framework added towards analysis, home checking, clinical solutions, clinical treatment, restoration, and advancement of Parkinson's illness with his patients. In the route of the most topical decade, the Remote Health Monitoring Framework has pulled in extensive consideration from the examination network and industry. Enhancement of a few ML calculations and classifier exhibitions similar to weighted cooperative classifiers were accounted for in the identification of heart variations from the norm [8].

Sensors' physiological information acquire by the planned framework utilized clinical groups. The multi-bouncing procedure had been executed to build the working degree, and a clinical entryway remote panel had been utilized in such a manner. The creator had singled out some clinical groups to decrease the interference flanked by the sensors and other active gadgets. Singh *et al.* [9] proposed structural equation modeling (SEM), and fuzzy cognitive map (FCM) planned a coronary illness forecast framework. The Canadian Community Health Survey 2012 dataset had been approved by SEM for the information. They utilized 20 noteworthy properties. SEM was utilized, which at that point anticipated a chance of cardiovascular sicknesses in the FCM representation to create the load structure. The connection between coronary collateral circulation (CCC) 121 alongside 20 properties for an SEM model is characterized. It is changeable, which characterizes whether the respondent has a coronary illness. Ghadge *et al.* [10] for large information examined an astute respiratory failure anticipation construction. Respiratory failure should be analysed opportune and viable in view of its put on pedestal normalness. A model of an astute cardiovascular failure expectation framework realized the fundamental target of this examination commentary, and it was that utilizes huge information and information withdrawal presenting methods. This framework could assemble obscured information concerning coronary illness from a guaranteed coronary illness database.

Numerous ongoing investigations address the issue of an early determination of coronary illness [11–13]. Here, we briefly talk about those who are legitimately identified with our work. Alizadehsani *et al.* [11] applied a few conventional AI techniques to a few of its occurrences and anticipated coronary artery disease (CAD). These creators introduced 87.23%, 84.35%, and 85.65% precision scores which were obtained with regards to in the early hours in the left anterior descending (LAD) acknowledgment vein, right coronary artery (RCA) supply route (right coronary conduit) instances of CAD, and left circumflex course, individually. In another investigation, Tayefi *et al.* [12] set forward another replica for anticipating CHD (coronary heart disease). Further, a CHD expectation mock-up utilizing choice trees was portrayed by Tayefi *et al.* Their model has given the usual CHD expectation precision of 96.7%. Another half and half ML reproduction to recognize CAD was proposed by Arabasadi *et al.* [34]. Moreover, the exhibition of the particle swarm optimization (PSO) calculation was contrasted with the C4.5 calculation. The usual PSO exactness technique was indicated by Alkeshuosh *et al.*, which outflanked the C4.5 calculation. It was approximately 88%. Babič *et al.* [14] tended to the issue of CAD recognition by applying unique AI strategies to three genuine CAD datasets. Abdar [15] applied four notable DT calculations and information. As indicated by the outcomes of that review, the C5.0 calculation gave the best precision of 85.33% among the contending strategies. A few basic rules were additionally produced by C5.0.

A hereditary calculation what is more, an artificial neural system was consolidated. The technique discussed that a generally decent presentation on the Z-Alizadeh Sani information with the precision, affectability and specificity scores equivalent to 94.68%, 96%, and 93%, individually by Arabasadi *et al.* Then again, Alkeshuosh *et al.* [16] created various guidelines for CAD location utilizing ML. For this reason, the creators are appropriated the notable PSO (molecule swarm advancement) transformative calculation.

The *k*-NN (*k*-closest neighbour) calculation [17] and preprocessing stride for identification was proposed. An artificial immune acknowledgment system in light of a fluffy asset designation instrument was afterward recommended to perceive patients' CAD. The best CAD forecast precision detailed by Polat *et al.* was 87%. These creators concentrated on the two after bearings: (1) guileless Bayes classifier, neural systems, and choice trees, a prescient CAD examination with support vector machine (SVM), and (2) a graphic computer-aided design examination utilizing affiliation and choice principles. The SVM was the finest entertainer among the strategies looked by Babič *et al.* and was demonstrated.

The best in class or all the more precisely state pattern strategies which appeared as of late are introduced to audit the different important, significant, and viable research commitments dependent on a few AI and fluffy rationale (FL)-based grouping strategies for coronary illness analysis. The current conventional obtrusive strategies used to analyse coronary illness depend on clinical times past of a patient just as relatives' genealogical history, corporeal assessment report which incorporates, however not constrained to these components just, far above the ground blood cholesterol, hypertension, corpulence, smoking, and clinical specialists appraisal for the side effects included. A large portion of these strategies causes mistaken conclusions in light of human intercession, messes up, and is regularly deferred in the analysis results. The human-arranged process likewise causes significant expense and is confounded as far as calculation and requires critical time for appraisal [17].

To defeat the impact of these conventional variables, a non-obtrusive clinical dynamic demonstrative framework dependent on prescient models of AI such as SVM, FL, *k*-NN, Naïve Bayes (NB), DTs, RF, logistic regression (LR), unpleasant sets, and a lot added has been created and utilized by academicians and scientists from industry and the scholarly world and is by and large normally utilized for the analysis of coronary illness. With the help of these master clinical dynamic emotionally supportive networks dependent on AI, the cardiovascular mortality proportion has been decreased [17].

In writing, the coronary illness finding through ML prescient models is generally utilized, and critical execution measurements have been accounted for over UCI heart malady Cleveland dataset.

14.2.1 Various methods for diagnosis of heart disease using ML

Numerous information mining apparatuses are given to actualize AI calculations. Some often utilized, free, and open-source apparatuses for simulations of heart disease are TANAGRA, RapidMiner, MATLAB®, Apache Mahout, WEKA, and so on. Some of the diagnosing methods are as follows.

14.2.1.1 Naïve Bayes classifier

NB is a staggeringly ground-breaking calculation for prescient demonstrating. It is the measurable classifier which expects no reliance between credits endeavouring to boost the back likelihood in deciding the class. Hypothetically, a categorizer has the base blunder velocity, yet not used case consistently. Mistakes are brought about by presumptions because of class contingent freedom and the absence of accessible probability information. This model is related through two probabilities that know how to be determined from the preparation dataset legitimately: (1) the contingent probability of each category with every x esteem. (2) Each category probability following equation shows the Naïve theorem, and the NB classifier depends on it:

$$P(A|B) = \frac{P(A) \times (P(B))}{P(B)}$$

Bayesian classifier ascertains contingent probability of an example having a place with each class, in light of the previous equation, and based on such restrictive likelihood information, the occurrence has delegated the class with the most noteworthy contingent likelihood.

14.2.1.2 Random forest

RF is famous, also nearly all ground-breaking AI calculations. It is one sort of AI calculation that is called bootstrap aggregation or bagging. To assess esteem from an information test, for example, mean, the bootstrap is an exceptionally ground-breaking factual approach. Here, bunches of tests of information are in use, the mean is determined, following that the entirety of the mean qualities is found of the mean value to give a superior expectation of the genuine mean worth. In packing, a similar technique is utilized; however, as opposed to evaluating the mean of each datum test, choice trees are commonly utilized. Here, various tests of the preparation information are thought of, and models are created for each datum test. While an expectation for any information is required, each model gives a forecast, and these expectations have arrived at the midpoint of showing signs of improvement estimation of the genuine yield esteem. Figure 14.2 illustrates the RF classifier for ML.

14.2.1.3 Simple logistic regression

LR could be a machine system taking in which it is in use on or after the pasture of insights. This technique is able to be utilized on behalf of parallel grouping, where esteems are recognized with two modules. Calculated relapse is like straight relapse, where the objective is to figure the estimations of the coefficients inside each information variable. In contrast to straight relapse, here, the forecast of the yield is built utilizing a non-direct capacity, which is called a strategic capacity. The calculated capacity changes any incentive inside the scope of 0–1. The forecasts made by strategic relapse are utilized as the likelihood of an information case worried to moreover category one or category 0. It could importantly be meant for issues anywhere, and an added method of reasoning meant for a forecast is required. Calculated relapse mechanisms well again at what time ascribes are random to yield uneven in addition to credits related to each other are expelled. Figure 14.3 shows the output of the simple LR classifier.

14.2.1.4 Artificial neural networks

Artificial neural systems additionally described are identified naturally propelled due to multilayer perceptron, and it is fit for displaying incredibly complex nondirect capacities. Artificial neural networks (ANNs) are solitary of the significant devices utilized in AI. Seeing that the given name 'neural' recommends, it is cerebrum arranged frameworks so as to be proposed towards copy the technique and

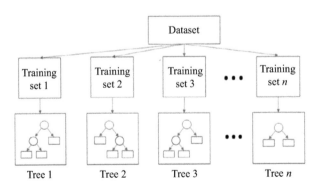

Figure 14.2   Random forest classifier

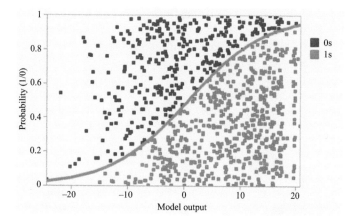

Figure 14.3 Simple logistic regression classifier

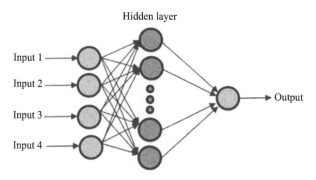

Figure 14.4 Artificial neural networks

people learn. Neural systems comprise three information layers, yield in addition to the layer of shrouded. By and large, a covered-up level includes components to change the contribution to an example to facilitate the yield layer controls. ANNs are incredible apparatuses to discover designs with the purpose of so mind-boggling otherwise uncertain en route used for an individual software engineer towards concentrating along with educating the machine what way perceive. Neural systems are being used because the 1950s as well as more than the most recent decades it encompasses turn into a significant piece of human-made consciousness because of the form of another system, which is designated 'back-propagation', that authorizes the organization to realize how in the direction of adjusting its shrouded neuron's layers in suitcases everywhere the results do not coordinate through the maker's desire. In Figure 14.4 the interconnection flanked by the layers become visible.

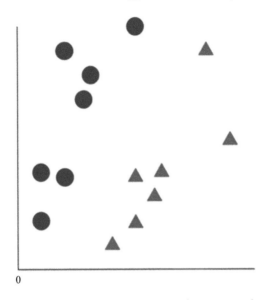

Figure 14.5   Support vector machine principles

14.2.1.5   Support vector machine

SVM has a process intended for inference together as the crow also flies, non-straight information. It applies a non-straight planning policy with the objective that it can change the grounding in sequence keen on a superior measurement. A hyperplane is a type of stripe which segregates the erratic info space in SVM. The hyperplane can isolate the focuses in the uneven information gap enclosing their group that is either '1' otherwise '0'. Within two measurements, one can picture a line and accepted that each input meeting point could be isolated by this line. The separation among the hyperplane furthermore neighbouring information organizes is described edge. The stripe that has the most prominent edge capable of recognizing the two categories that are identified as the ideal hyperplane. Those focuses are described as bolster vectors, and it characterizes or sustains the hyperplane. An advancement calculation that is used to ascertain the qualities for the parameters is expanded the edge. Figure 14.5 portrays the component change procedure.

14.2.1.6   Architecture flow for heart disease using ML

Figure 14.6 shows the steps to be followed to measure heart disease using an ML algorithm. Initially, the datasets are collected and checked for clinical criteria. The risk factor has to be checked related to dataset. It must undergo risk stratification to find the fine-tuned result augments and the dataset with labelling. It again is performing data partition along with a balanced distribution factor. The prepared data gain classified without and with random sampling. Then it undergoes risk progression evaluation. Moreover, finally, it can be used for testing and induction. The gained results have to evaluate performance.

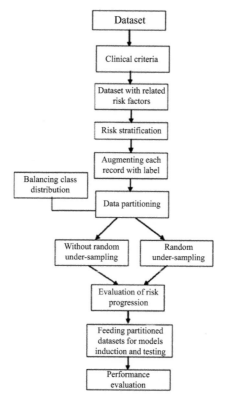

Figure 14.6   Linear steps to detect the heart disease using ML

14.3   Breast cancer diagnosing system using machine learning

The main application of AI and ML in the framework of medical and healthcare is image based and digital dragonizing. ML detects the pattern of the particular disease matching in an electronic heartcare pattern and conveys the contradictions to the physicians. In this situation, ML is the core, and AI is the second core, which estimates that particular diseases based on the information are gathered through a large set of datasets and millions of previous observations of caused diseases.

To illustrate this ML with the medical tool, examining and detecting breast cancer datasets are used. Here, for example, Wisconsin Data Set (Diagnostic) is used for predictions and dragonizing, which is available as an open source. The different examples are available for tumours in the dataset. The sample tumours are fixed as two parameters: all the tumours may be non-cancerous (benign) or cancerous (malignant). The properties of non-cancerous do not spread and grow locally. The properties of cancerous tissues are spread or penetrated to other tissues of the body. This is the two main properties of breast cancer; based on the pattern and properties, the tissues of the body can be scanned digitally and originated.

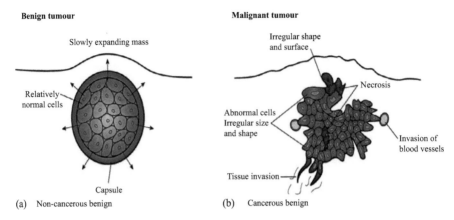

Figure 14.7   Benign and malignant data representations from sample

Figure 14.7 shows the datasets of cancerous (Benign) and non-cancerous (malignant) identifications.

Normally the cancer representations using ML having various steps as follows:

Step 1: classifying the dataset
Step 2: defining a set of metrics
Step 3: evaluating the prediction and diagnosing models
Step 4: creating an ML model
Step 5: evaluating the targeted output
Step 6: evaluating output quality through various parameters
Step 7: visualizing the decision boundaries

The first step is the classification of datasets with different functionalities, such as error removal from the datasets, training the datasets, testing the datasets, and choosing the valid datasets. Usually, 70% of datasets are used for training, and 30% of datasets are used for testing. The second step sets the various parameters for verifications. The verification parameters are false-positive and negative, true positive and negative, accuracy, precision, recall, etc. The third step is evaluating the model using the various parameters mentioned in step 2. For example, the score calculation using precision (P) and recall (R) is as follows:

$$\text{Score} = \frac{2 \times (R \times P)}{(R + P)}$$

The fourth step has tuned the model using ML techniques. The models produce different results based on the tuning. Some of the models are neural network model (NNM) and deep NNM, etc. The fifth step evaluating the targeted output is to fix the target output, which is based on the target values. For example, if the target output is 98% based on the targets, they tune the evaluating models or train them. The sixth step is to evaluate the fixed or targeted output, which is matched with the predefined curve. Finally the predicted data is visualized with the help of various representations. The various ML techniques for breast cancer predictions are described in the following.

14.3.1 k-*NN method for breast cancer prediction*

k-NN is the best example of the classification and categorization of data. The *k*-NN method is qualitative or quantitative and used to group certain data based on some specific points. The way of decision making is based on certain boundaries or classifications. In this method, *k* is the operator trying to find more data related to the operator. In AI and ML, the *k*-NN is used to push the relevant data based on the *k*-operator. Based on the operator, different neighbours and different relations are traced in individual datasets. The *k*-NN is not enough to find the exact data from the datasets. For example, regression and decision values tracing this *k*-NN are not reliable because more possible predictions are available in certain boundaries.

Similarly, in the guided and unguided learning, different methods are used to predict the data. The *k*-NN is precisely used in guided or supervised learning environments. The guided environments having certain parameters and predefined neighbours that match the datasets, based on those classifications, are performed. The classifications are performed based on the matching successive rate, and data is predicted from the datasets. From the experimental point of view, different approaches are used in a different way to predict or classify the data. Using *k*-operator, different suggestions are performed.

The *k*-NN is used in different situations and real-time classifications. Commonly, this method is used in understanding the natural process and behaviour of untraceable situations. Notably, in this section, *k*-NN is applied in the breast cancer disease environment. The breast cancer environment is considered unpredictable environments. The entire body and its parts have complicated structures. The whole-body part does not behave explicit or rational. This *k*-NN algorithm helps one to predict similar and non-similar data from the non-relational environments. Initially, the scanning process of the body or prediction is based on the assumptions of specific points. Based on the assumption points, the entire part of the scanning is categorized. If any unwanted prediction is performed, based on the prediction remaining whole part is mapped. The Wisconsin Data Set two parameters are categorized, such as cancerous (benign) and non-cancerous (malignant). Based on the two parameters, entire datasets are classified or grouped with the help of *k*-NN. The diagrammatic representations of the *k*-NN method [18] are shown in Figure 14.8, where blue represents sample test data, pink represents benign data, and green represents malignant data.

Some of the other methods for breast cancer predictions are DTs, neural networks, digital mammography, and Bayesian classifier. In neural networks, the structures contain different layers such as input, subtle, and output layer. The input layer represents the elements of a dataset, whereas the output layer contains the one that confuses the human. The weight between layers is changed using training data for breast cancer dataset using a back-propagation learning and following neural network learning method.

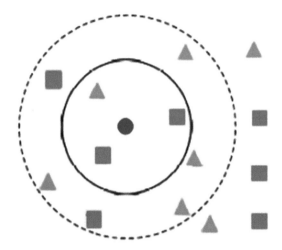

Figure 14.8   k-NN representation for breast cancer prediction

14.4   Neurological diseases diagnosing system using machine learning

Among neurological diseases, ML approach based diagnosing system provides multiple ways to relate the behaviour of an individual with their brain activation patterns. Nowadays, ML is applied to neuroimaging technologies progressively. The modernized ML techniques deal with some of the related specific samples with proper sizes, some appropriate sizes of features of the images, the predictor sizes effect, embedding selection of features, and bootstrap aggregation. Most of the ML algorithms are designed to process only the multicollinearity and low signal to noise. The common diseases in the nervous system, like peripheral and cranial nerves, spinal cord, and the brain cells, are named neurological disorders.

The problem may include epilepsy, dementia and vascular diseases, and Alzheimer's diseases (AD) that may include migraine, strokes, headaches-related disorders, Parkinson's diseases, brain diseases, brain cancers, and nerve-related disorders caused because of malnutrition. Neurodegenerative disorders become a severe problem of all well-settled countries. Early diagnosis confirms a respectable eminence of life for patients. The computer-aided-diagnosis tools might be adopted for significant support to the doctors [19]. At present, the identified neurologic diseases are 600 in numbers. Maximum of the diseases are categorized into a type related to the fault in the genes like Huntington's diseases, nervous system glitches (spina bifida), degenerative nerve disorder (AD and Parkinson's disease), injuries affected with the spinal cord as well as brain, tumours, central nervous system (CNS) infections (meningitis), neurocutaneous syndrome, stroke, and seizure disorders (epilepsy) [20]. In order to analyse the conditions through convolutional neural networks (CNNs), recurrent neural networks (RNNs), and

ANNs, machine training techniques are employed. These are the major neurological diseases that occurred in the human brain and spinal cord.

The ML methods mentioned just before might play a progressively critical part in the neurological investigation, attempting complications surrounded by numerous subdomains. To start with, radiological image order and division have been a conventional locus of deep learning improvement endeavours. Image grouping and division assignments are interestingly fit deep learning because of the high-dimensional nature of neuroimaging information, which is troublesome to manual examination, joined with the normally computerized nature of most current imaging. Besides, AI has been applied to functional mind mapping and correlational examinations utilizing functional magnetic resonance imaging (MRI) information for assignments, for example, the expectation of postoperative seizure. Finally, demonstrative anticipation with deep learning, the hang of utilizing different information types, including lab esteems, pictures, notes, among others, has been utilized to dole out malady hazards. The ML-based approaches adopted towards these tasks are discussed here.

For the diagnosis of epilepsy, Wang *et al.* [21] used symlet wavelet processing and grid search optimizer for detecting the features. A gradient boosting machine classifier is used, which leads to 96.5% accuracy. In 2018, Monteiro *et al.* [22] introduced a novel hybrid GA-BFOCM algorithm for classification with regularized LR with a secured accuracy of 92.6%. Rabeh *et al.* [23] utilized normalized least mean squares filter methodology and Bayes probability classifier, which resulted in 92% accuracy. Ullah *et al.* [24] found the diseases by using the CNN feature extraction method and SVM classifier with an accuracy of 80.25%. Cheng and Liu [25] introduced a 3D-CNN feature extraction method alone to classify neurological diseases. After this decade, the SoftMax classifier plays a major role in disease detection. IT works along with the deep convolutional neural network (D-CNN) technique, CNN-RNN technique, and cascaded CNN techniques, which resulted in 93%, 91.2%, and 93.26%, respectively [26–28]. For the treatment of Alzheimer's, the isolated wavelet transition is used with various methods to minimize dimensionality, primarily for the detection of different forms of Parkinson's disease.

14.4.1   Detecting the neurodegenerative diseases and the traumatic brain related injuries using D-CNN

The diagnosis, along with the evaluation of degenerative neuron diseases and TBIs (traumatic brain injuries), is facing vulnerable difficulties. All the problems create some functional deflects because of focal axonal swellings (FAS). As the ability is limited due to accessing of damaged neurons, the abovementioned problem is challenging to provide a prediction mechanism. This effect might be simulated using a model of discernment called CNNs [29,30]. We use biophysically important measurable information going on FAS for harming the associations in CNN's happening in a practically significant method. The vitality imperatives are consolidated on the mind employing trimming the CNNs on the way to be less overbuilt. Subjectively, it is exhibited that the harm prompts human-like slip-ups [31]. The investigations additionally give quantifiable evaluations by what means precision might get influenced through different sorts and heights of harm. The shortage coming about because of a fixed measure of harm extraordinarily relies upon which associations are haphazardly harmed, giving instinct to why it is hard to foresee weaknesses. There is an enormous level of subjectivity in deciphering psychological shortages from complex frameworks, such as the human cerebrum. Notwithstanding, we give significant knowledge and a quantitative structure for scatters in which FAS is embroiled [32].

The FAS damage is developed into three various CNNs by using a tensor flow framework. Every network might have its properties, and hence they were trained by using various kinds of datasets for each task. Initially, the classification of digits is done by considering the dataset, which is already trained, i.e., Modified National Institute of Standards and Technology (MNIST) dataset [31]. This network is trained for classifying the images, which consists of black images along with white images series with the pixel range (28×28). The tensor flow frameworks [32] are used for training the CNN. For our testing purpose, some of the subset's images can be taken. The accuracy of 98.74% is obtained.

In this, the input image considered is 'a handwritten 2'. This is fed as input to the MNIST network. Already for each valued image, some values are assigned as scores: for 2 it is 0.9998 and for 1 (0.000013); hence for our input, the value is easily identified as 2. Then the network gets damaged into some 50 separate classes. The damaged set of neurons will be identified by setting $p=0.01$, which will be overlapped with the targeted neurons in $p=0.02$ case. It is notified that about 12% of damage to the network provides the result to be less confident. The network will deliver a mistaken output by considering the value as 1, and this will cause 30% damage. Another set of damage may occur by arising the classes to the confused state between 1 and 2 (Figure 14.9). The classification of the object is identified in the network 2, where the image of bell peppers is taken as input to the network. This also assigns a certain value as a score to the images. This will create damage to it and the damage increases ($p=0$, 0.02 to 0.3). Here also, the damage arises to 12%. The total images trained for this network is about 1.2 million image sets.

The changes in each class of the damaged networks are shown in Figure 14.9. The CNN acknowledges a picture of a hand-written symbol as info and yields scores for every conceivable digit, 0–9. In these two graphs, the first system effectively and unhesitatingly orders the digit. If the harm level is incremented, then the certainty drops to a particular level, and the classes in the long run become confounded. For significant stages of harm, all modules might have comparative scores.

Here the effects due to the network damage are observed for the cataloguing of specific images. At that time, the number of mistakes is analysed statistically. By considering certain variations in the network settings, FAS models the phenomena like ageing and neurogenerative disorders.

For simulating the belongings of TBI based on CNN, the convolutional and completely connected layers are used for the determination of those values. Only

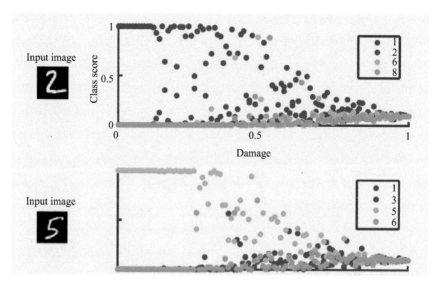

Figure 14.9   CNN method for prediction

the injuries due to the blockage are being found. The acquaintances among the neurons, along with the biased weights, were targeted. Normally CNNs are not used for a number of connections and hence by damaging the biased weights may not damage the connections. The human brain might have provided with a compromise stuck between the neural acquaintances and the adeptness. CNN will not be attacked by the overfitting problem. Hence, the scarification of CNN is thus helped in suppressing the overfitting problem. The sparsification is a method of information processing in the brain with some necessary constraints. CNN is sparsified initially, and the point of trade-off is fixed, which will filter the weak point, i.e., 69.4% of the links. This will reduce the accuracy form at 98.74%–91.47%.

Surveying levels of intellectual deficiencies in patients is, to a great extent, an abstract undertaking, with markers, for example, regardless of whether the patient and those near them have seen troubles with memory. There are a few devices accessible, together with the mini-mental state examination. This might dole out a groove subsequent to challenging execution on a concise arrangement of assignments, for example, recognizing items and adhering to composed directions. The obtained score might have been utilized for quantitatively follow the vicissitudes in an individual's subjective capacity. Additionally, in this chapter, we compute the adjustment in precision on related undertakings, for example, perusing manually written statistics and marking substances. The broad direct examinations by means of several degrees of damage, while accepting that by recreating FAS scheduled to our exemplary of perception, might lead towards consciousness addicted to the multifaceted procedures underlying neurodegeneration and TBI. In the entirety of the past trials, we mimicked TBI by suddenly applying axonal wounds. Here we rather re-enact maturing and its neurodegenerative impacts by step-by-step

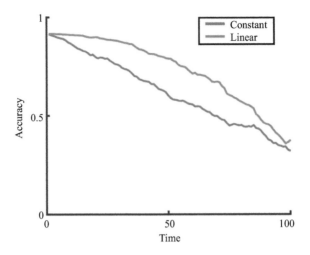

Figure 14.10   Aggregation harm

gathering arbitrary harm. We keep on utilizing the sparsified arrange and the heterogeneous FAS dispersion. Figure 14.10 shows that when harm is continuously introduced, it aggregates harm after some time. Axons trauma is acquired for some time, rather than a one-time attack, through maturing or neurodegenerative infection. We attribute the consistency of certain associations that have sustained harm per time to the fact that the amount of associations affected decreases over time. At the point when harm increments after some time, the underlying misfortune in exactness is moderate and the later misfortune is quicker.

Using the previous method, the analysis can be done effectively by understanding the evolution of CNN in the analysis of disorders like Parkinson's, TBI, linking damage, AD, and other diseases that create changes in cognitive behaviour.

14.4.2   Diagnosis using 3D-CNN

There are several techniques available for AD detection from the inputs obtained from the MRI images. The deep learning background is applicable for building the content-based image retrieval for aiding the AD. The 3D capsule network method is used along with CNN. It has a 3D autoencoder that is already trained that shows the performance of prediction to be better in its performance when compared to deep learning-based CNN. The 3D capsule networks are proficient for faster learning. It can handle a very tiny dataset and sharp images effectively. This method produces an accuracy of about 98.42% in the classification of AD.

The autoencoder is used to learn the unsupervised data, and it is capable of extracting some of the details from the images. This can be done by extracting the image parts from the tiny image datasets. The architecture is given in Figure 14.11.

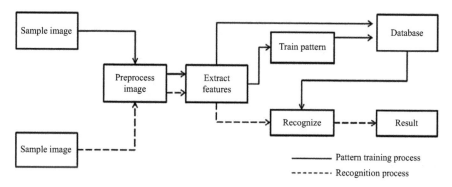

Figure 14.11 Architecture for Alzheimer's disease classification

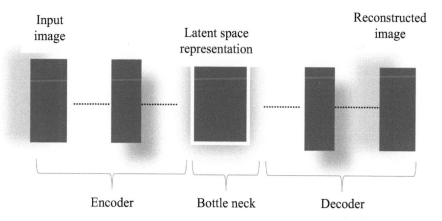

Figure 14.12 Autoencoder structure

14.4.3 Training of 3D sparse autoencoder and 3D-CNN

The 3D autoencoder shown in Figure 14.12 is trained by using 300 images, in which the datasets are obtained from the 3D MRI images for training. These can be mined to obtain more than 1,000 paths. The next level is training the 3D-CNN. Here, one pooling layer and a couple of successive layers are used, and one Softmax layer is used along with this. The retrieval process might be accompanied by brain MRIs, which are then used to operate the CNNs. It requires datasets that might include some spatial rotations, and the transformations might get improved because of their comprehensible simplifications. CNNs have been most appropriate for layer-pixel pooling method of picture advances, getting to information as numerous clusters.

This hand-off information data got as a contribution from layer to layer, otherwise called directing. Regardless, CNNs, for the most part, require a genuinely massive number of datasets to process for preparing; however, they cannot deal with the info information changes appropriately and disregard essential subtleties now and again. CapsNet requires less dataset for preparing when contrasted with CNNs. The CapsNet forms a clinical MRI picture dataset and handles all the more productively with strong dynamic directing, which are identified with explicit characters (size, area, direction, and so forth) and turns, concerning clinical subtleties [33].

The examination utilized 3D-CapsNet and saw it as an increasingly strong (94.06%) exactness for AD recognition over CNNs, and different structures talked about in this chapter. The proposed design is valid for 100 ages and registered the outcomes, and it was seen that in the underlying stages, the preparation was quicker and the absolute variable misfortune relied upon the CapsNet misfortune. Furthermore, the CapsNet paradigm will allow clinical research staff to produce reliable and successful outcomes in an incredible way. Additionally, CapsNet is fit for taking care of enormous datasets with low preparing turns and small example sizes, which is the explanation behind its prosperity [30].

14.5 Challenges and future direction of medical diagnosing system

The medical diagnosing system has different challenges and different works to consider future research in disease prediction and diagnosing. Some of the challenges and future direction of medical diagnosing systems are as follows:

- The developer improves the training model based on identifying the diagnosis system's future issues such as fractures and tumours.
- They develop a model for future prediction of disease status and the spreading of disease, also challenging tasks in the diagnosing system, for example, the type of cancer and spreading areas having till difficult to analyse.
- The data collection, sharing, and processing are having different difficulties from scanning to screening the entire process.
- The matching of symptoms with biomedical are having still open research areas for the suggestion, recommendation for medicine.
- The quality data collection and assessment are checking until having a lot of difficulties in diagnosing the system.
- The development of different segmentation tools for diagnosing and affected areas of prediction.
- Foreground and background extraction tools for inner and outer segmentation of diagnosing parts of the body.
- Develop new classification algorithms, and data mining approaches for predictions and diagnosing various diseases.
- Develop a better interaction between humans and algorithms for diagnosing systems.

14.6 Conclusion

The AI and ML techniques are used to automatically increase the predicting rate and accuracy using prior experience. Various AI and ML algorithms are used to predict and classify the data. Basic ML algorithms are *k*-NN, deep neural network, DT, CNN, and 3D-NN. These ML algorithms are applied to the different medical diagnosing system. Some of the medical diagnosing systems are breast cancer predictions, heart diagnosing system, and neurological diagnosing system, etc. This chapter presents the state of arts of the medical diagnosis system and three primary medical diagnoses, such as the heart, the diagnosis of the system, breast cancer diagnosis system, and neurological diagnosis system. First, heart diagnosing system with various ML algorithms such as DT, Bayesians classifier, and procedure for prediction of heart disease predictions are mentioned. Second, the breast cancer diagnosing system prediction and diagnosing using *k*-NN with various steps of prediction and diagnosing procedures are mentioned. Third, neurological medical diagnosing system using D-CNN, 3D-CNN, and encoder methods are presented in this chapter. Finally, various challenges and future direction of the medical diagnosing system are presented in this chapter.

References

[1] Bishop, C.M. Pattern Recognition and Machine Learning. Berlin, Heidelberg: Springer-Verlag; 2006. ISBN: 0387310738.

[2] Fatima, M. and Pasha, M. (2017). Survey of Machine Learning Algorithms for Disease Diagnostic. Journal of Intelligent Learning Systems and Applications, 9, 1–16.

[3] Hazra, A., Mandal, S., Gupta, A. and Mukherjee, A. (2017). Heart Disease Diagnosis and Prediction Using Machine Learning and Data Mining Techniques: A Review. Advances in Computational Sciences and Technology, 10, 2137–2159.

[4] Patel, J., Upadhyay, P. and Patel, D. (2016). Heart Disease Prediction Using Machine learning and Data Mining Technique. Journals of Computer Science & Electronics, 7, 129–137.

[5] Weng, S.F., Reps, J., Kai, J., Garibaldi, J.M. and Qureshi, N. (2017). Can Machine-Learning Improve Cardiovascular Risk Prediction Using Routine Clinical Data? PLoS One, 12, e0174944. https://doi.org/10.1371/journal.pone.0174944.

[6] Zhao, W., Wang, C. and Nakahira, Y. (2011). Medical Application on Internet of Things. In: IET International Conference on Communication Technology and Application (ICCTA 2011), Beijing, 14–16 October 2011, pp. 660–665.

[7] Chiuchisan, I. and Geman, O. (2014). An Approach of a Decision Support and Home Monitoring System for Patients With Neurological Disorders Using Internet of Things Concepts. WSEAS Transactions on Systems, 13, 460–469.

[8] Soni, J., Ansari, U. and Sharma, D. (2011). Intelligent and Effective Heart Disease Prediction System Using Weighted Associative Classifiers. International Journal on Computer Science and Engineering (IJCSE), 3, 2385–2392.

[9]   Singh, M., Martins, L.M., Joanis, P. and Mago, V.K. (2016). Building a Cardiovascular Disease Predictive Model Using Structural Equation Model and Fuzzy Cognitive Map. In: IEEE International Conference on Fuzzy Systems (FUZZ), Vancouver, 24–29 July 2016, pp. 1377–1382. https://doi.org/10.1109/FUZZ-IEEE.2016.7737850.

[10]   Ghadge, P., Girme, V., Kokane, K. and Deshmukh, P. (2016). Intelligent Heart Attack Prediction System Using Big Data. International Journal of Recent Research in Mathematics Computer Science and Information Technology, 2, 73–77.

[11]   Alizadehsani, R., Zangooei, M.H., Hosseini, M.J., *et al.* (2016). Coronary Artery Disease Detection Using Computational Intelligence Methods. Knowledge-Based Systems, 109, 187–197.

[12]   Tayefi, M., Tajfard, M., Saffar, S., *et al.* (2017). hs-CRP is Strongly Associated With Coronary Heart Disease (CHD): A Data Mining Approach Using Decision Tree Algorithm. Computer Methods and Programs in Biomedicine, 141, 105–109.

[13]   Mahmoodabadi, Z. and Tabrizi, S.S. A New ICA-Based Algorithm for Diagnosis of Coronary Artery Disease. In: Intelligent Computing, Communication and Devices. New Delhi, India: Springer; 2015. pp. 415–427.

[14]   Babič, F., Olejár, J., Vantová, Z. and Paralič, J. (2017). Predictive and Descriptive Analysis for Heart Disease Diagnosis. In: Proc. Federated Conf. Comput. Sci. Inf. Syst. (FedCSIS), Prague, Czech Republic, September 2017, pp. 155–163.

[15]   Abdar, M. (2015). Using Decision Trees in Data Mining for Predicting Factors Influencing of Heart Disease. Carpathian Journal of Electronic and Computer Engineering, 8(2), 31–36.

[16]   Alkeshuosh, A.H., Moghadam, M.Z., Al Mansoori, I. and Abdar, M. (2017). Using PSO Algorithm for Producing Best Rules in Diagnosis of Heart Disease. In: Proc. Int. Conf. Comput. Appl. (ICCA), Dubai, United Arab Emirates, September 2017, pp. 306–311.

[17]   Polat, K., Özşen, S. and Güneş, S. (2007). Automatic Detection of Heart Disease Using an Artificial Immune Recognition System (AIRS) With Fuzzy Resource Allocation Mechanism and *k*-NN (Nearest Neighbour) Based Weighting Preprocessing. Expert Systems with Applications, 32(2), 625–631.

[18]   Yue, W., Wang, Z., Chen, H., *et al.* (2018). Machine Learning With Applications in Breast Cancer Diagnosis and Prognosis. Designs, 2, 13..

[19]   Liu, M., Cheng, D., Wang, K. and Wang, Y. (2018). Alzheimer's Disease Neuroimaging Initiative. Multi-Modality Cascaded Convolutional Neural Networks for AD Diagnosis. Neuroinformatics, 16(3–4), 295–308.

[20]   Tagaris, A., Kollias, D., Stafylopatis, A., Tagaris, G. and Kollias, S. (2018). Machine Learning for Neurodegenerative Disorder Diagnosis—Survey of Practices and Launch of Benchmark Dataset. International Journal on Artificial Intelligence Tools, 27(03), 1850011.

[21] Wang, X., Gong, G. and Li, N. (2019). Automated Recognition of Epileptic EEG States Using a Combination of Symlet Wavelet Processing, Gradient Boosting Machine, and Grid Search Optimizer. Sensors, 19(2), 219.

[22] Monteiro, M., Fonseca, A.C., Freitas, A.T., *et al.* (2018). Using Machine Learning to Improve the Prediction of Functional Outcome in Ischemic Stroke Patients. IEEE/ACM Transactions on Computational Biology and Bioinformatics, 15(6), 1953–1959.

[23] Rabeh, A.B., Benzarti, F. and Amiri, H. (2017). New Method of Classification to Detect Alzheimer Disease. In: 14th International Conference on Computer Graphics, Imaging and Visualization. Marrakesh, Morocco: IEEE; pp. 111–116.

[24] Ullah, H.M., Onik, Z., Islam, R. and Nandi, D. (2018). Alzheimer's Disease and Dementia Detection from 3D Brain MRI Data Using Deep Convolutional Neural Networks. In: 3rd International Conference for Convergence in Technology (I2CT). Pune, India: IEEE; 2018, pp. 1–3.

[25] Cheng, D. and Liu, M. Classification of AD by Cascaded Convolutional Neural Networks Using PET Images. Wang, Q, *et al.* (eds.). MLMI 2017. LNCS, vol. 10541. Cham: Springer International Publishing AG; 2017. pp. 106–113.

[26] Islam, J. and Zhang, Y. (2018). Brain MRI Analysis for Alzheimer's Disease Diagnosis Using an Ensemble System of Deep Convolutional Neural Networks. Brain Informatics, 5(2), 2.

[27] Liu, M., Cheng, D. and Yan, W. (2018). Alzheimer's Disease Neuroimaging Initiative. Classification of Alzheimer's Disease by Combination of Convolutional and Recurrent Neural Networks Using FDG-PET Images. Frontiers in Neuroinformatics, 12, 35.

[28] https://medlineplus.gov/neurologicdiseases.html (accessed on 25th September 2020).

[29] Lusch, B., Weholt, J., Maia, P. D. and Kutz, J. N. (2018). Modeling Cognitive Deficits Following Neurodegenerative Diseases and Traumatic Brain Injuries With Deep Convolutional Neural Networks. Brain and Cognition, 123, 154–164.

[30] Sabour, S., Frosst , N. and Hinton , G.E. (2017). Dynamic Routing Between Capsules. In: Advances in Neural Information Processing Systems. UK: MIT press, pp. 3856–3866.

[31] Abadi, M., Agarwal, A., Barham, P. (2016). TensorFlow: Large-Scale Machine Learning on Heterogeneous Distributed Systems. arXiv preprint arXiv:1603.04467.

[32] Deng, L. (2012). The MNIST Database of Handwritten Digit Images for Machine Learning Research [Best of the Web]. IEEE Signal Processing Magazine, 29(6), 141–142.

[33] Kruthika, K.R., Maheshappa, H.D. and Alzheimer's Disease Neuroimaging Initiative (2019). CBIR System Using Capsule Networks and 3D CNN

for Alzheimer's Disease Diagnosis. Informatics in Medicine Unlocked, 14, 59–68.

[34]   Arabasadi, Z., Alizadehsani, R., Roshanzamir, M., Moosaei, H. and Yarifard, A.A. (2017). Computer Aided Decision Making for Heart Disease Detection Using Hybrid Neural Network-Genetic Algorithm. Computer Methods and Programs in Biomedicine, 141, 19–26.

Chapter 15

Python for healthcare analytics made simple

Sumathi Doraikannan[1] and Prabha Selvaraj[1]

Machine learning (ML) is found to be an element of healthcare industries for the past two decades after it was initially implemented for monitoring the antibiotic doses for patients who suffer from various infections. Nowadays, the volume of electronic healthcare records (EHR) gets increased, and thus, it leads to the huge massive of genetic sequential data which in turn directs the healthcare's importance in ML. A brief discussion about the common data sources in healthcare would be explained in detail. From various inferences, it is found that Python is a go-to language for developers, and it is extensively used in several fields. This chapter gives a brief description of the characteristics of data and the significance of the data quality in healthcare. Data has to be extracted from various sources for better analysis. Hence, the chapter puts forth an overview of challenges that must be resolved, and various types of extraction tools would be discussed. To describe the perceptions that are obtained through the analysis of the large data sets, data visualization is immensely used. In this world of healthcare, data analytics is huge, and it could include an extensive variety of organizations and other uses cases such as emergency rooms (ER), intensive care units, hospitals, and medical equipment manufacturers. The function of data visualization in the data science process flow could be discussed in detail in addition to the several techniques used to denote the complex data. It also covers advanced visualization techniques that emphasize grid, wordcloud, heatmap, and geospatial. Data analytics is a buzzword that refers to the diversified types of analysis. Perception is required since more information is required by the users for an extensive analysis. Certain techniques for the management of the data and analysis need more efforts and continuous attention particularly for data aggregation, data capture, real-time data streaming, analytics, and other visualization solutions, so that the integration could be done further for the improved utilization of electronic medical record (EMR) with the healthcare. Finally, this chapter briefs about the challenges that could be identified with the vast amount of data composed as EMR.

[1]School of Computer Science and Engineering, VIT-AP University, Amaravati, India

15.1 Introduction

The rapid increase in the population seems to be perplexing due to the huge volume of information about the patients. Data collection differs due to the application of standards and technologies that range from laboratories to pharmacies. The automatic process of data could be done with the help of various ML techniques. Implementation of ML carries a great development in medical science, and the complex medical data could be analysed. Huge progress in healthcare recently arises due to the retort towards the digitization of the healthcare information which forms as the motivating factor for the industries to implement the data analytics to derive the business decisions. The initiation for the healthcare information is the term 'Data' and how it is collected and maintained. The primary sources of health information are the clinical and demographical data stored in the patient's medical record. It provides a great value to the field of medical science and healthcare management by maintaining its accuracy, reliability, and accessibility based on the need.

15.1.1 Data

Data is distinguished as primary and secondary data [1]. Data collected by the staff working at the hospital and clinic are documented for further reference. Daily ward census reports that are recorded in the hospitals are considered as the primary data. Data sets that are derived from the primary data are known as secondary data. Summarization of the healthcare data that is found in the report is treated as the secondary data. Normally, the secondary data includes healthcare statistics, archives of diseases, master patient's index, disease, and technique indexes. Data thus collected has to be organized so that information could be generated. Data quality must be ensured based on the two key factors, namely, data validity and data accuracy. Effective communication is possible only when the data is valid, and it must adapt to the expected range of values. The efficacy of healthcare services could be enhanced by obtaining accurate information about the resources that are delivered entirely in all levels of healthcare. The data must be in an organized manner to make the interpretation process rapidly. Data gets transformed into the information after it is organized. It is observed from [2] that a data is significant element in the program planning and evaluation. The data quality must be ensured based on the two predominant factors, namely, data validity and data accuracy. The communication process is made efficient by assuring the validity of the data and data accuracy. Once data is collected, it has to be processed efficiently. Various research works have been done to resolve the issues that arise during the manipulation of the data, a transformation of data into information by creating it as an easy identification for the users. The data analysis process could be depicted as shown in Figure 15.1.

15.1.2 Importance of data quality in healthcare

The most significant and foremost step in ML is to achieve good-quality data. The need for accurate and reliable healthcare data is to

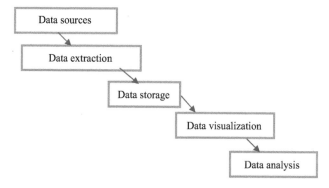

Figure 15.1   Data analysis flow

- serve the research in clinical and health services and outcomes of the health-care interference;
- provide accurate and trustworthy information regarding the treated diseases and medical actions that are carried out in the hospital and the community, as well as vaccination and screening programmes which include the details such as number and type of the members;
- identify the enduring and impending maintenance of the patient's health under all situations;
- plan healthcare services.

To retain the quality of the data, data must possess certain attributes as per the suggestions given by [1]

- precise and comprehensive,
- economical,
- applicable,
- organized manner,
- accessible to users whenever needed,
- readability,
- confidentiality and security.

15.1.3   Elements of data quality

Elements of the data quality and examples have been described in Table 15.1.

Resource management is done by delivering the required information which is accurate and needed under any situation. Maintenance of healthcare optimally, continuing healthcare, exploring the area of health service, organization, and administration of health systems are the few activities that are carried out.

15.1.4   Ensuring data and information quality

When the qualities of data are confirmed to a recognized standard, then data is considered as high quality. As of now, there are no standards in existence today.

Table 15.1   Elements of the data quality

S. No.	Elements	Examples
1	Reliability after the process of data collection, processing, storing, and information display, data must be consistent	The patient's name and age that have been recorded must be the same on all recorded pages
2	Completeness	Medical records must possess all relevant documents through comprehensive and suitable documentation
3	Accessibility needed data must be available for patient care	Clinical information must be accessible when required
4	Accuracy and validity	Codes mentioned for the representation of diseases must be confirmed with existing standards The patient's details such as address and identification must be documented clearly

The data quality standards have to be published by the healthcare organizations since the data must be used for further analysis. It is observed that there are two data quality standards, namely, the Medical Records Institute (MRI) which publishes a group of significant ethics of healthcare documentation and the American Health Information Management Association (AHIMA) which publishes data quality managing tool.

MRI principles of healthcare documentation:

Qualities of data must be

- Constant
- Complete
- Reliable
- Appropriate
- Interoperability
- Availability

AHIMA data quality model:

The AHIMA data quality model has been depicted in Figure 15.2.

Application: It identifies the tenacity for which the data is collected.

Analysis: Data has to be analysed and transformed into information.

Warehousing: A storehouse that stores data.

Collection: Accumulation of the data must be done.

15.2   Data extraction

It is defined as a method of retrieving the essential information from various sources. The way of extracting the data relies on the nature of the data. When structured data has to be

Figure 15.2   Data quality characteristics

extracted, then the process is done in the source system. It could be performed with the help of full extraction and incremental extraction. The extraction of unstructured data needs more focus on data preparation in such a way that data could be extracted. Moreover, the data needs to be cleaned and preprocessed for further analysis.

In the field of healthcare, the significant information which is required for determining the predictions and suggestions precisely is found to be present in the form of an unstructured manner. One needs significant data for making out proper decisions in healthcare. Therefore, data extraction is considered to be the most important task for extracting vital data for further analysis. Usually, documents such as reports from laboratory, notes from the doctors, medical records, and discharge statements are in unstructured manner. The objective of the data extraction is to retrieve the required information for further organization. Several techniques could be applied for the text analysis so that the valuable information could be obtained in a structured format.

From various studies, it has been observed that the cutting-edge algorithms of Natural Language Processing such as Named Entity Recognition (NER) models, word embedding, and entity resolution models related to healthcare have been applied. The objective of the NER is to identify the entities, and then semantic classification is done [3]. Conventional NER systems use rule-based methods, learning-based methods, or hybrid approaches [4]. These algorithms make use of various training models, so that the words related to that query of the consumer could be obtained from the text. It is the initial phase for extracting the information which is used to find and categorize the named entities such as the names of locations, persons, percentages, expressions of times, measures, financial values. It could be built with the two libraries, namely, NLTK and SpaCy.

15.2.1   Implementing NER with NLTK

Step 1: Import the required libraries.

Step 2: For instance, a tweet from healthcare is taken for analysis.

statement = 'from Google reviews, every day an average of 15 people are diagnosed with ALS – more than 5,000 people in per year. As many as 30,000 Americans may be currently affected by ALS. Annually ALS is responsible for 2 deaths per 100,000 people'

Step 3: Word tokenization is applied and part-of-speech tagging is implemented.

```
def preprocess(sentence):
    sentence = nltk.word_tokenize(sentence)
    sentence = nltk.pos_tag(sentence)
    return sentence
```

The input sentence has to be preprocessed, and, therefore, the output will be displayed in terms of tuples that contain the discrete words in that particular sentence and part of speech.

sentence = preprocess(statement)

sentence

The output is shown in Table 15.2.

The noun phrase is chunked so that the named entities are determined with the help of a regular expression. It comprises rules which are used to represent the way of chunking the sentences. In this code, the chunk pattern comprises a rule in such a way that the noun phrase denoted by NP could be formed when there is an occurrence of an optimal determiner, then adjectives JJ and at last, ended with a noun NN. Therefore, it is represented as given in the following:

Step 4: Chunk parser is created and tested.

pattern = 'NP: {<DT>?<JJ>*<NN>}'

cp = nltk.RegexpParser(pattern)

The chunk parser is tested for the given sentence.

cs = cp.parse(sentence)

The output of the testing is given by using the print statement, and it is displayed in Table 15.3.

print(cs)

There are two chunking utility functions, namely, tree2conlltags and conlltags2tree:

Table 15.2   Output of preprocessing

```
[('from', 'IN'),
('google', 'JJ'),
('reviews', 'NNS'),
(',', ','),
('Every', 'NNP'),
('day', 'NN'),
('an', 'DT'),
('average', 'NN'),
('of', 'IN'),
('15', 'CD'),
('people', 'NNS'),
('in', 'IN'),
('europe', 'NN'),
('are', 'VBP'),
('diagonised', 'VBN'),.....
```

Table 15.3   The output of the testing

```
(S
  from/IN
  google/JJ
  reviews/NNS
  ,/,
  Every/NNP
  (NP day/NN)
  (NP an/DT average/NN)
  of/IN
  15/CD
  people/NNS
  in/IN
  (NP europe/NN)
  are/VBP
diagonised/VBN
  with/IN
  ALS -/NNP
  more/JJR
  than/IN
  5000/CD
  people/NNS
  in/IN
  per/IN
  (NP year.As/NN)
  many/JJ
  as/IN
  30,000/CD
  Americans/NNPS
  may/MD
  be/VB
  currently/RB
  affected/VBN
  by/IN
  ALS.Annually/NNP
  ALS/NNP
  is/VBZ
  responsible/JJ
for/IN
  2/CD
  deaths/NNS
  per/IN
  100,000/CD
  people/NNS
  ./.)
```

Table 15.4   Output of training the parser

```
[('from', 'IN', 'O'),
('google', 'JJ', 'O'),
('reviews', 'NNS', 'O'),
(',', ',', 'O'),
('Every', 'NNP', 'O'),
('day', 'NN', 'B-NP'),
('an', 'DT', 'B-NP'),.....
```

Table 15.5   Output of the tree-based tagger

```
(S from/IN
  google/JJ
  reviews/NNS
  /,
  (PERSON Every/NNP)
  day/NN
  an/DT
  average/NN
  of/IN
  15/CD
  people/NNS
  in/IN
  europe/NN
```

- tree2conlltags function is used to obtain the words in triples, tag, and chunk for each token.
- conlltags2tree function is used to create a parse tree from the produced triples.

Step 5: Parser has to be trained with the functions.

These functions are used for training the parser. The chunk tags used a regular standard format termed IOB format. I denotes Inside, O means Outside, and B symbolizes Begin.

The output of training the parser is depicted in Table 15.4.

Step 6: Tree-based tagger is constructed.

The sentence is tokenized first, then it is POS-tagged, and later it is chunked before it is transferred to the tree-based tagger. The output is displayed as each word is tagged suitably with both the part of the speech and named entity class.

```
ne_tree = ne_chunk(pos_tag(word_tokenize(statement)))

print(ne_tree)
```

The output of the tree-based tagger is shown in Table 15.5.

Here, in this output, Every is recognized as person.

Table 15.6   Entity types

Type	Column heads
PERSON	People
ORG	An organization such as institutions and companies
LOC	A non-GPE location such as hills, mountains, and rivers
GPE	Countries, cities, and states
PRODUCT	Food, vehicles, and objects
EVENT	Sports, wars and matches, etc.
NORP	Religious, national groups
LANGUAGE	Any languages
DATE	Absolute or relative dates or periods
TIME	Time less than in a day
MONEY	Monetary values
CARDINAL	Numerals

15.2.2   Implementing Named Entity Recognition using SpaCy

OntoNotes 5 corpus is used for training NER, and several entity types are supported. Table 15.6 describes the entity types.

SpaCy is a new framework, and recently, it is treated as an effective library. The following code shows the deployment of SpaCy for NER. DisplaCy is used for visualization of the dependency tree.

Step 1: Importing the required libraries.

```
import spacy

from spacy import displacy
```

Step 2: Importing the English language.

SpaCy comprises various models. The default model for the English language is en_core_web_sm.

It is downloaded and assigned to an object named as nlp_obj

```
import en_core_web_sm
nlp_obj = en_core_web_sm.load()
```

Step 3: For example, a sentence has been taken, and entity types for the sentence are analysed.

sentence = nlp_obj('From google reviews every day an average of 15 people are diagnosed with ALS- more than 5000 people in per year. As many as 30,000 Americans may be currently affected by ALS. Annually ALS is responsible for 2 deaths per 100,000 people ')

```
print([(X.text, X.label_) for X in sentence.ents])
```

As mentioned in Table 15.6, the label of the input is shown as the output in Table 15.7.

Step 4: Token-level entity annotation could be done based on the BILOU tagging mechanism in order to label the boundaries of the entity. I – In tag – refers to the inner token, O – Out tag – denotes the outer token, and B – Begin tag – refers to the first token.

```
print ([(X, X.ent_iob_, X.ent_type_) for X in sentence])
```

The output of the token types of the input is shown in Table 15.8.

Step 5: Identification of various attributes is done.

The token class provides various attributes, namely, index, lemmatized word, checks for punctuation, space, and POS tagging.

Certain attributes are shown for the sample input in Table 15.9.

Step 6: A clear visualization of the Named Entity for the annotated sentence could be viewed in Table 15.10. Using for loop, the text and label are printed.

displacy.render(sentence, style='ent', jupyter=True)

Table 15.7 Entity types of input data

Output:
[('every day', 'DATE'), ('15', 'CARDINAL'), ('more than 5000', 'CARDINAL'), ('As many as 30,000', 'CARDINAL'), ('Americans', 'NORP'), ('ALS', 'ORG'), ('Annually', 'GPE'), ('2', 'CARDINAL'), ('100,000', 'CARDINAL')]

Table 15.8   Token types for the sample input

[(From, 'O', ''), (google, 'O', ''), (reviews, 'O', ''), (, 'O', ''), (every, 'B', 'DATE'), (day, 'I', 'DATE'), (an, 'O', ''), (average, 'O', ''), (of, 'O', ''), (15, 'B', 'CARDINAL'), (people, 'O', ''), (are, 'O', ''), (diagnosed, 'O', ''), (with, 'O', ''), (ALS-, 'O', ''), (more, 'B', 'CARDINAL'), (than, 'I', 'CARDINAL'), (5000, 'I', 'CARDINAL'), (people, 'O', ''), (in, 'O', ''), (per, 'O', ''), (year, 'O', ''), (., 'O', ''), (As, 'B', 'CARDINAL'), (many, 'I', 'CARDINAL'), (as, 'I', 'CARDINAL'), (30,000, 'I', 'CARDINAL'), (Americans, 'B', 'NORP'), (may, 'O', ''), (be, 'O', ''), (currently, 'O', ''), (affected, 'O', ''), (by, 'O', ''), (ALS, 'B', 'ORG'), (., 'O', ''), (Annually, 'B', 'GPE'), (ALS, 'O', ''), (is, 'O', ''), (responsible, 'O', ''), (for, 'O', ''), (2, 'B', 'CARDINAL'), (deaths, 'O', ''), (per, 'O', ''), (100,000, 'B', 'CARDINAL'), (people, 'O', '')]

Table 15.9   Attributes for the sample input

Output:							
From	0	from	False	False	Xxxx	ADP	IN
google	5	google	False	False	xxxx	PROPN	NNP
reviews	12	review	False	False	xxxx	NOUN	NNS
	20		False	True		SPACE	_SP
every	21	every	False	False	xxxx	DET	DT
day	27	day	False	False	xxx	NOUN	NN
an	31	an	False	False	xx	DET	DT
average	34	average	False	False	xxxx	NOUN	NN
	NUM	CD					
people	229	people	False	False	xxxx	NOUN	NNS

Table 15.10   Named entity for the input

Output
every day DATE
15 CARDINAL
more than 5000 CARDINAL
As many as 30,000 CARDINAL
Americans NORP
ALS ORG
Annually GPE
2 CARDINAL
100,000 CARDINAL

From google reviews every day <u>DATE</u> an average of 15 <u>CARDINAL</u> people are diagnosed with ALS- more than 5000 <u>CARDINAL</u> people in per year. As many as 30,000 <u>CARDINAL</u> Americans <u>NORP</u> may be currently   affected   by ALS <u>ORG</u> . Annually <u>GPE</u> ALS   is   responsible   for 2 <u>CARDINAL</u> deaths per 100,000 <u>CARDINAL</u> people

Step 7: Construction of dependency parser.

Also, SpaCy displays the dependency parser as per the code: the dependency tree illustrates the relationship among the headwords and its dependents. In the next output, the root word that does not have the dependency is identified as 'From'. It is mainly used to represent the grammatical structure as shown in Table 15.11.

Table 15.11   Grammatical structure output for the sentence

Output:
From/IN <--ROOT--From/IN
google/NNP <--compound--reviews/NNS
reviews/NNS <--pobj--From/IN
/_SP <----reviews/NNS
every/DT <--det--day/NN
day/NN <--npadvmod--From/IN
an/DT <--det--average/NN
average/NN <--nsubjpass--diagnosed/VBN
of/IN <--prep--average/NN
15/CD <--nummod--people/NNS
people/NNS <--pobj--of/IN
are/VBP <--auxpass--diagnosed/VBN
diagnosed/VBN <--relcl--day/NN
with/IN <--prep--diagnosed/VBN
ALS-/NNP <--punct--people/NNS
more/JJR <--amod--5000/CD
than/IN <--quantmod--5000/CD
5000/CD <--nummod--people/NNS
people/NNS <--pobj--with/IN
in/IN <--prep--people/NNS
per/IN <--prep--in/IN
year/NN <--pobj--per/IN
./. <--punct--diagnosed/VBN
As/RB <--advmod--30,000/CD
many/JJ <--amod--30,000/CD
as/IN <--quantmod--30,000/CD
30,000/CD <--nummod--Americans/NNPS
Americans/NNPS <--nsubjpass--affected/VBN
may/MD <--aux--affected/VBN
be/VB <--auxpass--affected/VBN
currently/RB <--advmod--affected/VBN
affected/VBN <--ROOT--affected/VBN
by/IN <--agent--affected/VBN

Step 8: Visualization is presented as shown in Figure 15.3.

Yet, to bring a clear visualization among its dependents, displaCy is used.

display.render(sentence, style='dep', jupyter=True, options={'distance': 90})

The authors have done a detailed study of various NER tools, and from that tools, they had chosen the public tools for the validation of the outputs. Evaluations exhibit reliable results on the selected tools. In the end, hybrid NER tools have been built with the combination of the best tools to deploy for the applications [5].

From [6], it has been stated that there is a necessity for the advanced data preparation before the information extraction from the unstructured data that must possess the semantic and context property. Therefore, computationally efficient extraction systems are required to overcome the issues that arise due to the multidimensional unstructured data.

15.3   Data visualization and tools

Nowadays, data volume increases higher than before in all domains. Therefore, it is not possible to depend on obsolete data presentation tools. As the volume of the

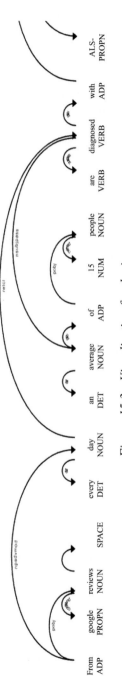

Figure 15.3 Visualization for the input

data is increased, it is a tedious process to generate and futile to consume especially with the huge volume of data. From a current review, it has been observed that nearly 70% of organizations find the difficulty in identifying the crucial data comprehensions or in determining the right data for making the decision. Hence, a necessity arises in all domains so that the users' task would be easier in the analysis of results, finding out the results and patterns, communicating to build a strong decision in that corresponding fields. Therefore, the process of examining the huge amount of data and the results must be in an interactive manner in terms of visual framework so that the users could understand easily and act accordingly. It is termed data visualization.

Data visualizations in healthcare are as follows:

Data visualizations could be used in various fields such as the management of sepsis, public health presentations, board presentations, and social determinants of health. Techniques used for data visualization have to follow the following steps:

Step 1: A Pilot project has to be identified.

The project to select as a pilot project must possess certain features such as visibility, high value, success, and deliverable in a short duration.

Step 2: Determine the data sources.

Data sources have to be explored for the pilot project, and a detailed study of attributes is required which helps in further analysis.

Step 3: A data visualization model has to be developed.

A model could be created with the help of available data visualization tools.

Step 4: Preparation of data.

Data transformation has to be done so that it could be used in the visualization process. The complete data visualization development could be performed by preparing the data.

Step 5: Improve data visualization.

Choose the proper data visualization tool and configure it to construct every part of the data visualization. Based on the feedback, adjust the configuration and test it.

Step 6: Test and implementation.

Acceptance testing has to be performed. Train the users with the tool. Recommendations are incorporated, and the improvement is done. Finally, an additional release is done.

The most common methods of data visualization aided in understanding the trend, association, distribution, assessment, and composition of the data values.

A clear perception could be obtained through data visualization. It is observed that Python consists of the utmost interactive data visualization tools. Some of the data visualization libraries are as follows:

1. Plotly: A web-based toolkit that has a rich API. It consists of a certain range of capabilities such as 3D charts, contour plots, and dendrograms. In addition, several types of charts, plots also could be presented.
2. Matplotlib: A 2D visualization library that provides a cooperative and collaborative environment for the users. Through this, various types of charts, plots, power spectra, and histograms could be produced.

3. Seaborn: This library depends on the Matplotlib. A rich feature of API has been provided for the construction of KDE-based visualizations. PyData Stack is incorporated with the Seaborn for facilitating the NumPy and pandas. Exploration and understanding of data become easier. Informative plots could be generated with the help of semantic association and mathematical combination which could be functioned on data frames and arrays.

4. Altair: It is a demonstrative arithmetic visualization library with a simple API. Efficient and beautiful visualizations could be made possible with a small amount of code.

5. ggplot: It is an implementation done in Python for the Grammar of Graphics of R programming language. It is incorporated with pandas.

Data visualization using Seaborn – An example: interpretation of heart disease: Problem definition: To check the count of the patients with and without diseases. Step 1: As the first step, the data set has to be read.

```
import numpy as np
import matplotlib.pyplot as plt
import seaborn as sns
import pandas as pd
from scipy import stats
dataframe=pd.read_csv("e:\project1\heart.csv")
```

Step 2: The data set comprises various attributes and its details are represented with the following command.

df.info() displays the attributes such as resting blood pressure, serum cholesterol, fasting blood sugar, resting cardiographic results, and exercise-induced angina.

```
<class 'pandas.core.frame.DataFrame'>
RangeIndex: 1025 entries, 0 to 1024
Data columns (total 14 columns):
age       1025 non-null int64
sex       1025 non-null int64
cp        1025 non-null int64
trestbps  1025 non-null int64
chol      1025 non-null int64
fbs       1025 non-null int64
restecg   1025 non-null int64
thalach   1025 non-null int64
exang     1025 non-null int64
oldpeak   1025 non-null float64
slope     1025 non-null int64
ca        1025 non-null int64
thal      1025 non-null int64
target    1025 non-null int64
dtypes: float64(1), int64(13)
memory usage: 112.2 KB
```

Step 3: To understand the data set, we can use a histogram. It is used for envisioning and understanding the probabilistic distribution of numerical data or image data.

```
def draw_histograms(dataframe, features, rows, cols):
fig=plt.figure(figsize=(20,20))
    for i, feature in enumerate(features):
        ax=fig.add_subplot(rows,cols,i+1)
        dataframe[feature].hist(bins=20,ax=ax,facecolor='blue')
        ax.set_title(feature+" Distribution",color='Red')

    fig.tight_layout()
    plt.show()
draw_histograms(df, df.columns,6,3)
```

Figure 15.4 shows the histogram Output for the features of the exhibited data set.

This is used to display the number of patients those who have diseases and who do not have.

df.target.value_counts()

Output:

1 526

0 499

Name: target, dtype: int64

Visualization is shown in terms of

sns.countplot(x='target',data=df)

Figure 15.5 displays the graph that shows the patients with and without diseases.

15.4   Advanced visualization methods

1. Heatmap

In this, colours are used to denote the numbers in a spreadsheet. Different colours are used to denote the smallest, middle, and highest range values.

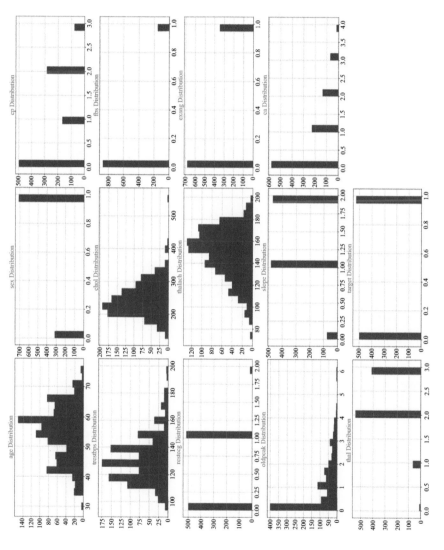

Figure 15.4 Histogram output for the features

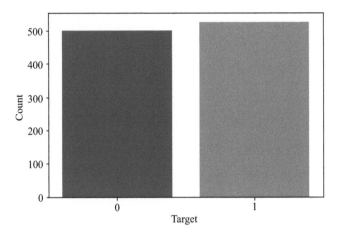

Figure 15.5   Graph for patients with and without diseases

Heatmap depends on numerical values. For example, consider the 'Prediction of house price' data set in which the attributes are all of the numerical values.

Step 1: Libraries are imported for processing.

```
import numpy as np
import matplotlib.pyplot as plt
import seaborn as sns
import pandas as pd
from scipy import stats
dataframe=pd.read_csv("e:\project1\heart.csv")
```

Step 2: With the help of Matplotlib, a graphical chart is plotted. Implementing Seaborn is very interesting to visualize. The collinearity of the multiple variables in the data set could be represented with the following code.

```
fig, ax = plt.subplots(figsize=(8,6))
sns.heatmap(dataframe.corr(), center=0, cmap='Blues')
ax.set_title('Multi-Collinearity of heart attributes')
```

Figure 15.6 displays the multicollinearity of heart attributes.
Output:

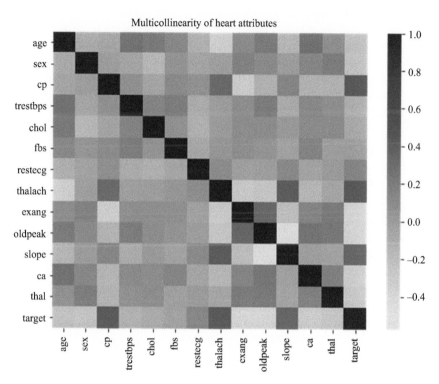

Figure 15.6   Heatmap to show multicollinearity

2. Geospatial charts
   Variables are plotted on physical addresses so that they hold the organizations to decide the methods for the construction of several clusters. Colour
   index or size is used as a metric for denoting the variables.
3. Grid
   Two metrics are used horizontally and vertically. A grid could be plotted
   against the desired category, and then colours are used to denote the data.
4. Wordcloud

It is used to denote the text data. It is a graphical representation of frequently
used words that have been stored in a collection of text files.

A fact is that the medical data is considered to be subtle, which results in
crucial problems if it is influenced. Hence, data science could be deployed in
healthcare to protect this data. The hasty evolution in the sensor data offers substantial potential to control healthcare. Data thus gathered needs processing, transformation in order to infer some knowledge. Hence, a need arises to develop data

analytical tools to do the process. Also, the heterogeneity in the sources of medical data leads to the exploration of techniques that emerged from several fields of data analytics. Nowadays, the healthcare industry undergoes several metamorphic revolutions when there is a transformation in business from volume-based to value-based. It is observed that there is a need for the healthcare providers to offer much care towards the patients which in turn must increase the life expectancy and enhance the control over the prolonged and communicable diseases. Thus, as in big data, predictive analytics contributes towards the decision-making in such a way that a strong relationship could be enabled among the patients and providers as mentioned in [7]. Various types of analytics provide insight into the data.

15.5   Data analytics

Data analytics could be divided into the following four types [8–10]:

- Descriptive analytics
- Diagnostic analytics
- Predictive analytics
- Prescriptive analytics

15.5.1   Descriptive analytics

The objective of this analytics is to comprehend the actions that happen historically and need to respond to the queries as follows:

- What is the count of patients those who have been hospitalized previously?
- What is the percentage of patients those who have left home therapy in the last month?
- What is the ratio of bone mineral metabolism (BMM) laboratory values for the patient population?

Responses could be prepared based on the historical data by applying statistical methods such as averages, percentages, counts, and standard deviation. It is also used to learn about various healthcare decisions and their inferences on the clinical results and outcomes [11]. Besides, it also identifies the patterns associated with hospital functionalities and aids in balancing the capacity and cost [12].

15.5.2   Diagnostic analytics

This makes one to know the reasons for the incidents, and few queries could be answered. The questions that are raised are as follows:

- State the reasons for the patients who visited the hospital the previous week.
- Find out the reasons for the patients those who have left home therapy.
- Justify the reasons for the patients not satisfying the BMM targets.

To answer these queries, more analysis is required on the data or it could be found out from the information gained through descriptive analytics. In this analysis, certain investigations could be carried out, and the reasons should be understood by applying various statistical methods. For instance, patient-related, organization-related, and provider-related services could be tracked down [10,13,14].

15.5.3 Predictive analytics

This is mainly for the creation of predictions like as suggested in [15]:

- Identify the patients those who might be prone to the risk of admitting to the hospital next week.
- What is the count of patients those who would like to shift from home therapy to the centre in the following month?
- What would be the forthcoming month's BMM values for the patients?

The models are trained based on historical data, and further events are predicted through the implementation of several ML algorithms. Through these models, patterns from the database are identified. The risk score for all the patients is computed. From this score, the identification of the risky patients is done to provide special attention. But it does not specify the methods of prevention of adversarial events such as hospitalization.

15.5.4 Prescriptive analytics

This provides information about the activities that are required to modify the forecasting action. Five constituents such as usage of hybrid data, both structured and unstructured data types, combining the estimations and prescriptions, considering the side effects with the help of the algorithms could be designed so that it could handle any situation along with the feedback methods [15].

The authors [16] have investigated the various analytics methods and suggested efficient solutions so that the performance of the ER has been augmented. An extensive literature study has been done which mainly focused on taking decisions clinically and administratively. In this work, the EMR is considered for analysis. In addition, analytics is performed on social media data [17].

Comparison of data analytics:

A detailed analysis in terms of comparison is given in Table 15.12.

Currently, the custom of storing health records is done digitally all over the globe. Normally the health records could be defined as personal health records (PHR), EHR as in [18], and EMRs. The comparison of all records is shown in Table 15.13.

Researchers [19] have deployed a model based on data mining for the prediction of 5 years' mortality using EHR. The Ensemble Rotating Forest algorithm with a decision tree is used to categorize the patients into two kinds of life expectancy, i.e., equal or greater than 5 years and less than 5 years. A study discovered that the usage of EMR systems results in the efficiency of healthcare delivery, better in the clinical decision process, and efficacy in sustaining the cooperation among the healthcare providers.

Table 15.12   Comparative analysis

Descriptive analytics	Diagnostic analytics	Predictive analytics	Prescriptive analytics
Historical data is used	Descriptive data is used	Historical data is used	Historical data is used
Stakeholders understand the information	It is also known as root cause analysis	Decision analysis is carried out risks and opportunities are identified	Fraud detection is possible
Tells about history	Deeper analysis is done	Prediction is done	Apart from predictions, activities and consequences for every action are provided

Table 15.13   Comparison of health records

EMR	EHR	PHR
These files carry the required information about the patient's condition to the treatments	The documents could be about the descriptions of the patient's information which could be used by the appropriate healthcare providers	It illustrates the information about the patient
Certain information such as the origin of the clinical data, medical terminologies related to the patient's disease, medical reports, and other documents	Data comes from all the resources such as prescriptions, reports, history, developments during the treatment	Data that has been collected follows the interoperability standards fixed by the nation
This kind of data is needed in healthcare organizations so that the data could be obtained, processed, and it provides a clear understanding. The organizations could improve their financial effects, clinical operations through the clear vicinity of the data	The recipients of the employee health insurance get the EHR data which results in controlling the costs in the benefits of health insurance	Appointment reminders for the patients as per the medication reminders, notifications about the immunization for the children notices about the regular health check-ups
An accurate diagnosis could be done. Public health could be improved	Data could be retrieved in a fast manner and the important healthcare quality indicators could be shown to the organizations	It represents the tracking of health information

From various studies, it has been observed that there is a tremendous progress in the healthcare field and better collaboration among the providers. Also, the prompt clinical decisions are taken [20,21].

15.6 Healthcare and technology: open issues

Various resolutions about the data in the healthcare industries obstruct the prevalent utilization of data analytics. Nowadays, the data in the healthcare industries seems to possess various formats in such a way that the construction of the perspective, grainy database is a complex process. Thus, it results in the cost increase for the usage of the data despite storing the necessary information in some method. Additionally, well-structured data is also not accessible by the researchers for carrying out further investigations. Mostly, all organizations that deal with electronic healthcare find issues related to data access, maintaining the quality of the data, data privacy, protection, reliability, and integration of data. Apart from that, complexity arises in the retention of data, management of data, data interoperability, and data interpretation.

15.6.1 Data remanence

It is the residual exemplification of data which has been deleted. This might lead to the occurrence of the involuntary data confidentiality attack. Data integrity and confidentiality are not adequate when the freshness of the data is considered. Hence, it implies that the heath records always must possess recent information. During the emergency, delays that occur due to the storage and transferring the obsolete statements and reports lead to the data inconsistency.

15.6.2 Data interoperability

The predominant issue related to data interoperability is that there might be a huge disparity in understanding the health terms and in its various coding standards. Annotation of data and events varies from professionals to professionals. An international standard which is been followed by various agencies and healthcare organizations is the Logical Observation Identifiers Names and Codes. But these standards are not used in EHRs. Health records are stored on centralized servers and in different formats, which hampers interoperability. Several benefits of EHRs are assisting in medical recommendations, augmenting disease management, and also in drop of crucial medication errors. But EHRs possess limitations with respect to interoperability [22,23].

15.6.3 Data staging

The processes of data migration, database-to-database conversion, translation from machine to machine, and data integration are involved in the process of staging.

Data that has been collected from various single-organizations must possess consistency. The limitation is that the EHR data from various regions must be combined, and it lacks in the storage of demographic and geographic diversity.

Identification of illness and mortality might be a challenging task. It is clear that the most important outcome that has to be monitored and investigated is the death; however, it is very complex to discover from the discrete EHR data. The death factor is presented in the discharge disposition which is an attribute of the encounter record.

15.6.4   *Application of big data in biomedical research*

Recent growth in the generation of a massive volume of data, collection of data, and analysis has led to the prospects in the medical domain. The usage of next-generation technology (NGS) results in increasing the volume of the data which originates from the transcriptomic and genomic study. The patient's profile could be studied clearly with the help of the combination of the proteomics, metabolomics, genomic, and transcriptomic data. Treatment could be improved further by the efficient and combined investigation of omics data along with the healthcare analytics, and it is depicted in Figure 15.7 [24,25].

Data could be collected from various genomics-based investigations, EMRs, prescriptions from the doctors, insurance details, and NGS-related information. Issues might arise due to the combination of various structured data. The decision-making process could be more complicated due to the amalgamation of various data types and massive data [26].

15.7   Conclusion

Recently, the healthcare system has a great uplift by adapting the digitization in the medical data which in turn leads to the generation of massive data. Analysis of medical data becomes quite difficult due to the nature and combination of the data. This chapter described the common data sources in healthcare. The significance of the quality of the data is discussed. Visualization of data is explored with the libraries. In addition, the practical implementation of libraries has been explained. Finally, the open issues related to healthcare have been discussed in detail, which could act as a game changer for the technology which attracts more focus by various researchers and academicians.

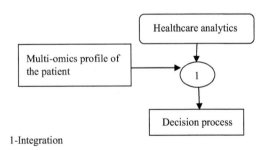

Figure 15.7   Integration of omics data and healthcare analytics

References

[1]   Abdelhak, Mervat, Grostick, Sara, Hankin, Mary Alice, and Jacobs, Ellen, "Health information: management of a strategic resource", 1996. WB Saunders, Philadelphia, PA.

[2]   Allee, Nancy, Alpi, Kristine, Cogdill, Keith Wilson, Selden, Catherine, and Youngkin, Molly, "Public health information and data: a training manual" [Internet], 2004. National Library of Medicine, Bethesda, MD. Available at: http://www.phpartners.org/pdf/phmanual.pdf.

[3]   Marrero, Mónica, Urbano, Julián, Sánchez-Cuadrado, Sonia, Morato, Jorge, and Gómez-Berbís, Juan Miguel, "Named Entity recognition: fallacies, challenges and opportunities", 2013, Computer Standards and Interfaces. 35(5):482–489.

[4]   Abdallah, Zahraa S, Carman, Mark, and Haffari, Gholamreza, "Multi-domain evaluation framework for named entity recognition tools", 2017, Computer Speech & Language. 43:34–55.

[5]   Jiang, Ridong, Banchs, Rafael E., and Li, Haizhou, "Evaluating and combining named entity recognition systems", 2016, Proceedings of the Sixth Named Entity Workshop, Joint With 54th ACL, Berlin, Germany, August 12, Association for Computational Linguistics, pp. 21–27.

[6]   Adnan, Kiran and Akbar, Rehan, "An analytical study of information extraction from unstructured and multidimensional big data", 2019, Journal of Big Data. 6:91.

[7]   Jeble, Shirish, Kumari, Sneha, and Patil, Yogesh, "Role of big data and predictive analytics", 2016, International Journal of Automation and Logistics. 2:307–331. https://doi.org/10.1504/IJAL.2016.10001272.

[8]   Burke, Jason, "Health analytics: gaining the insights to transform health care", 2013, vol. 69, Cary, North Carolina, USA: SAS Institute Inc.

[9]   Delen, Dursun and Demirkan, Haluk, "Data, information and analytics as services", 2013, Journal of Decision Support Systems. 55(1):359–363.

[10] Shao, Guodong, Shin, Seung-Jun, and Jain, Sanjay, "Data analytics using simulation for smart manufacturing", 2014, Proceedings of the 2014 Winter Simulation Conference, Savannah, GA, USA, December 7–10. IEEE/ACM, pp. 2192–2203.

[11] Raghupathi, Wullianallur, "An overview of health analytics", 2013, Journal of Health & Medical Informatics. 04. https://doi.org/10.4172/2157-7420.1000132.

[12] Lavalle, Steve, Lesser, Eric, Shockley, Rebecca, Hopkins, Michael, and Kruschwitz, Nina, "Big data, analytics and the path from insights to value", 2011, MIT Sloan Management Review. 52:21–32.

[13] Banerjee, Arindam, Bandyopadhyay, Tathagata, and Acharya, Prachi, "Data analytics: hyped up aspirations or true potential?", 2013, Vikalpa. 38(4):1–11.

[14] Corcoran, Michael, "The five types of analytics", Technical Report, 2012. Information Builders. pp. 68–69. http://www.informationbuilders.co.uk/sites/www.informationbuilders.com/files/intl/co.uk/presentations/four.

[15]   Riahi, Youssra, "Big data and big data analytics: concepts, types and technologies", 2018, International Journal of Research and Engineering. 5:524–528. https://doi.org/10.21276/ijre.2018.5.9.5.

[16]   Basu, Atanu, "Five pillars of prescriptive analytics success", March/April 2013, Analytics.

[17]   Khalif, Mohamed and Zabani, Ibrahim, "Utilizing health analytics in improving the performance of healthcare services: a case study on a tertiary care hospital", 2016, Journal of Infection and Public Health. 9:757–765.

[18]   Islam, M. S., Hasan, M. M., Wang, X., Germack, H. D., and Noor-E-Alam, M. "A systematic review on healthcare analytics: Application and theoretical perspective of data mining", 2018, Healthcare, Basel, Switzerland, 6(2):54. https://doi.org/10.3390/healthcare6020054

[19]   Ozair, Fouzia, Nayer, Jamshed, Sharma, Amit, and Aggarwal, Praveen, "Ethical issues in electronic health records: a general overview", 2015, Perspectives in Clinical Research. 6:73–76. https://doi.org/10.4103/2229-3485.153997.

[20]   Waithera, Lynn, Muhia, Joy, and Songole, Rogers, "Impact of electronic medical records on healthcare delivery in Kisii Teaching and Referral Hospital", 2017, Journal of Medical and Clinical Reviews. 3(4:21):1–7.

[21]   Mathias, Jason, Agrawal, Ankit, Feinglass, Joe, Cooper, Andrew, Baker, David, and Choudhary, Alok., "Development of a 5-year life expectancy index in older adults using predictive mining of electronic health record data", 2013, Journal of the American Medical Informatics Association—JAMIA. 20:e118–e124. https://doi.org/10.1136/amiajnl-2012-001360.

[22]   Cheng, Edward C, Le, Ying, Zhou, Jia, and Lu, Yang, "Healthcare services across China – on implementing an extensible universally unique patient identifier system", 2018, International Journal of Healthcare Management. 11(3):210–216, https://doi.org/10.1080/20479700.2017.1398388.

[23]   Poongodi, T., Sumathi, D., Suresh, P., and Balusamy, B. "Deep learning techniques for electronic health record (EHR) analysis". In: Bhoi, A., Mallick, P., Liu, C.M., Balas, V. (eds) Bio-inspired Neurocomputing. Studies in Computational Intelligence, vol 903, 2021. Springer, Singapore. https://doi.org/10.1007/978-981-15-5495-7_5.

[24]   Dash, Sabyasachi, Shakyawar, Sushil Kumar, Sharma, Mohit, and Kaushik, Sandeep, "Big data in healthcare: management, analysis and future prospects", 2019, Journal of Big Data. 6:54. https://doi.org/10.1186/s40537-019-0217-0.

[25]   Ristevski, Blagoj and Chen, Ming, "Big data analytics in medicine and healthcare", 2018, Journal of Integrative Bioinformatics. 15(3):20170030. https://doi.org/10.1515/jib-2017-0030.

[26]   Nikhil Kapu, Prabha Selvaraj, Vijay Kumar Burugari, and Anupama Namburi. "Secured electronic health ledger using block chain as a service", 2020, Journal of critical review. 7(6):2176–2185.

Chapter 16

Identification and classification of hepatitis C virus: an advance machine-learning-based approach

Janmenjoy Nayak[1], Pemmada Suresh Kumar[2], Dukka Karun Kumar Reddy[2] and Bighnaraj Naik[3]

Hepatitis C virus (HCV) is identified as one of the leading sources of liver disease transmitted through blood-to-blood contact worldwide. HCV contamination is flattering a foremost universal health challenge, and due to its complications, more than 3 million new infectious patients along with 350,000 deaths are occurring every year. In the future, hepatitis C (HC) may be considered as one of the reasons for malaise and fatality of human, as it has been estimated that nearly 170 million have been infected by this. The last decades of medical research are evident that detecting and finding solutions for HC has remained a major concern in Egypt. As Egyptian blood donors were found highest among other blood donors from all nationalities, HCV became a major community health concern. To cope with such a problem, some of the statistical-based approaches are being developed and became a partial solution to some extent. To address the challenges of healthcare, a wide range of tools, techniques, and frameworks have been offered by machine learning (ML). As ML approaches have the capability of determining and recognizing patterns in complex datasets, they are identified as the best connectionist systems to predict the future outcomes of the HCV. In this chapter, we propose experimental investigations on the study of various ML approaches for the diagnosis of associated risk factors, cofactors promoting its progression, complications in the prevention and control of HCV in Egypt. Further, the project will focus on some of the basic ML strategies along with the challenges of handling the HC disease.

[1]Department of Computer Science and Engineering, Aditya Institute of Technology and Management (AITAM), Tekkali, India
[2]Department of Computer Science and Engineering, Dr. Lankapalli Bullayya College of Engineering, Visakhapatnam, India
[3]Department of Computer Application, Veer Surendra Sai University of Technology, Burla, India

16.1   Introduction

The inflammation of the liver due to viral infection causes hepatitis. Hepatitis is an infectious disease in which the mode of transmission takes place through infected persons. This may happen through the sharing of reused medical needles. HCV is a major virus behind chronic hepatitis. About 130–170 million people have infectious HC throughout the world. In the 1970s only, scientists learned about HCV, and in the year 1989, finally, they have confirmed that the HCV exists. It is usually passed by blood-to-blood contact (when HC patient's blood is in contact with the bloodstream of another patient). There is a probability of HCV occurrences transmitted through the non-sterile checkup equipment (unclean medical equipment after being utilized on a contaminated person), usage of intravenous drug, and blood transfusions (when an individual is provided the blood that came from an unhygienic person). The impact of HCV will be either sensitive or chronic. Acute HCV is a diminutive infection where the virus may be cured within 6 months, and chronic HCV is long-lasting infection where there is the chance of liver cancer and even death. Dark yellow urine, fever, joint pain, loss of appetite, pain in abdomen, fatigue, and jaundice (eyes and skin will become yellowish) are the symptoms of HCV. Therefore, HCV can be treated by antiviral drugs advised by an expert who generally treats HC, and it can also be prohibited by keeping away from contact with the body fluids and blood from any HCV-infected person. Due to a lack of proper treatment, more than 1 million people are dying every year from HCV diseases and 300 million people are continually contaminated with HC.

Many times, various individuals came to know that they have HCV from a blood test at the time of a routine physical checkup or after donating blood in blood donation camps. This problem has mainly arisen in Egypt as they have more donors. It is evident that over a decade, Egypt people faced major economic and health problems due to HCV, and hence, Egypt was placed as a peak of the countries with serious HCV burden. Approximately 10 million Egyptians disclosed to the infectious HCV and about 5–7 million patients were considered as the most vulnerable to HCV in Egypt. Handling as well as the elimination of this specific infectious HCV disease in Egypt has become the major concern from the year 2007. To cope up with such problems and to deal with the disputes of healthcare, several statistical methods have been employed [1]. However, these approaches were limited to use only some enzyme factors, and still there is no use of factors such as ALT enzyme. Also, techniques such as binary linear regression were limitedly used, and there is a need to use other statistical approaches such as outlier analysis and link analysis, which became one of the drawbacks. Moreover, ML methods are also applied for resolving such problems and found to be efficient, and hence, they are being developed day-by-day.

ML is an application of artificial intelligence that offers the capability to mechanically learn and enhance from experience without being openly programmed. ML can be used to make freehand alternatives by independently expanding input from the information. Several earlier studies found that ML techniques offered a broad range of tools, methods, challenges, etc. to address the healthcare problems. From the past few decades, many researchers have used ML approaches to build the forecasting models that relay on clinical data such as forecasting the feedback of therapy in HCV patients based on their biochemical as well as clinical data [2]. These techniques have the ability to identify and determine the patterns in difficult problems. The complexity in the pattern of a dataset will be measured through the number of control parameters as well as instances contained in it.

The capability of an ML approach for controlling HCV disease can be identified through its factors, cofactors as well as complications. Several cofactors and associated risk factors can be considered for the diagnosis of HCV by using ML approaches. Platelet count, age, splitting factors, etc. are identified as some of the risk factors. Characteristics such as age, gender, body mass index (BMI), albumin, glucose, hemoglobin (HGB), and white blood cell (WBC) have been used for accurate prediction of HCV with the help of DTLA (decision tree (DT) learning algorithm) [3]. However, there is a limitation in DTLA on some parameter metrics in which the required performance evaluation can be performed through fine tuning of parameters [3]. Other parameters such as active smoking, passive smoking, allocation concealment, and selective reporting have been used for HCV diagnosis using Naïve Bayes (NB) method [4], and this method has the limitation that a lower number of trials are done in the experimental analysis which results in the change in exploration. Some standard parameters such as bilirubin, SGOT enzyme, Alk phosphate, PROTIME, CLASS [5], R^2, SE [6], standard deviation, MAE [7], soft margin, and Gaussian kernel have been used to predict HCV-related infections with the help of support vector machine (SVM), and this technique has a limitation that only some performance criteria are considered for the analysis. Benchmark features of HCV patients such as age, sex, HCV RNA level, hepatobiopsy, genotype, ribavirin, and treatment interval have also been used for identifying HCV. Some other features such as ALP, CHE, GOT, HPT, GPT, LAP, APTT, PT, total cholesterol, total protein, and lymphocyte were also considered as factors for HCV prediction using ML approaches. However, only some factors have been considered, which become a limitation in [8]. Control parameters such as polarity, amino acid positions, and physicochemical were used with ML approaches such as artificial neural network (ANN), and this technique has the limitation that hepatic enzymes need to be used for the study of HCV. Amino acid composition, pseudo amino acid composition, and tissue information are some other characteristics that are considered for HCV detection with the help of ML methods such as random forest (RF), and it has the limitation that only some ML techniques were used and still there is a need to use other advance ML techniques. Apart from these mentioned parameters, still many other important parameters can be used and those parameters are available in the dataset considered in this study.

Moreover, this chapter mainly focuses on the identification and classification of HCV disease using intelligent ML methods. The highlights of this research work are mentioned as follows:

- Four ML algorithms have been considered for the analysis of HCV.
- Proposed a novel bagging approach for effective analysis of HCV.

- Several associated risk factors, cofactors as well as complications for the prevention of chronic HCV have been demonstrated.
- The benchmark dataset named HCV for Egyptian patients having 29 attributes and 1,385 instances from the UCI repository [9] is considered for the study.

This chapter proposed a bagging-classifier-based approach that is one of the ensemble learning methods, and its performance is compared with various classifiers such as Extra Trees classifiers, RF, *k*-nearest neighbor (*k*-NN), and DT classifiers. Section 16.2 is having a literature survey that consists of ANN, RF, DT, and SVM. Section 16.3 consists of proposed methodology. Section 16.4 explains experimental setup that contains, dataset description, data processing, evaluation metrics, and environmental setup. Section 16.5 demonstrates the result analysis using the different ML methods along with the proposed method. Finally, Section 16.6 gives the conclusion of the chapter with possible future prospects.

16.2　Literature survey

In this section, various researches for the resolution of HCV complications have been summarized and explained briefly. The ML techniques that have already been used for analyzing and resolving the problems of HCV in Egypt were observed and described in the subsections.

16.2.1　Artificial neural network

One of the benchmark ML algorithms is ANN. ANN is used in almost every field for resolving major problems of healthcare as well as other fields. Jilani *et al.* [10] have proposed a contemporary method for classifying the HC patients with the ML approach and named the method as principal-component-analysis-based ANN (PCA-ANN). The authors have considered age, bilirubin, Alk phosphate, SGOT, albumin, PROTIME, CLASS as the factors for HCV analysis. An accuracy of 100% obtained for testing data and 99.15% for training data has been obtained for HC patient classification. Lara *et al.* [11] have proposed a novel model for identifying the latest conditions of HCV by employing the RBFNN (radial basis function neural network) classifier and some PhyChem (physical–chemical) characteristics of HVR1 (hyper variable region 1). The concerned PhyChem factors are enthalpy, protein-DNA twist, helix coil transition, slide rise, etc. An accuracy of 95.7% on fully trained data has been employed with the proposed method. To predict the antigenic activity in the NS3 protein of HCV, Lara *et al.* [12] have developed a new approach using the ANN technique. Amino acid positions were considered as factors for analyzing HCV antigenic conditions. Later, the authors stated that the proposed ANN method acts as an efficient tool for predicting the HCV NS3 protein.

16.2.2   Random forest

For exploring the NS5B polymerase inhibitors of HCV, Wei *et al.* [13] have developed a novel strategy by employing RB-VS (RF-based virtual screening), PB-VS (e-pharmacophore-based virtual screening), and DB-VS (docking-based virtual screening) methods. The high prediction was obtained for discovering those inhibitors in terms of SE (sensitivity), SP (specificity), and *Q* (overall accuracy) with the proposed approach. Singal *et al.* [14] have developed a modern approach for the prediction of hepatocellular carcinoma of HCV using the ML approach named HALT-C (hepatitis C antiviral long-term treatment against cirrhosis). Higher accuracy for diagnosing and identifying the patients at high risk who suffer from cirrhosis was found.

16.2.3   Decision tree

DT is a kind of supervised ML, where the data is constantly divided according to a certain parameter. DTs can be used majorly for resolving the complex problems of the HCV. Shousha *et al.* [15] have introduced a novel technique to contrast and assess the accurateness of fibrosis-4 (FIB-4) and aminotransferase-to-platelet ratio index (APRI) for predicting the HCV-linked fibrosis. To construct a DT, authors have used reduced error pruning tree methods by analyzing data mining (DM) approaches. They intended to calculate the prediction accurateness of FIB-4 and APRI against the techniques of data mining. They have also preferred multi-layer perceptron (MLP) as the best projecting algorithm with 0.825, 0.811, and 0.880 as sensitivity, specificity as well as receiver operating characteristic (ROC) curve area, respectively. Better results were found with MLP when compared to APRI, REPTree, and FIB-4. Ayeldeen *et al.* [16] have utilized a DT classifier to forecast the stages of individuals' liver fibrosis. Authors have intended to recognize the fibrosis stage in HC Egyptian patients that are given from individual laboratories and followed the DT technique as an ML approach. In their study, they got a higher range accuracy rate as 93.7% by using the DT classifier. ElHefnawi *et al.* [17] have proposed a technique that accurately predicts the response of interferon-based therapy in Egyptian patients with chronic HC by using ML technique. Authors have used both DT and ANN models. They have utilized the classification and regression trees (CART) algorithm for DT. They found 0.76 and 0.80 as best and average accuracy of ANN as well as 0.96 and 0.72 for DT, respectively. Compared with other methods, higher accuracy was found with DT method.

16.2.4   Support vector machine

An SVM is a supervised ML model that is useful for examining the information for both classification and regression. It became a high-performance classifier, which is extremely popular in various fields as well as bioinformatics. HCV is one such area where SVM proved its efficiency in solving diagonal issue problems. Soliman and Elhamd [5] have introduced a hybrid classification scheme by utilizing both particle swarm optimization (PSO) and least squares SVM for HCV diagnosis. In order to excerpt the feature vector, authors have employed PCA. The projected system was developed and assessed on the standard HCV dataset that is taken from the UCI repository of the ML database. They got 98.86% of the classification accuracy rate in the experimental results. Jiang *et al.* [18] have aimed to build a common model to differentiate among patients having mild or no fibrosis (METAVIR F0–F1) vs. clinically major fibrosis (METAVIR F2–F4). They have examined 204 repeated chronic HC patients retrospectively. Thirty-four serum indicators through the period of infection, age, and gender were evaluated for the classification of fibrosis with an SVM classifier. Their results proved a high amount of exactness and acted as a replacement for liver biopsy. Quantitative structure–activity relationship (QSAR) models by utilizing several training and descriptor set techniques were discovered by Qin *et al.* [7] to forecast the bioactivity HCV NS3/4A protease inhibitors with the usage of both the techniques such as SVM and multiple linear regressions (MLRs). Authors have constructed various QSAR approaches on 512 HCV NS3/4A protease inhibitors dataset and used a Kohonen's self-organizing map technique for dividing it (dataset) into the train and test sets, respectively. Their final study has outperformed as sub dataset models and found accurate results when compared to other models. Also, authors have proved that SVM is superior to MLR and suggested to use the grouping of both sub and whole SVM models to get more accurate results in upcoming days. Some more ML-based approaches for HCV are shown in Table 16.1.

16.3   Proposed methodology

The proposed model framework is an integration of many independent processes. The framework represents the overall system process as shown in Figure 16.1. Dataset collection is the initial procedure framework, where the collected dataset is studied strictly to discover the types of data. Data preprocessing is executed on the required dataset through data cleaning and data visualization measures. These measures transform the data into meaningful attribute vectors. These attribute vectors are then sliced into an 80:20 ratio for training and testing.

16.3.1   Bagging classifier

Bagging classifier is also called as bagging aggregated classifier. This is one of the ensemble meta-estimator learning techniques proposed by Breiman [29]. In this method, it will consider multiple predictors from which it will calculate the aggregated predictor. It is a procedure that will create classifiers in an ensemble way by considering random samples that are replaced from the dataset and then construct a classifier for every bootstrap sample. The decision of the final classification is done by voting or aggregating that will reduce the variance over the class labels built by classifiers. In other words, we can infer bagging built classification trees by considering bootstrap samples that are taken from training data and combine all the predictions to get finalized meta-predictor.

Table 16.1 Various machine learning approaches for solving hepatitis C-virus problems

S. no.	ML technique used	Factors considered	Result obtained	Reference
1	Principle-component-analysis-based ANN (PCA-ANN)	Age, bilirubin, Alk phosphate, SGOT, albumin, PROTIME, class	An accuracy of 100% obtained for testing data and 99.15% for training data has been obtained	[10]
2	SVM, RF (random forest)	5' NCR, CORE, E1, and NS5B genotypes	Obtained an accuracy of 99% for classifying HCV with the proposed technique	[19]
3	Sequential-forward-floating-selection-based SVM (SFFS–SVM)	Age, male/female, platelet count, AST, ALT, ALP, albumin prothrombin time, hyaluronic acid, etc.	Proposed SFFS–SVM successfully identified CHC (chronic hepatitis-C) patients having fibrosis and mild fibrosis with an accuracy of 96%	[18]
4	QSAR (quantitative structure activity relationship) classification model based on SLRM (sparse logistic regression model)	–	Higher prediction rate for classifying anti hepatitis C was found with the combination of SLRM (sparse logistic regression model) and QSAR	[20]
5	REP (reduced error) tree algorithm for data mining and MLP for prediction of advanced fibrosis	Age and PLT (platelet)	MLP successfully predicted advanced stage of fibrosis rather the compared ones: APRI (aminotransferase-to-platelet-ratio-index), FIB-4 (fibrosis-4), REP tree	[15]
6	ANN	Polarity, amino acid positions, and physicochemical factors	Results guided a focused rational design of antigenic targets with improved diagnostically relevant properties through a cyclic process of experimental evaluation using ANN	[12]
7	Ensemble learning models (RF, SVM, NB, MLP)	Amino acid composition, pseudo amino acid composition, tissue information features	An accuracy of 83% and specificity of 94.5% was found with the proposed method for predicting the interactions of protein–protein in between human and HCV	[21]
8	Hybrid rough genetic algorithm	Splitting factor	Good classification accuracy	[22]

(Continues)

Table 16.1 (*Continued*)

S. no.	ML technique used	Factors considered	Result obtained	Reference
9	Hybrid *k*-means, hierarchical clustering, FCM	Primer pattern, index position, similarity, and distance	Attained an accuracy rate of 0.998 for both sensitivity as well as specificity	[23]
10	PSO, genetic algorithm, MLR and DT algorithms	Age, albumin AST, AFP, PC, INR, WBC, Hb, ALT	Considered factors were found to be statistically noteworthy to advanced fibrosis with an accuracy rate of 84.4%	[24]
11	SVM	—	Global descriptors, 2D and 3D property auto-correlation descriptors were calculated from the program ADRIANA. Code and got 88.24% of highest accuracy of 2D autocorrelation descriptors	[25]
12	Radial basis function neural network classifier (RBFNN)	HVR1 sequence data, PhyChem features	Trained RBFNN on the features of PhyChem intra-host HVR1 variants got 94.85% classification accuracy (CA)	[11]
13	RF	—	Candesartan cilexetil was identified as an existing pro drug for hypertension that was recognized as a potential anti-HCV drug	[26]
14	DT, Naïve Bayes and SVM, NN	Count of hydrogen, oxygen, CA, cytosine, uracil, and nitrogen	Prediction of HCV 1a and 1b therapy responders from nonresponders with an accuracy rate of 75% and 85%. Also, categorized therapy responders with 82.50% accuracy rate and relapsers with 84.17% accuracy rate	[27]
15	SVM and RF	Age, ALT, GGT, gender, and Hb	The predicted immunoassay of HCV was found to have more accuracy than results of HBV immunoassay that are associated with matching usual pathology predictor variable data	[28]

The procedure of the proposed bagging classifier is as follows:

Algorithm: Multi-class bagging with decision tree as base model

---

1. Let $D = (D_i, c_i)_{i=1}^N$ be the hepatitis dataset where $D_i = (D_{i,1}, D_{i,2}, \ldots, D_{i,m})$ is the attribute's value of the *ith* instance and c_i is the corresponding class label. Here m is the number of features.

2. Repeat for $t = 0$ to T

(i) Randomly sample with replacement of n samples from the training set D.

(ii) Construct a decision tree sequentially $DT^t(D^t)$ by using splitting along features by using information gain computation (Equation (16.1)) and using the Gini index (Equation (16.2)).

$$InfoGain\left(F_{D^t}, f_{D^t}^j\right) = InfoMeasure(F_{D^t}) - \frac{F_{D^t}^L}{F_{D^t}} InfoMeasure\left(F_{D^t}^L\right)$$

$$-\frac{F_{D^t}^R}{F_{D^t}} InfoMeasure\left(F_{D^t}^R\right) \tag{16.1}$$

$$InfoMeasure_{gini}\left(D^t\left[F_{D^t}^S\right]\right) = 1 - \sum_{c_i \in c} P(c_i|D^t), S \in \{L, R\} \tag{16.2}$$

In (16.1) and (16.2), $f_{D^t}^j \in F_{D^t}$, $F_{D^t} = \{f_{D^t}^1, f_{D^t}^2, \ldots, f_{D^t}^m\}$ is the selected feature for splitting of D^t, where F_{D^t} is the feature vector of D^t. $F_{D^t}^L$ and $F_{D^t}^R$ are the features at left and right subtree of the DT^t.

3. Repeat for $t = 0$ to T

(i) Predict the disease type (Equation (16.3)) from trained model $DT^t(D^t)$. $c^t = DT^t(D^t)$

(ii) Return final prediction of bagging model by using majority voting.

4. Return the final prediction (Equation (16.3)):

$$c = P_{Bagging}(D) = majority\_voting\langle c^1, c^2, \ldots, c^T \rangle \tag{16.3}$$

16.4 Experimental setup

In this section, we have discussed about dataset and their attributes, data processing, various evaluation metrics to evaluate the results by proposed method as well as other competitive ML-based methods.

16.4.1 Data preprocessing

Exploratory data observation and analysis are the major criteria required for ML research. Feeding data with an appropriate classifier is the principal task for a

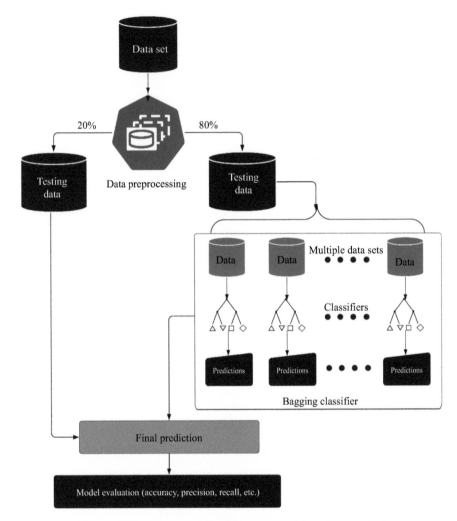

Figure 16.1   Framework of the proposed bagging method

classification model. Therefore, missing data is the initial step to deal with. In the HCV for Egyptian patients' dataset, columns do not hold any missing values. The open-source dataset with 29 features consists of 1,385 samples of categorical data. For the process of multiclass classification to take place, the ***baseline histological staging*** of the data is classified to form four classes. The dataset is further divided into training and testing datasets in the ratio of 80%:20%, respectively, i.e., 80% data is considered for training and the other 20% data is considered for testing.

16.4.2   Dataset description

HCV for Egyptian patients' dataset is described where Egyptian patients underwent treatment dosages for HCV about 18 months. This dataset contains 1,385 samples of data with 29 features, namely, age, gender, BMI, fever, nausea/vomiting, headache, diarrhea, fatigue and generalized bone ache, jaundice, epigastric pain, WBC, red blood cells, HGB, platelets, AST 1 aspartate transaminase ratio, ALT 1 alanine transaminase ratio 1 week, ALT 4 alanine transaminase ratio 12 weeks, ALT 12 alanine transaminase ratio 4 weeks, ALT 24 alanine transaminase ratio 24 weeks, ALT 36 alanine transaminase ratio 36 weeks, ALT 48 alanine transaminase ratio 48 weeks, ALT after 24-week alanine transaminase ratio 24 weeks, RNA base, RNA 4, RNA 12, RNA end-of-treatment, RNA elongation factor, baseline histological grading, and baseline histological staging. All the features are nominal by nature. The baseline histological staging is being classified into four types.

16.4.3   Attribute information

The dataset contains the data of Egyptian patients who had treatment for the HCV which is about 18 months. It has 29 attributes and 1,385 instances, having a multi-label-independent variable as shown in the following.

Age	Age is measured within a range of minimum age of 32 years and a maximum age of 61 years
Gender	The males are considered as 1, with 707 and females are considered as 2, with 678
BMI	The body mass index is measured to be within a range of minimum body mass index of 22 and maximum body mass index of 35
Fever	This feature with fever is considered as 1 with a count of 671 and no fever is considered as 2 with a count of 714
Nausea/vomiting	This feature with nausea or vomiting is considered as 1 with a count of 689 and no nausea or vomiting is considered as 2 with a count of 696
Headache	This feature with having a headache is considered as 1 with a count of 698 and not having a headache is considered as 2 with a count of 687
Diarrhea	This feature with having diarrhea is considered as 1 with a count of 689 and not having diarrhea is considered as 2 with a count of 696
Fatigue and generalized bone ache	This feature with having fatigue and generalized bone ache is considered as 1 with a count of 694 and not having fatigue and generalized bone ache is considered as 2 with a count of 691
Jaundice	This feature with having jaundice is considered as 1 with a count of 691 and not having jaundice is considered as 2 with a count of 694
Epigastric pain	This feature with having epigastric pain is considered as 1 with a count of 687 and not having epigastric pain is considered as 2 with a count of 698
WBC	The white blood cell count is measured within a range of minimum count of 2,991 and maximum count of 12,101
RBC	The red blood cells count is measured within a range of minimum count of 3,816,422 and maximum count of 5,018,451

(Continues)

(*Continued*)

HGB	The hemoglobin scale is measured within a range of minimum scale of 10 and maximum scale of 15
Plat	The blood platelets are measured within a range of minimum count of 93,013 and maximum count of 226,464
AST 1	The aspartate transaminase ratio feature within a range of minimum count of 39 and a maximum count of 128
ALT 1	The alanine transaminase ratio feature for 1 week is within a range of minimum count of 39 and a maximum count of 128
ALT 4	The alanine transaminase ratio feature for 12 weeks is within a range of minimum count of 39 and a maximum count of 128
ALT 12	The alanine transaminase ratio feature for 4 weeks is within a range of minimum count of 39 and a maximum count of 128
ALT 24	The alanine transaminase ratio feature for 24 weeks is within a range of minimum count of 39 and a maximum count of 128
ALT 36	The alanine transaminase ratio feature for 36 weeks is within a range of minimum count of 5 and a maximum count of 128
ALT 48	The alanine transaminase ratio feature for 48 weeks is within a range of minimum count of 5 and a maximum count of 128
ALT	The alanine transaminase ratio feature after 24 weeks is within a range of minimum count of 5 and a maximum count of 45
RNA base	This feature is within a range of minimum value of 11 and the maximum value of 1,201,086
RNA 4	This feature is within a range of minimum value of 5 and the maximum value of 1,201,715
RNA 12	This feature is within a range of minimum value of 5 and the maximum value of 3,731,527
RNA EOT	This feature RNA end-of-treatment is within a range of minimum value of 5 and the maximum value of 808,450
RNA EF	This feature with elongation factor is within a range of a minimum value of 5 and maximum value of 810,333
Baseline histological grading	This feature is within a range of minimum value of 3 and the maximum value of 16
Baseline histological staging	These are classified into categorical values. The total number of values of 1 are counted as 336, 2 are counted as 332, 3 are counted as 355, and 4 are counted as 362

16.4.4   *Evaluation metrics*

This section will give overview on the performance metrics used during the experimental analysis.

16.4.4.1   Confusion matrix

The prediction results in the form of a confusion matrix or error matrix are a synopsis on the classification model by identifying confusion between classes. The confusion matrix enlightens classification problem through prediction results. It gives us errors made by a classifier and the types of errors that are being made at classification.

The confusion matrix is given by true positive (TP), false positive (FP), false negative (FN), and true negative (TN), where TP is considered to be positive and is predicted to be positive. FN is considered to be positive but is predicted to be negative. TN is considered to be negative and is predicted to be negative. FP is considered to be negative but is predicted to be positive.

16.4.4.2 Accuracy

It gives the correctness of the classifier through the overall number of samples from a given test dataset as shown in the following equation:

$$Accuracy = \frac{(TP + TN)}{(TP + TN + FP + FN)} \tag{16.4}$$

16.4.4.3 Error

It is also known as misclassification rate and gives the rate of incorrect classification as shown in the following equation:

$$Error = \frac{FP + FN}{(TP + TN + FP + FN)} \tag{16.5}$$

16.4.4.4 Precision

The number of TPs compared to the number of positives is considered as precision and is shown in the following equation:

$$Precision = \frac{TP}{(TP + FP)} \tag{16.6}$$

16.4.4.5 Recall

It is also known as sensitivity or true positive rate, where the number of TPs compared to the number of TPs and FNs. it claims as shown in the following equation:

$$Recall = \frac{TP}{(TP + FN)} \tag{16.7}$$

16.4.4.6 False positive rate

The number of FN compared to the number of TPs and FNs. it claims as shown in the following equation:

$$FPR = \frac{FP}{(TN + FP)} \tag{16.8}$$

16.4.4.7 *F*1 score

It evaluates the harmonic mean of the recall and the precision as shown in the following equation:

$$F1 - Score = \frac{2 \times TP}{(2 \times TP + FP + FN)} \tag{16.9}$$

16.4.5   Environmental setup

This work has been experimented on system setup of an HP (ProDesk 600 G2 MT) desktop with Windows 10 Pro 64-bit (10.0, Build 17134), Intel® Core™ i7-6700 processor. The system has the memory of an 8 GB RAM. For analyzing the data, various software packages such as Pandas framework, Imblearn framework, and NumPy framework are used. Similarly, for data visualization, Matplotlib framework and mlxtend framework and for data analysis, Scikit-learn framework and classification-metrics framework are used. In the proposed method, DT is used as a base classifier, and the number of estimators considered is 500. The proposed method is compared with various ML algorithms such as extra-tree classifier, RF, *k*-NN, and DT, where extra-tree classifier parameters are as follows: the number of estimators is 100, the criterion is "Gini." Parameters considered in RF classifiers are as follows: the number of estimators is 60, the maximum depth is 21, and criterion is "Gini." In the *k*-NN, the neighbor is 1, *p* is considered as 10, and the number of jobs is 6. In DT, the maximum depth is taken into consideration is 24, criterion is entropy and used the best split in the experimentation.

16.5   Result analysis

This section represents the result analysis of the proposed bagging algorithm with *a base estimator as* a DT and various ML algorithms on HCV dataset. The simulated dataset contains 1,385 scenarios with multi-classification (staging-1, staging-2, staging-3, and staging-4) from the UCI ML repository; these scenarios were experimented and predicted. To validate the performance of our proposed method with different ML methods, we considered performance measures such as TP, TN, FP, FN, TPR/recall, false positive rate (FPR), precision, support, and accuracy. The confusion matrix of the bagging classifier is shown in Figure 16.2. From the confusion matrix, it is a clear observation that all the classes are classified correctly. Table 16.2 shows the results such as TP, TN, FP, FN, TPR, FPR, precision, and *F*-score using a bagging classifier, where the accuracy of the classifier is 100% and remaining ML algorithms *k*-NN, DT, Extra Trees, and RF classifiers are having accuracies of 84%, 84%, 84%, and 85%, respectively, and the accuracy comparisons of different classifiers are shown in Figure 16.3.

The performance of different ML algorithms with individual class results is presented in Tables 16.3–16.6. Table 16.3 with *k*-NN represents the case of recall for "staging-2" and "staging-4" with 0.85 and 0.86, and FPR for "staging-1, 2,

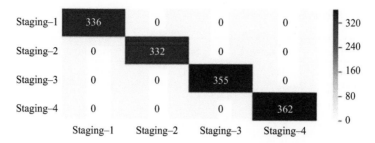

	Staging–1	Staging–2	Staging–3	Staging–4
Staging–1	336	0	0	0
Staging–2	0	332	0	0
Staging–3	0	0	355	0
Staging–4	0	0	0	362

Figure 16.2   Confusion matrix of a bagging classifier

Table 16.2   Performance measure using bagging

Bagging	Staging-1	Staging-2	Staging-3	Staging-4
True positive	336	332	355	362
True negative	1,049	1,053	1,030	1,023
False positive	0	0	0	0
False negative	0	0	0	0
TPR/recall	1	1	1	1
FPR	0	0	0	0
$F1$ score	1	1	1	1
Precision	1	1	1	1
Accuracy	1	1	1	1
Over all accuracy	**1**			

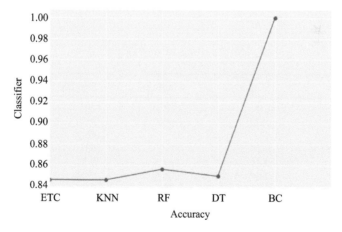

Figure 16.3   All classifiers' accuracy

Table 16.3   Performance measure using k-NN

k-NN	Staging-1	Staging-2	Staging-3	Staging-4
True positive	277	284	297	314
True negative	997	1,002	971	972
False positive	52	51	59	51
False negative	59	48	58	48
TPR/recall	0.82	0.85	0.83	0.86
FPR	0.04	0.04	0.05	0.04
*F*1 score	0.83	0.85	0.83	0.86
Precision	0.84	0.84	0.83	0.86
Accuracy	0.91	0.92	0.91	0.92
Over all accuracy	**0.84**			

Table 16.4   Performance measure using decision tree

Decision tree	Staging-1	Staging-2	Staging-3	Staging-4
True positive	281	288	292	316
True negative	1,006	993	980	968
False positive	43	60	50	55
False negative	55	44	63	46
TPR/recall	0.83	0.86	0.82	0.87
FPR	0.04	0.05	0.04	0.05
*F*1 score	0.85	0.84	0.83	0.86
Precision	0.86	0.82	0.85	0.85
Accuracy	0.92	0.92	0.91	0.92
Over all accuracy	**0.84**			

Table 16.5   Performance measure using extra-tree classifier

Extra tree	Staging-1	Staging-2	Staging-3	Staging-4
True positive	275	292	292	313
True negative	1,005	1,000	984	953
False positive	44	53	46	70
False negative	61	40	63	49
TPR/recall	0.81	0.87	0.82	0.86
FPR	0.04	0.05	0.04	0.06
*F*1 score	0.83	0.86	0.84	0.84
Precision	0.86	0.84	0.86	0.81
Accuracy	0.92	0.93	0.92	0.91
Over all accuracy	**0.84**			

Table 16.6   Performance measure using random forest

Random forest	Staging-1	Staging-2	Staging-3	Staging-4
True positive	282	288	293	323
True negative	1,011	1,009	987	949
False positive	38	44	43	74
False negative	54	44	62	39
TPR/recall	0.83	0.86	0.82	0.89
FPR	0.03	0.04	0.04	0.07
$F1$ score	0.85	0.86	0.84	0.85
Precision	0.88	0.86	0.87	0.81
Accuracy	0.93	0.93	0.92	0.91
Over all accuracy	**0.85**			

and 4" gives 0.04 compared to "staging-3" with 0.05. The individual accuracy of each class for "staging-1–4" has resulted as 0.91, 0.92, 0.91, and 0.92.

Table 16.4 for DT represents the case of recall for "staging-2" and "staging-4" with 0.86 and 0.87 and FPR for "staging-1 and 3" gives 0.04 compared to "staging-2 and 4" with 0.05, and the individual accuracy of each class for "staging-1–4" has resulted as 0.92, 0.92, 0.91, and 0.92. Table 16.5 for extra tree represents the case of recall for "staging-2" and "staging-4" with 0.87 and 0.86, and FPR for "staging-1–4" gives 0.04, 0.05, 0.04, and 0.06, and the individual accuracy of each class for "staging-1–4" has resulted as 0.92, 0.93, 0.92, and 0.92. Table 16.6 for RF represents the case of recall for "staging-2" and "staging-4" with 0.86 and 0.89, and FPR for "staging-1–4" gives 0.03, 0.04, 0.04, and 0.07, and the individual accuracy of each class for "staging-1–4" has resulted as 0.93, 0.93, 0.92, and 0.91. For all the classifiers, the TPR/recall for classes "staging-2–4" has given higher values than the "staging-1–3" for all classifiers. The FPR for all the "staging" classes is between 0.04 and 0.05. The average $F1$-scores of "staging-1–4" classes calculated for Tables 16.3–16.6 are 0.84, 0.85, 0.83, and 0.85. Similarly, the average precision of "staging-1–4" classes calculated for Tables 16.3–16.6 are 0.86, 0.84, 0.85, and 0.83. The accuracy of "staging-1–4" classes for Tables 16.3–16.6: the "staging-1" accuracy is in between 0.91 and 0.93, the "staging-2" accuracy is in between 0.92 and 0.93, the "staging-3" accuracy is in between 0.91 and 0.92, and the "staging-4" accuracy is in between 0.91 and 0.92. In the same way, all values in the TP, TN, FP, and FN performance for all class are nearly similar.

The proposed method with DT as a base estimator has performed well in terms of TP, TN, FP, FN, TPR, and FPR. The performance of the proposed method is good as FP and FN are zero. The proposed method has performed well in the case of $F1$-score, precision, and accuracy. The proposed method for "staging-1–4" is compared to ML algorithms in terms of all metrics and found to be superior.

AUC-ROC curves of the proposed method and various ML methods are plotted in between TPR and FPR those are as shown in Figure 16.4(a)–(e).

Table 16.7 shows some of the early developed methods and their accuracies using ML algorithms. From the table, it is evident that our proposed method

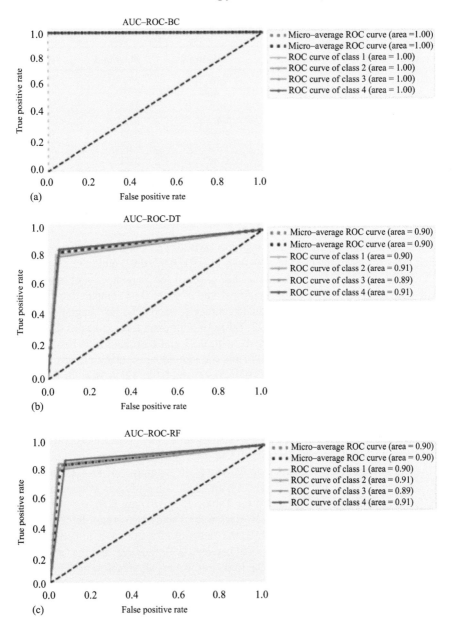

Figure 16.4   AUC-ROC curves of various classifiers: (a) bagging classifier, (b) decision tree, (c) random forest, (d) k-nearest neighbor, and (e) extra-tree classifier

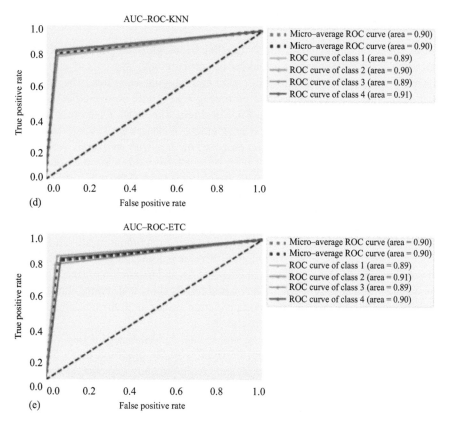

Figure 16.4   (*Continued*)

Table 16.7   *Comparison with previous work*

S. no.	Year	Intelligent method	Accuracy (%)	Reference
1	2006	SVM	96	[18]
2	2009	SVM, RF	99	[19]
3	2011	PCA-ANN	99.15	[10]
4	2014	Ensemble learning models	83	[21]
5	2014	DT, NB, SVM, NN	85	[27]
6	2017	RBFNN	94.8	[11]
7	2019	Hybrid *k*-means, hierarchical clustering, FCM	99.8	[23]
8	**2020**	**Bagging**	**100**	**This work**

outperformed well as compared to previously developed ML-based models. Our proposed method achieved the accuracy of 100%, and it signifies that the bagging method is able to classify the HCV data in an efficient way.

16.6   Conclusion

In this study, the predicted attribute "baseline histological staging" from the HCV dataset of Egyptian patients is a multi-class attribute with staging-1–4 classes and classified by using k-NN, RF, ETC, DT, and bagging classifier. The proposed method (bagging) gives much more promising results with an overall accuracy of 100% when compared to traditional ML classifiers. The recall, $F1$-score, precision, and with individual class accuracies for staging-1–4 classes are 100%, whereas the RF is the second-best model after the proposed method with an overall accuracy of 0.85, and the classes staging-1–4 values of recall are 0.83, 0.86, 0.82, and 0.89, $F1$-score are 0.85, 0.86, 0.84, and 0.85, precision is 0.88, 0.86, 0.87, and 0.81 and with individual class accuracies are 0.93, 0.93, 0.92, and 0.91. The maximum TP and TN values for the classes ETC, k-NN, and DT are staging-4 and staging-1. The minimum FN and FP values for the classes ETC, k-NN, and DT are staging-2 and staging-1. The classifiers ETC, k-NN, and DT having maximum recall value are for staging-4 and staging-2 class, minimum FPR value is for staging-1 class, maximum $F1$-score value is for staging-2 and staging-4 class, and maximum precision value is for staging-1 and staging-4 class. The overall results show that staging-1, staging-2, and staging-4 classes are having good prediction values in all the classifiers metric evaluation values compared to other classes.

The study evidently proves that a simple model consisting of patients of Egypt taking 18 months treatment dosage for HCV with the proposed method is categorized in the staging phase of the patients with clinically considerable stages as staging-1–4 classes with elevated degree of accuracy. Therefore, the appliance of this model representation possibly will act as a substitute for staging the HCV for the patients. As a future work, some other ensemble learning models may be adopted for analyzing the HCV data as well as other countries HCV data.

References

[1]   Yasin H, Jilani TA, and Danish M. Hepatitis-C classification using data mining techniques. Int J Comput Appl [Internet]. 2011;24(3):1–6. Available from: http://www.ijcaonline.org/volume24/number3/pxc3873888.pdf.

[2]   Abd El-Salam SM, Ezz MM, Hashem S, *et al.* Performance of machine learning approaches on prediction of esophageal varices for Egyptian chronic hepatitis C patients. Inform Med Unlocked [Internet]. 2019;17: 100267. Available from: https://doi.org/10.1016/j.imu.2019.100267.

[3]   Hashem S, Esmat G, Elakel W, *et al.* Accurate prediction of advanced liver fibrosis using the decision tree learning algorithm in chronic hepatitis C Egyptian patients. Gastroenterol Res Pract [Internet]. 2016;2016:1–7. Available from: http://www.hindawi.com/journals/grp/2016/2636390/.

[4]   Cure S, Diels J, Gavart S, Bianic F, and Jones E. Efficacy of telaprevir and boceprevir in treatment-naïve and treatment-experienced genotype 1 chronic hepatitis C patients: an indirect comparison using Bayesian network

meta-analysis. Curr Med Res Opin [Internet]. 2012;28(11):1841–56. Available from: https://www.tandfonline.com/doi/full/10.1185/03007995. 2012.734798.

[5] Soliman OS and Elhamd A. Classification of hepatitis C virus using modified particle swarm optimization and least squares support vector machine. Int J Sci Eng Res [Internet]. 2014;5(3):122–9. Available from: http://www.ijser.org.

[6] Khuntwal K, Yadav M, Nayarisseri A, Joshi S, Sharma D, and Suhane S. Credential role of van der Waal volumes and atomic masses in modeling hepatitis C virus NS5B polymerase inhibition by tetrahydrobenzo-thiophenes using SVM and MLR aided QSAR studies. Curr Bioinform [Internet]. 2013;8 (4):465–71. Available from: http://www.eurekaselect.com/openurl/content. php?genre=article&issn=1574-8936&volume=8&issue=4&spage=465.

[7] Qin Z, Wang M, and Yan A. QSAR studies of the bioactivity of hepatitis C virus (HCV) NS3/4A protease inhibitors by multiple linear regression (MLR) and support vector machine (SVM). Bioorg Med Chem Lett [Internet]. 2017;27(13):2931–8. Available from: http://dx.doi.org/10.1016/j.bmcl.2017.05.001.

[8] Yang J, Nugroho AS, Yamauchi K, *et al.* Efficacy of interferon treatment for chronic hepatitis C predicted by feature subset selection and support vector machine. J Med Syst [Internet]. 2007;31(2):117–23. Available from: http://link.springer.com/10.1007/s10916-006-9046-8.

[9] Dua D and Graff C. UCI Machine Learning Repository [Internet]. 2017. Available from: http://archive.ics.uci.edu/ml.

[10] Jilani TA, Yasin H, and Mohammad Yasin M. PCA-ANN for classification of hepatitis-C patients. Int J Comput Appl [Internet]. 2011;14(7):1–6. Available from: http://www.ijcaonline.org/volume14/number7/pxc3872530. pdf.

[11] Lara J, Teka M, and Khudyakov Y. Identification of recent cases of hepatitis C virus infection using physical-chemical properties of hypervariable region 1 and a radial basis function neural network classifier. BMC Genomics [Internet]. 2017;18(S10):880. Available from: https://bmcgenomics.biomedcentral.com/articles/10.1186/s12864-017-4269-2.

[12] Lara J, Wohlhueter RM, Dimitrova Z, and Khudyakov YE. Artificial neural network for prediction of antigenic activity for a major conformational epitope in the hepatitis C virus NS3 protein. Bioinformatics [Internet]. 2008;24 (17):1858–64. Available from: https://academic.oup.com/bioinformatics/article-lookup/doi/10.1093/bioinformatics/btn339.

[13] Wei Y, Li J, Qing J, *et al.* Discovery of novel hepatitis C virus NS5B polymerase inhibitors by combining random forest, multiple e-pharmacophore modeling and docking. PLoS One [Internet]. 2016;11(2):e0148181. Available from: https://dx.plos.org/10.1371/journal.pone.0148181.

[14] Singal AG, Mukherjee A, Elmunzer JB, *et al.* Machine learning algorithms outperform conventional regression models in predicting development of

hepatocellular carcinoma. Am J Gastroenterol [Internet]. 2013;108(11): 1723–30. Available from: http://dx.doi.org/10.1038/ajg.2013.332.

[15] Shousha HI, Awad AH, Omran DA, Elnegouly MM, and Mabrouk M. Data mining and machine learning algorithms using *IL28B* genotype and bio-chemical markers best predicted advanced liver fibrosis in chronic hepatitis C. Jpn J Infect Dis [Internet]. 2018;71(1):51–7. Available from: https://www.jstage.jst.go.jp/article/yoken/71/1/71_JJID.2017.089/_article.

[16] Ayeldeen H, Shaker O, Ayeldeen G, and Anwar KM. Prediction of liver fibrosis stages by machine learning model: a decision tree approach. In: Proc 2015 IEEE World Conf Complex Syst WCCS 2015; Morocco: IEEE Xplore, 2016.

[17] ElHefnawi M, Abdalla M, Ahmed S, *et al.* Accurate prediction of response to interferon-based therapy in Egyptian patients with chronic hepatitis C using machine-learning approaches. In: 2012 IEEE/ACM International Conference on Advances in Social Networks Analysis and Mining [Internet]. Istanbul: IEEE; 2012. p. 771–8. Available from: http://ieeexplore.ieee.org/document/6450170/.

[18] Jiang Z, Yamauchi K, Yoshioka K, *et al.* Support vector machine-based feature selection for classification of liver fibrosis grade in chronic hepatitis C. J Med Syst [Internet]. 2006;30(5):389–94. Available from: http://link.springer.com/10.1007/s10916-006-9023-2.

[19] Qiu P, Cai X-Y, Ding W, Zhang Q, Norris ED, and Greene JR. HCV geno-typing using statistical classification approach. *J Biomed Sci* [Internet]. 2009;16(1):62. Available from: http://www.jbiomedsci.com/content/16/1/62.

[20] Algamal ZY, Lee MH, Al-Fakih AM, and Aziz M. High-dimensional QSAR classification model for anti-hepatitis C virus activity of thiourea derivatives based on the sparse logistic regression model with a bridge penalty. J Chemom [Internet]. 2017;31(6):e2889. Available from: http://doi.wiley.com/10.1002/cem.2889.

[21] Abbasali E, Bahram G, Javad Z, and Reza E. Predicting of protein–protein interactions between human and hepatitis C virus via an ensemble learning method. Mol Biosyst [Internet]. 2010;6(1):30–7. Available from: http://xlink.rsc.org/?DOI=B907925B.

[22] Eissa MM, Elmogy M, Hashem M, and Badria FA. Hybrid rough genetic algorithm model for making treatment decisions of hepatitis C. In: 2014 International Conference on Engineering and Technology (ICET) [Internet]. Cairo, Egypt: IEEE; 2014. p. 1–8. Available from: http://ieeexplore.ieee.org/document/7016784/.

[23] Al Kindhi B, Sardjono TA, Purnomo MH, and Verkerke GJ. Hybrid K-means, fuzzy C-means, and hierarchical clustering for DNA hepatitis C virus trend mutation analysis. Expert Syst Appl [Internet]. 2019;121:373–81. Available from: https://doi.org/10.1016/j.eswa.2018.12.019.

[24] Hashem S, Esmat G, Elakel W, *et al.* Comparison of machine learning approaches for prediction of advanced liver fibrosis in chronic hepatitis C

patients. IEEE/ACM Trans Comput Biol Bioinform [Internet]. 2018;15 (3):861–8. Available from: https://ieeexplore.ieee.org/document/7891989/.

[25]   Wang M, Wang K, Yan A, and Yu C. Classification of HCV NS5B polymerase inhibitors using support vector machine. Int J Mol Sci [Internet]. 2012;13(4):4033–47. Available from: http://www.mdpi.com/1422-0067/13/4/4033.

[26]   Weidlich IE, Filippov IV, Brown J, *et al.* Inhibitors for the hepatitis C virus RNA polymerase explored by SAR with advanced machine learning methods. Bioorg Med Chem [Internet]. 2013;21(11):3127–37. Available from: http://dx.doi.org/10.1016/j.bmc.2013.03.032.

[27]   KayvanJoo A, Ebrahimi M, and Haqshenas G. Prediction of hepatitis C virus interferon/ribavirin therapy outcome based on viral nucleotide attributes using machine learning algorithms. BMC Res Notes [Internet]. 2014;7 (1):565. Available from: http://bmcresnotes.biomedcentral.com/articles/10. 1186/1756-0500-7-565.

[28]   Richardson AM and Lidbury BA. Enhancement of hepatitis virus immunoassay outcome predictions in imbalanced routine pathology data by data balancing and feature selection before the application of support vector machines. BMC Med Inform Decis Mak [Internet]. 2017;17(1):121. Available from: http://bmcmedinformdecismak.biomedcentral.com/articles/10.1186/s12911-017-0522-5.

[29]   Breiman L. Bagging predictors. Mach Learn [Internet]. 1996;24(2):123–40. Available from: http://link.springer.com/10.1007/BF00058655.

Chapter 17

Data visualization using machine learning for efficient tracking of pandemic – COVID-19

Supriya Khaitan[1], Priyanka Shukla[1], Anamika Mitra[2], T. Poongodi[1] and Rashi Agarwal[3]

From the first case in December 2019 to more than 2.92 million cases in just 3 months, COVID-19 became a pandemic. COVID-19 is spreading all around the world, and due to this pandemic situation, humans' life is at risk. On one side, healthcare and sanitization workers are stretching themselves to deal with this situation at the frontline, and on the other, data scientists and machine learning (ML) experts are researching to provide data in an understandable form to the world. This chapter provides the details of different ways of processing and visualizing the huge amount data generated on this pandemic. This includes the clusters on the basis of symptoms in different age groups, effects of COVID-19 on different countries, etc.

17.1 Introduction

Corona virus (CoV) is a large family which has caused for the pandemic created because of illness in both humans and animals. In humans, this has caused respiratory infections from common cold and cough to Middle East respiratory syndrome (MERS) and severe acute respiratory syndrome (SARS). The novel CoV disease, also known as COVID-19 (and SARS-Cov2) by the World Health Organization (WHO), is a rapidly evolving pandemic. COVID-19 is highly transmittable and pathogenic viral disease, with low respiratory infections primarily detected in Wuhan, Hubei province of Mainland China [1]. According to WHO, COVID-19 is a viral disease that has emerged and spread to different parts of the world and is causing serious health issues. Several viral epidemics have

[1]School of Computing Science and Engineering, Galgotias University, Greater Noida, India
[2]Department of Computer Science and Engineering, School of Engineering and Technology, Sharda University, Greater Noida, India
[3]Department of Computer Applications, Galgotias College of Engineering and Technology, Greater Noida, India

caused in the last two decades, such as SARS-CoV in 2002–03, H1N1 influenza in 2009 and MERS CoV in 2013 [2].

In the year 2002, SARS-CoV, a novel CoV, emerged in China, which proved to be having very high transmissibility in the humans, which led to infecting lakhs of people in more than dozens of the countries [3]. WHO has declared its outbreak as Public Health Emergency of International Concern on 30 January 2020 and on 11 March 2020 as a pandemic [4].

Many economically poor countries are demanding technical and financial support to successfully combat this COVID-19 effect, in which many African, Asian and Latin American nations are rapidly developing testing kits. There is significant strain difference and changes in the sequence structure. There are many evidences which link the sequence information with transmissibility of COVID-19. COVID-19 has infected many healthcare workers in China, India, USA and many more countries [5,6]. Today, China which has been the source of infection has now prevented and controlled the pandemic. It has been found that 85% of the human-to-human transmission has occurred in family clusters and because of which healthcare workers are infected [7].

It also has focused that the close and unprotected exposure is required for transmission by direct contact or any immediate environment activity surrounded by the infection. Case finding and contact tracing are being done by every country to find the chain of the virus. Many ML-enabled text and data mining technologies are being implemented. There can be many statistical estimation models that can find out the spread of the virus. They are as follows:

- assumption of the disease and its source
- estimation of the days of infection to occur before symptom onset
- city lockdown period

Based on the earlier baseline factors, the effect can be reduced or can be used to investigate the spread of the virus. Also, ML technology is being used to collect the data, and with the help of that data, the source can be found. It is said that obtaining timely understanding of the transmission of the virus is vital in order to evaluate the effect on the mankind. It could also help to provide important data for intervention strategies to understand the outbreak. Exploratory data analysis (EDA) is the most important aspect and the first step towards understanding this data.

17.2 Data preprocessing

Information is genuinely viewed as an asset in this day and age. According to the World Economic Forum, by 2025, we will produce around 500 exabytes of information every day. However, question here is, 'Is this information sufficiently fit to be utilized by AI? How would we conclude that?'. This makes us investigate the subject of information pre-preparing, i.e. changing the information with the end goal that it becomes machine-intelligible [8].

17.2.1   Importance of data preprocessing

Data can be found in different forms: it may be unstructured, structured or semi-structured. The data preprocessing is used to transform or encode the data, so that data can be parsed by a machine easily. It helps the ML algorithm to understand the features of data. A collection of data objects is known as dataset also known as vectors, patterns, records or entities [9]. Features describe data objects that capture the characteristic of an object. Features are also known as attributes, fields or characteristics. Data can further be divided into categorical and numerical data.

17.2.1.1   Categorical

They are the features that consist of defined set of values. Examples of categorical data are colour {red, blue, green}. Categorical data is further divided into two types:

- *Nominal:* Categorical variables without any implied order example car model, colour.
- *Ordinal:* Categorical variables with some implied order; however, scale of difference is not implied, Designation {Assistant, Clerk, Officer, Manager, General Manager} Size {XS, S, M, L, XL, XXL} are examples of ordinal.

17.2.1.2   Numeric

They are the features that are integer valued or continuous. Examples are speed and blood pressure reading.

- *Interval:* They are numeric values with defined interval and measurement unit. Examples are date and temperature.
- *Ratio:* They are numeric values with defined measurement unit where both ratios and difference are meaningful. Examples are age, electric current, mass, etc.

17.2.2   Data preprocessing consist of following steps

17.2.2.1   Data clean-up

It is normal to have missing and inconsistent values in dataset. It might have occurred during information assortment, or perhaps because of certain data validation; yet in any case, missing qualities must be mulled over (Figure 17.1). Some methods to deal with missing and inconsistent values are as follows:

- Eliminate lines with missing information: Straightforward and in some cases successful methodology. Falls flat if numerous items have missing qualities. In the event that an element has for the most part missing qualities, at that point that includes itself, can likewise be wiped out.
- Estimate missing values: On the off chance that all alone sensible level values are missing; at that point, we can likewise run straightforward insertion strategies to fill in those qualities. Be that as it may, most regular technique for

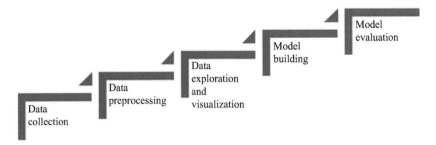

Figure 17.1   Data preprocessing steps

managing missing qualities is by filling them in with the mean, mode or median estimation of the particular element.
- Performing data assessment to deal with inconsistent values, and removing duplicate values.

17.2.2.2   Aggregation

It is a technique of combining two or more attributes together. The advantage of data aggregation is as follows:

- Data reduction: The data that we collect is vast and may contain some attributes that we do not require for analysis. Aggregation reduces the number of attributes
- Aggregate data has less variability
- It leads to change in data scale

17.2.2.3   Sampling

A sample is a subset of population. It is one of the data reduction techniques. It is a subset of data. If handling of data is time-consuming or expensive, sampling is the best solution. It is of two types:

- Random sampling: In this, probability of selecting an item is the same for all datasets.
- Stratified sampling: Random samples are drawn from different partitions of data.

17.2.2.4   Dimensionality reduction

With the increase in number of dimensions, data becomes sparse. This makes outlier detection and clustering difficult to apply as they depend on distance among any two points. Thus, it is important to reduce dimensions to avoid curse of dimensionality. The advantages of dimensionality reduction are as follows:

- efficient time complexity
- reduced memory consumption
- ease of data visualization
- elimination of irrelevant features

Methods used in dimensionality reduction are principal component analysis (PCA), feature subset selection, etc.

17.2.2.5 Discretization

It is mainly used for classification and converting continuous valued attributes to ordinal values. It can be done either as supervised or as unsupervised discretization. Binning is one of the methods of discretization.

17.3 Exploratory data analysis

This is an approach for data analysis that incurs many techniques. It is fundamentally a creative process. Specific statistical techniques can be used, such as creating histograms or boxplots. EDA is not a set of techniques or procedures; you may say it as a 'philosophy':

- Maximize insights into a dataset
- Uncover underlying structure
- Detect outliers and anomalies
- Test underlying assumptions
- Develop parsimonious models
- Determine optimal factor setting

Rather you may say, EDA is an inferential statistics, which tends to be rigid with rules and formulas. EDA is about your curiosity. Say there is some data of advertisers and their daily revenue numbers for a search engine. So we can define the business problem as follows.

How can a search engine want to improve its revenue? The question that comes to your mind will be as follows:

1. What will you look for?
2. Do you know what to look for?
3. Will you immediately run an R/Python code to find the mean, median and mode?

All you know is your objective is to understand the data. The most important step in that process is 'ask the right questions'. The first step of any EDA is to list down as many questions as you can on a piece of paper. You have the data, what do you want to know? What are you curious to know?

17.3.1 Univariate analysis

It focuses on one variable and analyses one variable at a time.

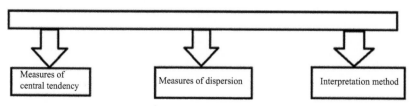

17.3.1.1   Measures of central tendency

- Mean: It is calculated by totalling all the values in a dataset and dividing by the number of values.
- Median: It is the central value in a dataset.
- Mode: It is the most frequently occurring value in the dataset.

17.3.1.2   Measures of dispersion

Dispersion is the extent to which values in a distribution differ from the average of the distribution. To quantify the extent of the variation, there are certain measures, namely

- Range: It is the difference between the largest (L) and the smallest value (S) in a distribution. Thus, $R=L-S$. A higher value of range implies higher dispersion and vice versa.

  Note: Range is unduly affected by extreme values. It is not based on all the values. As long as the minimum and maximum values remain unaltered, any change in other values does not affect range. It cannot be calculated for open-ended frequency distribution.

- Variance: It measures the dispersion around the mean.
- Standard deviation: It is the positive square root of the mean of squared deviations from mean. So, if there are five values $\times 1$, $\times 2$, $\times 3$, $\times 4$ and $\times 5$, first their mean is calculated. Then deviations of the values from mean are calculated. These deviations are then squared. The mean of these squared deviations is the variance. Positive square root of the variance is the standard deviation.

17.3.2   Bivariate analysis

Bivariate analysis is one of the simplest forms of quantitative (statistical) analysis. It involves the analysis of two variables (often denoted as X, Y), for the purpose of determining the empirical relationship between them.

- Comparison of two variables at a time.
- The variable may be qualitative or quantitative.

17.4   Data visualization techniques

Data visualization is a simple way to present and correlate the data – a technique to understand the data in an easier way. Choosing the right technique to represent the data is key to make data understandable. Choice of data visualization techniques is based on the following:

- *Audience:* It is basic to change data depiction to the expected intrigue gathering. On the other hand, if data bits of information are gotten ready for examiners or experienced ones, it can go past fundamental charts.

- *Content:* The sort of data chooses the systems. For example, if its estimations change after some time, you in all likelihood will use line diagrams to show the components. To show the association between two segments, you will use a scatter plot. Consequently, visual diagrams are perfect for relationship examination.
- *Context:* You may use different approaches to manage the way in which your diagrams look and in a similar manner read depending upon the particular situation. To highlight a particular figure, for example certifiable advantage advancement diverged from various years, you may need to use the shades of one concealing and pick the awe inspiring one for the hugest segment on the diagram. In fact, to isolate parts, you will use separate shades.
- *Dynamics:* There are various types of data, and all of them recommend a substitute pace of progress. For example, cash-related results can be assessed month to month or yearly, while time game plan and following data are persistently developing.
- *Reason:* The target of data portrayal has certified effect in the manner it is executed. In order to make a perplexing assessment of a system or merge different sorts of data for a continuously noteworthy view, observations are amassed into dashboards with controls and channels.

Many data visualization techniques are available, and following are the details of most common of all [10].

17.4.1   Box plot

Boxplot is a method for portraying numerical information graphically through their quartiles. Boxplot is divided into four quartiles and is a five-number summary, which includes min, quartile 1, median, quartile 3 and max. The difference between Q3 and Q1 is known as interquartile range (IQR). Anything that goes beyond 1.5*IQR is known as outlier. Boxplots are used when

- multiple datasets are compared;
- the significant features of dataset are analysed, not the details;
- summarizing data from another graph;
- there is insufficient data for creating a histogram.

Boxplots are not suitable for random data (Figure 17.2).

17.4.2   Charts

Charts are easiest way to show the visualization of data. It is one of the most common data visualization tools. It is used to show trends, historical low and high and also helps in finding outliers. It is effective if we can split our data into many categories. It is of many types such as bar chart, pie chart (Figure 17.3).

17.4.2.1   Bar chart

Bar outlines are one of the most well-known information representations. You can utilize them to rapidly think about information across classifications, feature

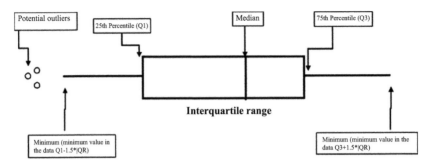

Figure 17.2   Box plot

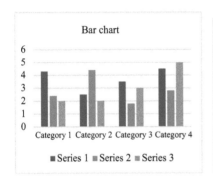

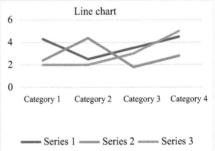

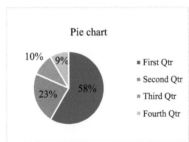

Figure 17.3   Charts

contrasts, show patterns and anomalies and uncover chronicled highs and lows initially. Bar outlines are particularly powerful when you have information that can be part into numerous classes.

17.4.2.2   Line chart

The line outline, or line chart, associates a few unmistakable information focuses, introducing them as one nonstop development. Use line outlines to see slants in information, for the most part after some time (like stock value changes more than 5 years or site visits for the month). The outcome is a basic, direct approach to imagine changes in a single worth comparative with another.

17.4.2.3   Pie chart

Pie outlines are incredible for adding subtlety to different representations. Alone, a pie graph does not give the watcher an approach to rapidly and precisely think about data. Since the watcher needs to make setting all alone, key focuses from your information are missed. Rather than making a pie graph the focal point of your dashboard, give utilizing them to bore down a shot different perception.

17.5   Maps

Maps are an easy decision for imagining any sort of area data, regardless of whether it is postal codes, state contractions, nation names or your own custom geocoding. On the off chance that you have geographic data related with your information, maps are a straightforward and convincing approach to show how area corresponds with patterns in your information (Figure 17.4).

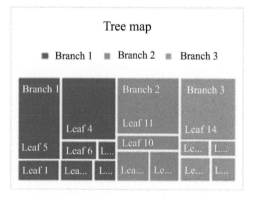

Figure 17.4   Map

17.5.1   Thickness maps

Thickness maps uncover examples or relative focuses that may somehow be covered up because of a covering mark on a guide – helping you recognize areas with more noteworthy or less quantities of information focuses. Thickness maps are best when working with an informational collection containing numerous information focused on a little geographic territory.

17.5.2   Tree map

Tree maps relate various fragments of your information to the entirety. As the name of the diagram recommends, every square shape in a tree map is partitioned into littler square shapes, or sub-branches, in view of its extent to the entirety. They utilize space to show per cent aggregate for every class.

For additional sorts of graphs, visual models, tips and data, download our whitepaper. In this chapter, you will find out about various diagram (and diagram) types – from bar graphs to thickness maps to box-and-stubble plots. You will additionally realize when to utilize one diagram over another, alongside tips on the best way to use these outline types for greatest effect.

17.6   Disperse plot

Disperse plots are a powerful method to explore the connection between various factors, appearing on the off chance that one variable is a decent indicator of another, or in the event that they will in general change autonomously. A dissipate plot presents heaps of particular information focused on a solitary outline. The outline would then be able to be improved with investigation such as group examination or pattern lines (Figure 17.5).

17.7   Gantt chart

Gantt diagrams show a venture timetable or show changes in action after some time. A Gantt outline demonstrates steps that should be finished before others can start, alongside asset portion.

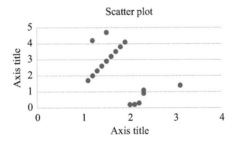

Figure 17.5   Scatter/disperse plot

17.8 Importance of data visualization in healthcare

Fortunately, probably the sharpest and most experienced science and clinical groups far and wide are handling the overwhelming work of understanding the instruments behind the spread of this pandemic. Examination is giving new bits of knowledge dependent on monstrous measures of information to stem the uptick in new cases and help address society's issues. Here are some different ways individuals are utilizing investigation to improve reactions to the coronavirus flare-up.

- Utilizing information perception to follow the coronavirus flare-up.
- Having the option to imagine the spread of the infection can help bring issues to light, uncover its effect and at last aid anticipation endeavours.
- Learn more about the status, area, spread and pattern examination of the coronavirus.

For a considerable length of time, even decades, numerous health officials approach specialists supported a lean social insurance framework that debilitated unused beds and underused offices. Questions here are, how would health be able to mind frameworks quickly grow limit when confronted with a pandemic? Also, since assets are hard to come by, what basic resources are required in every area? Fully expecting a surge of patients, clinics around the world cleared whatever number beds as could be allowed. Dropping elective medical procedures was a moderately simple advance. Yet, the essential and considerably more mind-boggling task is figuring out where and when beds will be required as COVID-19 travels through different populaces [11].

By utilizing investigative strategies to all the more proficiently designate accessible bed space and emergency clinic assets, even to neighbouring well-being frameworks, well-being authorities want to lessen death rates in zones hardest hit by the infection. These logical strategies include

- applying and refining epidemiological models to extend COVID-19 diseases inside a locale;
- predicting the potential number of contaminated individuals that will require clinical intercession and what the degree of care may resemble;
- forecasting the number of required guardian's dependent on situation demonstrating.

It is important to use all data that can be available to any health organization [12,13]. It can help the officials to be informed and give an insight to when, where and how to intervene. This can improve the care and life saving capabilities.

The way data can be represented is also important. It helps in easy understanding of data and improving the response. The experiences produced by examination could lead human services frameworks to take a few activities or a blend of them:

- Repurposing beds for a more significant level of care.
- Using day medical procedure/outpatient focuses as new bed space.

- Exploring the chance of reviving covered offices.
- Reallocating clinicians, essential hardware and supplies to where they are required most.

In an industry where human lives remain in a precarious situation consistently, there is ostensibly not any more significant time than now to utilize every single accessible asset.

17.8.1   Uses of data visualization

- A way to explore data with presentable results
- Preprocessing of data in process of data mining
- Helps in finding missing values and can be used for dealing with missing values
- Means to find the variable to be included in data analysis
- Helps in data reduction by combining categories
- Country-wise confirmed cases

17.9   COVID-19 gripping the world

In the midst of a flood of data on COVID-19, handling the pertinent material can be testing. While some have totally disengaged themselves from the sequence of media reports, others are normally following their news source to all the more likely see how to battle COVID-19. This requires they not just gain admittance to checked data of these turns of events but also in addition get important bits of knowledge from the enormous measure of information that has been produced over the most recent couple of months over the world. In this setting, information visualization has permitted individuals to comprehend and retain data in a fast and precise way. Virtual products such as Tableau and Microsoft Power BI have incorporated these intricate systems by picturing information, identifying shrouded examples and transforming them into visual stories. Without depending on individuals to filter through quantitative information or numbers on a spreadsheet, this permits them to get data applicable to their circumstance and, subsequently, respond in a better way.

This could be accomplished by moulding the course of events of the pandemic, reporting the spread of the infection in a specific region and recognizing hotspots, among others. Likewise, these assorted arrangements of perceptions have additionally helped political pioneers and network individuals plan all the more successfully, along these lines, having a significant genuine effect notwithstanding this emergency. In this part of the chapter, Tableau is used to generate graphics where current situation of the COVID-19 in the world is analysed. Figure 17.6 shows the spread of COVID-19 across the world, which can be clearly seen that United States is the most hit country, after Italy and China [14–16].

The spread of the novel CoV all through the world is influencing representatives, managers and the economy. Various states, provinces and districts are

Figure 17.6   A world map of COVID-19 spread

necessitating people remain inside, abstain from social event places, such as bars, restaurants, gym, and are asking people to work from home. These adjustments in conduct have a broad effect – especially on organizations that rely upon face-to-face cooperation – inciting cutbacks, lost income and, now and again, business terminations. This could mean more extensive financial changes: higher jobless-ness, diminished utilization because of lost wages and terminations, decreased business venture because of lost income and, at last, falling total national output. How arranged are businesses to change in accordance with new working condi-tions? What enterprises most straightforwardly affected by ongoing changes, and what exercises can be gathered from past downturns? All these answers can be easily understood by visualizing [13,17].

As instances of COVID-19 multiply over the globe so have information related with these. This remembers data for the number of influenced patients, the number of individuals they are probably going to contaminate, hardware that is accessible for human services labourers, just as the passing and recuperation rates, among others. This information should be effectively passed on to individuals, since in the case of a pandemic like this, instinct cannot fill in for realities to see how the spread is progressing [18]. The methodology that is required ought to include examining, sharing and utilizing information. Here, picturing the information can help clarify the creating occasions in a reasonable and concise manner or individuals to deci-pher information well, coax out examples and get on patterns. Figure 17.7 shows the jobs lost in United States due to COVID-19; data has been taken from The Economic Times.

It is important to use control and preventive measures along with the hand hygiene and waste management in COVID-19 spread. Doctors and healthcare workers who deal directly with COVID patients need protective equipment such as gloves, face shield, goggles coverall, boots, etc. Many governments have made it

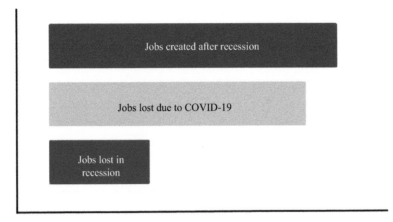

Figure 17.7   Job lost in United States due to COVID-19

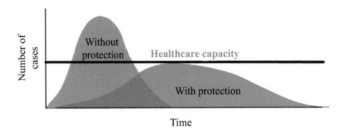

Figure 17.8   Usage of healthcare system capacity with and without gears

compulsory for all to use masks as it is airborne disease. Figure 17.8 shows the number of cases over time with and without protective gear. It can be clearly seen that without the use of protective gear the healthcare system will not be able to manage.

The Coronavirus Resource Centre dashboard from Johns Hopkins University has developed as a dependable source that gives both a miniaturized scale and large scale see on the pandemic. Fusing information from different associations, including WHO, the stage is refreshed every day with rich infographics on the COVID-19 episode [19]. The graphics catches the instances of positive cases and related patterns, infographics on the number of medical clinics in general vicinity, its ability to treat COVID-19 patients, the rate at which cases are being distinguished and the number of individuals requiring hospitalization, etc. Some of the statics of the top 10 countries with COVID-19 cases w.r.t. total confirmed cases, total recovered cases and total deaths are given in Figure 17.9. The data taken for visualization is till 20 April 2020. It can be clearly seen that maximum confirmed cases and highest death rates are in the United States. However, a maximum number of people are recovered in China.

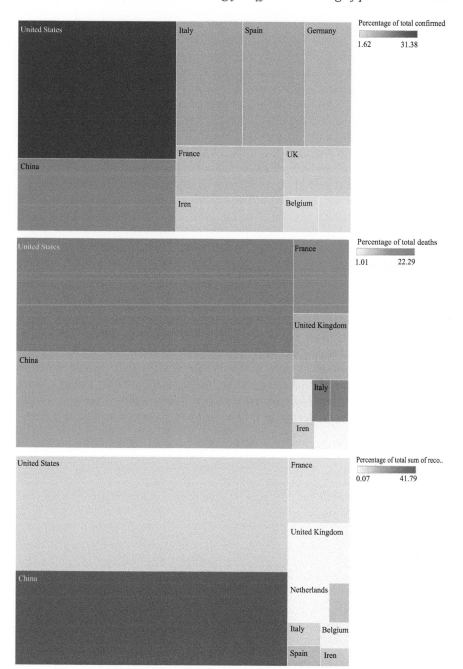

Figure 17.9   Top 10 countries with (a) a maximum number of confirmed cases, (b) a maximum number of deaths reported, (c) a maximum recovery cases

It has yielded exceptional conduct transforms, one model being the idea of 'levelling the bend', effectively outlined in different information perception diagrams. This has inspired the general population to rehearse social removing and, in this manner, effectively take part in battling COVID-19. With nations over the world setting up movement limitations – and a few, similar to India, upholding across the nation lockdowns – visual portrayals of monstrous information have educated these methodologies [20,21].

For instance, Colorado in the United States has taken different proactive measures to utilize Tableau to picture the episode's movement. The site is refreshed regularly at 4.00 p.m., giving specialists sufficient opportunity to audit the information and improve its exactness. It involves a case synopsis of the whole state, including the number of cases, those hospitalized, the number of individuals tried and the number of passing recorded. Similar platforms have been adopted by many countries [22].

17.10   COVID-19 India situation

The loss of life due to COVID-19 in India has crossed 900 as on 28 April 2020. Since 24 March 2020, India has been under the nation lockdown across, presently stretched out by the government to 3 May 2020, to control the spread of the new infection. India is not among the most noticeably awful hit nations, yet its horribly under-subsidized and sketchy open well-being framework, with gigantic varieties between various states, presents unique challenges for the nation's health system [23]. Age-wise graphs with different types of symptoms are shown in Figure 17.10. In the earlier graph, fever and cough are the mostly seen symptoms at the age group

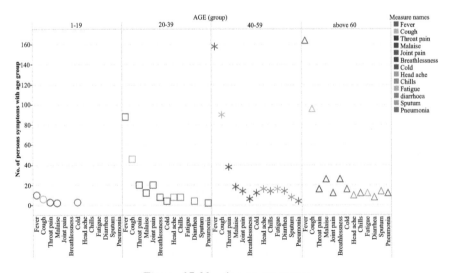

Figure 17.10   Age vs symptoms

40–50 years and above 60 years [29]. People below the age of 20 years are less affected from COVID-19 [24].

Initially, the rates of testing have been low. Reasons may be different and wide such as huge population, political issues and operational feasibility. However, efforts have been made later on to change the situation by implementing hundreds of testing kits made available, and many private as well as govt. companies and laboratories are working and also have received approvals. Testing requirements is to be increased exponentially as well as strategically as a tool to provide epidemiological evidence. Response time of India initially was limited by the shortage of healthcare workers, but later it has been mobilized by recruiting additional healthcare workers from different sources [27].

Threat to the COVID-19 response in India has come up because of the spread of misinformation driven by fear, stigma and blame. Favourable condition for India has been its young population (65% aged <35 years). The lockdown is tremendously having the desired effect of flattening the epidemic curve. The immediate challenge in front of the Indian Government is to keep infections at manageable levels. Rapid testing, tracing and isolating patients are required to ensure the success of lockdown [24].

Over the past weeks, there have been a few revealed cases of patients attempting to escape detachment wards in government clinics and conceal travel history. Numerous with introduction to associated cases with COVID-19, people have additionally attempted to avoid the obligatory home isolate.

These are stressing improvements in the background of India's most recent regulation arrangement, a 20-page report, which explicitly discusses 'non-pharmaceutical mediations' (Figure 17.11). 'Isolate and confinement are significant pillar of bunch regulation', the report states. Isolate alludes to partition of people who are not yet sick yet have been presented to COVID-19 and in this way can possibly turn into sick [28]. Disengagement alludes to detachment of people who are not well, suspected or affirmed COVID-19 cases. There have been rehashed reports of individuals getting away from emergency clinics or isolation in the previous week. How would this be able to affect the progressing control measures for COVID-19? One key issue is the trust shortage in the general well-being framework in numerous pieces of the nation. Other significant components incorporate dread of confinement and shame connected to the individuals who are being isolated and confined. Disease transmission experts and general well-being specialists state that expanding consumption in the general well-being framework is vital to building trust. '[Escaping quarantine] is for the most part out of dread and shame, and needing to be with one's family since it is for a delayed time just as need of pay' [25,26]. It is hard for individuals in India to comprehend the significance of segregation and isolate, despite the fact that it is a reaction to a pandemic. The confidence in the general well-being framework cannot develop quickly as a reaction to the pandemic. An overstretched open medicinal services framework powers a great many Indians to go to the unregulated private medicinal services division.

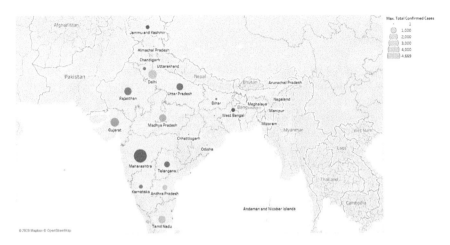

Figure 17.11   An India map of COVID-19 spread

The province of Kerala, which effectively managed a Nipah episode in year 2018, offers helpful exercises. 'Treatment for COVID-19 is right now engaged in government emergency clinics. In many pieces of the nation, these emergency clinics have been underfunded, not disparaged by the rich and incredible; their staff are unsettled. This doesn't change overnight. Trust in government is a significant segment in a crisis wellbeing reaction. We saw what trust can do when we dealt with the Nipah reaction. Kerala has consistently been pleased with the specialized nature of its administration. Since 2005, the state government venture has gone up significantly. Kerala government's The Aardram venture has further raised the profile of government medical clinics; considerable speculations have been made'. Figure 17.12(a) shows the confirmed cases with respect to states in India. Maharashtra is having maximum confirmed cases. In Maharashtra, Delhi and Gujarat, change in positive cases increased in the first week of April. Figure 17.12 (b) represents the active cases which are calculated removing death cases and recovered cases from the confirmed cases.

India's count of COVID-19-positive cases has arrived at 29,000, and the number of fatalities right now remains below 1,000. India is continually over-hauling its testing abilities to keep in mind the spread of coronavirus diseases in the nation. The number of tests has increased just about multiple times since 1 April to a normal 15,000 day by day in the previous 5 days. While Maharashtra has directed the most elevated number of tests on a flat-out premise, Delhi bests the outlines with most noteworthy COVID-19 tests for each capita premise. Delhi has so far led 11,709 tests, which converts into 7 tests for each 10,000 people. It is trailed by Kerala and Rajasthan, with proportions of 4.2 and 3.6, individually, on similar measurements. West Bengal and Uttar Pradesh have the least thickness, with 0.5 and 0.3 COVID-19 tests for every 10,000 population. By and large, India has a proportion of 1.3 tests per 10,000 population.

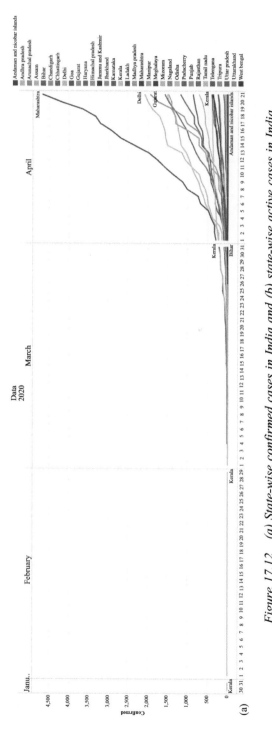

Figure 17.12   (a) State-wise confirmed cases in India and (b) state-wise active cases in India

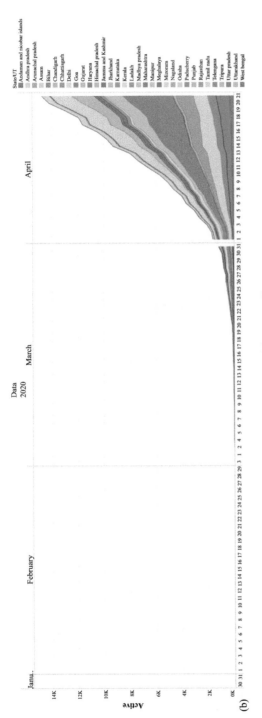

Figure 17.12 (Continued)

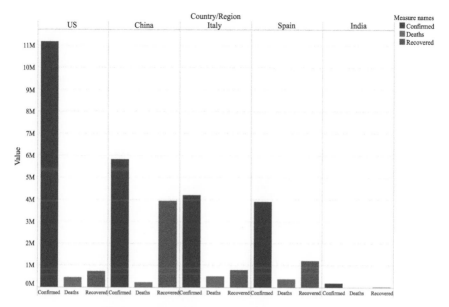

*Figure 17.13   Comparison of confirmed death and recovered COVID-19 cases
India vs the top four countries*

The country has been divided into red, green and orange zones, and Maharashtra, Gujarat and many other places have been converted into hotspots, and the movement is totally stopped by the government. In India, the number of deaths confirmed and recovered rates are much lesser as compared with some other countries in the world as shown in Figure 17.13.

Pictures from the best in class emergency clinics in the United States, Italy and Spain of COVID-19 patients heaving for air and biting the dust are activating alerts over the world. The United States and Italy which have seen more than 9,000 deaths, the most noteworthy among countries, went above and beyond and prohibited burial service administrations to confine social affairs with an end goal to contain the spread of the novel coronavirus contaminations.

India, which has a population of 1.3 billion, needs to seize such a circumstance from creating. Its delicate medicinal services framework will not have the option to adapt to such an episode. Thus, the administration settled on a two-dimensional technique: lock down the whole country to break the contamination tie and rapidly increase it worn out human services offices to confront the pandemic. Each Indian state today has comparative needs, including new beds, increment limit of escalated care units, demand parts of private emergency clinics, request lifesaving ventilators, clinical experts. Many train coaches, universities and private hospitals are being converted into quarantine centres to fulfil the increasing demand. Figures 17.14 and 17.15 show some statistics of hospital beds.

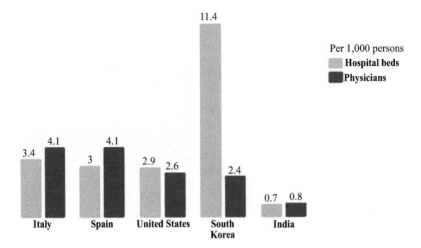

Figure 17.14   Hospital beds vs number of doctors per 1,000 people

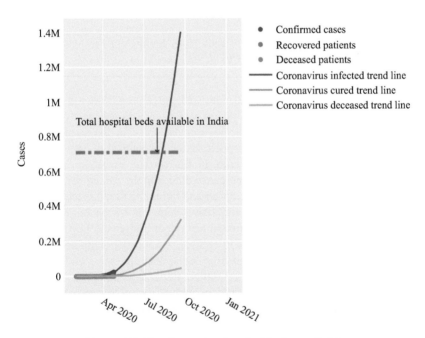

Figure 17.15   Case-wise hospital beds available

17.11   Issue and challenges

COVID-19 has affected the whole world; the fastest growing economies are under lockdown, and the world has stopped. Dealing with this pandemic is itself a challenge. The world is facing new challenges, and the reports show the thriving economies are also not prepared for the challenges that COVID-19 has brought. Some of the challenges are listed as follows:

- Spreading of infection, COVID-19 is highly infectious disease, understanding the transmission and symptoms is the first step.
- Stopping the infection spread.
- Shortage of hospital staff, medicines and equipment.
- Acceptance among people for importance of social distancing.
- Economic slowdown.
- Loss of work for daily wagers, their hunger.
- Quick and effective vaccine and its large-scale production.

17.12 Conclusion

Data visualization is the best way for easier interpretation of data. A dashboard that contains the patient records, hospital details, the number of cases is more effective than textual information about the same. In this chapter, a Tableau tool is used for visualization of COVID-19 dataset for whole world and India. Initially, China was having the maximum confirmed case of COVID-19 but now the graph has changed; the United States have maximum confirmed cases among the world according to dataset. The analysis regarding the different states and the number of beds is done in the chapter.

References

[1] Pengfei Sun, Xiaosheng Lu, Chao Xu, Wenjuan Sun, and Bo Pan, "Understanding of COVID-19 based on current evidence." Journal of Medical Virology, vol. 92, no. 6, pp. 548–551, 2020.

[2] Catrin Sohrabi, Zaid Alsafi, Niamh O'Neill, *et al.*, "World Health Organization declares global emergency: a review of the 2019 novel coronavirus (COVID-19)." International Journal of Surgery, vol. 76, pp. 71–76, 2020.

[3] Zi Yue Zu, Meng Di Jiang, Peng Peng Xu, *et al.*, "Coronavirus disease 2019 (COVID-19): a perspective from China." Radiology, vol. 296, pp. 200490, 2020.

[4] World Health Organization. "Coronavirus disease 2019 (COVID-19): situation report, 72." 2020.

[5] Tao Zhou, Quanhui Liu, Zimo Yang, *et al.*, "Preliminary prediction of the basic reproduction number of the Wuhan novel coronavirus 2019-nCoV." Journal of Evidence-Based Medicine, vol. 3, pp. 3–7, 2020.

[6] Chaolin Huang, Yeming Wang, Xingwang Li, *et al.*, "Clinical features of patients infected with 2019 novel coronavirus in Wuhan, China." The Lancet, vol. 395, pp. 497–506, 2020.

[7]   WHO, "Novel coronavirus (2019-ncov) – situation report – 22", 2020. https://www.who.int/docs/default-source/coronaviruse/situation-reports/20200211-sitrep-22-ncov.pdf? sfvrsn¼fb6d49b1_2. (Accessed 20 February 2020).

[8]   Puneet Misra and Arun Singh Yadav, "Impact of Preprocessing Methods on Healthcare Predictions", In Proceedings of 2nd International Conference on Advanced Computing and Software Engineering (ICACSE), 2019.

[9]   Han, Jiawei, Jian Pei, and Micheline Kamber, "Data mining: concepts and techniques." Elsevier, 2011.

[10]   Pathak, Shreyans, and Shashwat Pathak, "Data Visualization Techniques, Model and Taxonomy." In Data Visualization and Knowledge Engineering, Cham: Springer, pp. 249–271, 2020.

[11]   Samrat K. Dey, Md Mahbubur Rahman, Umme R. Siddiqi, and Arpita Howlader, "Analyzing the epidemiological outbreak of COVID-19: a visual exploratory data analysis approach." Journal of Medical Virology, vol. 92, no. 6, pp. 632–638, 2020.

[12]   Fahima Khanam, Itisha Nowrin, and M. Rubaiyat Hossain Mondal, "Data visualization and analyzation of COVID-19." Journal of Scientific Research and Reports, vol. 26, no. 3, pp. 42–52, 2020.

[13]   Fotios Petropoulos and Spyros Makridakis, "Forecasting the novel coronavirus COVID-19." PLoS One, vol. 15, no. 3, 2020.

[14]   Jordan Soren and Andrew Q. Philips, "Cointegration testing and dynamic simulations of autoregressive distributed lag models." The Stata Journal, vol. 18, no. 4, pp. 902–923, 2018.

[15]   Nanshan Chen, Min Zhou, Xuan Dong, *et al.*, "Epidemiological and clinical characteristics of 99 cases of 2019 novel coronavirus pneumonia in Wuhan, China: a descriptive study." The Lancet, vol. 395, no. 10223, pp. 507–513, 2020.

[16]   Maimuna S. Majumder and Kenneth D. Mandl, "Early in the epidemic: impact of preprints on global discourse about COVID-19 transmissibility." The Lancet Global Health, doi: 10.1016/S2214-109X(20)30113-3, 2020.

[17]   Ma H, Hu J, Tian J, *et al.*, "Visualizing the novel coronavirus (COVID-19) in children: what we learn from patients at Wuhan children's hospital." SSRN Electronic Journal, 2020. Available at SSRN 3556676.

[18]   Wang, Li-Sheng, Yi-Ru Wang, Da-Wei Ye, and Qing-Quan Liu, "A review of the 2019 Novel Coronavirus (COVID-19) based on current evidence." International Journal of antimicrobial agents, 105948, 2020.

[19]   WHO, "Coronavirus disease 2019 (Covid-19) – situation report – 33." 2020. https://www.who.int/docs/default-source/coronaviruse/situation-reports/2020 0222-sitrep-33-covid-19.pdf?sfvrsn¼c9585c8f_2. (Accessed 24 February 2020).

[20]   Bo Xu, Bernardo Gutierrez, Sumiko Mekaru, *et al.*, "Epidemiological data from the COVID-19 outbreak, real-time case information." Scientific Data, vol. 7, pp. 106, 2020. https://doi.org/10.1038/s41597-020-0448-0.

[21] Samuel Asumadu Sarkodie and Phebe Asantewaa Owusu, "Investigating the cases of novel coronavirus disease (COVID-19) in China using dynamic statistical techniques, Heliyon, Article e03747, vol. 6, no. 4, 2020.

[22] Hien Lau, Veria Khosrawipour, Piotr Kocbach, *et al.*, "Internationally lost COVID-19 cases." Journal of Microbiology, Immunology and Infection, vol. 53, pp. 454–458, 2020.

[23] Talha Burki, "Outbreak of coronavirus disease 2019." The Lancet Infectious Diseases, vol. 20, no. 3, pp. 292–293, 2020.

[24] Anuradha Tomar and Neeraj Gupta, "Prediction for the spread of COVID-19 in India and effectiveness of preventive measures." Science of the Total Environment, vol. 728, no. 138762, p. 1, 2020.

[25] Roosa, K., Y. Lee, R. Luo, *et al.*, "Real-time forecasts of the COVID-19 epidemic in China from February 5th to February 24th, 2020." Infectious Disease Modelling, vol. 5, pp. 256–263, 2020.

[26] Meg Miller, "2019 novel coronavirus COVID-19 (2019-nCoV) data repository." Bulletin-Association of Canadian Map Libraries and Archives (ACMLA), vol. 164, pp. 47–51, 2020.

[27] Qun Li, Xuhua Guan, Peng Wu, *et al.*, "Early transmission dynamics in Wuhan, China, of novel coronavirus–infected pneumonia." The New England Journal of Medicine, vol. 382, pp. 1199–1207, 2020.

[28] Chaolin Huang, Yeming Wang, Xingwang Li, *et al.*, "Clinical features of patients infected with 2019 novel coronavirus in Wuhan, China." The Lancet, vol. 395, no. 10223, pp. 497–506, 2020.

[29] Supriya Khaitan, Anamika Mitra, Priyanka Shukla, and Sudeshna Chakraborty, "Statistical investigation of novel corona virus COVID-19." International Journal of Control and Automation, vol. 13, no. 2s, pp. 01–06, 2020.

Index